Sacajawea
and the
Wright Brothers

A vintage postcard of Sacajawea from a statue by sculptor Leonard Crunelle located in North Dakota.

Photograph of Wilbur and Orville Wright taken outside their home in Dayton shortly before Wilbur's death.

Sacajawea and the Wright Brothers

*The Definitive Biographies of Three Individuals
Who Changed American History Forever*

SPECIAL EDITION
Edited by Gary Brin

Condensed from the works by
Grace Raymond Hebard and Fred C. Kelly

LIST OF TITLES USED FOR THIS COLLECTION

Sacajawea A Guide and Interpreter of the Lewis and Clark Expedition was originally published in 1933. It remains the definitive account of Sacajawea's life.

The Wright Brothers A Biography Authorized by Orville Wright was originally published in 1943. It is the only biography verified by Orville Wright before his death.

BOTH TITLES CAN BE FOUND AT THE SITE LISTED BELOW
www.nancyhankslincolnpubliclibrary.org

Spelling errors and visible publishing mistakes found in the original versions listed above were corrected or slightly adjusted whenever necessary for this edition. Original text was left intact to preserve the historical accuracy of the writings.

BOTH BOOKS USED FOR THIS EDITION HAS BEEN REFORMATTED FROM THE ORIGINAL 1933 AND 1943 PUBLISHED VERSIONS.

Images of Sacajawea and the Wright Brothers displayed in this book are courtesy of the Library of Congress. All photographs were digitally restored for this edition.
Cover design and book layout © 2022 by Standish Press
Compilation © 2022 by Standish Press

FIRST EDITION

ALL NEW MATERIAL AND CORRECTIONS
Copyright © 2022 by Standish Press

All rights reserved. No part of this book may be reproduced by any means whatsoever without written permission from the publisher.

For more information about reprint rights please visit
www.standishpress.com

ISBN—978-1-945510-09-0

Library of Congress Control Number
2022944504

MANUFACTURED IN THE UNITED STATES OF AMERICA

In Remembrance of

Sacajawea and the Wright Brothers

Though they lived in vastly different times and in different worlds—they managed to achieve impossible goals that most of their contemporaries could only dream about.

This book is also dedicated in memory of

Milton Wright and Katharine Wright Haskell

No one can dream without an exceptional father and sister who allowed the Wright Brothers to achieve the impossible.

Contents

Page 11
Foreword

Page 13
Sacajawea

Page 125
Wright Brothers

Page 345
Afterword

Page 348
Additional Notes

Page 364
About the Series Editor

Foreword

What else can be said about Sacajawea and the Wright Brothers? They changed history—guaranteed that they would never be forgotten by historians and schoolchildren alike.

Sacajawea began her life in the late 1780s unaware that over two centuries later she would be firmly entrenched as part of the fabric of American history for simply agreeing to lead a band of travelers across a country that at the time was unknown—even to members of her own tribe. The trek across the vast wilderness from the Plains to the shores of the Pacific had never been attempted at this point in the history of the United States. It must be assumed that others—intrepid white men—had attempted it previously and possibly succeeded. But no record exists of such daring travels before the Lewis and Clark Expedition made their way through the Plains and the treacherous Rocky Mountains toward the shores of the vast Pacific Ocean. Today, such travel seems boring—easy to attempt over a period of a week—but in a time when there when cars, trains, and airplanes existed only in the feverish fantasies of would-be inventors—traveling across vast stretches of wilderness was a terrifying prospect. Yet, when it was over, the men of the Lewis and Clark Expedition were legends in their own time and Sacajawea was rightfully credited for her accomplishments. Grace Raymond Hebard's account of Sacajawea's life was the first attempt to cover every aspect of the life of the unofficial guide of the Lewis and Clark Expedition and although through the years it has been criticized by revisionist historians, it remains an important volume about the life of an American Indian that proudly stands alongside her male peers.

When Wilbur and Orville Wright were young boys growing up in the Midwest, they could never have imagined that one day they would accomplish the impossible and create something that would propel them into history for an invention that many had dreamed about but no one had achieved. In December 1903 when they realized their "aeroplane" had lifted into the air, the thoughts going through their minds are impossible to imagine. In the years following, the Wright Brothers didn't publish a memoir of their experiences, though they published several accounts of their first flight. Fred C. Kelly's biography of Wilbur and Orville Wright is the closest thing to an autobiography of the Wright Brothers that history buffs can have. Authorized by Orville Wright before publication, it remains one of the most important factual accounts of the lives of two brothers that changed history.

Gary Brin
Series Editor

Sacajawea

Sacajawea
A Guide and Interpreter of the Lewis and Clark Expedition

Preface

The St. Louis Exposition of 1904 created a widespread interest in the historic background of the Louisiana Purchase, whose centennial it officially commemorated, and brought new significance to that great epic of western exploration, the Lewis and Clark Expedition. Among the many by-products of this interest was the search for a typical model for a statue to be erected at the outer gates of the exposition. This search led to a study of the life and services of Sacajawea, the guide of the Lewis and Clark Expedition, and to an interest in the career of that remarkable woman, which has continued unabated for nearly thirty years. This volume is the product of that interest. For three decades, with the aid of trained assistants, the author has prosecuted her search for authentic historical material which would enable her to rescue Sacajawea from the semi-oblivion into which her name had fallen, and give to her her legitimate place in the history of the great northwest. In this volume the author has also sought to unravel the tangled skein of Sacajawea's family life, to trace the career of her son, Baptiste, the papoose of the Lewis and Clark Expedition, and of her adopted son, Bazil, one of the signers of the treaty of 1868 at Fort Bridger, to portray as accurately as possible her personal traits and characteristics, to trace her wanderings far and wide through the west, and especially to record the significant services she rendered not only as guide to Lewis and Clark but also for many years and on many occasions as counselor to her own people and to the whites. In this long study much significant information heretofore unknown has been brought to light, many facts misinterpreted or seen in false perspective have been given their proper setting, new light has been thrown on numerous controversial issues, and much that was confused has been cleared of uncertainty and presented in its true setting.

Among some of the specific contributions of the volume are the verification of Baptiste's journey to Europe with Prince Paul of Wurttemberg, the proof that Baptiste and Toussaint Jr., whose common father was old Charbonneau, were born of different mothers, the explanation of the real motives which led Sacajawea to leave Charbonneau, the true interpretation of the word Sacajawea, commonly but erroneously given as "Bird Woman," the account of Sacajawea's "lost years" among the Comanches and of her return to her own people, the Shoshones, and the story of her long life thereafter among them on the reservation. In the Thwaites edition of the Lewis and Clark *Journals*, published in 1904, a letter written in 1806 by Captain William Clark to Charbonneau appeared for the first time.

A great deal of confusion was created by Clark's use in this letter of certain names and expressions such as "*your famn Janey*," "*Pomp*," "*your dancing boy, Baptiste*," etc. From the material appearing later in these pages it will be shown that "Janey" was Sacajawea, the "famn" of Charbonneau, and that the "dancing boy, Baptiste," was the child of Sacajawea and

Charbonneau, born in 1805 at the Mandan villages and spoken of as the papoose of the expedition. He was also called *"Pomp"* according to the Indian custom of so designating the oldest child. Read in this way, the letter enables us to understand Captain Clark's expenditures for the education of Baptiste Charbonneau in St. Louis a few years later. The facts bearing on this matter are brought out in detail in later chapters. Verification has also been found, in the work of Dr. Charles A. Eastman and in the researches of Mr. and Mrs. W. H. Clift among the Comanches on behalf of the author, for the statements of Andrew Bazil, the (adopted) grandson of Sacajawea, regarding his grandmother's life among the Comanches. But most unexpected of all was the corroboration of the testimony of Sacajawea's descendants that Baptiste had visited a land to the east beyond the "Big Waters" and there learned to speak a number of languages.

When the Indians on the reservation told of the big houses on the water and of people on the other side who wore wooden shoes, "Wobenamptiko," the author naturally recorded their statements with some wonder and skepticism. She could not openly question them, however, or show her astonishment, for the interview would then have ended immediately, because the Indians spoke as to a friend without "forked tongues," and any question of their truthfulness would have constituted an unpardonable offense. The startling verification of Baptiste's education in Germany, revealed by a study of the Stuttgart archives, confirmed unmistakably the trustworthiness and value of Indian testimony. The researches in the Stuttgart archives were carried out by a trained archivist, Herr Friedrich Bauser, who brought to light the writings of Prince Paul of Wurttemberg, with their account of the prince's travels in the United States and the mentioning of the Indian boy, Baptiste. Prince Paul's request for permission to make the inland voyage in 1823, and Captain Clark's reply were discovered in the Missouri archives, and the quaint drawings of the prince's artist are given to the world again after many years. The material in the volume has been carefully examined for errors by numerous authorities familiar with the field and, while mistakes may have been made in the details of the narrative, the work rests upon authentic and carefully verified sources. Much of the information and a large part of the testimony upon which the narrative is based have never appeared before in print, and maps and illustrations have been made available for the first time. The printed sources upon which in part the volume is based will be discussed in subsequent pages.

Some explanation should be given here, however, as to the Indian testimony which constitutes so large a part of the contents of the volume. Although the Indians have no written history, their memories are trained to a remarkable degree to retain tribal history, and Indian verbal testimony is, therefore, as much to be relied upon as the writings of any other race. In seeking information from Indian sources, care was taken to see that during an interview all other Indians were excluded except the Indian being examined and the necessary witnesses thereto. In all such interviews, a government interpreter was nearly always employed, and the questions and answers were recorded by a trained stenographer. In order to insure absolute accuracy, two Shoshone witnesses, who also understood English, certified that the questions in English had been accurately rendered in Shoshone, and that the answers were as accurately translated into English by the interpreter. After the material secured at these interviews had been typewritten, the Indian interviewed and the Indian witnesses signed the document by "thumbprint." Other witnesses signed by name. No hearsay evidence was accepted, and every effort was made to prevent collusion. Thus, on one occasion, three Indians living long distances apart were interviewed on the same morning to prevent any chance of consultation between them. As to the other authorities whose statements have been used in the preparation of the volume, their names are sufficiently well-known to establish the value of their testimony. Among these may be listed the Reverend John Roberts, spiritual leader of the Shoshones for nearly a half century, Mrs. James Irwin, Mr. Fincelius G. Burnett, agricultural adviser on the reservation since 1871, John C. Burnet, and James

I. Patten, teacher and missionary. To those who have assisted through their collaboration and research—the author desires to express her appreciation—and also to that large number of historical writers who have made this publication possible.

Especially do I desire to express my gratitude to the Indians on the Shoshone Reservation, many of whom are descendants of Sacajawea and some of whom knew her personally, for the information they have placed at my disposal. I desire also to express my gratitude to the Reverend John Roberts, missionary-clergyman of the Protestant Episcopal Church to the Indians in Wyoming, to Mr. Lawrence J. Burpee, Canada, Mr. Fincelius G. Burnett, the Reverend James I. Patten, Mr. John C. Burnet, Mrs. A. D. Lane, James E. Compton, interpreter, and the stenographers who gave willingly and abundantly of their time and skill, to those in the Indian field service, H. E. Wadsworth, Chester E. Faris, and R. Paul Haas, to Mrs. Eva Emery Dye, to the state librarians, historians, and historical societies of Wyoming, North Dakota, South Dakota, Montana, Utah, Idaho, Colorado, Oregon, Washington, Kansas, Wisconsin, Missouri, and Oklahoma, to the University of Wyoming librarians who have for thirty years furnished needed information for this and other publications, to Mrs. Calvin Page, artist, to the historical department of the Church of Jesus Christ of the Latter Day Saints at Salt Lake City, to the Jesuits of Missouri, through Father Charles Van Tourehout, St. Genevieve archives of St. Louis University, to the Episcopalians of Wyoming and Colorado, to which denomination the Shoshones have been assigned, to the Comanche Indians of the Oklahoma country, a very few of whom remember the Shoshone woman, to United States Senators Francis E. Warren, Joseph M. Carey, John B. Kendrick, and Robert D. Carey, to Representatives Charles E. Winter and Vincent Carter, to Brigadier-General Walter S. Schuyler and Colonel Richard H. Wilson, to William A. Carter Jr., E. A. Carter, John E. Rees, and James K. Moore Jr., to Miss Stella M. Drumm, librarian of the Missouri Historical Society, Mrs. Daniel R. Russell, daughter of W. C. Kennerly, William E. Connelley of Kansas and LeRoy

Hafen of Colorado, to Mrs. Laura T. Scott, Miss Jean Bishop, and Fred Lockley, to Chancellor M. A. Brannon, to Friedrich Bauser of Germany, Professor Louis C. Butscher, Mrs. L. M. Wells, Albert W. Johnson, Earle R. Forrest, and Milo M. Quaife, to the publishers for written consent to reprint from their publications, to the several US departments at Washington DC, particularly to the commissioner of Indian Affairs, to Mr. W. H. Clift and his wife, Edith Connelley Clift (daughter of the Honorable William E. Connelley), who together conducted the research among the Comanches of Oklahoma, to Mr. Willard O. Walters of the Henry E. Huntington Library and Art Gallery, California, to William M. Camp, J. Neilson Barry, Olin D. Wheeler, Agnes C. Laut, Reuben Gold Thwaites, General William Clark Kennerly, Alfred J. Mokler, J. Cecil Alter, George Bird Grinnell, E. N. Roberts, Charles Alexander Eastman, and, finally, to Dr. June E. Downey of the University of Wyoming for a lifetime friendship and faith in this work, and to Professor Wilson O. Clough of the University of Wyoming for constructive criticism on the manuscript.

Introduction

Before discussing the contributions of Sacajawea to the Lewis and Clark Expedition, it is desirable to describe briefly the sources upon which our knowledge of this "national epic of exploration" rests, and to say something of the capacity and training of the two leaders, Meriwether Lewis and William Clark, for the great task entrusted to them. Lewis was born in Virginia in 1774. His early education and training developed in him unusual powers of observation and gave him knowledge and an understanding of nature which proved of great value to him as the leader of the Expedition. He also served for three years prior to the expedition as private secretary to President Jefferson, and was thus a man of unusual educational and cultural attainments. Captain William Clark, in his turn, had seen service under General Scott and "Mad Anthony" Wayne as an engineer in the construction of roads and forts. This experience gave him more than ordinary skill in topography and in the drafting of maps.

The two men thus supplemented each other, and together supplied all the qualifications essential for the success of so great an undertaking. Each had confidence in and affection for the other, an attitude clearly expressed by Lewis when he wrote to Clark, "*I could neither hope, wish or expect from a union with any man on earth more perfect support or further aid in the discharge of the several duties in the mission than that which I am confident I shall derive from being associated with yourself.*" Detailed written instructions were given to the commanders of the expedition by President Jefferson concerning the keeping of journals and the collecting and recording of scientific data. Both Lewis and Clark followed these instructions with remarkable faithfulness and painstaking care, so that neither the trying conditions of exploration in unknown country, the threat of Indian attack, or weariness and fatigue could prevent them from recording the experiences they encountered day by day, and of noting down significant scientific data. The journal which Captain Clark kept is more complete than that of Captain Lewis. It contains a daily record for all but ten days of the entire journey, and even the events of this brief period are covered in a single entry.

In Lewis's journal, on the other hand, the records of four hundred forty-one days of the expedition are lacking. It is possible indeed that the original journals showed no such omissions and that someday these long missing portions will be found. At least there is no known reason, such as prolonged sickness, to account for the great gap in his journal. Often the record of Lewis closely parallels that of Clark, and vice versa, for the two sometimes copied even verbatim from each other. Generally, however, each described an event in his own way, using his own characteristic phraseology. In addition to the journals kept by Lewis and Clark, the leaders of the expedition also urged individual members of the party to keep journals or diaries for themselves. Apparently three of the twenty-three privates and four sergeants complied with these instructions. The three privates who recorded their experiences were Joseph Whitehouse, Robert Frazer, a former dancing master from Vermont, and George Shannon, the youngest member of the expedition. Whitehouse's journal covers only the period from May 14, 1804, to November 6, 1805. Whitehouse is said to have given the manuscript of his diary to his confessor on his death bed, and the latter in turn sold it in 1894 to a private collector, from whom it was purchased by the publisher of Reuben Gold Thwaites's *Early Western Travels*. Thwaites considered the journal authentic and of definite historical value, although some of the entries are not in Whitehouse's own handwriting. Among other contributions of value to this volume, Whitehouse definitely establishes the fact that Charbonneau, the interpreter for Lewis and Clark, had at least two other wives besides Sacajawea. The whereabouts of the journals of the other two privates are unknown. Of the journals kept by the four sergeants, that of Nathaniel Pryor, "one of the nine men from Kentucky," afterward ensign and eventually captain in the army, has been lost.

Charles Floyd of Kentucky, the only member of the expedition to lose his life while in service, kept a faithful record of the expedition until his death on August 20, 1804. His journal was lost for eighty-five years but was found in its original form in 1894 by Dr. Thwaites and published by him in the original journals of Lewis and Clark. Since Floyd's record ends before the expedition reached the Mandan villages, where Sacajawea first joined the expedition, it finds no further mention in this volume. Patrick Gass, who was elected sergeant after Floyd's death, was born in Pennsylvania in 1771 of Scotch-Irish parentage and was thus the oldest member of the expedition with the possible exception of Captain Clark. His education was limited to fourteen days in school, but the journal which he kept is one of the chief sources of the Expedition, and was first published in 1807, seven years before the journals of Lewis and Clark. Within five years after its first publication in Philadelphia, it was republished three times in the United States and printed also in London and Paris. For our purpose the chief value of Gass's journal lies in the fact that it definitely states that Charbonneau, the interpreter, had more than one wife and also throws light upon a number of other controversial subjects. The journal of John Ordway, another sergeant of the expedition, was lost for more than a century.

It too was finally discovered by Dr. Thwaites, who found portions of it in possession of the heirs of Captain William Clark and other portions in the Nicholas Biddle estate where it had been filed with the journals of Lewis and Clark. Ordway's journal gives a complete daily record of the expedition from beginning to end. Whatever gaps occurred, therefore, in the journals of Lewis, Clark, Gass, Floyd, and Whitehouse were thus bridged over by Ordway's careful narrative. Ordway was one of the best educated of the enlisted men, a fact which clearly increases the importance of his diary. He carried his manuscript for safekeeping under his shirt through all the vicissitudes of the expedition, and finally sold it to Lewis and Clark for the sum of ten dollars. Upon the return of the expedition to St. Louis in September, 1806, Lewis and Clark set about the task of preparing their report for President Jefferson. The original records of the two leaders of the expedition were all re-transcribed in red morocco, gilt-edged notebooks which have in part been preserved to the present day. The original notes, however, unfortunately were mostly destroyed. Captain Clark, a draftsman of unusual ability, made for his journal numerous maps of the routes followed by the expedition as well as many rough drawings of birds, rivers, fishes, and the like. These were put into systematized form, and became a valuable asset to the final records of the Expedition.

It was the intention of the two leaders to arrange for the publication of their journals immediately after making their report to the president, but unexpected developments made this impossible. Lewis was appointed governor of the new Louisiana territory, and Clark was made superintendent of Indian Affairs. These new responsibilities for some years rendered it impossible for the leaders to prepare the final revision of their journals, and to edit them for publication. In 1809, however, at the earnest request of President Jefferson, Lewis started east in order to undertake the long-delayed task of preparing the journals for the publishers. His death en route at the hands of a murderer—left to Captain Clark alone the task of putting the records into proper form for publication. The next year Clark secured the services of Nicholas Biddle to edit the manuscripts, and engaged George Shannon, the youngest member of the expedition, to act as his assistant. In this capacity Shannon was able both to interpret the notes made by the diarists—and also to add much valuable material from his own personal experiences as a member of the Expedition and from the vast fund of information he had gained from conversations with other members of the company.

Clark, on his part, aided the undertaking by frequent correspondence with the editors, and finally made a special journey to Philadelphia to assist in the actual assembling and editing of the material. In the preparation of the Lewis and Clark journals the editors also had the use of the original copy of Sergeant Ordway's journal and of the already published work of Sergeant Gass. Sixteen months were required to complete the undertaking—from March 25, 1810, to July 8, 1811. Then when the task was finished it was difficult to find a publisher for the work. Finally, under the supervision of Paul Allen, two small volumes were issued in 1814. This edition, however, omitted the carefully-prepared, scientific data, including Captain Clark's maps and atlas. These were not published until the Thwaites edition of 1904. The Biddle edition, moreover, comprised less than a fourth of the original manuscripts, which contained over a million and a half words. Such a reduction necessarily involved the omission of much material that was of genuine value. Nevertheless, the volumes have fittingly been ranked by Dr. Thwaites as among the most important and interesting books of American travel. The Biddle edition was later reprinted in England, and also translated and published in the Dutch, German, and French languages.

In evaluating this edition, it must be remembered that it was produced with the aid and under the supervision of the actual members of the Expedition, therefore, where corrections were made in the spelling of proper names or revisions effected in the narrative, it must be assumed that these changes reflect the best judgment of both Clark and Shannon. This fact has a direct bearing on several matters about which there has been much dispute. This is especially true of the proper pronunciation and spelling of the name Sacajawea. It was probable, indeed, that the spelling of unusual words was the peculiar contribution of George Shannon to the Biddle edition. Shannon, who by 1810 had completed part of his college education, seems to have had an unusually keen and discriminating ear for Indian pronunciations. The Indians whom the expedition encountered, of course, had no written language, and the spelling of proper names was therefore wholly a matter of choice on the part of the white man who was seeking to reduce their statements to writing. Shannon's suggestion for the spelling of these Indian proper names was, moreover, approved personally by Captain Clark, who not only collaborated with Biddle and Shannon, as we have seen, but also passed on the entire manuscript before it was published.

Consequently, in the matter of the correct pronunciation and spelling of the Indian proper names, the Biddle edition must be accepted as probably the most accurate of all the accounts of the Lewis and Clark Expedition. Following the publication of the original Lewis and Clark journals in the Biddle edition of 1814, no authoritative edition of the narrative of the expedition appears again until 1893. In that year Elliott Coues issued the *History of the Expedition Under the Command of Lewis and Clark* in four volumes. It was the intention of Dr. Coues to follow the Biddle text with scrupulous fidelity in this edition, but after the manuscript had been placed in the hands of the printer, the editor learned of the discovery of the original manuscript of the journals of Lewis and Clark. This new material, however, Coues preferred to use as the basis for copious editorial footnotes rather than to change the original plan of publishing an exact reproduction of the Biddle text of 1814. In 1904 Dr. Reuben Gold Thwaites, the insatiable student of western exploration—published the definitive edition of the Lewis and Clark Expedition in eight volumes under the title, *Original Journals of Lewis and Clark, 1804* to 1806. In this edition the original manuscripts were followed closely, even to the reproduction of curious orthography and varied spelling. The work of the diarists in revising their manuscripts and putting them into final form for publication is also shown in the text by many erasures, interpolations, interlineations, corrections of a later date made in red ink, words in parentheses "dug out with a knife" and entries made of events before the events themselves had actually occurred.

☐☐☐☐☐☐☐☐☐☐

The treaty by which France ceded the Louisiana Territory to the United States was signed April 30, 1803, and ratified by Congress on October 26 of the same year. It was not until December 20, however, that the formal transfer of the territory, embracing approximately 1,020,571 square miles, actually occurred. The cost of this enormous empire was $15,000,000, or about two and one-half cents an acre. The American most interested in this transaction, and in many ways most responsible for it, was Thomas Jefferson. As early as 1786 we find him lending his support in Paris to John Ledyard, the "Connecticut Yankee" who dreamed of crossing Asia, sailing to the northwest coast, and making his way overland to the American settlements in the Mississippi Valley. Six years later, more than a decade before the confirmation of the Louisiana Purchase, Jefferson, then Secretary of State, began to discuss the advisability of sending an exploring party to navigate the Missouri River to its source. His object was to open commercial relations with the Indians, secure for our government some of the riches of the region which were being monopolized by traders from Canada, discover, if possible, a waterway to the Pacific, and open a route that would enable us to share in the trade of the Orient. At that time, however, no one had the slightest conception of the vastness of the territory lying beyond the Missouri, although in 1792 Robert Gray, a ship captain from Boston, had sailed around the cape to the Pacific in the ship *Columbia*, and cast anchor in the harbor at the mouth of the river to which he gave the name of his vessel. From this time on many

English and Yankee ships sailed along the northwest coast gathering furs—and the region about Vancouver Island thus became definitely known. But the territory between the Missouri and the Pacific was as yet unexplored except as a few adventurous trappers had ascended the Missouri River a thousand miles or so and set their steel beaver traps along its tributaries. In 1793 Jefferson engaged the services of Andre Michaux, a French botanist, to explore the territory between the Missouri and the Pacific, instructing him specifically to *"seek for and pursue that route which shall form the shortest and most convenient communication between the higher parts of the Missouri and the Pacific Ocean."* Michaux set out upon the expedition, but before he reached the Mississippi was recalled by his own government. Three months, moreover, before the treaty transferring the Louisiana Territory to the United States was actually signed, Jefferson sent a confidential letter to Congress asking for an appropriation of twenty-five hundred dollars to be used to equip an expedition to explore the country drained by the Missouri River. It is interesting to note that an appropriation for even so small an amount to explore a region that now has taxable wealth of more than seven billion dollars was difficult to secure. In preparing for the expedition that was finally authorized, Jefferson selected the leaders with extraordinary care. As already stated, the chief command was given to his former private secretary from Virginia, Captain Meriwether Lewis, and he in turn selected Captain William Clark, likewise a native of Virginia but at that time a resident of Kentucky, to be his companion.

Preparatory to its final organization, the Expedition went into winter quarters at the mouth of the Wood River about twenty miles above St. Louis. Besides the two leaders, the party at this time included twenty-seven men—among whom was Clark's colored body servant, named York, who proved a rare curiosity to the natives. Three other men were added to this number before the expedition started on its westward journey.

These included the hunter, Drewyer, or Drouillard as it is correctly spelled, a head boatman, Cruzatte, and a water man named Labiche. Fifteen soldiers, commanded by Warfington, escorted the Expedition as a guard. Twenty of the thirty men comprising the body of the expedition completed the entire journey. Of these none was married. As already stated, the instructions which President Jefferson issued to the commanders of the expedition were minute and complete. They were expected to make careful observations of the country through which they passed and to keep complete records of these observations. They [the Expedition] were also to serve as naturalists, botanists, geologists, paleontologists, astronomers, engineers, meteorologists, minerologists, ornithologists, and ethnologists. Especially were they charged to be diplomatic and conciliatory in their dealings with the Indians, for in this capacity, they were the official representatives for the government of the United States. As already [previously] explained, because of these instructions the journals kept by Lewis and Clark and the other members of the company became veritable storehouses of valuable information regarding nearly every aspect of the country through which the Expedition passed, and of the various Indian tribes of the northwest. The Expedition left its winter quarters at the mouth of Wood River on May 14, 1804. In ascending the Missouri River, the party employed three boats, the largest of which was fifty-five feet long, drew three feet of water, and was propelled by one large, square-shaped sail and twenty-two oars.

The other two boats were of six and seven oars respectively. Two horses were taken along to assist whenever possible in dragging the boats upstream, and to carry to the boats the game killed by the hunters. The largest boat had a swivel gun, or a small cannon swinging on a pivot, which often did efficient service if in no other way than by its terrifying noise. Because of the tortuous streams, unknown channels, countless snags, sandbars, and swift currents, the progress of the company was slow and the Expedition ordinarily counted itself fortunate to make as much as fifteen miles a day. One hundred sixty-five days were required to reach the Mandan villages, sixteen hundred miles from St. Louis. On the return journey the same distance was covered in thirty-seven days. There were, of course, no charts or maps for the explorers to follow, the territory was unnamed, uncharted, unexplored. Naturally for an expedition of this magnitude, a vast and varied amount of supplies was necessary. These included food, clothing, camp equipment, firearms and ammunition, and large quantities of articles to be used in bartering with the Indians. It was expected, naturally, that much of the necessary food would be supplied by hunting and fishing from day to day. Powder was carried in small canisters made of lead. These canisters not only served as containers for the powder but also were melted up for bullets. Each canister furnished sufficient bullets to correspond to its original content of powder, so that in this way there was no lost weight.

The supplies were packed in bales, each of which contained a portion of all the articles taken. Thus in case of accident or the loss of a single bale, the entire supply of any one commodity would not be destroyed. Articles to be used as presents to the Indians comprised fourteen additional bales. These consisted of bright-colored beads, tinsel and red cloth, lace coats, brass kettles, fish hooks, looking glasses, small bells, thimbles, handkerchiefs of various colors, flags, medals, knives, tomahawks, articles of dress, and anything else that might please the fancy of bartering Indians. Among the beads, those of a blue color were most popular because they were known as the "chief's beads," and commanded a higher value than those of other colors. Lewis and Clark also took with them three sizes of medals representing varying degrees of honor which were to be given to the chiefs of the tribes with whom they came in contact. The first stages of the journey which lasted several months were for the most part uneventful. The weather was generally mild and wild game plentiful. Not infrequently the explorers, making headway against the muddy current of the Missouri, met the crude boats of trappers loaded to the gunwale with hides and pelts, floating down the river to St. Louis—the forerunners of the vast fur trade soon to be in operation up and down the Missouri River. On August 3, 1804, Lewis and Clark held their first formal council with the Indians. At this council Lewis told the chiefs about the new government to which they must in the future give their allegiance, and assured them of that government's protection.

The chiefs expressed their pleasure at this change of government and sent their greetings to their "Great Father," the president. The place where this council was held was called Council Bluffs. The site of this council was on the west bank of the river, in what is now Nebraska, about twenty miles north of the site of the present city of Council Bluffs in Iowa. On October 26, the explorers reached the Mandan Villages, near the site of the present city of Bismarck, North Dakota. This site was about five days's journey further up the river from the original Mandan villages discovered by [Pierre] LaVerendrye in 1738.

The Expedition members spent the winter of 1805 in these villages, housing themselves in huts and stockades which they constructed under the supervision of Sergeant Patrick Gass, the head carpenter. The winter was occupied in making boats, mending clothes, jerking meat, and studying the language, habits, and customs of the Indians. While the Expedition was in winter quarters at the Mandan villages, Lewis and Clark secured the services of an interpreter named Toussaint Charbonneau, a French-Canadian trapper who had spent his life in the northwest. Charbonneau's career will be described more at length in a later chapter—it is sufficient to note here that his training and experience were such as to fit him to be of great value to the Expedition. Charbonneau brought with him his three Indian wives, one of whom was Sacajawea, the chief figure of this volume. His arrival at the headquarters of the Expedition is recorded in nearly all of the journals. Clark, in his entry of November 4, 1804, wrote as follows, *"A Mr. Charbonneau, interpreter from the Gross Ventre Nation, came to see us and informed that he came down with several Indians from a hunting expedition up the river to hear what we had told the Indians in council. This man wished to hire as an interpreter."* Similarly Ordway, on November 4, wrote, *"A Frenchman's squaw came to our camp who belongs to the Snake Nation. She came with our* interpreter's wife and brought with them four buffalo robes and gave them to our officers." An entry of the same date in the Biddle edition reads, "We received a visit of two squaws, prisoners from the Rocky Mountains, purchased by Charbonneau." Gass, in speaking of Charbonneau's wives in his entry of December 25, writes as follows, "At half past two another gun was fired, as a notice to assemble at the dance, which was continued in a jovial manner till eight at night, and without the presence of any females except three squaws, wives to our interpreter, who took no other part than the amusement of looking on. None of the natives came to the garrison this day, the commanding officers having requested they should not, which was strictly attended to. During the remainder of the month we lived in peace and tranquility in the garrison, and were daily visited by the natives." Sacajawea, as stated by Ordway, was a member of the Snake, or Shoshone tribe of Indians. For this reason it was felt that she would be a most essential addition to the company, because it was known that the route of the Expedition lay through the territory occupied by this tribe. As a child she had been captured by the Minnetarees, Hidatsas, or Gros Ventres of the upper Missouri. These Hidatsa Indians lived in the vicinity of the junction of the Knife and Missouri Rivers in North Dakota. From these Indians, Charbonneau either purchased her or won her by gambling, and later married her, probably, as we shall see, at the insistence of Lewis or Clark. While the expedition was still in winter quarters, Sacajawea gave birth to a boy. The event is recorded by four of the diarists of the Expedition. Lewis, on February 11, 1805, wrote as follows, "About five o'clock this evening one of the wives of Charbonneau was delivered of a fine boy. It is worthy of remark that this was the first child which this woman has borne." Gass, on February 12, says "On the twelfth we arrived at the fort and found that one of our interpreter's wives had, in our absence, made an addition to our number." Ordway writes on February 11 "An interesting occurrence of this day was the birth of a son of the Shoshone woman." The event is also confirmed by Whitehouse, but is not mentioned in the Biddle narrative. At five o'clock on the afternoon of April 7, 1805, two expeditions left the Mandans, one returned to St. Louis with letters to President Jefferson and with furs, stuffed and live animals, bones, articles of Indian dress, bows and arrows, the other, with thirty-two members in six canoes, turned its steps toward the uncharted northwest. Charbonneau and Sacajawea of course accompanied this latter company as interpreters. Lewis, in speaking of the departure of the Expedition wrote on April 7, *"Our party now consists of the following individuals, interpreters George Drouillard and Toussaint Charbonneau, also a black man of the name of York, servant to Captain Clark, an Indian woman, wife to Charbonneau, with a young child."* Clark, in turn, on the same date mentions, *"my servant, York, George Drouillard, who acts as hunter and interpreter, Charbonneau and his Indian squaw to act as interpreter and interpretress for the Snake Indians—one Mandan, and Charbonneau's infant."* The Biddle narrative, in turn, under the date of April 7 says, *"The wife of Charbonneau also accompanied us with her young child and we hope may be useful as an interpreter among the Snake Indians. She was, herself, one of that tribe but having been taken in war by the Minnetarees by whom she was sold as a slave to Charbonneau, who brought her up and afterwards married her."* During its progress up the Missouri River, the members of the Expedition found a great abundance of game such as deer, buffalo, elk, geese, ducks, and prairie chickens. Bear also were very numerous and sometimes dangerous. During this stage of the Expedition, Sacajawea made herself useful in many small ways. Lewis, on April 9, says that when the expedition halted for dinner the squaw, *"busied herself in search for the wild artichokes which the mice (gophers) collect and deposit in large hordes. This operation she performed by penetrating the earth with a sharp stick about some collection of driftwood. Her labors soon proved successful and she procured a good quantity of these roots."* Clark, on April 18, writes that he left the boat and went on foot across a great bend of the river, accompanied by Charbonneau and Sacajawea with her papoose. Lewis also mentions on April 30 that Clark spent the greater part of the day walking along the shore, accompanied by Charbonneau and Sacajawea. Not long after this, Sacajawea performed a service of inestimable value to the Expedition and one that doubtless greatly raised her in the esteem of its leaders. Clark records this incident, under date of May 14, at some length, as follows, "*we proceeded on very well until about six o'clock. A squall of wind struck our sail broadside and turned the pirogue nearly over, and in this situation the pirogue remained until the sail was cut down, in which time she nearly filled with water. The articles which floated out were nearly all caught by the squaw who was in the rear. This accident had like to have cost us dearly, for in this pirogue were embarked our papers, instruments, books, medicine, a great proportion of our merchandise, and, in short, almost every article indispensably necessary to further the views and insure the success of the enterprise in which we are now launched to the distance of 2,200 miles.*" Captain Lewis also pays his tribute to Sacajawea for her coolness and bravery in this emergency, writing as follows, "*by four o'clock in the evening our instruments, medicine, merchandise, provisions, were perfectly dried, repacked, and put on board the pirogue. The loss we sustained was not so great as we had at first apprehended, our medicine sustained the greatest injury, several articles of which were entirely spoiled, and many considerably injured. The balance of our losses consisted of some garden seeds, a small quantity of gunpowder, and a few culinary articles which fell overboard and sunk. The Indian woman—to whom I ascribe equal fortitude and resolution with any person on board at the time of the accident—caught and preserved most of the light articles which were washed overboard.*" Probably in recognition of this great service which Sacajawea had rendered to the Expedition, Lewis records—May 20—that a river was named in her honor. His entry, both because of the spelling of the name and its interpretation, is of definite significance. It reads as follows, "*About five miles above the mouth of Shell River, a handsome river of about fifty yards in width discharged itself into the Shell River on the starboard or upper side. This stream we called Sacajawea or 'Bird Woman's River,' after our interpreter, the Snake woman.*" At the junction of the Marias and the Missouri Rivers, the Expedition cached part of its supplies. The common method employed by the mountain men to make such a cache was as follows—a good dry spot was selected—the sod was carefully removed and placed to one side, so that when it was replaced it would not show that it had been disturbed. After the sod was removed a hole was dug, and the extra earth that would not be needed to fill up the hole was carried to the stream and thrown into the water so that no trace of it might be seen. Then twigs and branches were placed in the bottom of the hole, and on these were placed the goods to be cached or hidden, these were then covered with hides and skins to keep out moisture or water, over all of this was placed enough of the dirt to fill the hole, leaving space enough for the sod, which was carefully replaced. Sometimes a fire was made on the spot to destroy any sign of the work, or horses were picketed over the cache, or night camps were established. If the greatest care was exercised, even the skilled eye of the Indian could not detect the hiding place. On May 29, soon after leaving this spot, the Expedition reached an abandoned Indian encampment, and from the fragments of moccasins lying about, Sacajawea concluded that the former occupants, though not of the Shoshoni tribe, belonged to one of the other Rocky Mountain groups. On the thirteenth of June, 1805, the party reached the Great Falls of the Missouri. It was necessary to portage the supplies and baggage of the company around these falls, a task which occupied a month.

  The men themselves carried much of the baggage on their backs, but most of the supplies were transported in a cart, the wheels of which were made of a cottonwood tree twenty-two inches in diameter. During these operations the men, whose feet were protected only by moccasins, suffered severely from the prickly pear, or cactus, through which they had to walk. The thorns of this plant easily pierced the rawhide moccasins and left the feet sore and festering. This, added to the heat, fatigue, and hard work, constituted a fearful strain on the members of the company. Here, also, Sacajawea fell seriously ill. Both Lewis and Clark record this incident in considerable detail. Lewis, on June

10, writes, "*Sacajawea, our Indian woman, is very sick this evening. Captain bled her.*" Clark, on the same date, confirms Lewis's statement as follows, "*Sacajawea, our Indian woman, very sick. I bled her.*" The next day Clark repeated the bleeding, an operation which he said, "*appeared to be of great service to her.*" On June 12, Clark wrote, "*The interpreter's wife very sick, so much so that I moved her into the back part of our covered part of the pirogue, which is cool, her own situation being a very hot one in the bottom of the pirogue exposed to the sun.*" Clark's entries on the thirteenth and fourteenth record the growing seriousness of Sacajawea's illness. On the sixteenth, Clark records that the poor little Indian woman is, "*very bad and will take no medicine whatever until her husband, finding her out of her senses, easily prevailed upon her to take medicine. If she dies it will be the fault of her husband.*" Lewis, on the same date, speaks at considerable length of the gravity of Sacajawea's illness, of the means employed to bring about a cure, and especially of the great importance he attached to her services in negotiating with the Indians whom they expected to encounter. His entry reads as follows, "*About 2 PM I reached the camp, found the Indian woman extremely ill and much reduced by her indisposition. This gave me some concern, as well as for the poor object herself, then with a young child in her arms, as from her condition of her being our only dependence for a friendly negotiation with the Snake Indians, on whom we depend for horses to assist us in our portage from the Missouri to the Columbia River. One of the small canoes was left below this rapid in order to pass and repass the river for the purpose of hunting as well as to procure the water of the sulpher spring, the virtues of which I now resolved to try on the Indian woman. I caused her to drink the mineral all together. When I first came down I found that her pulse was scarcely perceptible, very quick, frequently irregular, and attended with strong nervous symptoms, that of the twitching of the fingers and the leaders of the arms, now the pulse has become regular, much fuller, and a gentle perspiration had taken place, the nervous system has also in a great measure abated, and she feels herself much free from pain.*" The day following Sacajawea was much better. Lewis's entry on June 17 records this improvement. *"The Indian woman much better today, I have still continued the same course of medicine, she is free from pain, clear of fever, her pulse regular, and eats as heartily as I am willing to permit her, of broiled buffalo well seasoned with pepper and salt and rich soup of the same meat. I think, therefore, that there is every rational hope of her recovery."* The next day he wrote, *"The Indian woman is recovering fast. She set up the greater part of the day and walked out for the first time since she arrived here. She eats heartily and is free from fever or pain."* The day following, however, the patient's ill-advised diet of raw apples and dried fish came near proving her undoing. Lewis writes of the incident in the following way, *"The Indian woman was much better this morning. She walked out and gathered a considerable quantity of the white apples of which she ate so heartily in this raw state, together with a considerable quantity of dried fish without my knowledge that she complained very much and her fever again returned. I rebuked Charbonneau severely for suffering her to indulge herself with food, having been previously told what she must only eat."* This was the crisis of Sacajawea's illness.

The next day she was free from pain and fever, and celebrated by going fishing. On the twenty-fourth, Lewis records that she was perfectly recovered. A few days after Sacajawea's recovery, a sudden cloudburst almost swept Sacajawea, her baby, Charbonneau, and Captain Clark, with his Negro servant York, to destruction, and if it had not been for Clark's bravery and presence of mind, Sacajawea, Charbonneau, and the baby would almost certainly have been drowned. Lewis, in his entry of June 29, records the near tragedy as follows, *"He [Clark] determined himself to pass by the way of the river to camp in order to supply the deficiency of some notes and remarks which he had made as he first ascended the river but which he had unfortunately lost. Accordingly, he left one man at Willow Run to guard the baggage and took with him his black man, York. Charbonneau and his Indian woman also accompanied Captain Clark. On his arrival at the falls he perceived a very black cloud rising in the west, which threatened* immediate rain, he looked about for a shelter but could find none without being in great danger of being blown into the river should the wind prove as violent as it sometimes is on those occasions in these Plains. At length, about a fourth of a mile above the falls, he discovered a deep ravine where there were some shelving rocks under which he took shelter near the river with Charbonneau and the Indian woman, laying their guns, compass, etc., under a shelving rock on the upper side of the ravine where they were perfectly secure from the rain. The first shower was moderate, accompanied by a violent rain, the effects of which they did, but little feel. Soon after, a most violent torrent of rain descended, accompanied with hail. The rain appeared to descend in a body, and instantly collected in the ravine and came down in a rolling current with irresistible force, driving rocks, mud, and everything before it which opposed its passage. Captain Clark fortunately discovered it a moment before it reached them and, seizing his gun and shot pouch with his left hand, with the right he assisted himself up the steep bluff, shoving occasionally the Indian woman before him who had her child in her arms. Charbonneau had the woman by the hand, endeavoring to pull her up the hill, but was so much frightened that he remained frequently motionless, and but for Captain Clark, both himself and his woman and child must have perished. So sudden was the rise of the water that before Captain Clark could reach his gun and begin to ascend the bank, it was up to his waist and wet his watch, and he could scarcely ascend faster than it arose until it had obtained the depth of fifteen feet with a current tremendous to behold. One moment longer and it would have swept them into the river just above the great cataract of 87 feet, where they must have inevitably perished. Charbonneau lost his gun, shot pouch, horn, tomahawk, and my wiping rod, Captain Clark his umbrella and compass or circumferenter. They fortunately arrived on the plain safe, where they found the black man, York, in search of them. York had separated from them a little while before the storm in pursuit of some buffalo, and had not seen them enter the ravine. When this gust came on, he [York] returned in search of them and not being able to find them for some time was much alarmed. The bier in which the woman carries her child, and all its clothes were swept away as they lay at her feet, she having time only to grasp her child—the infant was therefore very cold and the woman also, who had just recovered from a severe indisposition, was also wet and cold." Clark gives substantially the same account, but adds a few significant details. His version reads as follows, "*I determined myself to proceed on to the falls and take the river, according we all set out. I took my servant and one man, Charbonneau our interpreter, and his squaw accompanied. Soon after I arrived at the falls, I perceived a cloud which appeared black and threatened immediate rain. I looked out for a shelter, but could see no place without being in great danger of being blown into the river if the wind should prove as turbulent as it is at sometimes. About one fourth of a mile above the falls I observed a deep ravine in which was shelving rocks under which we took shelter near the river and placed our guns, the compass, etc., etc. under a shelving rock on the upper side of the creek, in a place which was very secure from rain. The first shower was moderate, accompanied with a violent wind, the effects of which we did not feel. Soon after a torrent of rain and hail fell more violent than ever I saw before, the rain fell like one volley of water falling from the heavens and gave us time only to get out of the way of a torrent of water which was pouring down the hill into the river with immense force, tearing everything before it, taking with it large rocks and mud. I took my gun and shot pouch in my left hand, and with the right scrambled up the hill pushing the interpreter's wife (who had the child in her arms) before me, the interpreter himself making attempts to pull up his wife by the hand, much scared and nearly without motion. We at length reached the top of the hill safe, where I found my servant in search of us, greatly agitated for our welfare. Before I got out of the bottom of the ravine, which was a flat dry rock when I entered it, the water was up to my waist and wet my watch. I scarcely got out before it raised ten feet deep with a torrent which was terrible to behold and by the time I reached the top of the hill, at least fifteen feet of water. I directed the party to return to the camp at the run as fast as possible to get to our load, where clothes could be got to* cover the child, whose clothes were all lost, and the woman, who was but just recovering from a severe indisposition, and was wet and cold. I was fearful of a relapse. I caused her, as also the others of the party, to take a little spirits, which my servant had in a canteen. I lost at the river in the torrent the large compass, an elegant fusee, tomahawk, umbrella, shot pouch and horn with powder and ball, moccasins, and the woman lost her child's bier and clothes, bedding, etc." The same incident is much more briefly recorded by Gass under date of July 1, and Ordway and Biddle under date of June 29. Biddle, instead of speaking of the basket in which Sacajawea carried her baby as a "bier," calls it a "net."

Near the close of July the Expedition began to draw near to the forks of the Missouri River and came into the country of the Shoshone Indians. On July 19 Lewis found several Indian camps of willow brush which had been occupied earlier in the spring. He also found pine trees from which the Indians had stripped the bark for the purpose, as Sacajawea explained, of obtaining the sap and tenderer part of the wood and bark for food. On the twenty-second, Lewis records, *"The Indian woman recognizes the country and assures us that this is the river on which her relations live and that the three forks are at no great distance. This piece of information has cheered the spirits of the party, who now begin to console themselves with the anticipation of shortly seeing the head of the Missouri, yet unknown to the civilized world."* On the twenty-eighth, the same diary contains this entry, *"Our present camp is precisely on the spot that the Snake Indians were encamped at the time the Minnetarees of the Knife River first came in sight of them five years since. From hence they retreated about three miles up Jefferson's River and concealed themselves in the woods. The Minnetarees pursued, attacked them, killed four men, four women, a number of boys, and made prisoners of all the females and four boys. Sacajawea, our Indian woman, was one of the female prisoners taken at that time, though I cannot discover that she shows any emotion of sorrow in recollecting this event, or of joy in being again restored to her native country. If she has enough to eat and a few trinkets to wear, I believe she would be perfectly content anywhere."* The expedition was now at the Three Forks of the Missouri, approximately 2,850 miles from home. The three streams, which here came together to make the Missouri, were named the Jefferson, the Madison, and the Gallatin. Here Clark fell sick, and it was not until July 30 that the Expedition was able to continue its ascent of the Jefferson River. The same day, according to Clark, *"the company passed the place the squaw interpretess was taken."* On August 8, the company came to a familiar landmark known as Beaverhead Rock, which Lewis described in some detail, at the same time emphasizing the grave necessity of finding Indians who would be able to supply the expedition with horses. His account runs as follows, *"The Indian woman recognized the point of high plain to our right, which she informed us was not very distant from the summer retreat of her nation on a river beyond the mountains which runs to the west. This hill she says her nation calls the beaver's head from a conceived resemblance of its figure to the head of that animal. She assures us that we shall either find her people on this river or on the river immediately west of its source, which, from its present size, cannot be very distant. As it is now all important with us to meet with these people as soon as possible, I determined to proceed tomorrow with a small party to the source of the principal stream of this river and pass the mountains to the Columbia, and down that river until I found the Indians, in short, it is my resolution to find them or some others, who have horses, if it should cause me a trip of one month, for without horses we shall be obliged to leave a great part of our stores, of which, it appears to me, that we have a stock already sufficiently small for the length of the voyage before us."*

On August 14, both Lewis and Clark record that Sacajawea was badly treated by her husband, who was severely reprimanded by Captain Clark in consequence. The next day Lewis mentions that Clark and Sacajawea narrowly escaped being bitten by a rattlesnake, a fact which is also confirmed by Clark in his entry of the same date. The day following, Ordway records that Sacajawea found and gathered *"a fine parcel of serviceberries"* and that on the sixteenth, Clark, Charbonneau, and

Sacajawea, while walking along the bank, found great quantities of these berries—*"the largest and best I ever saw"*—and gathering a bucket full gave them out to the party at noon, when they stopped for dinner. On August 13, when Captain Lewis, with three companions, was proceeding ahead of the main body of the Expedition, he saw in the distance an Indian riding on horseback. Although the captain made the sign of friendship customary with the Missouri River and Rocky Mountain Indians, of holding his blanket in both hands at the two corners, throwing it above his head and unfolding it when he brought it to the earth as if spreading it out on the ground and inviting them to come and sit on it, he failed to induce the Indian to come to him. Then he ran toward the Indian with a looking glass (mirror) and trinkets, calling—"tabba bone, tabba bone"—words that Sacajawea had taught him to use, meaning—"white man, white man"—at the same time rolling up his sleeves and opening his shirt to show the white skin of his arms and chest, for his face and hands were browned and tanned to the color of an Indian from the exposure to the wind during months of outdoor life. But despite all his efforts the Indian fled. The next day, however, Lewis overtook some squaws who conducted him to a camp where he met a chief and about sixty warriors, all [described as] well-mounted.

This chief, named Cameahwait, Lewis later discovered was the long-lost brother of Sacajawea—and after much bartering and bickering, he agreed to furnish horses and a guide to pilot the Expedition over the mountains. While Lewis was carrying on his negotiations with the Shoshone chief, the main body of the Expedition under Clark was dragging its boats up the Beaverhead River. On the seventeenth, in a charming valley near the present village of Armstead, Montana, where Lewis and Cameahwait had made their camps, Clark and his party came into view. The reunion of Sacajawea with her people which here occurred, her recognition of her brother in the person of Chief Cameahwait, and her meeting with the companion who had been with her when she was taken captive but who had escaped and returned to her people, are graphically given both by Lewis and

Clark. Of these events Lewis wrote on August 17 and 19 as follows, "Shortly after, Captain Clark arrived with the interpreter, Charbonneau, and the Indian woman, who proved to be a sister of the Chief Cameahwait. The meeting of those people was really affecting, particularly between Sacajawea and an Indian woman who had been taken prisoner at the same time with her and who had afterwards escaped from Minnetarees and rejoined her nation—we formed a canopy of one of our large sails, and planted some willow brush in the ground to form a shade for the Indians to set under while we spoke to them, which we thought it best to do this evening. Accordingly, about 4 PM, we called them together and through the medium of Labiche, Charbonneau, and Sacajawea, we communicated to them fully the objects which had brought us into this distant part of the country, in which we took care to make them a conspicuous object of our own good wishes and the care of our government." Lewis also relates the following complication which arose from Sacajawea's unexpected homecoming, "The father frequently disposes of his infant daughters in marriage to men who are grown who have sons for whom they think proper to provide wives. The compensation given in such cases usually consists of horses or mules which the father receives at the time of the contract and converts to his own use. Sacajawea had been disposed of before she was taken by the Minnetarees. The husband was yet living with this band. He was more than double her age and had two other wives. He claimed her as his wife, but said that as she [Sacajawea] had had a child by another man, who was Charbonneau, that he did not want her." Clark's description of Sacajawea's meeting with her people reads as follows, "I had not proceeded on one mile before I saw at a distance several Indians on horseback coming towards me. The interpreter and squaw, who were before me at some distance, danced for the joyful sight, and she made signs to me that they were her nation. As I approached nearer them, I discovered one of Captain Lewis's party with them, dressed in their dress. They met me with great signs of joy. The great chief of this nation proved to be the brother of the woman with us, and is a man of influence, sense, and easy and reserved manners, [who] appears to possess a great deal of sincerity." The description of Sacajawea's return to her tribe in the Biddle edition is significant not only because of the wealth of detail which it adds, but also (especially for the purpose of this narrative), because it records the adoption by Sacajawea of the son of her eldest sister. This is particularly important in tracing the family relations of Sacajawea and in establishing the connection between her and the Indian named Bazil of whom frequent mention is made in subsequent pages of this volume.

Biddle's lengthy account herewith follows, "*The Indians were all transported with joy, and the chief, in the warmth of his satisfaction, renewed his embrace to Captain Lewis, who was quite as much delighted as the Indians themselves. The report proved most agreeably true. On setting out at seven o'clock, Captain Clark, with Charbonneau and his wife, walked on shore. but they had not gone more than a mile before Captain Clark saw Sacajawea, who was with her husband one hundred yards ahead, begin to dance and show every mark of the most extravagant joy, turning round him and pointing to several Indians, whom he now saw advancing on horseback, sucking her fingers at the same time to indicate that they were of her native tribe. We soon drew near to the camp, and just as we approached it a woman made her way through the crowd towards Sacajawea, and recognizing each other, they embraced with the most tender affection. The meeting of these two young women had in it something peculiarly touching, not only in the ardent manner in which their feelings were expressed, but from the real interest of their situation. They had been companions in childhood, in the war with the Minnetarees they had both been taken prisoners in the same battle, they had shared and softened the rigors of their captivity till one of them had escaped from the Minnetarees, with scarce a hope of ever seeing her friend free from the hands of her enemies. While Sacajawea was renewing among the women the friendships of former days, Captain Clark went on, and was received by Captain Lewis and the chief, who, after the first embraces and salutations were over, conducted him to a sort of circular tent or shade of willows. Here he was seated on a white robe, and the chief immediately tied in his hair six small shells resembling pearls, an ornament highly valued by these people, who procured them in the course of trade from the seacoast. The moccasins of the whole party were then taken off, and after much ceremony the smoking began. After this the conference was to be opened, and glad of an opportunity of being able to converse more intelligibly, Sacajawea was sent for, she came into the tent, sat down, and was beginning to interpret, when in the person of Cameahwait she recognized her brother, she instantly jumped up and ran and embraced him, throwing over him her blanket and weeping profusely, the chief himself was moved, though not in the same degree. After some conversation between them she resumed her seat, and attempted to interpret for us, but her new situation seemed to overpower her, and she was frequently interrupted by her tears. After the council was finished the unfortunate woman learned that all her family was dead except two brothers, one of whom was absent, and a son of her eldest sister, a small boy, who was immediately adopted by her."* On the seventeenth, Lewis and Clark held a council at which it was agreed that the next day Clark should set out in advance of the main body with eleven men furnished with axes and other tools necessary for making canoes, together with their arms and as much baggage as they could carry. Clark was also to take with him Charbonneau and Sacajawea and leave them at the Shoshone camp so that they might hasten the return of the Indians with their horses to the main camp of the Expedition near the forks of the Beaverhead. Clark, however, and his company were to continue to the Columbia, and there construct canoes for the use of the larger party if they found the river navigable. On the eighteenth, Clark succeeded in purchasing three horses from the Shoshone chief, for which he gave *"a chief's coat, some handkerchiefs, a shirt, leggings and a few arrow points."* Two of his own coats he gave to two under chiefs *"who appeared not well-satisfied that the first chief was dressed so much finer than themselves."* Charbonneau and Sacajawea, in accordance with the prearranged agreement were left at the Indian camp to persuade the Indians to bring their horses as soon as possible to the main body of the Expedition under Lewis. On August 22 the Indians under Cameahwait met with Lewis near the crest of the Rocky Mountains, and for a number of days the latter bargained with them for the purchase of their horses. Lewis, in two entries of August 22 and 24, records these negotiations. "*At 11 AM Charbonneau, the Indian woman, Cameahwait, and about fifty men with a number of women and children arrived. They encamped near us. After they had turned out their horses and arranged their camp, I called the chiefs and warriors together and addressed them a second time. I gave him a few dried squashes which we had brought from the Mandans. He had them boiled and declared them to be the best thing he had ever tasted, except sugar, a small lump of which it seems his sister, Sacajawea, had given him. I had now nine horses and a mule, and two which I had hired made twelve. These I loaded and the Indian women took the balance of the baggage. I had given the interpreter some articles with which to purchase a horse for the woman which he had obtained. For each horse I gave an ax, a knife, handkerchief, and a little paint, and for the mules the addition of a knife, a shirt, handkerchief, and a pair of leggings.*" Biddle, under entries of the same date, describes this horse trading episode as follows, "*We then produced some battle axes which we had made at Fort Mandan, and a quantity of knives, with both of which they appeared very much pleased, and we were soon able to purchase three horses by giving for each an axe, a knife, a handkerchief, and a little paint. To this we were obliged to add a second knife, a shirt, a handkerchief, and a pair of leggings, and such is the estimation in which those animals are held, that even at this price, which was double that for a horse, the fellow who sold him took upon himself great merit in having given away a mule to us. They now said that they had no more horses for sale, and as we had now nine of our own, two hired horses and a mule, we began loading them as heavily as was prudent, and, placing the rest on the shoulders of the Indian women, left our camp at twelve o'clock. We were all on foot, except Sacajawea, for whom her husband had purchased a horse with some articles which we gave him for that purpose, an*

Indian, however, had the politeness to offer Captain Lewis one of his horses to ride, which he accepted in order better to direct the march of the party." As the Expedition left this spot, Lewis learned with grave concern that Cameahwait had sent a messenger ahead to summon the remaining Indians on the Lemhi River to join him in the annual buffalo hunt on the Missouri.

This hunt, usually undertaken in July, had already been delayed to a late start because of the councils with Lewis and the negotiations over the horses. Afraid that the Indians would leave him without sufficient horses for the journey over the mountains if they started on this hunt, Lewis prevailed upon Cameahwait to countermand his order until the Expedition should reach the Lemhi Indians, whose help was seriously needed.

Credit was given to Sacajawea for saving the Expedition in this emergency. Lewis, on August 25, describes the incident as follows, "*This morning loaded our horses and set out a little after sunrise, sometime after we had halted, Charbonneau mentioned to me with apparent unconcern that he expected to meet all the Indians from the camp on the Columbia tomorrow on their way to the Missouri—he then informed me that the first chief had dispatched some of his young men this morning to this camp requesting the Indians to meet them tomorrow and that he himself and those with him would go on with them down the Missouri, and consequently leave me and my baggage on the mountain or thereabouts. I was out of patience with the folly of Charbonneau who had not sufficient sagacity to see the consequences which would inevitably flow from such a movement of the Indians, and although he had been in possession of this information since early in the morning when it had been communicated to him by his Indian woman, yet he never mentioned it until the afternoon.*" Ordway even more definitely speaks of the inestimable value of the Indian woman's services in this connection. "*Whilst at dinner we learned by means of Sacajawea that the young men who left us this morning carried a request from the chief that the village would break up its encampment and meet his party tomorrow, when they would all go down the Missouri into the buffalo country. Alarmed at this new caprice of the Indians, which if not counteracted, threatened to leave ourselves and our baggage on the mountains, or even if we reached the waters of the Columbia, prevent our obtaining horses to go on farther, Captain Lewis immediately called the three chiefs together." In September, 1805, the party crossed the Bitterroot Mountains amidst snow and drifts and hailed with delight the first westward flowing streams. Here, having branded their horses, they left them in care of a Nez Perce chief.

Building themselves canoes, they floated down the Clearwater River to its junction with the Snake River, where Lewiston, Idaho and Clarkston, Washington, now stand.

On they continued, down the swift flowing Snake that sped to its junction with the Columbia, a short distance above the present site of Kennewick and Pasco in the State of Washington. Embarked on the broad Columbia, their course was rapid and easy, save for the excitement of shooting an occasional rapid or making a portage. Soon Mt. Hood was seen to the south and Mt. Adams to the north. East of the mountains game had been very plentiful, furnishing the explorers with an abundance to eat.

On the west side of the continental divide, however, they actually suffered for food. Sometimes, indeed, they were reduced to such straits that they were obliged to buy puppies from the Indians from which they made stews that were greatly relished. Horse flesh was also eaten by all the white explorers, but Sacajawea, being a Shoshone, refused to eat the meat either of the horses or the puppies. On October 28, the explorers were visited by some Indians, one of whom wore a round hat and a sailor's pea jacket, another had a British musket, still others possessed a cutlass, a brass tea kettle, and bright colored cloths. Lewis and Clark therefore knew that they were near the end of their outward journey, for such articles could only have been obtained from trading vessels along the coast. On November 8, the eyes of the weary explorers were rested and their hearts rejoiced by the sight of the goal of so many months of toil and travel—the western sea, the object for which Pierre LaVerendrye had sought so long ago in vain. One week later Lewis and his party reached the ocean, four thousand one hundred thirty-four miles from home. A few miles from the sea on the south side of the mouth of the Columbia, on a small stream afterward called Lewis and Clark River, they built Fort Clatsop. Here establishing their winter quarters, they stayed until March 23, 1806. After their long journey across the continent, the men were almost naked. Clothes had to be made for immediate wear and for the return journey. During the winter the men made over four hundred pairs of moccasins and clothes of all kinds from the skins of elk, deer, beaver, and sea otter. Many gallons of salt were also made by evaporating sea water, and numerous packs of jerked venison were prepared for the return journey. The blubber of a whale, discovered on the beach, was also made into oil for the use of the Expedition. In describing these matters on January 5, 1806, Lewis writes, "*Willard and Weiser returned—they informed us—they could find a convenient place for making salt, that they had at length established themselves on the coast about fifteen miles southwest from this, near the lodge of some Tillamook families, that the Indians were very friendly and had given them a considerable quantity of the blubber of the whale which perished on the coast some distance southeast of them. Part of this blubber they brought with them. It was white and not unlike the fat of pork, though the texture was more spongy and somewhat coarser. I had a part of it cooked and found it very palatable and tender, it resembled the beaver or the dog in flavor.*" On the same date Clark also writes, "*The Indians were very friendly and had given them a considerable quantity of the blubber of the whale which perished on the coast some distance southeast of them. It was white and not unlike the fat of pork, though the texture was more spongy and somewhat coarser.*" Sacajawea, hearing of the "large fish," begged to be allowed to go to the beach, seventeen miles distant by the shortest route, or thirty-five miles of easier travel. As the Indian woman had not yet visited the ocean, she was permitted to take the journey. Lewis's entry of January 6 reads, "*Captain Clark set out after an early breakfast, with the party in two canoes as had been concerted last evening, Charbonneau and his Indian woman were also of the party, the Indian woman was very importunate to be permitted to go, and was therefore indulged." Sacajawea never forgot this experience, and long years afterward in her home on the reservation in Wyoming she used to describe this visit to the sea and the enormous "fish" lying on the sand.

While in winter quarters at Fort Clatsop, Lewis and Clark were visited by many Indians with whom they carried on a limited trade and from whom they received much interesting information. The daily events at this camp, the site of which Sacajawea was largely instrumental in selecting, judging from Clark's entry of November 24 are pictured in the following extracts from the various diaries. On November 20, Clark wrote, *"Found many of the Chinooks with Captain Lewis, of whom there was two chiefs, Comcomly and Chillarlarwil, to whom we gave medals and to one a flag. One of the Indians had on a robe made of two sea otter skins. The fur from them was more beautiful than any fur I had ever seen. Both Captain Lewis and myself endeavored to purchase the robe with different articles. At length we procured it for a belt of blue beads which the squaw wife of our interpreter, Charbonneau, wore around her waist. We gave the squaw a coat of blue cloth, for the belt of blue beads we gave for the sea otter skins purchased from an Indian."* On November 30 Clark wrote, *"The squaw gave me a piece of bread made of flour she had reserved for her child and kept until this time, which has unfortunately got wet and a little sour. This bread I eat with great satisfaction, it being the only mouthful I had tasted for several months past."* His entry of December 3, 1805, reads, *"The squaw broke the two shank bones of the elk after the marrow was taken out, boiled them, and extracted a pint of grease or tallow from them—after eating the marrow out of two shank bones of an elk, the squaw chopped the bones fine, boiled them, extracted a pint of grease, which is superior to the tallow of the animal."* Again, on December 25, Clark writes *"I received a present of Captain Lewis of a fleece hosiery, shirt, drawers and socks, a pair of moccasins of Whitehouse, a small Indian basket of Goodrich, two dozen white weasel's tails of the Indian woman, and some black root of the Indians before their departure."* On March 23, 1806, after presenting Chief Comcomly with Fort Clatsop and the equipment, Lewis and Clark pushed their boats from the shore and the home journey began.

On April sixteenth, Captain Clark, in company with Charbonneau, Sacajawea, and nine men, undertook to trade with the Indians for horses, employing a large part of the remaining stock of merchandise for that purpose. On the route to the Walla Wallas, some difficulty was encountered over the theft of a robe belonging to Captain Clark, but on April 28 Lewis records that they found a Shoshone woman *"prisoner among these people by means of whom and Sacajawea we found the means of conversing with the Walla Wallas. We conversed with them for several hours and fully satisfied all their inquiries with respect to ourselves and the objects of our pursuit. They were much pleased."* Clark, in turn, makes a similar statement. *"We found a Shoshone woman, prisoner among those people by means of whom and Sacajawea, Charbonneau wife, we found means of conversing with the Walla Wallas."* On the return journey Sacajawea proved to be of as much value to the expedition as she had been on the journey to the Pacific. Thus, on May 11, 1806, Clark wrote of her services as an interpreter to the Chopunnish Indians *"The one-eyed chief, Yoomparkkartim, arrived, and we gave him a medal of the small size and spoke to the Indians through a Snake boy, Charbonneau, and his wife. We informed them who we were, where we came from and our intentions towards them, which pleased them very much, we drew a map of the country with a coal on the mat in their way, and by the assistance of the Snake boy and our interpreters were enabled to make ourselves understood by them although it had to pass through French, Minnetaree, Shoshone, and Chopunnish languages."* In the Biddle edition the same incident is described in a little more detail, as follows, under date of May 11, *"It was not without difficulty, nor until after nearly half the day was spent, that we were able to convey all this information to the Chopunnish, much of which might have been lost or distorted in its circuitous route through a variety of languages, for in the first place we spoke in English to one of our men, who translated it into French to*

Charbonneau, he interpreted it to his wife in the Minnetaree language, and she then put it into Shoshoni, and the young Shoshoni prisoner explained it to the Chopunnish in their own dialect." At times the Expedition found it difficult to secure supplies from the Indians because the merchandise, so necessary for trade, was almost exhausted. When the company left the coast it had on hand for exchange only, *"six blue robes, one of scarlet, five made out of the old United States flag that had floated over many a council, a few old clothes, Clark's uniform, coat, and hat, and a few little trinkets that might be tied in a handkerchief."*

At the Clearwater River the leaders of the expedition had to render medical service to the Indians in order to obtain necessary supplies. Eye water was at a premium, and cures for rheumatism in great demand, and by the relief thus afforded to the suffering Indians, Lewis and Clark won their goodwill. Finally, however, the medicine chest was exhausted, brass buttons had departed from the soldiers's uniforms, needles, thread, fish hooks, files, and awls had been exchanged for food, and now these "made-to-order" doctors had to resort to every device to obtain from the natives the commonest commodities. In the eyes of the Indians they were wonderful "medicine men." One can fancy how mystified the red men were over a watch, with its even ticking inside the case, the magnet, with its power to make a piece of steel move without touching it, phosphorus, invisible in the daytime but ghastly at night, the spyglass, bringing objects at a distance within reach of the hand, the burning glass, stealing fire from heaven, and the air gun, with its terrifying noise.

No wonder the Indians thought the white men were more than human beings, and that the exhibition of these mysteries brought to the party the much-needed food and supplies.

Sacajawea also acquainted the members of the expedition with the virtues of fennel roots, and gathered large quantities of this food for use in the passage of the Rocky Mountains. After crossing the Rocky Mountains, the Expedition was divided into four parties to carry out further explorations. These parties were instructed to unite at the mouth of the Yellowstone. One of these companies, under command of Captain Clark, included Sacajawea and Charbonneau. Clark was under instructions to proceed to the Yellowstone River and descend this river in canoes to its junction with the Missouri. Here he would await the arrival of Captain Lewis and the rest of the expedition. Describing this incident on July 3, Clark wrote, "*Took my leave of Captain Lewis and his Indians. Set out with nineteen men, interpreter Charbonneau and his wife and child (as an interpreter and interpretess) for the Crow Indians and the latter for the Shoshoni with fifty horses.*" Three days later Sacajawea pointed out the gap in the mountains now known as Bozeman Pass, and described the surrounding country in some detail to Captain Clark.

Clark mentions this in his journal in the following paragraph, "*The Indian woman, wife to Charbonneau, informed me that she had been in this plain frequently and knew it well, that the creek which we descended was a branch of Wisdom River, and when we ascended the higher part of the Plain we would discover a gap in the mountains in our direction to the canoes, and when we arrived at that gap we would see a high point of a mountain covered with snow in our direction to the canoes.*" Ordway also mentions the incident in an entry of the same date, and in the Biddle edition under date of July 6 appears the following, "*In the afternoon we passed along the hillside north of the creek, till in the course of six miles we entered an extensive level plain. Here the tracks of the Indians scattered so much that we could no longer pursue it, but Sacajawea recognized the plain immediately. She had traveled often during her childhood, and informed us that it was the great resort of the Shoshones, who came for the purpose of gathering Camassia quamash and cows, and of taking beaver, with which the Plains abounded. Surrounded on all sides by high points of mountains covered with snow, among which was the gap pointed out by the squaw, bearing south 56 east.*" The next day the Biddle narrative mentions the fact that the party was now nearing the spot where a cache had been made the preceding August, and the record of the eighth reads, "*We proceeded down the west branch of Jefferson River, and at the distance of nine miles* reached its forks, where we had deposited our merchandise in the month of August. We found everything safe, though some of the goods were a little damp and one of the canoes had a hole."

On the ninth, Clark records that Sacajawea brought him a plant the root of which was eaten by the Indians. "*This root resembled a carrot in form and size and something of its color, but a paler yellow than that of our carrot.*" On July thirteenth, Clark started in the direction of Bozeman Pass, taking with him Charbonneau, Sacajawea and her papoose, and his Negro servant, York. On that date he wrote, "*I observe several leading roads with appear to pass to a gap of the mountain in the east northeast direction about 18 or 20 miles distant. The Indian woman, who has been of great service to me as a pilot through this country, recommends a gap in the mountains more south which I shall cross.*" On August 3, the company started its descent of the Yellowstone, an event which Clark describes as follows, "*I descended in two small canoes lashed together in which I had the following persons, John Shields, George Gibson, William Bratton, Francois Labiche, Toussaint Charbonneau, his wife and child, and my man York. The Rochejhone or Yellowstone River, is large and navigable with but few obstructions quite into the Rocky Mountains.*" The Biddle edition, under entry of the next day, speaks of the great annoyance caused by the mosquitoes during this stage of the expedition. "*Captain Clark therefore determined to go on to some spot which would be free from mosquitoes—he proceeded down the river to the second point and encamped on a sandbar, but here the mosquitoes seemed to be even more numerous than above. The face of the Indian child is considerably puffed up and swollen with the bites of these animals, nor could the men procure scarcely any sleep during the night.*" On August 9 Clark wrote that Sacajawea brought him a "large and well-flavored gooseberry of a rich crimson color, and a deep purple berry of the large cherry of the current species and which is common on this river as low as the Mandans, the engages call it the Indian current." Captain Lewis, dissatisfied with his previous exploration up the Marias River, after his separation from Clark took with him

Drouillard, the interpreter and hunter, and the two Field brothers, and traveled northeast to what is now Great Falls, Montana, and then northwest, trying to find the source of the Marias River.

Here he had an unpleasant encounter with the Blackfeet, the most treacherous of all the Indians. In camp early one morning a Blackfoot stole Field's rifle, whereupon Field stabbed the thief to the heart and recovered his rifle, but in the heat of the struggle the Indians were discovered trying to drive away the horses. Without horses, Lewis and his men would have been helpless, miles from their party and in a strange country, surrounded by hostile Indians. In this emergency it was necessary to act vigorously and immediately. Lewis therefore at once opened fire, killing one of the Indians, and in exchange received a shot which fortunately only passed through his hair. His men then seized the horses of the Indians and fled for the Missouri.

The party rode sixty miles without stopping, covering over one hundred twenty miles in twenty-four hours, until they reached the junction of the Marias and the Missouri Rivers. Here Captain Lewis found another detachment of the Expedition. Opening the caches which they had made here the preceding year, the explorers found much of their buried goods spoiled by water, but fortunately the iron boat was in good condition. Turning the horses loose here on the prairies, the company sailed down the Missouri and met Clark, Charbonneau, Sacajawea, and the rest of the party at the mouth of the Yellowstone. Two days after this reunion, the entire Expedition arrived at the Mandan villages where they found that during their absence their fort had been destroyed by fire. Charbonneau and Sacajawea remained at the Mandan villages when the expedition continued on its way to St. Louis. The parting is described by Clark, Gass, and Biddle. The entries describing this incident from all of these journals are reprinted here because of the significant tribute they pay to Sacajawea and also because of the mention they make of Clark's offer to take Sacajawea's nineteen-months-old boy, Baptiste, to civilization with him. Of this incident Clark wrote as follows, *"Settled with Toussaint Charbonneau for his services as an* interpreter the price of a horse and lodge purchased of him for public service, in all amounting to five hundred dollars, thirty-three and one third cents. We also took our leave of T. Charbonneau, his Snake Indian wife, and their child, who had accompanied us on our route to the Pacific Ocean in the capacity of interpreter and interpretess. T. Charbonneau wished much to accompany us in the said capacity. I offered to take his little son, a beautiful, promising child who is nineteen months old, to which they both himself and his wife were willing, provided the child had been weaned. They observed that in one year the boy would be sufficiently old to leave his mother, and he would then take him to me if I would be so friendly as to raise the child for him in such a manner as I thought proper, to which I agreed, etc." The Biddle edition, under date of August 16, contains the following entry, "*The principal chiefs of the Minnetarees came down to bid us farewell, as none of them could be prevailed on to go with us. This circumstance induced our interpreter, Charbonneau, with his wife and child, to remain here, as he could be no longer useful, and notwithstanding our offers of taking him with us to the United States, he said that he had there no acquaintance and no chance of making a livelihood, and preferred remaining among the Indians. This man has been very serviceable to us, and his wife particularly useful among the Shoshones. Indeed, she has borne with a patience truly admirable the fatigues of so long a route encumbered with the charge of an infant, who is even now only nineteen months old. We therefore paid him his wages, amounting to five hundred dollars and thirty three cents, including the price of a horse and a lodge [a leather tent] purchased of him.*" After leaving the Mandan villages, Clark, on August 20, wrote at great length to Charbonneau showing his very deep interest in the interpreter and his family, and expressing an earnest desire to adopt Sacajawea's [infant] child, Baptiste. Clark's reference in this letter to "your little son" and "my boy Pomp" are of especial significance. Because of its importance, this letter, already referred to in the preface to this volume, is here reprinted in full. The text of it is as follows, "*Charbonneau, sir, your present situation with the Indians gives me some concern—I wish now I had advised you to come on with me to the Illinois where it most probably would be in my power to put you on some way to do something for yourself. You have been a long time with me and have conducted yourself in such a manner as to gain my friendship, your woman, who accompanied you that long dangerous and fatiguing route to the Pacific Ocean and back, deserved a greater reward for her attention and services on that route than we had in our power to give her at the Mandans. As to your little son (my boy Pomp) you well know my fondness for him and my anxiety to take and raise him as my own child. I once more tell you if you will bring your son Baptiste to me, I will educate him and treat him as my own child—I do not forget the promise which I made to you and shall now repeat them that you may be certain. Charbonneau—if you wish to live with the white people—and will come to me, I will give you a piece of land and furnish you with horses—cows and hogs. If you wish to visit your friends in Montreal, I will let you have a horse, and your family shall be taken care of until your return—if you wish to return as an interpreter for the Minnetarees when the troops come up to form the establishment, you will be with me ready and I will procure you the place—or if you wish to return to trade with the Indians and will leave your little son Pomp with me, I will assist you with merchandise for that purpose, and become myself concerned with you in trade on a small scale, that is to say not exceeding a pirogue load at one time. If you are disposed to accept either of my offers to you, and will bring down your son, "your famn Janey" had best come along with you to take care of the boy until I get him—let me advise you to keep your bill of exchange and what furs and peltries you have in possession, and get as much more as you can, and get as many robes, and big horn and cabra (goat) skins as you can collect in the course of this winter. And take them down to St. Louis as early as possible. Inquire of the governor of that place for a letter which I shall leave with the governor. I shall inform you what you had best do with your furs peltries and robes, etc. when you get to St. Louis write a letter to me by the post and let me know your situation. If you do not intend to go down either this fall or in the spring, write a letter to me by the* first opportunity and inform me what you intend to do that I may know if I may expect you or not. If you ever intend to come down this fall or the next spring will be the best time—this fall would be best if you could get down before the winter. I shall be found either in St. Louis or in Clarksville at the Falls of the Ohio. Wishing you and your family great success, and with anxious expectations of seeing my little dancing boy, Baptiste, I shall remain your friend." (William Clark) "Keep this letter and let not more than one or two persons see it, and when you write to me seal your letter. I think you best not determine which of my offers to accept until you see me. Come prepared to accept of either which you may choose after you get down." (Mr. Toussaint Charbonneau, Minnetarees Villages)

With the departure of the Expedition from the Mandan villages and the separation of Lewis and Clark from the interpreter Charbonneau, his wife Sacajawea, and "my boy Pomp" (Jean Baptiste Charbonneau) the history of these three comes to an end so far as the journals of Lewis, Clark, Gass, Ordway, and Whitehouse are concerned. Henceforth we must look to other sources for the further story of the Charbonneau family, which the later chapters of this book contain.

☐☐☐☐☐☐☐☐☐☐

In the letter from Clark to Charbonneau, quoted in the last chapter, the American commander proposed that Charbonneau come to St. Louis to live, and promised to aid him in securing land and property. [William] Clark's interest, however, was apparently far stronger in Sacajawea and her son, Baptiste, than in Charbonneau. In the letter he wrote, "*As to your little son, my boy Pomp, you well know my fondness for him and my anxiety to take and raise him as my own child. I once more tell you if you will bring your son Baptiste to me I will educate him and treat him as my own child.*" The same letter also urges Charbonneau to bring "*your famn Janey,*" or Sacajawea, to St. Louis to take care of the little dancing boy, Baptiste. In this invitation Clark showed true diplomatic skill. In order to bring Sacajawea and Baptiste to St. Louis it was necessary to win Charbonneau's goodwill and to avoid arousing his antagonism. This Clark did so successfully that within a few years we find Charbonneau, Sacajawea, and Baptiste living in St. Louis, which was then the great emporium of the fur trade. A number of the names used by Captain Clark in his letter to Charbonneau require brief interpretation. His expression "my boy Pomp" and "your boy Pomp" apply, of course, to the same child—the infant born to Sacajawea at the Mandan villages. He is also referred to in the letter as "your son Baptiste," and "my little dancing boy Baptiste." Pomp is a name often given to the oldest boy in a Shoshone family, and means "head" or "the leader."

    It is bestowed upon the oldest son, and thus becomes a title of primogeniture, and the bearer of it is recognized as one having authority. Two of the landmarks on the expedition were named for this little boy, Sacajawea's son. Both names apparently were given on the same day. One was a small stream flowing into the Yellowstone, called Baptiste Creek.

    The other was the great rock overlooking the Yellowstone, just north of the present site of Billings, Montana. This was designated on Captain Clark's map of 1814 as Pomp's Tower, but it is now called Pompey's Pillar. On one of the sides of this rock Captain Clark records that he marked his "name and the day of the month and year, William Clark, July 25, 1806." Prior to the publication of Captain Clark's letter to Charbonneau, Dr. Elliott Coues stated that the Baptiste Creek, referred to in the preceding paragraph, was named for Jean Baptiste LePage who was engaged by Lewis and Clark at the Mandan villages on November 3, 1804, to accompany the expedition. LePage was a French Canadian and a friend of Charbonneau, but since the discovery of Clark's letter, it is evident that the name was given in honor of Sacajawea's son, Baptiste. The little dancing boy was evidently exceedingly popular with the members of the Expedition, and as soon as he could stand alone, with his chubby hands holding fast to Sacajawea's fingers, he made his tiny moccasined feet move to the rhythm of the violin, and when he could balance himself and stand unsupported he danced with the men about the campfire—danced just as small Indian children dance today on the Shoshone Reservation where Sacajawea, in her later years, watched her grandchildren dance to the rhythm of modern Indian instruments. Charbonneau with his two Shoshone wives and his two sons reached St. Louis in August, 1806. Leaving his family here, the interpreter accepted an offer to trap for a fur company on the rivers of the southwest—perhaps branches of the Red or Arkansas—in territory inhabited by various Indian tribes including especially that branch of the Shoshones known as the Comanches. Four years later we find Charbonneau once more in St. Louis. Here, on October 30, 1810, he purchased from Captain Clark, who was then Indian agent for the Louisiana Territory, a tract of land on the Missouri River in Saint Ferdinand Township. Within a few months, however, Charbonneau disposed of this land to Captain Clark for the sum of one hundred dollars. The transaction is recorded in the records of the court for March 26, 1811. "*This instrument*," writes Miss [Stella] Drumm, "*indicates that Charbonneau bought this land with a view to settling down to civilized life but, becoming weary of it, transferred his property to Clark and returned to the Mandans.*" An entry in the Auguste Chouteau manuscript to the effect that Charbonneau on March 20 purchased from Chouteau fifty pounds of biscuit or hard tack, doubtless to be used on an expedition into the wilderness, evidently confirms Miss Drumm's conclusion that Charbonneau was leaving St. Louis for an extended period.

From other sources we learn that in April, 1811, Charbonneau entered the service of Henry Marie Brackenridge, the explorer, on his expedition up the Missouri. Brackenridge sailed from St. Louis on April 2, taking with him Charbonneau and one of the latter's wives known as the "Otter Woman." This woman, a Shoshone, was somewhat older than Sacajawea, with whom she was on friendly terms, and was the mother of one of Charbonneau's other sons, Toussaint Jr., a lad a few years older than his half-brother, Baptiste. Toussaint Jr. in later years was also frequently called "Tessou." When Charbonneau started on the expedition with Brackenridge, he left Sacajawea, Baptiste, and Toussaint Jr. in the care of Captain Clark at St. Louis. Captain

Clark acted as guardian for the two boys, though not in a legal capacity. The entry in Brackenridge's journal, which speaks of the departure of the expedition, reads as follows, "*We have on board a Frenchman named Charbonneau, with his wife, an Indian woman of the Snake nation, both of whom accompanied Lewis and Clark to the Pacific, and were of great service. The woman, a good creature, of a mild and gentle disposition, was greatly attached to the whites, whose manners and airs she tries to imitate, but she had become sickly and longed to revisit her native country, her husband also, who had spend many years amongst the Indians, was become weary of civilized life.*" In this account Brackenridge seems to identify the woman who accompanied his expedition with Sacajawea, but investigation shows this to be incorrect.

Charbonneau at this time had at least three wives, two Shoshone and one Mandan, and the woman mentioned by Brackenridge was not Sacajawea but his other Shoshone wife, the mother of Toussaint Jr. Baptiste was still too young to be left in St. Louis without his mother's care, since he was only six years old, and Sacajawea remained to care for her son and also to have oversight of the other boy, Toussaint Jr. Further confirmation of this fact will be found in a later chapter. It is desirable here to trace briefly the career of Charbonneau from this time on until his death. As already stated in an earlier chapter, Charbonneau was born in Canada, of French parentage, about the year 1758. In 1793 he is first mentioned as an engage of the Northwest Fur Company, serving as a trader at Pine Fort on the Assiniboine.

Two years later he moved into the Missouri Valley, where he became established among the Minnetaree or Gros Ventres on the Knife River at their central village, Mentaharter. In 1796 Charbonneau went to live in the Mandan villages, where he was the only white man in the territory. Since at that time there were no trade relations with St. Louis, he was obliged to purchase his supplies from the English traders further north. Some time prior to the Lewis and Clark Expedition, he entered the employ of the American Fur Company, and in 1803 and 1804 had charge of Fort Pembina with Alexander Henry. In addition to serving as guide for

Lewis and Clark, he also served with Major Stephen H. Long and with various later expeditions to the Rocky Mountains. In many respects, Charbonneau's character apparently left something to be desired. In sudden emergency or danger he was likely to prove himself an arrant coward, as was evidenced by his conduct in the sudden flood which nearly swept Captain Clark and his party to destruction. He also at times, shamefully abused his wife, Sacajawea, his conduct eventually forcing her to leave him, and at times his trustworthiness seems to have been seriously open to question. Shortly before the departure of Lewis and Clark from the Mandan villages in the spring of 1805, for example, Charbonneau apparently sought to break his engagement with the explorers to enter the service of the Northwest Company. This would have left the American expedition without an interpreter, and would have deprived it also of the services of Sacajawea. Clark wrote on March 12, 1805, "*Charbonneau sent a Frenchman to our party [to say] that he was sorry for the foolish part he had acted and if we pleased he would accompany us agreeably to the terms we had proposed and do everything we wished him to do, etc., etc. He agreed to our terms and we agreed he might go on with us.*" [Francois Antoine] Larocque of the Northwest Company, on the other hand, defends Charbonneau in this transaction. In his journal of 1804 and 1805 he wrote, "*Spoke to Charbonneau about helping as interpreter in the trade to the Big Bellies, he told me that, being engaged to the Americans, he could not come without leave from Captain Lewis, and desired me to speak to him, which I did, with the result that Lewis gave consent.*" As we have already seen, when Lewis and Clark returned to the Mandans from their expedition to the Pacific, they left Charbonneau and Sacajawea with these Indians while they continued their journey to St. Louis. As already stated in Clark's letter, quoted in the previous chapter, for his nineteen months of service to the Expedition, Charbonneau received the sum of five hundred dollars and thirty-three cents, including the price of a horse and a lodge, or leather tent, purchased from him. The value of the service that he rendered the explorers has been the subject of some dispute. Both Lewis and Clark, it is true, commend him as a useful servant, and Clark afterward offered to aid him if he wished to return to civilization, but this offer, as we have seen, may have been inspired in part by Clark's affection for the little boy, Baptiste. Apparently Charbonneau discharged his duties as interpreter in good faith, though his knowledge of the Indian languages was probably not as adequate as he pretended.

Among Charbonneau's most caustic critics is Dr. Elliott Coues, who makes numerous references to the unfortunate interpreter's clumsiness and boorish manners. Says Coues, "*In the light of the narrative he appears to have been a poor specimen, consisting chiefly of a tongue to wag in a mouth to fill, and had he possessed the comprehensive saintliness of his baptismal name he would have been a minus function in comparison with his wife, Sacajawea, who contributed a full man's share to the success of the expedition besides taking care of her baby.*" Dr. Coues also speaks scathingly of Charbonneau's attempt to desert the Expedition just before its start from the Mandan towns, saying, "*It is a wonder he was not frozen out of the garrison.*" Coues writes further of Charbonneau and Sacajawea, "*It could have hardly occurred to anyone in 1806, that Charbonneau's wife earned her wages too. What Charbonneau's services were, except on rare occasions when his wife interpreted to him, does not appear in the history to naked eyes. This individual remained among the Indians for many years. He was found by Maximilian in 1832-1834, and he 'candidly confessed' to the Prince of Wied that after a residence of thirty-seven years among the Minnetarees, he 'could never learn to pronounce their language correctly.' He must therefore have been a fool as well as the coward and wife beater that we know he was. But his linguistic accomplishments were equal to abuse of Sacajawea in more than one dialect, and interpreters received good pay in those days.*" Among his contemporaries, Charbonneau also had critics almost as sarcastic as Dr. Coues. [John] Luttig, in his journal, spoke in derision of him, accusing him of exaggeration and cowardice, and saying that he gave wild accounts of the dangers from the Indians to excite fear among the engages.

Again, when in 1834 James Kipp of the Columbia Fur Company took Charbonneau into his service, William Laidlaw, also of the Columbia Company and in charge of Fort Pierre, wrote his disapproval, saying, "*I am much surprised at your taking Charbonneau into favor, after showing so much ingratitude upon all occasions. The knave, what does he say for himself?*" Evidently, judging from these quotations, the old interpreter's reputation was not unblemished, and certainly Sacajawea's fondness for the white captains was due in part to the kindness and protection they gave her from this "loutish, brutal fellow." Despite all these limitations, however, Charbonneau on the whole, apparently discharged his duties as interpreter faithfully enough.

But his knowledge of the Indian tongue was not nearly so great as he pretended, and as a consequence he made at times some serious blunders. One of the most unfortunate of these was in causing the wrong interpretation to be given to the name Sacajawea, which in reality means "Canoe Launcher" instead of "Bird Woman." The [careless] error apparently arose in the following manner, when interrogated as to the meaning of the name of his Indian woman, Charbonneau attempted in his clumsy and self-important way to explain its meaning by Indian signs, which were understood to refer to the flight of a bird. He made signs of flying by motions of his hands and arms, working them at the level of his shoulders, which thus given were naturally interpreted as "Bird Woman." The proper signs for the Shoshone name, Sacajawea, however, should have been made with the arms and hands near the waist line to indicate the motion of one who propels a canoe or boat—thus giving to the word its true meaning, the "Boat or Canoe Launcher." During his thirty-seven years among the Mandans, Charbonneau himself acquired various names. These included "The Chief of the Little Village," "The Man who Possesses Many Gourds," "The Great Horse Came from Afar," "The Bear of the Forest." In addition to the frequent mention he received in the various journals of the Lewis and Clark Expedition, Charbonneau's name appears frequently in the writings of other explorers and travelers. Among these are Henry

Brackenridge and John Bradbury in 1811, John Luttig in 1812, Prince Paul of Wurttemberg in 1823, General Henry Atkinson, 1825, General Stephen W. Kearny, also in 1825, Maximilian, Prince of Wied, 1833, Charles Larpenteur, 1838, and "every fur trader and trapper of the early days in the upper Missouri regions." From these references, it is possible to reconstruct with some degree of accuracy the outline of Charbonneau's career after he left St. Louis in 1811. As we have seen, Charbonneau accompanied Henry Brackenridge on his expedition up the Missouri in 1811. In July, 1816, he was engaged by Julius de Mun (also DeMun) for Auguste Pierre Chouteau and company, to go from St. Louis on a trading voyage up and down the Arkansas and Platte Rivers. The engagement was for one year. Three years later his name appears on the payroll of Captain Clark, the superintendent of Indian Affairs, for "salary as interpreter, $200, from July 17—December 31, 1819." General Henry Atkinson in 1825 makes several references to Charbonneau, one of which was to the effect that at the time Charbonneau with his wife and her brother were at the Mandan villages. Major Stephen Kearny, in his journal of August 11, 1825, mentions Charbonneau Creek, named for "a Frenchman who accompanied Lewis and Clark across the mountains," and whom he saw living at the Mandans, plying his trade as a trader among these Indians. On the records of the United States agent, John Francis Alexander Sanford, on the upper Missouri, is to be found under date of February 29, 1828, a notation of wages paid to Toussaint Charbonneau, interpreter for the Mandan and Gros Ventre Indians. In the books of the Mandan sub-agency, covering a period of six years, it is recorded that payments were made to Toussaint Charbonneau, interpreter, which equaled the sum of $2,437.32 from November 30, 1828, to September 30, 1834. Charbonneau served at this fort as interpreter between the agents and the Mandans, Gros Ventre, Minnetaree and Crow Indians. The letter books at Fort Clark under date of May 30, 1830, contain the accounts of purchases made in the name of "His Royal Highness," Prince Paul of Wurttemberg. These include goods to be delivered to James

Kipp, who in turn "*is to send the purchase to Charbonneau at the Gros Ventres village.*" On May 5 the same royal explorer [Prince Paul] bought additional goods, including powder and tobacco for Charbonneau. Two weeks later he visited Fort Union, where he made further purchases which were to be given to the "interpreter, Charbonneau." In 1833 Kipp, while among the Mandans, carried on a conversation, "*by the help of the old interpreter, Charbonneau, who had lived thirty-seven years in the villages of the Mandans.*" This item and date establish rather definitely the length of Charbonneau's residence among the Mandans. And the fact that even after this long period he could not "correctly pronounce" Indian names, may help to explain in part why the orthography and pronunciation of the word "Sacajawea," which he attempted to give to Lewis and Clark, appeared with many variations in the journals of the Expedition. Maximilian, Prince of Wied, also spoke of the inability of Charbonneau to pronounce Mandan words correctly.

He generally lives at Awatichay (Hidatsa village), the second village of the Manitaries (Hidatsa) and excepting some journeys, has always remained at this spot, hence, he is well acquainted with the Manitaries and their language, though as he candidly confessed he could never learn to pronounce it. In 1833 the famous royal traveler, above referred to, secured from the American Fur Company the privilege of passing the winter at Fort Clark, where he built for himself a small house within the stockade and later engaged the services of Toussaint Charbonneau, "former interpreter of Lewis and Clark."

In April, 1833, Prince Maximilian received from Captain William Clark, then superintendent of Indian Affairs at St. Louis, a passport to travel up the Missouri to the Indian Territory. With Maximilian, when he reached the Mandans was "old Charbonneau" whom he frequently mentions from this time onward in his journal. In June, 1833, a short time after the arrival of the party at the Mandans, when the Indians tried to force him to trade his compass for a horse, Maximilian wrote, "*It was only by the assistance of old Charbonneau that I escaped a disagreeable* and, perhaps, violent scene." Again, on this same day, he says, "Charbonneau acted as interpreter in the Manitari language."

Charbonneau told Maximilian many of the incidents which had occurred during his thirty-seven years of residence in the Minnetaree and Mandan villages. He stated that he had reached the Mandans, who at one time dwelt near the Heart River "*at the end of the last century,*" at a time when the Indians used the shoulder blade of a buffalo for plowing, and flint for arrowheads. He said also that the "*father's brother is called father and the mother's sister, mother—and that cousins were called brothers and sisters.*" Prince Maximilian speaks, for the most part, in favorable terms of Charbonneau, saying that he was indebted to the old French Canadian for many valuable accounts concerning the manners, morals, and habits of the different Indian tribes with which the interpreter was acquainted. On the other hand, speaking of a document or treaty which was shown him, he said, "*This document was written on long paper in English and Manitari language. Most of the Indian names, which were doubtless given by Charbonneau, were incorrectly written.*" In October, 1834, old Charbonneau, then well-advanced in years, went with one of his squaws in quest of a runaway wife. The incident is recorded in Francis Chardon's *Journal at Fort Clark* (published 1932) under date of October 22, as follows, "*Charbonneau and his lady started for the Gros Ventres on a visit (or to tell the truth) in quest of one of his runaway wives—for I must inform you he had two lively ones. Poor old man.*" Another entry of September 10, 1837, reads, "*Charbonneau arrived last night from the Gros Ventres—all well in that quarter, the disease [a steamer had recently arrived with smallpox aboard] had not yet broke out among them, except his squaw, who died four days ago.*" On October 27, 1838, when four score years of age, Charbonneau made his last venture into matrimony. Chardon records, "*Old Charbonneau, an old man of 80, took to himself a young wife, a young Assiniboine of 14, a prisoner that was taken in the fight of this summer, and bought by me of the Rees (Arikara tribe), the young men of the Fort, and two Rees, gave to the old man a splendid charivari (mock parade) the drums, pans, kittles, etc., beating, guns firing, etc., the old gentlemen gave a feast to the men, and a glass of grog. The two Indians, who had never seen the like before, were under the apprehension that we were for killing of them, and sneaked off."*

In most accounts the story of Toussaint Charbonneau ends about this time. But in the spring of 1838 Charles Larpenteur and his party of fur traders met Charbonneau on the Missouri and were greatly rejoiced to learn through him that they were then only seventy miles from Fort Clark. Charbonneau further told Larpenteur that he had been forty years among the Missouri Indians and that when he came the river was so small that he could straddle it. Larpenteur's statement that Charbonneau at this time was wearing pants and a red flannel shirt would indicate that the old man had never wholly adopted Indian garb.

A more recent historical research, moreover, has brought to light one further reference to Charbonneau. In August, 1839, the old man appeared at the office of the superintendent of Indian Affairs in St. Louis, having made the journey from the Mandan villages, a distance of 1600 miles. Here the old interpreter, penniless and laboring under the infirmities of eighty winters, asked for the payment of salary due him for services long since rendered and as long since forgotten. *"This man,"* states Joshua Pilcher, who was then superintendent, *"has been a faithful servant to the government, though in a humble capacity—for the last fifteen years he has been employed as the government interpreter at the Mandan."* Whatsoever financial amount was due Charbonneau was paid him on August 26, 1839. This is the last official reference to Toussaint Charbonneau, interpreter for the Lewis and Clark Expedition. The exact date of the death of Toussaint Charbonneau has not been ascertained, and even his burial place is unknown. Vague rumors still persist among the Shoshone Indians of the Wind River Reservation, that Charbonneau married a Ute woman and eventually died and was buried among the Ute Indians in Utah. But there are no Charbonneaus on the Ute Reservation, and no one can be found there who claims relationship with the old interpreter.

In the preceding chapter, mention was made of the fact that in April, 1811, Henry Marie Brackenridge ascended the Missouri River, taking with him Charbonneau and one of the latter's Indian wives. At that time at the headquarters of the great fur trader, Manuel Lisa, on the upper Missouri, John C. Luttig was acting in the capacity of clerk, having come into the employ of the Missouri Fur Company three years before. On December 20, 1812, Luttig made the following entry in his journal, "*This evening the wife of Charbonneau, a Snake squaw, died of a putrid fever. She was the best woman in the fort, aged about twenty-five years. She left a fine infant child.*" This child, named Lizette, was born in August, and was thus about four months old at the time of her mother's death. It is evident, moreover, that this Indian mother was "Otter Woman" referred to by Brackenridge, and that she had only the one child with her at the time of her death. Had it been otherwise the fact would certainly have been noted in Luttig's journal. A number of Indian tribes were then hostile to American traders, and, as a consequence, Charbonneau left his motherless child with some of the Indian women at Lisa's headquarters when he accompanied the expeditions of the fur traders. From one of these expeditions Charbonneau failed to return to the Mandan country and Luttig, therefore, supposing that he was dead, took Charbonneau's baby, Lizette, to St. Louis in the fall of 1813 to have a guardian appointed for her. Her brother, Toussaint Jr., as we have already seen in a preceding chapter, was then already in St. Louis. When Luttig reached St. Louis, William Clark was temporarily absent from the city. As a consequence, the court named John Luttig temporary guardian of the two children, but when Clark returned to St. Louis, he relieved Luttig of this responsibility. The court record reads as follows, "*The court appoints John C. Luttig [this name is crossed out and that of William Clark substituted] guardian to the infant children of Toussaint Charbonneau deceased, to wit, Toussaint Charbonneau Jr., a boy about the age of ten years, and Lizette*

Charbonneau, a girl about one year old. The said infant children not being possessed of any property within the knowledge of the court, the said guardian is not required to give bond." At this time Sacajawea and her son Baptiste were also in St. Louis living under Clark's protection. Clark, however, did not assume the legal guardianship of Baptiste because the boy was still living with his mother and a guardianship was hence unnecessary. Sacajawea, indeed, had never left or abandoned her son to the care of anyone since his birth in the Mandan country eight and one half years before. It is also certain that Sacajawea had not returned with Charbonneau to the Mandans in 1811. This conclusion is amply confirmed by the report of Dr. Charles A. Eastman to the office of Indian affairs in 1925 as stated. "*The court record shows that Baptiste, the child of Sacajawea, was conspicuously absent. This means that Baptiste had been retained in St. Louis when Charbonneau and his other Snake wife had gone back to the Indian country as stated by Brackenridge. Baptiste was too young to be separated from his mother, and my knowledge of the Indian mother's traits and habits is such that she could not have permitted to be separated from her child at that age, especially those times. It would have been impossible for Clark to retain Baptiste without his mother, but as he determined either to adopt or educate the boy, the youngest member of the expedition across the continent, he had to provide for the Bird Woman in order to keep Baptiste in St. Louis so that he may see to his education. As he could not trust Toussaint Charbonneau to take the child back up the Missouri, therefore he retains him, and that is why Baptiste was not mentioned in the Orphans Court when Luttig applied for guardian.*" And again "*The evidence given by Poor Wolf, Chief of the Hidatsa, and Mrs. Weidemann, shows that Charbonneau did have two Shoshone wives, and a Mandan wife besides. They clearly stated that Charbonneau took both of his Shoshone wives with him when he visited St. Louis some time in 1807 to 1808, and it is evident that he had returned with but one Shoshone wife, who died on December 20, 1812.*" It is thus evident that, in 1811, Sacajawea and Baptiste were living in St. Louis under the protection of Captain Clark, and that Baptiste's half-brother and sister, Toussaint Jr. and Lizette, for whom Captain Clark was acting as legal guardian, were in 1813 also living in the same city. In the fulfillment of his promise to Charbonneau, Clark assumed responsibility for the education of Baptiste, and apparently undertook the same responsibility for his ward, Toussaint Jr. Various entries in Clark's abstract of expenditures when serving as superintendent of Indian affairs throw significant light upon the education of these two boys.

One account stood in the name of Reverend J. E. Welch, a Baptist minister who boarded and taught Indian and half-breed boys. He was paid for tutoring J. B. [Jean Baptiste] Charbonneau. Another account for [teaching] expenses incurred for Toussaint Charbonneau Jr. was paid to Reverend Francis Neil, a Catholic priest, who conducted a boys's school in St. Louis, which later became the present St. Louis University. Both of these accounts were made out to Captain Clark, and in them Baptiste and Toussaint Jr. were spoken of as "half-Indian boys." From July 1 to December 31, 1819, Charbonneau senior, the father of the boys, received $200 as compensation for serving as interpreter for Captain Clark. On January 22, 1820, Mr. Welch was paid an additional sum for *"two quarters tuition for J. B. Charbonneau, a half-Indian boy, and for firewood and ink for the same individual."* On March 31, an additional sum was paid for three months's boarding, lodging, and washing, to L. T. Honore for "J. B. Charbonneau" again on April 1, a payment was made to J. and G. H. Kennerly for school supplies and clothing for "Charbonneau, a half-Indian." Among other items appearing in this "Abstract of Expenditures" for Charbonneau are shoes, books, writing paper and quills, William Scott's *Lessons*, a dictionary, a hat, one ciphering book, a Roman history, a slate and pencils, and the sum of 62 cents in cash. On April eleventh of the same year [1820], Mr. Welch was again paid certain sums for tuition—and for fuel and ink for "J. B. Charbonneau, half-Indian boy." The teaching of these "half-Indian boys" was carried on in French, the language of their father and the language then taught in the schools of St. Louis. In this official record of expenses the entries all appear as having been paid to "T. Charbonneau," or "Charbonneau." Charbonneau in turn paid his sons's teachers. Since these various items for tuition, board, and lodging are all for "half-Indian boys," it is ridiculous to suppose that they represent sums paid for the education of old Charbonneau himself as some have unthinkingly suggested. Charbonneau not only gloried in the fact that he was a full-blooded white man, but at the time was over sixty years of age. It would be preposterous to suppose that he attended school at Captain Clark's expense and was there listed as a "half-Indian boy." Further confirmation of the fact that both Toussaint Jr. and Baptiste were educated in St. Louis by Captain Clark is derived from a more recent source. In 1902, Mrs. Eva Emery Dye had a personal interview in St. Louis with Captain William Clark Kennerly, a nephew by marriage of Captain Clark. Captain Kennerly stated in this interview that he knew Charbonneau's boy, Baptiste, when the boy was in school in St. Louis.

In December, 1906, and the two months following, the author of this volume received a series of letters, mentioned elsewhere, written by Captain Kennerly from his home in St. Louis, in which he affirmed that he had known Sacajawea and Charbonneau in St. Louis and had seen them frequently in that city. He added that he had also known their child, Baptiste, who was then being educated by Captain Clark. Later he met Baptiste at Fort Laramie in 1843, when the Indian was acting as guide and hunter for overland expeditions—and at the time was serving as "a cart driver" for Sir William Drummond Stewart. In a manuscript by William M. Boggs, which describes men and conditions at Fort Bent, mention is made both of Baptiste Charbonneau and of Toussaint Jr., who was at Fort Bent in 1844-1845. Boggs wrote, *"Another half-breed at the Fort was 'Tessou.' (Toussaint) His father was French and his mother (Otter Woman) an Indian, but the writer was not informed of what tribe. 'Tessou' was in some way related to (Baptiste) Charbonneau. Both of them were very high strung, but Tessou was quick and passionate. He fired a rifle across the court of the Fort at the head of a large Negro blacksmith, only missing his skull about a quarter of an inch, because the Negro had been in a party that chivaried (mocked) Tessou the evening before, and being a dangerous man, Captain Vrain gave him an outfit and sent him away from the Fort."* With this entry, the brief history of Toussaint Charbonneau Jr. comes to a close. So far at least, no later record of him has been found. The story of Baptiste, however, contains still further material of varied and peculiar interest. It is with this story that the remainder of this chapter is concerned. A number of authors writing of the early history of the fur trade and the fur traders of the far west make frequent [written] references to Charbonneau, whom they usually speak of as "a half-breed."

Some of them refer to his residence and education in Europe, and to the fact that he was familiar with several languages, including English, Shoshone, German, French, and Spanish. That "this classically" educated Indian boy was Jean Baptiste Charbonneau, the first child of Sacajawea, there is now no shadow of a doubt. The documentary evidence of Baptiste's travels abroad with a member of the royal family of Germany, however, remained unknown in many of its essential historical facts until very recently, and is here published for the first time.

Among the interesting personages who came to the United States to travel through the far west in the days of the fur traders, was Prince Paul of Wurttemberg. A brief summary of the prince's experiences and early travels in the west is given in the following account from historian Hiram Martin Chittenden.

"In 1823 an individual referred to in the Chouteau correspondence as Prince Paul of Wurttemberg, went up the river and passed the winter. He returned to New Orleans in the summer of 1824. In 1829 he again went up and was found among the Mandans April 22, 1830, by Joshua Pilcher, who was then returning from his tour of the Hudson's Bay Company posts. The purpose of his journey, as stated in the correspondence, was the pursuit of knowledge. He left Fort Tecumseh in August, 1830, and was in St. Louis in October of that year. In reference to this last visit, a local paper, under date of January 29, 1830, had the following, 'Paul William of Wurttemberg, nephew of the king of England, arrived at New Orleans the 1st instant, from Europe. About six years ago he

spent some time exploring the upper regions of the Missouri, but business requiring his return to Europe, he has revisited the American hemisphere and will, in the prosecution of his former plan, cross the Rocky Mountains and visit the continent of the Pacific. He is in his 33rd year. He does not seem to have crossed the continent at this time, for he was back in St. Louis in the fall of 1830. There is no record of his making any other trip up the Missouri.' "

    In this last statement Chittenden plainly is in error, as we shall presently discover. As already indicated, Prince Paul made his first journey to the United States in 1823, sailing in that year from Hamburg to New Orleans. He was granted permission by the secretary of state, John Quincy Adams, to enter and travel through the United States, and the federal authorities of the west were instructed to provide him with every means in their power to further and safeguard his movements and to furnish him military escort when it should be deemed necessary. On May 5, 1823, Prince Paul requested "General" Clark of St. Louis to furnish him a passport to travel up the Missouri River, stating that the sole object of his contemplated expedition was for his own instruction. This request was granted by the secretary of war on June 10, 1823. On this expedition the prince of Wurttemberg made the acquaintance of Jean Baptiste Charbonneau, and of his mother, Sacajawea, as well as of Charbonneau himself, whose services he used as an interpreter. The meeting with Jean Baptiste was near the mouth of the Kaw River on June 21, 1823. In his journal published in 1835 the prince describes this meeting and the fact of Baptiste's return with him to Europe. On June 21, 1823, he wrote, "*The settlements of the fur traders, two spacious dwelling houses, are found a short half-mile farther on the right bank of the Missouri, and I rode thither in order to visit their respective owners, the Messieurs Curtiss and Wood. But I failed to find them, though I did the wife of the latter, a Creole, and daughter of the aged Chauvin with whom I had spent a night not far from St. Charles. The entire population of the settlement consisted of but a few persons, Creoles and half-breeds, whose occupation is the trading with Kansas Indians, confined mostly to the chase and the cultivation of the soil. Here I found also a youth of sixteen, whose mother was of the tribe of Shoshone, or Snake Indians, and who had accompanied the Messieurs Lewis and Clark to the Pacific Ocean in the years 1804 to 1806 as interpretess. This Indian woman was married to the French interpreter of the Expedition, Toussaint Charbonneau by name. Charbonneau rendered me service also, some time later in this same capacity, and Baptiste, his son (the youth of sixteen) of whom I made mention above, joined me on my return and followed me to Europe and has remained with me ever since."* On December 3, Prince Paul sailed from St. Louis to New Orleans on the steamboat *Cincinnati*, and on the twenty-fourth of that month he and Baptiste embarked on the brig *Smyrna* for the Atlantic seaboard on the first leg of their long journey to Europe. In 1828, Prince Paul wrote an account of his western travels under the title *Trip to North America in the Years 1822, 1823, and 1824*. Only one copy of this book apparently was ever printed.

This is now preserved in the Henry E. Huntington Library and Art Gallery in San Marino, California, and at the request of the author, Mr. Willard O. Walters of the library permitted Professor Louis C. Butscher of the University of Wyoming to examine this volume. The volume, which was probably printed merely for the author's inspection, contains "hundreds of marginal manuscript notes" written in German script by the author. Prince Paul, although educated and trained for a military career, was more interested in science, literature, and philosophy, than in war. Consequently, he resigned his military position and devoted himself to the study of botany and zoology under the direction of Gay-Lussac, Cuvier, Jussien, and Hay. He came to the United States again in 1829, unattended except by "a hardy hunter and master of woodcraft." At St. Louis the royal traveler again petitioned Captain Clark for a passport to visit the Indian lodges in the north, and this courtesy, at Captain Clark's request, was granted by John Eaton, Secretary of War. This journey carried Prince Paul as far as the Mandan villages, the former home of Charbonneau and Sacajawea. The prince kept a complete journal of this journey (as he did of all the others), which he carefully prepared for publication, but despite diligent search, the manuscript has never been found. This is most unfortunate from the standpoint of the present volume, since it would undoubtedly throw great light upon Baptiste's stay in Europe, including as it did in addition to a record of the expedition, the history of the life of Prince Paul from the time he left America in December, 1823, until he returned to this country in 1829. Despite the fact that both on his earlier and later visits the prince was shown every courtesy by the officials of the American government, there was serious question in official quarters as to the real motives which lay behind his "search for knowledge," and whether this did not conceal a plan of establishing a German colony somewhere in North America, or of seeking to develop an extensive foreign fur trade by establishing new companies in the fur territory. Neither of these purposes, however, was in any way revealed by the prince's activities. A final reference is made by Prince Paul in his account of his travels in North America to the young half-breed Baptiste, who had been an inmate of his family for six years and for whom he had come to have a very genuine affection. This reference occurs in the account of his fourth journey, made nearly twenty years after his second expedition up the Missouri. This began in 1849, and carried him through west Texas, across Mexico to Acapulco, thence by steamer to San Pedro in California, and up the Pacific Coast to Sutter's Fort near Sacramento. In his journal he records in considerable detail his life and experiences while a guest of the hospitable Swiss land baron. In the course of the description, part of which is devoted to an account of the Indians in Sutter's employ, occurs this sentence, "*One of these Snakes was a fine young lad, quite intelligent, who reminded me strangely and with a certain sadness of Baptiste Charbonneau, who had followed me in 1825 to Europe, and whose mother was of the tribe of the Shoshones.*" From Sutter's Fort the Prince of Wurttemberg returned to New Orleans early in the spring of 1851 by way of the Isthmus of Panama, and continued on to St. Louis. This, instead of the rough border town of 5,000 inhabitants he had visited in 1823, he now found to be a city of 80,000 people. From St. Louis the prince traveled up the Missouri River and thence to the west, following the Platte and North Platte, by way of the old "covered wagon" road or Oregon Trail. In his journal he mentions Independence Rock, Devil's Gate, South Pass, the Great Salt Lake, and the Mormon colony in Salt Lake City. It was on this journey that he likewise fell in with Father DeSmet, near Ash Hollow on the Platte River. An extended account of this chance meeting in the wilderness between these two interesting men, the one a great missionary of the cross, the other an adventurous member of one of Europe's ruling families, is given in the following extract (from a translation by Louis G. Butscher of the University of Wyoming) from Father DeSmet's journal. *"Quite late in the afternoon of the 23rd of September, 1851, I bade farewell to the Creoles, Canadians, and half-bloods. I exhorted them to live well and to pray to God, and to hope that he would soon send them spiritual succor for their temporal and external happiness and that of their children. I shook hands for the last time with the great chiefs and with a large number of the Indians, and addressed them some encouraging words and promised to plead their cause with the great chiefs of the black gowns, and make known the desire, good intentions, and hopes they had expressed to me, while they would daily, in all sincerity of heart, implore the "Master of Life" to send them zealous priests to instruct them in the way of salvation, which Jesus Christ, his only son, came to trace to his own children on earth. I directed my course toward "the springs," situated about 14 miles distant, in the vicinity of Robidoux's trading house, for Colonel Mitchell had named this as the rendezvous for all those who proposed going directly to the United States. On the 24th, before sunrise we set out in good and numerous company. I visited, in my way, two trading houses in order to baptize five half-blood children. In the course of the day we passed the famous Chimney Rock, so often described by travelers. I had already seen it, in 1840 and 1841, in my first visit to the Rocky Mountains, and mentioned it in my letters. I found it considerably diminished in height. We cast around a last look upon the singular productions of nature, the castle and tower, which are* near the chimney, and resemble the ruins of lordly residences scattered over several acres, presenting a very elevated and broken surface amid a level plain. Arrived on the Platte, at the place known as Ash Hollow, we turned our steps toward the South Fork, fifteen miles away, over a beautiful rolling country of great elevation. Here we met Prince Paul accompanied only by a Prussian officer, on their way to enjoy a hunt in the Wind River Mountains. We exchanged our little news, and received with pleasure the interesting information which the prince gave us. His Excellency must be indeed courageous, to undertake at his age so long a journey in such a wilderness, with but one man as suite, and in a wretched little open wagon, which carried the prince and his officer as well as their whole baggage and provisions. Later I learned that the prince intends to choose a location suited to agriculture, for the purpose of founding a German colony. We live in an age when wonders multiply, we cannot say what, in the way of colonization, may not come to pass in a short time, after witnessing the success of the Mormons, who in less than five years have changed the face of a frightful desert and live there in great abundance. Yet, I am free to maintain that if the prince has really formed the plan ascribed to him which I scarcely credit. I pity from the bottom of my heart those who first embark in the expedition. The enemies whom they would have to meet are still too powerful. Crows, Blackfeet, Sioux, Cheyenne, Arapahos, and Snakes are the most feared and warlike of the desert. A colony established in such a neighborhood, and against the will of the numerous warlike tribes in the vicinity of those mountains, would run great dangers and meet heavy obstacles. The influence of religion alone can prepare these parts for such a transformation. The threats and promises of colonists, their guns and sabers, would never effect what can be accomplished by the peaceful sign of the black gown and the sight of the humanizing sign of the cross." Prince Paul was accompanied on this journey by his artist named Heinrich Balduin Mollhausen. For part of the way, at least, the two traveled "in a wretched little open wagon" which was also described as "an apparently crazy open vehicle." A month after their meeting with DeSmet, the prince and his companion narrowly escaped massacre at the hands of a marauding band of savages. The account of this experience, though it has no bearing upon the history of Sacajawea or Baptiste, is nevertheless appropriately recorded in this volume.

The prince's account reads as follows. "*On October 26, 1851, there was clear sunshine and north northwest wind early in the day. After I had traveled about five miles I recognized among some grazing buffalo two forms which I knew at once to be Indians. They were close to the road we were traveling. Soon I saw their blankets, and observed that they were Indian warriors with cavalry swords and otherwise armed to the teeth. They were leading a great, wolf-like hound between them, and approached our outfit shouting "Cheyenne." They seemed to be quite friendly, but at the same time they inspired me with suspicion, and they were more like Cayuga or Kiowa than anything else, evil, thieving Indians who are fond of killing off the white people and of robbing them. As we observed that their war party was approaching, all afoot and well armed with cavalry sabers, carbines, rifles, bows, and tomahawks, there seemed to be nothing for us to do but wait quietly and tranquilly what was to ensue. In such extremes the sole means of salvation lies in sheer courage and equanimity in order to pull oneself out of a serious situation such as that of being confronted by a troupe of wild people on the warpath. This body consisted of fourteen or fifteen savages, mostly young bucks completely armed, well dressed, and imposing looking. At first they pretended to be friendly. They wanted to look at my arms, and demanded foodstuffs and whiskey, both of which I willingly acceded to, inasmuch as I had mostly bacon in my grub-box, a viand (food) which the Indians of the west despise. Now they were growing even more importunate. They grabbed my double-barreled shotgun, a short, fine hunting knife, and an old but very fine traveling pistol of the make of von der Fecht, which I had carried with me for years during my travels. When they once had these arms in their possession they became quite insolent. They now tore my Mexican serape and my cap from me bodily, and then, at a signal from the leader, some of them took their firearms, cocked them, while others* drew their bows. Then one of them, an evil-looking ruffian, struck one of my horses with his tomahawk. Gradually advancing, the warriors, half a dozen or more, pushed their rifles against my breast and head. One young buck pointed his arrow within a hand's breadth of my right eye, and all gave to me and to Mr. Mollhausen, who was himself subjected to the same terror and who conducted himself with the utmost sangfroid, to understand that we were to suffer death, and that they would add our scalps to those that dangled, fresh and gory, from their belts. They declared themselves the mortal enemies of the Gankise (derogatory term for Yankee). I smiled at these threats, showed before them the greatest calmness, and remarked that I was a Washi (Indian term for French Creoles and Canadians). Quite coolly I showed my ten fingers raised above my head, and said, "squaw," then pointed to myself and Mr. Mollhausen and exclaimed "men," which should convey to them my opinion that ten to fifteen Gankise, or Ankise-hu, a corrupted term for Yankee used by many Indians, if they wanted to attack two unarmed men, were cowards, and if we two were Washi, they betrayed friends, also, that two brave white men did not propose to be intimidated by any number of warriors. This had an immediate and most startling effect. All weapons were lowered—all booty taken from us was—even to the smallest object, put back to the place from which it had been snatched, quietly and in an orderly manner. The chief, who seemed to be the most reasonable of all, restored to me with profound respect both cap and serape. Only a young buck, who had taken my cherished pistol, had vanished. So then the leader came forward again and placed a fine six chambered revolver on my wagon, pointing in the distance to where a slain buffalo lay, and in the crowd, with repeated protestations of friendship, dispersed and soon vanished from view. But in the melee Mr. Mollhausen has lost his diary, which contained a great number of fine sketches. The rest of the day passed serenely, and I made camp some fifteen miles farther on, with a violent, cool wind blowing from the southeast. The night was beautiful. We were a mile away from the river." The expedition of 1839-1841, by Prince Paul and the two subsequent to that date are described in a single manuscript volume of great interest and historic value, which was discovered by Herr Friedrich Bauser in Stuttgart in 1929. In the archives of the state library at Stuttgart, Herr Bauser also discovered a pencil sketch of the Indian surprise attack of the Kiowa on the Platte River, which pictures the Indians in the act of torturing Prince Paul and his artist companion. In October, 1930, the same investigator discovered another picture labeled "The Race of the Cheyenne Maidens." In the summer of 1927 the Reverend Henry Hartig of Minnesota, upon a visit to Stuttgart, his birthplace—saw in that city an oil painting in one of the "aulas" of a school building entitled "Prince Paul and his Indian boy."

Although diligent search was made for this painting by Herr Bauser, he was unsuccessful in locating it, but one is certainly justified in accepting Hartig's statement that he saw such a painting. Although there is altogether too scant mention of Baptiste's six years in Europe in Prince Paul's manuscripts, and though nothing further touching on this strange interlude in the young half-breed's life may ever be found, the evidence from these long-forgotten records furnishes strange and unexpected verification of statements made to the author of this volume, and carefully preserved on the Shoshone Reservation. When Baptiste's daughter and his nephew declared that Baptiste had been educated in the land to the east beyond the big waters, and told of the big houses on the water and of the people with wooden shoes (Wobenamptiko, or Wooden Shoe White Man, as Baptiste was called), it was difficult to believe that their statements were more than some misunderstood legend.

But only a few years later the discovery of the prince's manuscripts served at once to support the simple verbal testimony, and to make more certain the true identity both of Baptiste and Sacajawea. Baptiste's career from the time of his return to the United States with Prince Paul, until he went to live with his mother's people, the Shoshones, in the Bridger Valley on the Wind River Reservation in 1852, can be traced with some degree of accuracy in the frequent references made to him in the journals of western fur traders and explorers during this period. In the narrative of Warren Angus Ferris, one of the employees of the American Fur Company from 1830 to 1835, who trapped much of the territory explored by Lewis and Clark, Baptiste is mentioned in connection with one of his adventures. "*We spent the following morning in the charitable office conveying water to our enfeebled companions who lingered behind, and the poor beasts that had also been left by the way, and succeeded in getting them all to camp, except the person and animals of Charbonneau, one of our men, who could nowhere be found. This was the infant who, together with his mother, was saved from a sudden flood near the Falls of Missouri, by Captain Lewis—of Lewis and Clark's Expedition.*" (It was William Clark who saved the lives of Sacajawea and Baptiste not Meriwether Lewis, according to the published journals.) In the same year Thomas Fitzpatrick, known as "Broken Hand," William Sublette, and the "Blanket Chief" James Bridger, went to the Big Horn country with two hundred men, crossed the Yellowstone, and followed that river to its junction with the Missouri. From here the fur men ascended the Missouri to the Three Forks, and then trapped up the Jefferson. This is the country, it will be remembered, where Sacajawea in August, 1805, found her people, the Shoshones, and adopted her sister's son, Bazil.

Later the three members of the Rocky Mountain Fur Company turned eastward "*in time to reach the valley of the Powder River before winter set in.*" The Powder River Valley, in what is now Wyoming, was a favorite winter ground, and it was here that the three fur traders, with their hunters, exchanged furs, fights, beads, and bullets. During the winter, Joseph Meek was sent with an express from this encampment to St. Louis. On his way to the Platte, however, Meek "*fell in with an express on its way to St. Louis, to whom he delivered his dispatch, returning at once to the Powder River camp. On this journey he was accompanied only by a Frenchman, Charbonneau.*" In the writings of Nathaniel Wyeth, frequent mention is made of a Charbonneau, whom we may presume to have been Baptiste, during the years 1832 to 1833. Thus Wyeth records that Charbonneau, a half breed, was with Jim Bridger in August, 1832. On May 19 of the next year, he speaks of a half-breed, "Charloi," who was one of four hunters going to trap beaver in the Blackfoot country. Three of these hunters, among whom was a "Churboye," returned on June 21. On August 1 of that year, Wyeth writes *"Mr. Bridger sent four men to this river to look for us, viz, Mr. Smith, Thompson, Charbonneau, a half-breed."* Following an attack by Indians, Wyeth later wrote *"The Indians got seven horses—all there were. Charbonneau pursued them on foot and got his gun wet crossing a little stream and only snapped twice."* It may be remarked in passing that a vast amount of territory was covered on this hunt, which extended up Clark Fork to the source of the Salmon, covered the upper regions of the Green and the Popo Agie Rivers, came down the Snake within sight of the Grand Teton, to the source of the Wind River, and thence passed down the Big Horn to the Yellowstone. In 1839 we find "Charbonneau," the half breed son of Sacajawea, graceful, urbane, fluent, reciting his victories over the Indians to the fur men of Kit Carson's company. A somewhat extended reference is also made to Baptiste by (Elias) Willard Smith in his journal of 1839 to 1840. Smith mentions a Mr. Charbonneau who went down the Platte River two thousand miles from the mountains in sixty days, carrying peltries to the market in St. Louis. The same writer also speaks of the half-breeds who had been employed by Mr. Thompson, in command of a trading post on the western side of the mountains. *"One of these,"* he says, *"was the son of Captain Clark, the great western traveler and companion of Lewis. He had received an education in Europe during seven years."* On December 17, Smith's hunters were on the Green River where it crossed the boundary between Utah and Wyoming. Moving westward, they came to *"about twenty lodges of Indians of the Snake tribe. They call themselves Shoshones. We obtained a few trinkets. They are very good-looking Indians. The men are generally tall and slightly made, the women short and stout."* The hunters were now in the valley later to be known as Bridger Valley and Washakie Valley, where Baptiste, "Mr. Charbonneau," was in years to come to make his home with the Shoshones and live beside his brother, Bazil, the adopted (cousin) son of Sacajawea. After zigzagging over the boundary line of the present state of Wyoming and Colorado as well as into Utah, on July 3, 1840, Smith's party arrived in its boats at St. Louis. The afternoon of this arrival, "*Mr. Charbonneau went out a short distance from the river bank to shoot buffalo for his meat.*" General John Charles Fremont, in the journal of his expedition of 1842, mentions a Charbonneau who, in all probability, was Baptiste. On July 9, 1842, Fremont had his first glimpse of Long's Peak and the snowy summit of the Rocky Mountains. On this day he also met some white men hunting for lost horses. "*These men were in search of a band of horses that had gone off from a camp some miles down, in charge of Mr. Charbonneau about eight miles from our sleeping place we reached Bijou's Fork, an affluent of the right bank. In about two miles arrived at Charbonneau camp, on an island in the Platte. Mr. Charbonneau was in the service of Bent and St. Vrain's company, and had left their fort some forty or fifty miles above, in the spring, with boats laden with furs of the last year's trade. He had met the same fortune as the voyagers of the North Fork, and, finding it impossible to proceed, had taken up his summer's residence on this island, which he named St. Helena. Mr. Charbonneau received us hospitably. One of his people was sent to gather mint, with the aid of which he concocted a very good julep. July 10th. We parted with our hospitable host after breakfast the next morning, and reached St. Vrain's Fort, about forty miles from St. Helena, late in the evening.*" In 1842, Sir William Drummond Stewart organized a party in St. Louis to hunt buffalo. The party began its actual hunt at Fort Laramie, on the Oregon Trail in 1843. In this group of hunters with Stewart were William Sublette, Captain Jefferson Kennerly Clark, a son of Captain Clark of the Lewis and Clark Expedition, and William Clark Kennerly, a nephew of Captain William Clark, for whom he was named. The party included eighty other members, among whom were guides, drivers, and hunters. Among others engaged to join the expedition was Baptiste Charbonneau, who served in the capacity of "a cart driver." When at Fort Laramie, Baptiste saw young Clark and "at once welcomed him as the son of his old guardian." Fifty or sixty lodges of the Sioux Indians were then at the fort, and some of the chiefs recognized Jefferson Clark because of the strong resemblance to his father, whom they had known on his Pacific expedition, and at once called the young man "son of red-headed father." In 1906, Captain Kennerly was the last surviving member of the group which accompanied Stewart on this hunt in 1843.

Upon his death at St. Louis on September 5, 1912, his papers, manuscripts, and a small diary were given to the Missouri Historical Society. Among this valuable material is a manuscript which contains the following extract "*One of the drivers, Baptiste Charbonneau, was the son of an old trapper and Sacajawea, the brave Indian woman who had guided Lewis and Clark on their perilous journey through the wilderness. By singular coincidence he was again to make the journey and guide the son of William Clark through the same region.*" It is significant to note that the name of Sacajawea and that of Baptiste Charbonneau are thus spelled, in the Kennerly manuscript describing the buffalo hunt of 1843, precisely as they are today. One of the most extensive accounts of Charbonneau is to be found in the manuscript of W. M. Boggs, which was prepared in 1905, but remained unpublished until 1930. In this chronicle, covering the period between 1844 and that of 1845, Boggs wrote, "*I also learned considerable from the hunters of Bent's Fort, particularly from Charbonneau, an educated half-breed. His father was a French-Canadian, his mother said to be a Blackfoot squaw. His name was Baptiste Charbonneau. His father and mother accompanied the Lewis and Clark Expedition in their journey to the Pacific shores via the Columbia River as guides. Charbonneau and his squaw were very useful members of the Lewis and Clark Expedition. This Baptiste Charbonneau at Bent's Fort was only a papoose at the time of the Lewis and Clark Expedition, but his mother took him the entire route, according to General Clark's account in his published letters. The squaw was as useful as a guide as the man Charbonneau himself, being raised in the country they were passing over and familiar with mountain passes and trails. This Baptiste Charbonneau, or half-breed of the elder Charbonneau* that was employed by the Lewis and Clark Expedition to the Pacific Ocean, had been educated to some extent. He wore his hair long so that it hung down to his shoulders. It is said that Charbonneau was the best man on foot of the Plains or in the Rocky Mountains."

In addition to this commendation of Baptiste, Boggs further pays tribute to the fur company employees, "*Such men as these heretofore described were employed by the Bents, and were perfectly reliable and devoted to the interests of the company. The company would entrust them with thousands of dollars worth of goods, and send them to distant tribes of Indians to barter for robes, furs, and peltries, with pack animals to carry the outfit. The traders, thus outfitted, would remain away for months, or until the season for trade was over, and would then return to the fort with the robes and the peltries that they had accumulated, and I have never heard of one of these men being accused of abusing the confidence placed in them by their employers.*" Lieutenant George Frederick Ruxton, like Fremont, Boggs, and the others, includes Baptiste in his list of important fur traders. Thus he writes, "*Away to the headwaters of the Platte, where several small streams run into the south fork of the river and head in the broken ridges of the "divide" which separates the valleys of the Platte and Arkansas, were camped a band of trappers, on a creek called Bijou. They were a trapping party, on their way to wintering ground, in the more southern valley of Arkansas. There was old Sam Owins—him as got "rubbed out," "rubbed out" by the Spaniards. Bill Bent—his boys camped the other side of the trail, and they all were mountain men, wagh, and Bill Williams, and Bill Tharpe (the Pawnees took his hair on Pawnee Fork last spring), three Bills, and them three's all "gone under." Surely Hatcher went out that time, and wasn't Bill Garey along too? Didn't him and Charbonneau sit in camp for twenty hours, at a deck of Euker? Them was Bent's Indian traders up on the Arkansas. Singly and in bands numbering from two to ten the traders dropped into the rendezvous, some with many packs of beaver.—Fitzpatrick and Hatcher and old Bill Williams.—Sublette came in with his men from the Yellowstone and many of Wyeth's New Englanders were there. Charbonneau with his half-breeds brought peltries from the* country below. Charbonneau, a half-breed, was not lost in the crowd, and last in height, but first in every quality which constitutes excellence in a mountaineer—who was "taller" for his inches than Kit Carson?" In a report made by Lieutenant J. W. (James William) Abert on his journey to the upper Arkansas and through the country of the Comanche Indians in the fall of 1845, there are also frequent mentions of "Mr. Charbonneau" and his services as a guide from Bent's Fort to St. Louis. On August 9, he writes, "*Mr. Charbonneau called for me to accompany me to Fort Bent on a visit.*" On the same day Colonel [John Charles] Fremont met with Lieutenant Abert for a council, and also with the Indians. Later Mr. Fitzpatrick joined the expedition, expressing his delight with the usefulness of the guide, "Mr. Charbonneau." During these years, 1846-1847, much is said about "Charbonneau" (Baptiste Charbonneau) who was then serving as guide to Lieutenant Colonel Philip St. George Cooke. How useful Baptiste was to this conquest of New Mexico and California can only be learned from the numerous extracts taken from Colonel Cooke's journal.

From this report one gathers that Charbonneau was not illiterate, that he not only signed his name to a notice, but could also read, that he was a guide and hunter who knew by intuition, (like his mother before him when she led Captain Clark to the mouth of the Yellowstone in 1806), how to discover the gaps and passes in the mountains and the sources of streams. He could also understand and converse in the Mexican language.

Colonel Emory, on October 6, 1846, while en route to San Diego from Santa Fe, writes, "*I saw some objects on the hill to the west, which were first mistaken for large cedars, but dwindled by distance to a shrub. Charbonneau (one of our guides) exclaimed, 'Indians! They are Apaches.' His more practical eye detected human figures in my shrubbery.*" The prowess of Charbonneau is further illustrated by an extract from Colonel Cooke's report of November 25, 1846. "*Charbonneau, who had killed an antelope before the column reached the mountain, I found near the summit, while the baggage was slowly crawling up, in pursuit of grizzly bears. I saw three of them far up among the rocks, standing* conspicuously and looking quite white in the sun, whilst the bold hunter was gradually approaching them. Soon after he fired, and in ten seconds again, then there was a confused action and we could see one fall, and the others rushing about with loud and fierce cries that made the mountain ring. The firing having ceased, whilst the young bears were close by, I was much alarmed for the guide's safety, and then we heard him crying out in Spanish, but it was for more balls, and so the cubs escaped. The bear was rolled down and butchered before the wagons had passed." In his journal from November 16, 1846, to January 21, 1847, General Cooke mentions the services rendered the expedition by Charbonneau not less than twenty-nine times. He speaks of his skill in the selection of routes, trapping beaver, finding water, establishing camps, discovering passes, scouting, estimating distances, locating smoke signals, hunting bears, fighting Indians, and many other such valuable services. Cooke's forces reached the headquarters of the Mormon battalion at the mission of San Diego on January 30, 1847. "Thus marching half naked and half fed, and living upon wild animals," wrote Cooke, "we have discovered and made a road of great value to the country." A great deal of credit for the success of the expedition, it would seem, should be given to Charbonneau, who thus guided Cooke's expedition as his mother had guided that of Lewis and Clark, and who now looked again upon the waters of the Pacific which he had seen as an infant at the mouth of the Columbia River in the year 1805. From 1852 to 1885, Baptiste was with his mother's tribe, the Shoshones, in Bridger Valley and on the Shoshone Reservation in Wyoming.

In later life he seems to have deteriorated despite his education, his contact with civilization, and his efficient services in earlier years to explorers, government officials, and fur traders. Such reversion is not, of course, any isolated phenomenon among the Indians for it is a problem continually before our government even today. Baptiste thus apparently forgot his "classical education" and "superior attainments" though Indians and white men on the reservation all agreed that even as an old man he used the English language [he learned] with a limited vocabulary. Certainly, the fact that Baptiste reverted in later years to his Indian customs and manner of life does not in any way disprove the fact that it was he who was educated by Captain Clark in St. Louis—and accompanied Prince Paul to Germany. Examples without number have occurred of the same sort of reversion both among Indians and whites who have lived under similar conditions among savages or in the wilderness. Culture that is only a veneering is easily rubbed off by constant association with uneducated Indians and illiterate whites.

□□□□□□□□□□□

Just when Charbonneau made his reappearance in St. Louis, or what happened to him in the meantime, is not definitely known. We find, however, as already stated, that in July, 1816, he entered the employ of the firm of Auguste Chouteau to engage in a trading expedition along the Arkansas and Platte Rivers. This engagement lasted one year. Sometime before 1820 he came back to St. Louis bringing a new wife, named Eagle, of the Hidatsa tribe, with whom Sacajawea apparently made no objection to sharing her home. Later Charbonneau obtained employment with a fur company, taking with him his two wives, Eagle and Sacajawea, and his sons Toussaint Jr. and Baptiste. Later still, various members of the family appear to have acted as guides and interpreters at posts near Neosho and Washita.

Somewhere in this region, in what is now western Oklahoma and Kansas, the polygamous old interpreter took to himself another wife. This was a Ute woman, beautiful and youthful enough to become a discordant element in the household, and before long she and Sacajawea were engaged in a bitter domestic feud. During the temporary absence of the two sons, Toussaint Jr. and Baptiste, an incident occurred from which Sacajawea emerged triumphant at the expense of her Ute rival. Charbonneau, having nothing to fear in the absence of his sons, took the part of the younger woman and vented his anger upon Sacajawea by whipping her. This, as the records of the Lewis and Clark Expedition show, was certainly not the first time Sacajawea had suffered similar treatment at the hands of her esteemed husband. But in this instance, not so much because of the whipping itself as because of the disgrace of being beaten by her husband in the presence of the new and younger wife, Sacajawea disappeared from her tepee and left Charbonneau, never to return. When Toussaint Jr. and Baptiste returned and learned of Sacajawea's departure and what their father had done, "they made it very serious for Charbonneau and were never friends after that." Apparently they, too, left the old interpreter and were never reunited with him. Charbonneau, on his part, after Sacajawea's disappearance, accompanied a large body of fur traders to Salt Lake where many of the employees of the company were then trapping for beaver and trading with the Indians. The summer following this encampment, Charbonneau crossed the Rocky Mountains to the northeast and reached the Wind, Big Horn, Yellowstone, and Missouri Rivers, finally arriving at the villages of the Gros Ventre, which he was accustomed to look upon as his home. After Sacajawea left Charbonneau, she apparently wandered about for some time, finally making her home with a tribe of the Comanches. The language of these people she could understand, and they in turn could understand her, for they were in fact a branch of the Shoshones, and the two languages differed from each other in about the same degree that high Dutch differs from low Dutch. Here, in the course of time, Sacajawea married a member of this tribe with the aristocratic name of Jerk Meat. With this husband she lived harmoniously for a number of years, giving birth to five children, only two of whom, however, survived. One of these was a son called Ticannaf, and the other, the youngest of the five, a daughter named Yagawosier or Crying Basket. Shortly after the birth of this last child, Jerk Meat was killed in battle.

 From this time on Sacajawea "was not in harmony with her husband's people," and decided to leave the Comanches and seek her own tribe. The Comanches, informed of her intentions, "did not take her seriously." Nevertheless, she so completely disappeared that her whereabouts were unknown for many years, and the Comanches thereafter spoke of her as Wadzewipe, or Lost Woman. This name, it should be noted, is of Comanche origin, and does not belong to the Shoshone tongue. When she left the Comanches, Sacajawea took with her, her daughter, Yagawosier. For food she carried a small parfleche (buffalo hide) bag filled with dried buffalo meat and, thus equipped, started her long odyssey in search of her own people. Her Comanche son, Ticannaf, hunted diligently for her, as did the entire band, but they searched in vain. She was not to be found among the Wichita or the Kiowa. A number of routes led from the Comanche country to Sacajawea's old home among the Shoshones, and various authors do not agree as to which of these she followed. It was possible for her to follow up the Missouri to its source in Beaverhead Valley where she had been stolen when a young girl, and thence to travel south and east to the Shoshone tribe of Chief Washakie, or, she could leave the Missouri at the mouth of the Yellowstone, following that stream and the Big Horn to Fort Bridger. The most direct route, however, was that used by John Charles Fremont on his second exploring expedition, and ran directly north from the territory occupied by the Comanches, with whom Sacajawea had made her home. This route would also have enabled Sacajawea to avoid Charbonneau's country on the upper Missouri, as she unquestionably wished to do. In Fremont's account of his expedition, moreover, there is a [brief] passage describing an Indian woman returning to her people—the Shoshones—which gives every evidence of referring to Sacajawea. This account was written when Fremont was encamped at St. Vrain's Fort (Fort St. Vrain) in July, 1843.

  The passage is quoted here at length. "*Reaching St. Vrain's Fort on the morning of the 23rd of July, we found Mr. Fitzpatrick and his party in good order and excellent health, and with him my true and reliable friend, Kit Carson, who had brought ten good mules with the necessary pack saddles. Through this portion of the mountains also, are the customary roads of the war parties going out against the Utah and Shoshone Indians, and occasionally parties from the Crow nation make their way down to the* southward along this chain, in the expectation of surprising some straggling lodges of their enemies. Shortly before our arrival, one of their parties had attacked an Arapaho village in the vicinity, which they had found unexpectedly strong. A (French) engage at Lupton's Fort (Fort Lupton) in Colorado had been shot in the back on July 4th, and died during our absence to the Arkansas. The wife of the murdered man, an Indian woman of the Snake nation, desirous, like Naomi of old, to return to her people, requested and obtained permission to travel with my party to the neighborhood of Bear River, where she expected to meet with some of their villages. Happier than the Jewish widow, she carried with her two children, pretty little half-breeds, who added much to the liveliness of the camp. Her baggage was carried on five or six packhorses, and I gave her a small tent, for which I no longer had any use, as I had procured a lodge at the fort." On August 2, while traveling along the most western fork of Laramie River in Wyoming, Fremont wrote, "At this place I became first acquainted with the yampah (possibly wild carrots or dill) which I found our Snake woman engaged in digging in the low-timbered bottom of the creek. Among the Indians along the Rocky Mountains, and more particularly among the Shoshone or Snake Indians, in whose territory it is very abundant, this is considered the best among roots used for food."

On the eighteenth, after the expedition had crossed the South Pass and was on the old Oregon Trail beyond the Big Sandy and Green Rivers in the neighborhood of Hams Fork of the Blacks Fork of the Green River, Fremont wrote, "*The Shoshone woman took leave of us here, expecting to find some of her relations at Bridger's Fort (Fort Bridger), which is only a mile or two distant, on a fork of this stream. In the evening we encamped on a salt creek, about fifteen feet wide, having today traveled thirty-two miles.*" As already stated, Fremont's account of this Snake or Shoshone woman in all probability refers to Sacajawea. It was not at all strange that Sacajawea should have adopted the child of a (French) engage, even though the child might not have been her own, for it was customary for a Shoshone woman to adopt a child left without its parents even though there were no blood relationship between the woman and the child. Perhaps, indeed, Sacajawea had herself married this French trader, but of this there is no evidence. Andrew Bazil, grandson of Sacajawea, and son of the Bazil whom she adopted in 1805, told the author in a personal interview on the Shoshone Reservation that his grandmother returned to the Shoshones from the Comanches by the easiest route, which ran directly from the south through Colorado into Wyoming and along the Oregon Trail, and that when she returned she had with her two adopted daughters.

James McAdams, a great-grandson of Sacajawea, also confirmed the tradition that Sacajawea returned to her people along a direct route from the south, and that she brought with her a number of horses. The Shoshones at this time [1843] were under the chieftainship of Washakie and were not as isolated as one might believe, for well-beaten trails radiated from the valley of the Bridger and the Green, and were constantly in use by hunting parties, Indian raiders, and even white travelers. These paths led to the sources of the Missouri, where the lodges of the Lemhi Indians were located. To this day the Shoshones of the reservation in the Wind River country use these trails, deepened by generations of heavy travel, in their big game hunting.

At that time the territory contained thousands of buffalo and even today there are elk, moose, deer, and big horn sheep in the regions not frequently traveled. These paths are also still used semi-annually when the Shoshones visit the Indians, who live near the sources of the Salmon River where Sacajawea tarried for a week with her people in August, 1805. It is difficult indeed to realize how migratory the Indians were (and still are), and how far they sometimes traveled. In speaking of this trait of the Shoshones, Fincelius G. Burnett, an Indian instructor on the Shoshone Reservation for much of the time since 1872, makes this statement, "*There are Indians here who have traveled through the mountains and deserts to the California coast, and then have returned through Oregon, Washington, and Montana. Time is nothing to the Indian, his home is wherever his lodge is, and if there is plenty of game or fish, and grass for his pony, he is happy, and it* matters little to him, when he takes a notion to move, whether it is north, south, east, or west. There is one thing you can depend on that he will do, and that is that he will move in some direction every three or four days." The life of Sacajawea after her reunion with her tribe, the Shoshones, is described at length in a later chapter. Among these people she found her two sons, Baptiste, who was now an interpreter, guide, and hunter, and Bazil, the orphan, child of her dead sister, whom she adopted in 1805 when she was a member of the Lewis and Clark Expedition. The story of her life from this time on is based largely on the testimony of her friends and relatives on the Shoshone Reservation in the Wind River country. Some of this testimony was procured many years ago, some more recently, much of it could never be obtained again, for many of those from whom it came have gone to join their ancestors, carrying with them the fading memory of the trails and hunting grounds of long ago before the white man came to restrict the Indian's wanderings and to change his customs and habits. The Shoshone Indians of the Lemhi Valley in Idaho, who constituted the tribe to which Sacajawea belonged, in the course of time drifted into Bridger Valley in what is now the southwestern part of Wyoming, and set up their tepees along the Bear River and beside the sources and branches of the Green.

About 1840 a great Indian leader named Washakie became chief of these Indians in the Bridger Valley, and for sixty years filled this high office, winning for himself by his valor, skill in warfare, and constant loyalty to the government of the United States, the name of "White Man's Friend, Chief Washakie." As we have seen, one of the Lemhi chiefs who aided Lewis and Clark was Cameahwait, the brother of Sacajawea. This chief was killed in battle against the Pahkeeps about 1840, and was succeeded by his nephew, Nowroyawn [later known as Snag to the Mormons] who had distinguished himself by his bravery in this battle.

Fighting beside Nowroyawn was his cousin, Shoogan or Bazil, as he was more commonly called by the whites, the adopted son of Sacajawea. Bazil became, in time, one of the trusted sub-chiefs under Washakie, to whom he was related, and because of a wound which he received in a battle in 1862 in which Nowroyawn was killed, he was known to the Indians as the lame sub-chief of Washakie. In 1843 James Bridger established his blacksmith shop, post, and fort, in the valley of Blacks Fork and Green Rivers to supply the *"immigrants for Oregon and California with necessary supplies."* Bridger spoke of this new landmark on the Oregon Trail as a *"small fort with a blacksmith shop and a supply of iron, in the road of the immigrants."* It was not designed for a road house or a saloon, but as a "sanctuary in the midst of the immigrant's journey." It was near this fort, which was completed by the first of August, 1843, that Fremont took leave of the Shoshone woman with her two small children *"who expected to find relatives at Bridger Fort."* In 1847 the Mormons, under the leadership of Brigham Young, traveled the Oregon Trail from Council Bluffs to Salt Lake. Here they broke the sod, planted seed, and ploughed furrows for irrigation ditches to signalize their arrival in the land of promise. In the meantime, a company of Young's followers had been recruited by the United States Government in Omaha, and organized into the so-called Mormon battalion to assist in the conquest of California.

With these Mormons Baptiste Charbonneau, Bazil's brother, came in frequent contact while he was serving under General Cooke and the other leaders of the California expedition. East and north of the Mormon settlement at Salt Lake lay the Shoshone Reservation where Sacajawea, Bazil, and, in time, Baptiste came to live. Here from perhaps 1850 to 1871, when they migrated to the Shoshone Reservation further north, these three made their home, and Bazil at least, from his contact with the Mormons, learned something of agriculture and the cultivation of the soil. At the time of the construction of the Union Pacific Railroad through Bridger Valley it was necessary to secure the permission of the Indians for the right of way in order to avoid serious difficulty and probable bloodshed. The Shoshones naturally objected strongly to the construction through their territory of a railroad, which would drive away the game upon which they depended for their living. Washakie recognized the seriousness of the situation for his people, and therefore sought from the government a new reservation in the Wind River Valley where his people might find a new home and where the game would remain undisturbed. The Great Treaty, by which this was accomplished, was signed by government officials and Chief Washakie and his sub-chiefs on July 3, 1868. Under this treaty the Shoshones were granted some 2,784,400 acres, all of which lay north of the Oregon Trail. Subsequent treaties have reduced this territory to less than 525,000 acres. On the part of the Indians, the treaty was signed by Washakie and his sub-chiefs, of whom Bazil was one. Since no Indian was then able to read or write, the names of the signers appeared with "his X mark." A thorough search has been made of the files of the Indian office, but no record so far has been found of the minutes of the council at which this treaty was drafted, though such minutes should have been forwarded to Washington. The treaty is, of course, a matter of official record. Prior to this treaty, Bazil had also agreed to and signed the treaty of 1863, and his mark also appears on the treaty of 1872. With characteristic farsightedness, Chief Washakie cherished the desire that his people might be taught to raise crops on some of the land in the new reservation in order that they might have food when the game should have disappeared and the buffalo have been hunted out. Some of the tribe, indeed, had already learned their first lessons in agriculture, even before the move was made to the new reservation, from the Mormon immigrants who had settled in Bridger Valley. Here at Fort Supply these followers of Joseph Smith had grown the first crops in southwestern Wyoming. They had also learned to converse with the Shoshones and Bannocks, who had erected their lodges around Fort Bridger, studying the Shoshone language from a Mormon teacher who was married to a Shoshone wife.

  Here Bazil, among others, had been taught agriculture and the art of irrigating land, and had learned his lesson so well that by 1856 he was able to produce wheat and vegetables. The success of his experiment made him "feel good" and also inspired others to grow potatoes, beets, and peas. Washakie himself also learned the value of reclaiming land by irrigation. It is only natural that there should have been scant mention made of Sacajawea in the interval between the time that she rejoined her people and the change of the Shoshones to the Wind River Reservation, nor is it strange that such meager reference as there is should come from the statements of individuals, including both Indians and whites, rather than from official records, for until the treaty of 1868 the government had little, if any, interest in the Shoshone Indians and exercised only nominal control over the tribe. Such information as is available, however, clearly shows that Sacajawea exercised great and beneficial influence among her people and was of inestimable service to the whites and to the American Government. It is certain from the testimonies, here printed for the first time, that Sacajawea made her influence felt in the council of 1868 at Fort Bridger, and that she sought to persuade her people to accept the proposed reservation and to live at peace with the whites. Speaking on this subject, Andrew Bazil, son of the sub-chief Bazil and grandson of Sacajawea, said to the author in 1926, "*My father Bazil, my grandmother Porivo, Chief Washakie, and myself were at the Great Treaty, and my grandmother sat back where the women sat in a circle, where I could not hear the words of her speech. When my grandmother was living, my father used to say to me, 'You must respect your grandmother—all the white people respect her and honor her everywhere.' My father said he had made peace with the Mormon Church on behalf of his people. My father was noted among the Mormons. My father also had some papers that he carefully kept in a leather bag which he said were very valuable. Later I learned that these papers were given to my grandmother [Sacajawea] by some great white chiefs.*" Barbara Meyers, daughter of Baptiste, and granddaughter of Sacajawea, with a smiling face which resembled that of her grandmother, recalled Sacajawea's [notable] presence at the Great Treaty. "*Yes, Porivo, or Sacajawea, or Wadzewipe, was at the council of the Great treaty down at Fort Bridger when the Bridger Valley territory was exchanged by Washakie and his warriors for the present Shoshone*

Reservation. This Sacajawea was my grandmother, and my father was her son, Baptiste, the papoose who was carried to the big waters toward the setting sun. I was there at the council in 1868, but at that time, I was quite a young woman, and was one of the listeners at the council." Hebecheechee, in 1929, told the following to the author through the government interpreter, "Yes, I was at Fort Bridger at the time of the Great treaty, when the Bridger country was sold by Chief Washakie for the Shoshone Reservation. My uncle (my father's brother), Humpy, was one of the leaders of the Shoshones at the treaty, and one of Washakie's fighters in the council. In the council, Washakie asked my father to suggest what part of what is now Wyoming they should ask for a reservation, and what would be best for the Shoshones. My uncle told Washakie that he should ask for the "warm valley" where there was little snow, and there were hot springs for bathing. I remember that there were a lot of women in a circle at this council. I cannot remember whether Sacajawea was there or not. So many women were there, she might have been there and not noticed. I was not interested except in the part my uncle was taking." Enga Peahrora, daughter of Chief Washakie, stood at the open flap of her tepee and spoke of Porivo and her part in the council, called the Great treaty of 1868, as follows, "I knew Porivo, or Sacajawea, at Fort Bridger. She lived with her son Bazil. I was a young girl at the time, perhaps at the age of fourteen or fifteen. She lived with Bazil in an Indian tepee at Fort Bridger. I knew that Porivo took part in the council at Fort Bridger because I was right there and saw her in the council myself. She had a part in the meeting, and she spoke in the meeting, I know this, because I was there and saw her speak."

Quantan Quay, in a personal interview on the reservation [July 21, 1929], added his testimony. "I was at the council at the time that the treaty was made with our government at Fort Bridger. Sacajawea was at this council meeting. I know she was there. I saw her there. Bazil was one of the men speakers and spoke, but Baptiste [Charbonneau] did not speak or say a thing." Edmo St. Clair, son of an employee of the American Fur Company when it was [then] operating in the Bridger Valley country, knew

Sacajawea, Bazil, and Baptiste, particularly the sons, since they were always used as interpreters in dealing with the white traders and Indians. Mr. St. Clair testified, "*I met Sacajawea, mother of Baptiste and Bazil, sometime after we had moved to Fort Bridger, and after I had come to know her two sons. This was in 1863. I was at Fort Bridger when the treaty was made between the government and Chief Washakie and his people in 1868. Bazil, the son of Sacajawea, was one of the signers of the treaty. I saw Sacajawea at the treaty, and remember very well seeing her in the circle formed by the Shoshone women just back of the circle made by Chief Washakie and his men. They were sitting down. I also saw her standing up and making a short speech of some kind, but I cannot remember now what she said. It has been over sixty years ago. The last time I saw Sacajawea at Fort Bridger was in 1869, a year after the treaty.*" Mr. Fincelius G. Burnett, who knew Sacajawea longer and better than any other white man, said in an interview, "*At the time of the signing of the Great Treaty I was not there, since I did not come among the Shoshone Indians until 1871. It would have been an unthinkable thing under ordinary circumstances for a woman to be allowed to address a council of wise brave lords of creation, but she represented the white men as well as the Indians. There is no doubt that her influence was felt in all important questions that were discussed. Bazil was her mouthpiece and he was an eloquent speaker. Through him, her influence was felt on all important questions. Bazil was a man of noble and commanding presence. He was fully six feet tall and weighed over two hundred pounds. He had a deep, musical voice, and had a great influence in council. All questions of importance were discussed around the campfires and in their lodges. Here is where a woman's influence was felt. Many a brave warrior in council has spoken eloquent words of wisdom that his wife or mother put in his mouth while discussing important questions around the campfire. I have known Washakie and other chiefs to visit Sacajawea's home near the agency and listen intensely to her conversation for hours. When discontent arose for any cause among the Indians, Chief Washakie, his sub-chief Bazil, and Sacajawea could always be depended upon *as firm friends of the whites, although the government failed many times to fulfill their promises to them. The influence of Washakie, Bazil, and Sacajawea, caused all the mountain Indians to remain peaceful during the Indian wars, and saved the government great expense and the lives of many pioneers. Wyoming is under many obligations to these three noble, true and steadfast Indian friends. What a pity that their influence and worth were not recognized while they were living. There are but a very few men living who knew and appreciated them. Washakie understood English fairly well, but when conversing with Sacajawea, they talked the Shoshone language. Those who understood French said that both she and Bazil talked very good French. She and Bazil talked English very well. Sacajawea also talked several Indian languages."*

In a letter to the author dated December 9, 1931, the Honorable Alonzo M. Clark, acting governor of the state of Wyoming, commenting upon the book *Washakie*, asks this question *"What was the basic reason for Chief Washakie, under all conditions, ever and persistently remaining a loyal friend to the white people?"* In the influence of Sacajawea, as evidenced by the testimony given above, lay the answer to that question. For it is certainly evident that Sacajawea proved of the greatest value to the whites through her influence with her own people. She was able to understand the white man's point of view and to present this to the Indians, at the same time successfully interpreting the Indian's point of view to the whites. Her own people respected her council, and the whites valued her understanding and influence. The influence of Bazil, like that of his mother, was also of great value to the American government. The domestic relationships of Sacajawea were somewhat complex. She was the mother of Baptiste who, as already frequently stated, was born in 1805 in the Mandan villages just before the Lewis and Clark Expedition started for the west. She was stepmother of Toussaint Jr., the son of Charbonneau and the "other Shoshone woman" who died in 1812, and she was the aunt and foster mother of Bazil, the son of Sacajawea's oldest sister, who was born about 1802. The adoption of Bazil by Sacajawea followed the custom of the Shoshones, by which a sister adopts her deceased sister's children. At the time of the adoption, on August 17, 1805, near the Two Forks of the Jefferson River, Bazil was a "small boy." This expression to the Indians signified a small child who was able to walk, hence it is surmised that Bazil was about three years old at the time of his adoption. The incident of his adoption, as already stated, is recorded only in the Biddle edition of the Lewis and Clark journals. It will be remembered that after Sacajawea's adoption of Bazil, she continued with the Lewis and Clark Expedition, while her newly-adopted son remained with his people, the Shoshones. Apparently, therefore, he knew nothing of his foster mother until he was a man, grown, and she had returned to her tribe at Fort Bridger, sometime after 1840.

From that time on, however, it appears that the relationship between Bazil and Sacajawea was not only formally acknowledged, but was much more intimate and close than that of Sacajawea and her own son, Baptiste. Thus, Sacajawea became known as Bazil's mother, or Bazil umbea, and lived with him as part of his recognized household. Baptiste, whose history has previously been given in some detail in this volume, undertook the last of his more important missions when he served with the Mormon battalion on its march to California.

For twenty years thereafter the records contain almost no mention of his [Baptiste] name. By this time the trails and passes were well defined and extensively used, and the services of expert guides and interpreters were consequently less and less in demand. During these years Baptiste seems to have devoted himself to hunting and, perhaps in a minor way, serving also as a guide. Apparently he cared almost nothing for the agricultural interests of his [adopted] half-brother, Bazil. He played but a small part in the historical records and activities of the Shoshones, and, according to Andrew Bazil, almost never spoke in their councils. Bazil, on the contrary, always held an important and dignified position in the councils of his tribe. As already stated—he was one of the sub-chiefs of Washakie and, as such, signed three of the five major treaties which that great chieftain made with the government of the United States. These treaties were those of 1863, 1868, and 1872. On these documents, Bazil's name appears as Bazeel, though, of course, like most Indians, he was able to sign only with his mark. Bazil, as already recorded, early recognized the value of studying the agricultural methods of the whites. After he left the Lemhi Mission in Idaho he lived until 1871 in close contact with the Mormon settlers in Bridger Valley and from them learned much that was useful to his people. The records of the archives of the historical department of the Church of Jesus Christ of the Latter Day Saints, at Salt Lake City, attest to Bazil's friendly relations with these pioneers. As early as 1852 we find him one of the speakers at a harvest festival and pioneer celebration held by the Mormons at Fort Supply, near Fort Bridger. On this occasion he expressed himself as grateful for the training in agriculture he had received, saying in part, "*I feel well to see grain growing on the Snake land, now their children can get bread to eat, also butter and milk. Before you came here our children were often hungry, now they can get bread and vegetables when we are not fortunate in hunting meat.*" Elder Isaac Bullock, one of the missionaries of Fort Lemhi, writes in the fall of 1856 that, "*Baziel, one of the Snakes who has lived in the fort with us during the last year, has raised thirty bushels of wheat and some vegetables. He and his squaws have harvested it clean and neat, and appear to feel well-satisfied with their prospects for bread this winter.*" At a Fort Lemhi banquet of the same year, Bazil proposed the following toast, "*I want you to live and never die, that you may raise plenty of the good things we have had to eat today, for they make my heart feel good.*" Chief Bazil seems to have been a popular after dinner speaker, for the three speeches here recorded occurred at three different places—at Fort Supply and Fort Bridger, both then in Utah, and at Fort Lemhi in Idaho. It is probable also, that Bazil was actually baptized into the Mormon faith. The records of the Mormon Salmon River Mission of November 11, 1855, mention the baptism of sixty-five Indians, among, whom, appears the name of Snag, a cousin of Bazil's already referred to in a previous chapter, and chief of the

Shoshones after Cameahwait. Writes Andrew Jenson—assistant church historian—to the author. "*While the mission at Fort Lemhi was functioning from 1855 to 1858, Bazil lived there with his wives for about a year. The date of the baptism of Bazil is not recorded in those portions of the manuscript records of the Salmon River Mission, but it seems hardly credible that this chief remained with the missionaries that length of time and became somewhat prominent among them, unless he had received baptism at their hands.*" In 1871, Sacajawea, Bazil and his wives, Baptiste with his three wives, and Chief Washakie likewise with his three wives, migrated into the new reservation in the Wind River Valley, to the east and north of the Mormon lands, there to remain with their people for the rest of their lives. Sacajawea died in 1884, Baptiste in 1885, and Bazil in 1886. Chief Washakie lived until 1900.

Numerous descendants of these four Shoshones make their homes at the present time on the same reservation, and some of them, both at Fort Bridger and on the reservation, have made valuable contributions to the history of Sacajawea, Bazil, and Baptiste. The influence of Sacajawea and Bazil, and to a lesser degree of Baptiste, in interpreting the white man to their fellow tribesmen and in urging them to adopt his methods of agriculture, was of the greatest service to the government agents sent to the reservation for this purpose. One of the most important of these government agents was Mr. Fincelius Gray Burnett, previously referred to, who was sent to teach the Shoshones and Bannocks how to farm. This position was held by Mr. Burnett with great credit until 1924, and because of his long acquaintance with the Shoshones and his intelligent understanding, his testimony is of particular value and interest. In a personal interview with the author, Mr. Burnett made the following statement, "*Sacajawea was of the greatest help to the Indian agents, James Irwin and James I. Patten. Into her house about one hundred fifty yards from the agent's office, or into their office at the Wind River agency, she and they were going in and out many times a day and in this way they were kept in close touch with what was to the advantage of the agents to know about the* government's wards, the Shoshones. It was she who kept the affairs of the office straight as to information that was to be sent to Washington. The government interpreter for the Shoshones, during the early years of reservation life, talked very indifferent English, and experienced difficulty in translating the agent's English speeches into the Shoshone language for the Indians. Sacajawea and Bazil, both able to speak English and Shoshone, were of invaluable service as interpreters to the agent during a long and important period of this reservation life. During the first days when the Indians started to work in agriculture on the Shoshone Reservation under my supervision as instructor in agriculture, there was not an Indian or a horse that knew anything about farming. We finally got started with the assistance of Porivo [Sacajawea], Bazil and Baptiste, who had seen the great fields of grain in the south among the Comanches, or with the Mormons in the region of Great Salt Lake. Baptiste, too, had seen fields in his travels. With the help these three gave in their native tongue, and the confidence the Shoshones had in Sacajawea and her sons and their ability to tell the Indians what we wished to do, we got under way." As already stated, Mr. Burnett remembers Bazil as a *"fine, portly man, nearly six feet tall, who must have weighed over 200 pounds. His complexion was also very fair for a full-blooded Indian. He was crippled in one knee, and when walking, the toes only of one foot touched the ground. He and his mother were much attached to each other, and they lived together until Sacajawea's death. Sacajawea had another son who was identified as the babe she carried on her back on the expedition. He was called Baptiste. He was a small man, and had a complexion as dark as any full-blooded Indian. He was of course, a 'breed.' "* James I. Patten, who was officially identified with the Shoshone Reservation and the Wind River agency as teacher and lay missionary as early as 1871 and for many years thereafter, also corroborates Mr. Burnett's description of Bazil. *"Bazil was a sub-chief of the Shoshone tribe and usually quite active in tribal affairs. He was rather lighter in complexion than Baptiste, was lame in one of his limbs, five feet eight inches, about, in height, in weight about two hundred* seventy-five pounds, with thick lips and a very pleasant and good natured manner. He claimed Sacajawea as his mother, and gave her always all the attention and care that a son would be expected to show a mother." From 1868 to 1875, when supplies were carried by freighters over the Oregon Trail from Fort Laramie to Fort Bridger and thence to Salt Lake City, one of the best-known freighters was a man named Jim Faris, who was then well acquainted with the country and its Indian inhabitants.

In his statement to Charles Alexander Eastman, Faris made the following comments on Bazil and Baptiste, "*Bazil seemed to have had then a great influence with Brigham Young—in fact he made two or three agreements with him. He also was one of the strong men of James Bridger and Antoine Roubideaux, for he usually interpreted all their trading with his tribe. I have also known his brother, Baptiste. He was not a leader of the band, but he was [an] assistant to his brother in a way. Bazil once said to me that since he came back here he took the responsibility of guiding his uncle's band. His uncle had been dead before he came back, and it was led by another man, but not successfully. What Bazil said, I think was true, because ever since I have known him he was always considered the head of Henry's Fork Snakes. I know him to be a very reliable and conscientious man. He was practically old or middle aged when I met him, but in action he was a man of a great deal of physical activity and clear headedness. He was a very useful lieutenant to Chief Washakie. He never claimed very much honor, but it is a fact that he and his mother were the trump card when Washakie made the treaty with the United States in 1868. He did not as a rule volunteer information or tell much about his own life, except that he knew me very well and we talked over a good deal of western life in the past when we smoked in our own cabins. It appears from what he said he came into this country with Jim Bridger and Roubideaux from the southwest. After he arrived here, he devoted his time to his tribe and he was with them all the time, but his brother, Baptiste, became more or less a guide and trapper to the fur traders and hunters for a time, but he too after a while settled down with his brother's tribe.*" Further interesting information regarding the two brothers or cousins was given the author by Barbara Meyers, the daughter of Baptiste. "*Baptiste, my father, did not always live with Bazil, and did not say very much. He seldom spoke in public nor told of his different travels. My Uncle Bazil was more of a spokesman. My grandmother often spoke to me of having had a French husband and that Baptiste was the son of this French husband. Both Baptiste and Bazil spoke the Ute and French and English languages, as well as, of course, the Shoshone language. My father, Baptiste, often spoke to me of being across the big waters into another country toward the rising sun, and how funny the white people were over in that district. He saw many curious people and often spoke about this period of his life. Baptiste, my father, spoke several languages. At Fort Bridger he used to tell me of his many travels, and at that time when he was at Bridger when the treaty was made [1868] he was sixty-three years old.*" From the testimony of those who knew them, at least in later years, Bazil thus seems to have been a much stronger character than Baptiste. Quantan Quay, in describing the two men, says, "*Bazil was a man of fine character, physically splendid, a true specimen or type of Indian. He was always gentle in his speech and never loud or boisterous. On the other hand, Baptiste was a treacherous man, because he liked his firewater and used it often.*" This opinion is confirmed by Mr. James I. Patten, who thus describes Baptiste as he recalled him, "*He was a man of little force or importance in the tribe, about five feet six inches in height, quite dark complexion, stocky build, weight about two hundred pounds, thick lips and his mouth drawn well down at the corners. He was rather pleasant and sociable in manner, liked ease and enjoyed it. He had a wife and several children. He acknowledged Sacajawea as his mother, and that she accompanied the Expedition to the coast, but seemed to take but a passing interest in her.*" From the statements made above, the conclusion reached in chapter 3 is further strengthened—that Baptiste in later life suffered the usual fate of the half-breed who deteriorates from adopting the vices of the whites. In earlier years, however, he proved himself of great value to the fur traders and explorers because of his ability as an interpreter and his knowledge of the west. Returning to his mother's people in later years when changed conditions made his services as guide and interpreter no longer in demand, he lived the remainder of his life somewhat apart from the rest of his tribe, "in a lone lodge camping by himself," as Mr. Burnett records, talking little and mingling little with other people.

Bazil, on the other hand, was an active and valued leader of his people and a man whose services and friendship were also greatly appreciated by the whites. The testimony of his contemporaries unanimously ascribes to him exceptional qualities. The fact that both Bazil and Baptiste claimed Sacajawea as [their] mother and were in turn acknowledged by her as her sons adds substantial weight to the claim that she was [as stated] the guide of the Lewis and Clark Expedition.

□□□□□□□□□□□

One of the chief marks of greatness on the part of Chief Washakie, whose name has so frequently been mentioned in these pages, was his ability to look ahead into the future and prepare for the time when the buffalo would be gone and the Indian would be forced to raise his own food or perish from starvation. With this object in mind, Washakie, as we have already seen, succeeded in obtaining the Wind River Valley as a reservation for the Shoshone people from the United States government in 1868. The task of teaching the Indians to farm, however, upon this reservation was not without its difficulties. Mr. Fincelius G. Burnett tells the story of the beginnings of this effort in the following paragraph, *"We commenced to harness one team to the plow. I told the Indian to drive the horse, but the horse balked. The Indian said to his squaw, 'You lead them,' referring to the horses—and the Indian would hold on to the plow and at the same time he would have to hold his blanket around his body with his teeth, because he refused to abandon his blanket. At first we got along pretty well. The next horse reared and ran away. The next one had a woman at the plow and the man riding the horse. Finally we got the 320 acres ploughed and had good crops that year* through irrigation. We had ten acres of barley, and the rest was in wheat and oats, half and half. Those who measured the grain as it was thrashed vowed that the crop averaged seventy-five bushels to the acre, barley, wheat, and oats equally. That fall we had a little mill with some bolting cloth, which enabled us to do some grinding. This was the first wheat to be ground by Indians in Wyoming. I am inclined to believe and have always thought that this was the first wheat and first flour in the state." According to Burnett, as we have already seen, Sacajawea and Bazil rendered great service both in urging the Shoshones to learn to farm and in setting the example. Sacajawea told her people that the buffalo and other game animals would soon be gone, that the whites would become as numerous as grasshoppers, and that the Indians would have to learn to raise wheat and grind grain.

Sacajawea also told them how the Mandans on the Missouri raised corn, how good it was, and how it kept away the hunger. The irrigation ditches of the whites seemed to the Indians to lead the water uphill, and Washakie said that only white men and Mormons could do this and that Indians could not. The Indians looked through the surveyor's level or the transit, and wondered how the instrument achieved the miracle, calling it white man's medicine. Many other difficulties were encountered in the first agricultural work among the Shoshones.

Spotted fever took its toll, and the Indian suspected that evil agencies were responsible for this. Mr. Burnett tells how one Indian refused to have his land ploughed or to take care of it. When asked why, the Indian finally admitted, "*If I turn water into the gopher's hole, he will come out of the hole and sit up and look at me and I will die!*" That this superstitious fear was not entirely without foundation has been shown by recent tests which have demonstrated that the gopher carries the tick which spreads the dreaded spotted fever in the mountain districts. It was for this reason that the authorities at Washington, about 1894 and 1895, urged the extermination of the gopher as a dangerous pest. Dr. E. N. Roberts, a trained chemist and son of the Reverend John Roberts of the Shoshone mission, corroborates this fear of the

Indians of the gopher, and gives a similar explanation to account for it. "*Certain of the Shoshones have told my father that if a gopher comes out of its hole and looks at one, that one is liable to fall ill with the fever. Further, the Indian believes that if he goes out of his tepee in the morning and finds a pocket gopher facing the tepee door, with his head bowed and his forepaws drawn over the face, the Indian or members of his family will become ill and die. The Shoshones believed this to the extent that they would desert their abodes upon such a discovery, and move elsewhere immediately in the hope that they might escape disaster. Hence the Shoshone desire not to disturb the gopher by irrigation, or to run the risk of being seen by the animal. The idea of a gopher dying in front of an Indian dwelling is not necessarily "far-fetched," because during the season when spotted fever was particularly prevalent, a good many of the gophers also died of the disease, and when ill with it, a gopher would likely wander from his burrow and die in the open and perhaps near an Indian tepee, which he would not ordinarily closely approach. It is true, as far as I have observed, that white mice, rats, and guinea pigs, when ill from experimental inoculation with virulent bacterial cultures, generally assume a posture which is characteristic—a huddled position, remaining quiet with the feet under them, head down—and generally they die in that position and do not 'turn up their toes,' so the Shoshone description of a gopher dead from spotted fever sounds accurate and characteristic of rodents dying of such a cause.*"

Difficult as were these first problems to overcome, the Shoshones, in the course of time, adapted themselves to agriculture and, as we have seen, Sacajawea and her son Bazil contributed much to the success of this new experiment. It is our purpose in the remainder of this chapter to speak more in detail of the character and activities of Sacajawea as she lived on the reservation as her contemporaries remembered her. Apparently even in her late years, she was a person of restless spirit who traveled far and wide throughout the west. Thus she was seen at many of the well-known trading posts such as Fort Laramie and Fort Bridger, and her name appears at irregular intervals in their records. Charles William Bocker, pioneer of early Wyoming, who died at Laramie on November 20, 1929, prepared a written statement containing the recollections of Sacajawea and of events relating to her life and times. Part of this statement is considered of sufficient interest to be given here unedited. "*I came to the Oregon Trail from Sweden in 1857, and went over it through Wyoming with an emigrant to Utah, a friend of mother's, a widow. I cannot remember much on the route, but I do remember when we were at Fort Laramie. From there we went directly to Salt Lake, which was the end of our "home stretch." I went to Fort Bridger in 1858. My mother's cousin lived at Fort Supply. Fort Supply was a fort erected by the Mormons not far from old Fort Bridger. I commenced to work at Fort Bridger for the Judge W. A. Carter family and his brother in 1865, and a part of 1866 and 1867 were spent taking care of cattle and hauling hay cut on Hams Fork or Willow Creek. In 1868 I worked for the Union Pacific Railroad, working on the grade, driving spikes in the ties and helping lay the rails. I was working west part of the time toward Promontory. I frequently saw Jim Bridger at Fort Bridger. I remember that I first met him about 1866, when Judge W. A. Carter and I were walking by Bridger's house where he lived. Bridger, his wife and daughter, all three of them, were in front of the house. Judge Carter introduced me to Jim Bridger, his wife, and daughter at that time. The mother was a pretty, fair-looking woman. She was related to Shade Large, who married a relative of Sacajawea's, also to Mrs. Dick Hamilton. All these three women were related—Mrs. Shade Large, Mrs. Dick Hamilton, and Mrs. Jim Bridger—to Sacajawea. I saw Sacajawea with Bridger's wife walking, talking, and visiting many times. When I was introduced to Sacajawea at Fort Bridger, by Mr. Carter, I should judge at this time she must have been an old woman of about seventy years. Squaw ages are hard to tell. She was pretty good looking for an old woman, in fact, quite lovely looking for an old woman, and she could ride horses as well as any of them. She could talk a little English, but got it mixed up. At this time one of the Carters or Mr. Hamilton spoke to me about this Indian woman having been on an expedition with the white men. I* heard at that time when I was at Fort Bridger, as many times, that she had been with the white men. Everybody all around everywhere knew it, and it was common talk. Bridger knew it, Carter knew it, Hamilton knew it, the white men knew it, the Indians knew it." Mr. Bocker also recalled that Sacajawea came to Fort Bridger every year. She had her lodge somewhat north of the old fort, and came with the other Indians to exchange the articles which they had brought for money and trinkets at the Sutler store.

During these visits Mr. Bocker became so well-acquainted with Sacajawea that he could talk to her in her native tongue. She was commonly called Porivo or chief, the name by which she was known on the reservation, and she usually rode on horseback into the fort, dragging the usual Indian travois behind her horse.

This method of travel consisted of having a pole fastened on each side of the pony with cross bars reaching from one pole to the other on which baggage, papooses, or other burdens were carried. Continued Mr. Bocker, "*I remember of buying a pair of moccasins from Sacajawea in 1865 when she came down from her lodge, the articles costing me $1.50 plus a quantity of beads which I purchased for her from the Sutler store. In 1866, I again had a transaction with her on her second visit, when I purchased a buffalo robe from her for three dollars in cash and miscellaneous articles of value to an Indian. In 1867, I purchased from her an Indian blanket for which I attempted to pay her with "shin-plasters," but Sacajawea, not knowing the value of this, small paper money issued by our government during the war, refused to accept them and demanded coin or 'hard money.'* " As a result of a newspaper notice of the death of Mr. Bocker in 1929 the author received a letter from Mr. Tom Rivington of Gering, Nebraska, which in turn brought forth much additional interesting information regarding Sacajawea. The letter is full of touches of the old west, the wild escapades of the road agent, and reminiscences of the Indian woman. According to Mr. Rivington, during 1860 and 1861 Sacajawea made her home for part of the time with certain Indians living near [present day] Virginia City, Montana.

"*The white people,*" he says, "*had great admiration for her and did not require her to pay for anything she desired at the store.*" He also says that Slade, the notorious road agent then operating in Colorado, Wyoming, and Montana, gave Sacajawea money and a pass on the stagecoach, with orders to let her eat without charge at the stations along the road. Rivington, who as a boy "*slept in her tent many times,*" also recalls that once, when Sacajawea was about to board the stagecoach, a notorious character named Plummer, who was both outlaw and sheriff, gave her three sacks of flour to keep her from going. That night the stage was shot up—robbed. According to Rivington, Sacajawea also lived for a time with the Bannock Indians at Fort Hall, and used also to visit the Blackfeet at Fort Benton. Later she went to Fort Bridger, "*to live with Jim Bridger's Ute wife. Here is where she got in with the Shoshone Indians. They were the tribe that gave her the name of Sa-ca-ja-we. She made her home with them ever after. She told me that she visited the first time at Fort Laramie in 1856-1859-1863. She was a woman that was not satisfied anywhere, and the stagecoach companies helped to make her this way as they gave her free rides. She told me she was as far south as the Gila River in Arizona, but she did not like the Apache Indians for they were always at war, but she said the whites made them that way. She was over in California to see the Indians there, but said they were so poor, as the whites had taken all the country away from them, and she had been with the Nez Perce Indians in the state of Washington for several years. She had lived with different tribes up in Canada.*" Rivington also recalls that this Indian woman "*never liked to stay where she could not see the mountains, for she called them home. For the unseen spirit dwelt in the hills, and a swift-running creek could preach a better sermon for her than any mortal could have done. Every morning she thanked the spirits for a new day. She worshipped the white flowers that grew at the snow line on the sides of the tall mountains, for, as she said, she sometimes believed that they were spirits of little children that had gone away, but reappeared every spring to gladden the pathway of those now living. I was just a boy then, but those words sank deep in my soul. I believed then and I believe now, that if there is a hereafter that the Indian woman's name will be on the right side of the ledger. Sa-ca-ja-we is gone." In 1871, as already mentioned, Sacajawea came to the Shoshone Wind River Reservation to live with her people. Here she came in constant contact with various whites such as Mr. Fincelius G. Burnett, Reverend John Roberts, and others whose names have frequently been mentioned in this volume. Among other Americans who knew Sacajawea at this time were Mr. and Mrs. A. D. Lane, who were in charge of the store at the agency. In 1929, Mrs. Lane told the author that she "saw Sacajawea many times as she sat in the sun warming her aged bones. She was known to us and the small world in which she lived as Bazil's mother or Bazil umbea. A niece of Bazil's named Ellen, made her home with us, and often spoke of Bazil's mother and told how this Indian woman led the white men to a great body of water. Sacajawea's cabin, as well as her tent, was about one fourth of a mile east of Mr. Lane's trading store." Perhaps the American who knew Sacajawea most intimately during these days on the reservation was Mrs. James Irwin, the wife of the United States government agent on the Wind River Reservation. From Sacajawea, Mrs. Irwin learned how to speak and understand the Shoshone language, and in turn taught Sacajawea a better use and understanding of English. Mrs. Irwin had had unusual educational advantages, and was an astronomer of some ability as well as a botanist. After a time she began to keep a record of the statements made to her by Sacajawea covering her activities with the Lewis and Clark Expedition and her life elsewhere, but, unfortunately, a fire at the agency burned the government records and also destroyed Mrs. Irwin's manuscript, thus causing an irreparable loss to the history of Sacajawea. Mr. James I. Patten in 1871 became teacher and lay missionary to the Indians on the Wind River Reservation, and for many years following served on that reservation. Here he saw and talked with Sacajawea almost daily in Shoshone and in French and English, both of which languages she spoke "somewhat indifferently." Mr. Patten bears out the statement of the others who met Sacajawea that she was the guide of the Lewis and Clark Expedition and that her son Baptiste was the papoose she had carried with her to the coast. In the late fall of 1874, Bazil and Baptiste brought Sacajawea to the agency headquarters for care while they were to be away on a long buffalo hunt. At that time they spoke of her as their mother. Mr. Patten also remembers that once when he saw Sacajawea carrying a heavy burden, he remarked to Bazil, who had helped her rise with it, that she was pretty old for such a heavy load. "Yes," said Bazil, "*pretty old. She is my mother*" and mentioned Lewis and Clark. Sacajawea also told Mr. Patten that both Bazil and Baptiste were her sons. Baptiste, though he spoke of Sacajawea as his mother, appears to have had little interest in her. According to the Reverend John Roberts who went to the reservation in 1883 as missionary clergyman of the Protestant Episcopal Church, a post which he held until 1932, Sacajawea had many names in accordance with the Shoshone custom.

Thus she was called on the reservation "Bahribo" or "Water White Man," "Wadzewipe" or "Lost Woman," and "Booenive" or "Grass Maiden." A number of the older Indians on the reservation have also told their recollections of Sacajawea or Porivo to the author. In 1926 one of these, known as Grandma Herford, who was then about ninety-eight years old, told the author that she had met Porivo when she was herself a girl some twelve years of age, soon after Porivo's return to the Shoshones. "*I remember her telling my mother that when she was traveling with a large body of men over whom army officers were in charge, that the people became very hungry and killed some of their horses, and even dogs, for food. This meat Sacajawea did not eat, nor did the Shoshones.*" Quantan Quay, a name which means "She Held My Hand," also living on the Shoshone Reservation, told his recollections of Sacajawea in the musical Indian tongue.

He said that he knew the woman guide and her sons very well, and that the two men acted as interpreters with the whites near Fort Bridger and later traded in furs. He recalled that once when a band of his people were away all summer hunting in the Wind River country, they heard on their return that Bazil's mother had come back to Bridger. He also said that he had heard many times that the father of Bazil and Baptiste was a Frenchman, and that he had been left among the Utes. The tradition was widespread among the Indians, according to Quantan Quay, that Sacajawea had led a body of men in the early days to the waters of the west. "*I have no reason to doubt that she was the real Sacajawea of the Lewis and Clark Expedition, because both her sons were buried and are still buried here near her.*" Quantan Quay, also told of seeing Sacajawea at the council of 1868, and of hearing Bazil speak. Frequent mention has been made of Mr. Burnett, and frequent citations covering phases of Sacajawea's life have been quoted from his statements to the author. Like Mrs. Irwin, he was intimately acquainted with Sacajawea, and learned from her and her family how to use the Shoshone language. According to Burnett, Sacajawea and Bazil both spoke French. It was in 1871 that Sacajawea told him that she had been the guide with the Lewis and Clark Expedition, and gave him many of the details of the experiences of the Expedition.

He recalled especially her description of the difficulties she experienced in approaching close enough to the Shoshones, when the expedition reached their territory, to convince them that the white men were their friends—thus substantiating the statement already made that Sacajawea on this, as well as on other occasions, saved the party from attack by her presence. This is further borne out by the statements of a few very old Indians living in 1902 west of the mountains, who told how they hid in the grass and bushes, behind stones and trees, or in canyons watching the expedition, and were prevented from destroying the party only by the presence of the woman with the papoose on her back. According to Mr. Burnett, Sacajawea was modest in her behavior and could not easily be induced to talk.

Sometimes, however, she would tell him some of her recollections of her associations with Lewis and Clark. One of these ran as follows, "*I remember very distinctly that one day about 1872 a group of us including Doctor James Irwin, Charlie Oldham, some other white men, and a group of Indians were sitting* in a circle with Sacajawea. She was talking about her trip across the mountains, telling her story in the English language, and turning always to Bazil for verification, always speaking to him in French. She told that when she was out across the mountains with the Lewis and Clark people, word came to camp one day that a big fish had been found on the great sea, and that she begged the white men to allow her to go down and see the fish. She told about the fish she had seen, and the Indians at once whispered to each other, then called out, 'Ishsham! Ishsham!' Which being interpreted means 'A lie! A lie! Squaw a liar!' The Indians were incredulous and could not believe a fish could be as large as she indicated. They asked her how long it was. She indicated by a space that was from fifty to sixty feet, the distance between the hitching post and her tepee, and again the Indians could not believe it saying, 'White man, is this the truth?' I answered that there were fishes called whales that were as long and even longer than she indicated. At this the Indians burst out of one accord and said, 'Ishsham! Ishsham! White man a liar!' But Sacajawea stuck to her story, and again appealed to me for verification as to the size of the fish, saying, 'White man, is squaw a liar?' " At the time of this incident, Mr. Burnett had not read any of the accounts of the Lewis and Clark Expedition, and knew nothing of the story recorded in the journals of the discovery of the carcass of a whale on the shores of the Pacific, nor of the account by Lewis and Clark of Sacajawea's request that she be allowed to see the remains of this monstrous fish. He could easily, of course, guess that the Indian woman referred to a whale by her description. Sacajawea further told of the dark or brown people who lived on the rock at the edge of the big water, and who slipped into the water at the approach of the white men. Lewis and Clark in their account call them more accurately seals. The Indian woman also, according to Mr. Burnett, told of lashing two canoes together to make a larger boat, no trees being found large enough to make into boats to hold the instruments and supplies of the voyagers to the Pacific. This method of transportation is frequently mentioned in the journals of Lewis and Clark. Mr. Burnett also gave a personal description of

Sacajawea. She loved to dress like the whites and sometimes did so, but not often, because she did not like the ridicule of the others. Burnett described her as "*not dark in looks, but rather as light as a half-breed, medium of size, a very fine looking woman and much thought of by the other Indians. She weighed about one hundred forty pounds, was about five feet three inches tall. She was pleasing in appearance, a woman full of brightness and smartness, and you would have taken the son, Bazil, as the elder of the two.*" Of the various attempts in statuary to represent the Indian woman guide of Lewis and Clark, Mr. Burnett preferred the one by Henry Altman of New York, in which an Indian woman is represented on horseback. Of this statue he said, "*It comes nearer to being like Sacajawea as I knew her than any of the pictures or statues that I have seen. Sacajawea was as she is represented in the picture, small and squat and brown in color, although she was light complexioned for an Indian. The statue of Sacajawea in Portland, Oregon, is to my mind beautiful, but it is a typical representation of a Sioux woman rather than of Sacajawea, a Shoshone. Sacajawea was really very good looking, in fact, handsome, as many Shoshone women are.*" Further confirmation of Sacajawea's life among the Comanches was also obtained from many of the older Indians on the reservation. In fact, nearly everyone interviewed by the author among the Shoshones mentioned the fact that Sacajawea had lived for a time with the Comanches. When Andrew Bazil, for example, the grandson of Sacajawea, was interviewed by the author as he halted in his work in one of the finest hay fields on the reservation, he replied "*I remember very well my grandmother's story of her life among the Comanches. I used to get her to talk Comanche because it sounded funny. It was different from the Shoshone language, although they understood each other. I have cousins in that tribe, descendants of my grandmother, Porivo, who come to see me and I go to see them, but they did not know of her past when she came to them. They supposed she ran away, leaving a son, who was the son of her Comanche husband. On account of her disappearance, they called her 'Wadzewipe' or 'Lost Woman.' While she lived with this tribe she* was called 'Porivo' or 'Chief,' because the whites looked up to her as a big woman and respected her. When she came back here she was still called by that name, although it was not a Shoshone word." Bazil also stated that he had heard from other Indians that his grandmother had run away from the Comanches, and that it was they who gave her the name Wadzewipe. "*I received this information when I was in Oklahoma, and I visited the very scene from which my grandmother ran away from her Comanche husband.*" Bazil was at that time planning to go again to Oklahoma. Hebecheechee, an Indian, seventy-eight years old, who was born in the Wind River Valley, remembered Sacajawea at Fort Bridger, and recalled the story of how she ran away from the Comanches and returned to the Bridger country with some white people. "*She left a son among the Comanches and during recent years a daughter of that son visited us here on this reservation. I know this visitor well as she was a close friend of Andrew Bazil. One time when she was on the reservation she explained to me that she was a granddaughter of Sacajawea. The tradition was very common among this tribe of Indians that Sacajawea had led a large body of white men to the west to a body of big waters. All of this was a tribal tradition, never questioned, but accepted by all of her tribe and the Bannocks and white people.*" Barbara Meyers, daughter of Baptiste, also said "*My grandmother often spoke to me about being with the Comanche Indians for several years, and of her travels and exploits. My father also often spoke of having traveled with a large body of white men when they were hungry and making pemmican of buffalo meat—that is, pounding it up fine and mixing it with tallow and fat.*" Tasoondahipe, to whom extended reference has just been made, died in 1929, shortly after a visit to her grandmother's grave on the Wind River Reservation. She told the author that Sacajawea was the wife of Jerk Meat, and when he died, she ran away with her youngest child, Yagawosier, finally reaching her people, the Shoshones, in southwestern Wyoming. The Comanches mourned her as dead for many years. According to Tasoondahipe, it was not until Comanche boys from Oklahoma attended the Carlisle

School in Pennsylvania and met the Shoshone boys from Wyoming, that it was learned that Sacajawea had successfully reached her people. One of Sacajawea's great-grandsons, named James McAdams, contributed certain interesting information regarding the lost medal which Sacajawea had received from the government for her services. This medal bore Jefferson's head and his name, and had a gold rim about it. "*I have seen it many times. At Salt Lake the people, when they saw this medal, said to Porivo or Chief, 'Something grand!' and they gave Sacajawea and her people who were with her a big feast in honor of her wonderful achievements for the white people when they were on their way to the big waters. My great-grandmother Sacajawea gave Bazil, her son, some precious papers, and these papers were put in a leather wallet, which were then in the possession of Bazil and were buried with him. Mr. Eastman [Dr. Charles A. Eastman] dug up the bones of Bazil, but found them deeply embedded in wet earth, and the bones and the writing in the wallet were only dirt or mud, though the wallet was in good shape, made of thick, heavy leather and being about the size of a woman's pocketbook, perhaps four by six inches. I helped to bury the bones of my grandfather by the monument or marker of Sacajawea in the Wind River Indian Cemetery a short time after.*" McAdams said further that he had often seen the wallet Sacajawea carried, for she always carried papers with her "*to show she was worth something.*" According to McAdams, the wallet also contained a letter from Brigham Young, which he thought might have been a recommendation of some kind. McAdams, like Andrew Bazil, credited Sacajawea with introducing the sun dance among the Shoshone Indians.

He also said that Baptiste had told him of seeing Sacajawea at Fort Bridger, and that Bazil had said that he saw her and said to her, "*Here is my mother back again.*" He added that Sacajawea called her French husband Charbonneau.

He also had heard the story of her leaving Charbonneau because he had treated her roughly and had brought home a Ute wife with whom Sacajawea could not agree. "*She further told me several times of the fact that one of the 'Big Soldiers' (William

Clark) on the march in which she took part, wanted her son to educate him as his ward. Whenever she [Sacajawea] told this story she would throw out her arms and then clasp them close to her breast, saying, 'I wanted to hold my son right here.' "

☐☐☐☐☐☐☐☐☐☐

While Sacajawea was in the agency, as stated elsewhere in this volume, a number of white people who in one capacity or another were likewise attached to the reservation, made her acquaintance. One of these was Bishop George Maxwell Randall who, following the assignment by President Grant to the Protestant Episcopal Church of spiritual oversight of the Shoshone Indians came to the reservation in 1873 and established there a mission for the Shoshone and Bannock Indians.

Bishop Randall was a man of eloquence and courage, and one or two incidents related by Mr. Burnett, illustrative of the character of this first bishop to the agency, are well-worth recording here. On August 19, 1873, according to Mr. Burnett's account, Bishop Randall was holding services in a schoolhouse (later known as the Bishop Randall Chapel), which was ultimately moved to the Wind River Cemetery near the spot where Sacajawea lies buried. Here it now serves as a sort of mortuary chapel. "The schoolhouse was about two or three hundred yards from our residences and of course the Indians were hostile to the Shoshones and the white men, and were almost continually trying to get us. We never went anywhere, even to church, without our arms. On entering the church, we would stack our guns in the corner, but would keep on our cartridge belts and revolvers. Later it was learned that on this night we and our schoolhouse were surrounded by a large war party, which sneaked up to the little wooden building and peeped through the windows. The red men saw the guns stacked in the corner and learned that we were all fully armed, which fact made the red men conclude that the white men were putting up some kind of a game on them, so they slipped away and left us, all of us being unaware of their close presence to us. Three months after this event, Dr. James Irwin, our Indian agent at that time, was transferred to the Pine Ridge agency, where the Indians informed him that they had us surrounded in the schoolhouse that night in 1873. They asked Dr. Irwin why we were there. They also asked, 'Who was the Big Chief with the big voice who was talking to the white men?' The bishop was dressed in his ecclesiastical robes, different, of course, from the clothes worn by the ordinary white man. Hence, he was the chief of the gathering. Not only were there white men in the congregation, but there were some Shoshone Indians and a few of their women, among whom was Sacajawea." In the baptismal records of Bishop Randall appear the names of four of Sacajawea's great-grandchildren who were baptized in the mission room on August 19, 1873.

Three of these were children of "Battez" (Baptiste) and one a child of "Bazil." The sponsors of these and other Indian children were Mrs. Sarah Trumbull Irwin and James I. Patten. The names of the two sons of Sacajawea, as used by the Indians, were so near alike in pronunciation that it was difficult to know of which they spoke. "Pasce" was Bazil, and "Patseese" was Baptiste, according to Mr. Burnett, and in the record, various spellings of the two names appear. Other whites on the reservation from whom intimate details of Sacajawea's life were secured were Dr. James Irwin and Mr. James I. Patten, who early were identified with the work of the Episcopal Church among the Indians of the reservation. The Reverend John Roberts, who in 1883 was put in charge of the mission established by Bishop Randall, carried on his work for fifty years among the Shoshones and therefore became one of the chief authorities on the history and customs of that people. He was called "White Robes" by Chief Washakie and is still held in such respect that even today when he passes a group of Indians sitting on the ground gambling, they always arise and say with a bow, "How do you do, Father Roberts?" In the parish records kept by Mr. Roberts appears the official record of the death of Sacajawea.

The certified copy of the entry, furnished by Mr. Roberts and later verified by the personal examination of the author, reads as follows *(Date) April 9, 1884, (Name) Bazil's mother*

(Shoshone), (Age) One hundred, (Residence) Shoshone agency, (Cause of death) Old age, (Place of burial) Burial ground, Shoshone agency, (Signature of clergyman) J. Roberts. Mr. [John] Roberts conducted a Christian burial ceremony over Sacajawea's grave in the cemetery of the Shoshone Reservation on the day she died. Sacajawea had no last illness. She was found lifeless in her tepee on the morning of April 9, 1884. She was in her "shakedown" of blankets and quilts, and death had apparently come during the night. To the end of her life she retained her vigor and health, and she died alone, as she had so very often lived. One of Sacajawea's close neighbors at the agency gave the following account of the incident, which clearly describes the circumstances of her death. "One morning word was received that Bazil's mother was dead. Mr. Lane, the Indian trader, said, 'I'll go to the tepee.' At the door of the tent Bazil arrived with tears running down his face. Speaking to me, he said, 'Mrs. Lane, my mother is dead.' I saw Bazil's mother taken from the tepee wrapped in skins and sewed up for burial. The body was placed on her favorite horse, the horse being led by Bazil. Probably the body was to be taken to where the coffin was, for she was buried in a coffin according to the statement by Reverend Roberts and others. At the time of Sacajawea's death Bazil had two wives, and they all lived together, Sacajawea with them all the time and, at times, Baptiste was there also." The cemetery where Sacajawea lies buried is a forty acre tract of ground enclosed by a strong, durable fence made of cedar posts and twisted, barbed wire. When Sacajawea was buried, a small wooden slab was placed at the head of her grave. After this was worn away or removed, a small boulder was placed to mark her head and another to mark her feet. Today, however, a substantial cement stone column commemorates the spot. On the inclined face of this [site] is a bronze tablet bearing the following inscription.

SACAJAWEA
DIED APRIL 9, 1884
A GUIDE WITH THE
LEWIS AND CLARK EXPEDITION
1805-1806
Identified 1907 by Reverend J. Roberts
Who Officiated at Her Burial

This cement marker, which was placed on Sacajawea's grave by Mr. H. E. Wadsworth, Shoshone agent, was built with the assistance of Sacajawea's descendants, and the tablet was the gift of the Honorable Timothy F. Burke of Cheyenne, Wyoming, in 1909. The family of Sacajawea was not to be separated, even by death, for more than a few years. In 1885 Jean Baptiste Charbonneau died on the reservation. His body, according to Mr. Charles Lahoe, the government interpreter for the Shoshones, who knew both Baptiste and Bazil and assisted at their burials, was taken by a few Indians and carried into the mountains west of the agency and there let down between two crags about forty feet high. After the body had been lowered by a rope, a few rocks were thrown down upon the corpse, one of which struck the skull and crushed it. With the death of Baptiste in 1885, the last survivor of the Lewis and Clark Expedition had once more joined the other members of that gallant company. In view of the persistent belief that a medal given Toussaint Charbonneau by Lewis or Clark was worn by Baptiste at the time of his death and was buried with him, a search was made in recent years for the body, but an examination of the side of the mountain where the corpse had been left in 1885 showed that a mountain slide had forever buried from sight the bones of the man who as a child traveled on the back of his mother to the Pacific with the first expedition of whites to cross the continent.

In 1886, Bazil, the adopted son of Sacajawea and formerly a sub-chief under Washakie, also died. He was buried after the Indian custom. Wrapped in a sheet and blanket, the body was taken by a few Indians up to a stream called Mill Creek, and there placed in a new gulch which was dug into the bank and which caved down and covered the body. When Bazil was buried, a leather wallet or some similar receptacle containing a number of valuable papers, letters, and documents whose exact contents were unknown, was buried with him. These papers had at one time belonged to Sacajawea, and she had carried the packet containing them with her at all times. At her death, in accordance with the usual custom, these papers had been given to Bazil as the oldest son. It was reported that the leather case contained letters written by Lewis and Clark, together with certificates of good character given to Sacajawea by President Brigham Young of the Mormon Church, but the exact nature of the papers was known only slightly to persons outside of Sacajawea's immediate family. When the United States Government wished to make an appropriation to erect a monument over Sacajawea's grave, Dr. Charles Alexander Eastman, a Sioux, instituted an official search for this wallet together with the papers which it was reported to contain, for the discovery of this would serve to identify the grave and settle the controversy as to where Sacajawea was buried.

In the fall of 1924 Andrew Bazil, the grandson of Sacajawea, volunteered to locate the site of his father's grave, made nearly forty years before, and gave permission to have the grave opened. He recalled that his father was buried with the papers, and that he had stated that they belonged to Sacajawea and many of them had been obtained from the members of the Lewis and Clark Expedition, of which she was a member. The wallet was found, as many predicted it would be, in Bazil's grave lying underneath the skull. The contents of the bag, however, had been so ruined by moisture and the passage of time that nothing could be deciphered. It was only possible to determine that the papers discovered had, had writing on them at the time of Bazil's burial. The skeleton was found to be in poor condition. An old saddle lay across the feet, and beside the skeleton was a handsome pipe of peace. On January 12, 1925, the bones were reinterred beside those of Sacajawea, but because of the inclemency of the weather, it was impossible to hold a formal ceremony beyond the reading of the prayers for the dead.

In August, 1915, the author made a pilgrimage to the cemetery of the Wind River Reservation for the purpose of paying humble tribute to Sacajawea. There she placed a few flowers upon her grave—wild sunflowers, purple wood asters, and sweet smelling clover picked from the side of Andrew Bazil's irrigation ditch. This silent city of the dead was a part of the old hunting ground of Sacajawea's sons and of her tribal ancestors. The cemetery—barren, beggaring description—stands on an open desert tract of land surrounded in the distance by the Wind River mountain range with its ragged, eternally snow capped peaks. Around these few sacred acres was a five-strand barbed wire fence with an old-styled, seven-step stile over it. There were no evidences of life, the land—devoid of trees, shrubs, flowers, and grass—was as quiet and dead as the mortal bodies of the braves who were there taking their last sleep. Here and there the cemetery was dotted with spears, long and straight, placed at the heads of departed chiefs in order that those who were in their new happy hunting grounds might continue their activities with the same instruments of war they had used when upon the earth. On these spears, flying, fluttering in the wind, were bright pieces of cloth, giving the appearance of a gala day. On many of the graves was placed some chosen piece of property—the one most loved from the possessions of the dead—which could again be used in the new land to which the departed one had gone.

Among these sacred grave decorations, iron bedsteads held the most prominent place, for many of them were placed around the graves, the head and foot boards and the two sides making a small fence to protect the grave. Many wagons were likewise given an honored place, though the boxes and tongues had been removed from them. In 1915 there was but one marble tombstone in the entire cemetery, this was over the grave of an infant but three days old, and bore the inscription "Coffin the same as white man." The last view from the old-fashioned set of steps remains vividly in one's memory, weird, fascinating, oppressive, suggestive of the crowding of one civilization upon another. Gradually, however, the primitive method of grave marking is being displaced by white tombstones, by an occasional iron marker for the World War heroes, a bit of grass, flowers mostly of bright-colored paper, or an isolated tree. A well-beaten path from the wooden stile to Sacajawea's grave makes no guide post necessary. Annually thousands of people journey to this last resting place of the woman who served as guide to the Lewis and Clark Expedition. With the account of the death of Sacajawea and her two sons, the present volume logically draws to its close. It is believed that the evidence here presented proves conclusively that the central figure of the volume was in reality the famous guide of the Lewis and Clark Expedition, and that she was the mother of Baptiste and the foster mother of Bazil. All of this is substantiated by the testimonies of those—both men, and women, whites and Indians—who knew Sacajawea on the reservation and who heard firsthand the account and tradition of her services with the exploring party. Added to this testimony is that of Charles Alexander Eastman who, as already stated, made a thorough and detailed search on behalf of the United States government for the grave of Sacajawea, and who formally declared on March 17, 1925, in the city of Washington, that Sacajawea's last resting place was on the Shoshone Wind River Reservation in Wyoming. This decision, as Dr. Eastman says, must be accepted on the basis not only of the tribal tradition, but of other evidence that corroborates that tradition so strikingly that its truth cannot be questioned. In addition to the evidence already cited in this volume, it should also be pointed out that in more than a century and a quarter which has elapsed since the Lewis and Clark Expedition, no claim has been advanced on behalf of any other person as a rival to Sacajawea, and in spite of repeated efforts by careful investigators, no evidence has been discovered that points to anyone except the heroine of the Shoshone Valley as the guide of [Captains] Lewis and Clark.

If the objection is raised that no effort was made by Sacajawea to proclaim herself to the world as the guide of the Expedition, this is easily answered. Although Sacajawea, as a matter of fact, willingly told her story both to whites and Indians when they asked her about it, she was naturally not inclined to boast of an exploit which, by bringing the first white men into the territory of her people, eventually destroyed their hunting grounds and brought an end to their freedom. In other words, that which might be regarded as worthy of great praise among the whites—would be bitterly condemned by the Indians—and naturally she did not care to court such unpopularity. As to the argument that if it had been the real Sacajawea who died on the Shoshone Reservation nearly fifty years ago, there would have been a great deal of publicity given to the event and the death of such an important character would have aroused widespread interest instead of being lost in obscurity, one has only to cite the case of a vast number of other famous characters in history whose fame experienced a similar eclipse. To cite the fate of Columbus will be sufficient for our purpose. When this first of explorers died only fourteen years after his great voyage, it was written "*The event made no impression either upon the city or upon the nation. The world at large thought no more of the mournful procession which bore that wayworn body to the grave than it did of any poor creature journeying on his bier to the potter's field.*"

As time passes and a new century dawns since the young Indian woman guided the Lewis and Clark Expedition on its historic way, it is believed that the desire to commemorate her faithfulness and integrity will grow and prompt the erection of further monuments to her name. History has frequently had to seek the last resting places of its heroes to do them honor.

How many places claimed the blind poet after death, who, when living, had to beg for his very food. "*Seven cities warred for Homer, being dead, who living had no roof to shield his head.*"

Wright Brothers

The Wright Brothers
A Biography Authorized by Orville Wright

Author's Preface

The aim in this book has been to satisfy the curiosity of the average, non-technical reader regarding the work of the Wright Brothers, and to do so as simply as possible. No attempt has been made to go into minute technical details. Nor does the book cover the scientific researches and numerous inventions by Orville Wright since the death of his brother. To give credit to everyone who has been gracious with help in the preparation of what I have written would require so long a list, with risk of names being unintentionally omitted, that I shall not attempt it.

But one name naturally and obviously comes first and foremost—that of Orville Wright himself. He has read my manuscript and given generously of his time in verifying the accuracy of various statements and in correcting inaccuracies which otherwise would have appeared. Next in importance to that of Orville Wright has been the help received from his secretary, Miss Mabel Beck, whose memory and knowledge of Mr. Wright's voluminous files enabled her quickly to produce documentary evidence to make certain of accuracy.

Prologue

In a corner of the Pullman smoking compartment, by the window, the man who had been explaining the whole economic system mentioned inventors as an example of the fortunate relationship between desire for money and scientific progress. "Take the Wright brothers," he said, "Would they have worked all those years trying to fly just for their health?" Another passenger ventured to ask, "Don't people sometimes become curious about a problem and work to see what they can find out?" The man by the window chuckled tolerantly as he replied, "Do you think those Wright brothers would have kept on pouring money into their experiments and risking their lives if they hadn't hoped to get rich at it? No, sir! It was the chance to make a fortune that kept them going." Most of the other passengers in the compartment nodded in agreement. Not long afterward, one of those who had overheard that conversation was in Dayton, Ohio, and inquired of his friend Orville Wright, "Do you think the expectation of profit is the main incentive to inventors?" Orville Wright didn't think so.

He doubted if Alexander Graham Bell expected to make much out of the telephone. And it seemed to him unlikely that Edison started out with the idea of making money. Certainly, he said, Steinmetz had little interest in financial reward. All [Charles Proteus] Steinmetz asked of life was the opportunity to spend as much time as possible in the laboratory working at problems that interested him.—"And the Wright brothers?"—If they had been interested in invention with the idea of making money, said Orville Wright, looking amused, they "most assuredly would have tried something in which the chances for success were brighter."

From earliest years both Wilbur and Orville Wright were motivated by what Thorstein Veblen called the "instinct of workmanship." Their father, the Reverend Milton Wright, used to encourage them in this and never chided them for spending on their hobbies what little money they might have. But he did urge them to try to earn enough to meet the costs of whatever projects they were carrying on. "*All the money anyone needs,*" he used to say, "*is just enough to prevent one from being a burden on others.*" Both brothers were fascinated by mechanics almost from the time they were conscious of interest in anything.

The childhood events most vivid in the recollections of Orville Wright have had to do with mechanical devices of one kind or another. One of the high spots was the day he attained the age of five, because he received for a birthday gift a gyroscopic top that would maintain its balance and spin while resting on the edge of a knife blade. Shortly after that fifth birthday, and partly because of his inborn enthusiasm over mechanics, Orville began an association with another boy that had an important influence on his life. His mother started him to kindergarten. The school was within a short walking distance of the Wright home and Orville set out after breakfast each morning with just enough time to reach the classroom if he didn't loiter. His mother bade him return home promptly after he was dismissed and he always arrived punctually at the time expected. When asked how he was getting along, he cheerfully said all was going well, but did not go into details. At the end of a month his mother went to visit the kindergarten to learn just how Orvie was doing. "*I hope the child has been behaving himself,*" said the mother to the teacher. The teacher stared at her in astonishment. "*Why,*" said she, "*you know, since the first few days I haven't seen him. I supposed you had decided to keep him at home.*"

It turned out that Orville had almost immediately lost interest in kindergarten and instead had regularly gone to a house two doors from his own, on Hawthorne Street, to join a playmate, Edwin Henry Sines. With an eye on the clock to adjust himself to the kindergarten hours, he had stayed there and played with young Sines until about a minute before he was due at home. Orville's father and mother were not too severe when this little irregularity was discovered, because the boys had not been engaged in any mischief. On the contrary, their play had been of a sort that might properly be called "constructive." The thing that had occupied them most was an old sewing-machine belonging to Sines's mother. They "oiled" it by dropping water from a feather into the oil holes! Both Orville and Wilbur followed their father's advice and earned whatever money they spent. One source of income was from wiping dishes in the evening, for which their mother paid a flat rate of one cent. Sometimes she employed them to make minor household repairs. Orville seemed to find more outlets for money than did Wilbur, who was more saving, and from time to time he borrowed from Wilbur—but he kept his credit good by sticking to an arrangement they always made that the next money earned should be applied on the debt. One of Orville's early money-making ventures was the collecting of old bones in nearby alleys, vacant lots, or neighbors's yards, and selling them to a fertilizer factory. He and another boy first did this as a means for raising funds with which to buy candy for use while fishing. They accumulated a weight of bones that it seemed to them must represent a small fortune—and were somewhat shocked when the buyer paid them only three cents.

At first, Orville's associates in his projects were boys of his own age rather than Wilbur, who was more than four years older and moved in a different group, but a day came when the brothers began to share curiosity over a mechanical phenomenon. In June, 1878, when Orville was seven years old and Wilbur eleven, the Wright family left Dayton, because the work of the father, who had been made a Bishop of the United Brethren Church, was shifted to Cedar Rapids, Iowa. And it was in a house on Adams Street, in Cedar Rapids, not long after their arrival there that an event occurred which was to have much influence on the lives of Wilbur and Orville—as well as to have its effect on the whole human race. Bishop Wright had returned from a short trip on church business bringing with him a little present for his two younger sons. "*Look here, boys,*" he said to Wilbur and Orville, holding out his hands with something hidden between them. Then he tossed the gift toward them. But instead of falling at once to the floor or into their hands, as they expected, it went to the ceiling where it fluttered briefly before it fell. It was a flying machine, a helicopter, the invention of a Frenchman, Alphonse Penaud. Made of cork, bamboo, and thin paper, the device weighed so little that twisted rubber bands provided all the power needed to send it aloft for a few seconds. As the brothers were to learn later, Penaud, an invalid during most of his short life, had not only invented, as early as 1871, various kinds of toy flying machines—both the helicopter type and others that flew horizontally—but was the originator of the use of rubber bands for motive power. Simple as was this helicopter—they called it the "bat"—Wilbur and Orville felt great admiration for its ingenuity. Though it soon went the way of all fragile toys, the impression it left on their minds never faded. Not long afterward Wilbur tried to build an improvement on that toy helicopter.

If so small a device could fly, why not make a bigger one that could fly longer and higher? Orville was still too young to contribute much to the actual building of larger models, but he was keenly interested as Wilbur made several, each larger than the one preceding. To the brothers's astonishment, they discovered that the bigger the machine, the less it would fly, and if it was much bigger than the original toy, it wouldn't fly at all. They did not yet understand that a machine of only twice the linear dimensions of another would require eight times the power. Orville, meanwhile, had distinguished himself in another way, by organizing an army. His grade at school was dismissed one Friday afternoon, though the rest of the school was in session, and it occurred to Orville that it might be amusing to march by, throw gravel on the windows, and taunt those who were still at their lessons. Supported by his friend, Bert Shaffer, he proposed to a dozen other boys in the class that they form themselves into an army, and act not as individuals but as an organization. For having thought of the idea, Orville, who had been doing some reading about Napoleon, would be the General, but there would be Colonels and Captains as well. In fact, they used up all the military titles they knew. Lacking guns, they would have to carry wooden clubs, and these they got by removing some loose pickets from the school fence. All went well until the school janitor began to chase them, evidently intending to capture them. One of the boys made him pause by throwing a rock in his direction as he was crawling through a hole in the fence. After escaping into a distant alley, all in the army assumed they would probably be in plenty of trouble when they returned to school Monday morning. "*We'll be all right,*" said Orville, feeling bound, as their commanding General, to try to uphold the army's morale, "*if we stick together. They can't fire us all.*"

He mounted a box lying in the alley and outlined what they should do. The teacher would doubtless single out only two or three of them that had been recognized by the janitor and ask them to stay after school. But if the teacher asked one of them to stand up, they must all stand up, or, if she asked one to stay after school, all must stay, and show their solidarity. "*All for one, and one for all,*" he quoted. When they were back in school at the next session, the teacher said nothing to indicate that retribution was in the making, but when the class was dismissed at the end of the afternoon, she asked Orville to "remain." True to their pact, all the rest of the army stayed in their seats—or, rather, all except one undersized lad. A few minutes later, the teacher asked Orville to come to her desk. As he stepped forward, all the others started to do likewise. "*The rest of you sit down,*" commanded the teacher, and then added, "*I don't know why you're here at all.*" Her tone was such that all meekly sat down. When Orville reached her desk, she said, "*You were speaking of a song you could bring for the exercises next Friday*"—and went on to talk, pleasantly enough, of Orville's part in a forthcoming school entertainment. She didn't even seem to know about the daring behavior of the army in the schoolyard. Probably the janitor, embarrassed over his failure to capture the culprits, had not reported them. While in Cedar Rapids, Orville showed enterprise in another direction. He had enough intellectual curiosity to study lessons that the teacher had not yet assigned. When a little more than eight years old he told his father that he was tired of the Second Reader they were still studying at school and wished he had a Third Reader.

One morning, not long after that, at the middle of the school year, the principal came to the room Orville was in and announced that any pupils who showed enough proficiency in reading might be promoted at once, without waiting until the end of the year, and begin the Third Reader. The more promising members of the class, selected by the teacher, then stood toeing a chalk mark, up front, as was commonly done, and took turns at reading. In his alarm lest he might not do himself full justice, Orville, someone told him later, held his book upside down. That did not prevent him from reading accurately, as he knew the book by heart, and he was promoted. *"I'm now in the Third Reader class,"* he proudly announced when he reached home that noon. *"Well, that's a strange thing,"* said his father. *"Just this morning I bought the Third Reader you asked for. But,"* he added, *"you won't be able to use it today, because you're going to miss school this afternoon. I have arranged for you and Wilbur to go to the photographer's and have your pictures taken."* Orville's picture thus commemorated what had seemed to him an important event in his life. After three years in Cedar Rapids, the Wright family, in June 1881, moved to Richmond, Indiana, partly that Mrs. Wright, who was not in robust health, might have the companionship of her sister who lived there. It was in Richmond that Orville took up the building and flying of kites.

Though it interested him, Wilbur did not then take much part in this kite flying sport, because he feared it might be considered too juvenile for a boy of his size. Orville came to be considered an expert at kite making and sold kites to playmates as a convenient means of getting spending money. He made the framework of his kites as thin as possible, to reduce weight. Indeed, they were so thin that they would often bend in the wind and the kite formed an arc. But it did not then occur to Orville that this curvature of the kite's surface had any relation to its good flying qualities. Though he had turned his kite making to profit, Orville's best source of revenue in Richmond was a job of folding papers, a church publication. For additional spending money he entered the junk business. He would go after school or on Saturdays to pick up scraps of metal thrown out by a chain factory, and hauled this in his "express" wagon to a junk dealer's yard. One of his projects was the building of a small wooden lathe. It was too small to be quite satisfactory, and Wilbur offered to help him build a larger lathe, seven or eight feet long.

This was the first "big" mechanical job he and Wilbur worked on together. The lathe was considered a great success, especially by neighbor boys who thought it a privilege to work the foot treadle that provided the motive power. But Wilbur felt that it should be improved. He had noticed that bicycles were being equipped with ball bearings to give easy running quality and he said the lathe ought to have ball bearings. He looked about the barn for material that could be adapted and took some metal rings from an old set of harness. When two of these were held tightly side by side they formed the outer track for the ball bearings, but, instead of steel balls, marbles were used—the common kind, made of clay, that we used to call "commies."

Within this circle of marble bearings would rest the shaft of the lathe. The idea seemed so sound that the brothers's friends were much impressed. Many were on hand in the upper floor of the barn awaiting eagerly the final tinkering before the ball bearing "patent" could be demonstrated. As soon as the lathe was put into operation, there was a terrible noise and then it seemed as if the barn itself was beginning to sway and shake. It was evident that the marbles in the bearing had not been strong enough to withstand the stress, but why should the barn become so agitated? Orville went downstairs to find out if there could be any other cause. When he reached the outside he saw his sister Katharine held against the side of the house by an invisible force. A small cyclone was taking place! All the boys upstairs had been too absorbed to notice such minor phenomena as weather. Some of the enterprises Orville got into at Richmond were not of a mechanical nature, and Wilbur, if sharing in them at all, appeared only in the background, or as a consultant, for he was at an age when a boy gave thought to his dignity. Orville had noticed that many boys chewed small hunks of tar. It seemed to him that if the tar could be flavored with sugar to make it more palatable and small pieces were wrapped in tissue paper, a market for the product might be found. He and his friend, Harry Morrow, began a series of experiments in the Wright backyard, and they seemed well on their way to having a saleable article. But as they kept testing their samples, both became ill—some kind of stomach disorder—accompanied by nausea—and abandoned their plans. Wilbur, though not a partner in all this, was much interested and for years afterwards used to refer to "that chewing gum corporation." If Orville was "into" more different things at this time than his brother, it was mainly because Wilbur's great passion was for reading. And what he read, he absorbed. It wasn't long until he himself began to show a gift for writing. Because of that, Wilbur played an important part in one of Orville's early business ventures—though behind the scenes. One of Orville's friends was a boy living next door named Gansey Johnston, whose father made a hobby of taxidermy. They often played in the Johnston barn where the father had a collection of stuffed birds and animals. One day Orville's imagination was much stirred. He saw possibilities for putting those birds and animals to good use—especially when he noted that there was even a huge black bear and a grizzly. It was obvious to him that he and the Johnston boy should form a partnership and he asked Gansey how he would feel about such an arrangement. *"Partnership to do what?"* asked the boy. Why, said Orville, to give a circus! Though he had never thought of giving a circus, the Johnston lad caught the idea and soon was enthusiastic. They then decided to take in Orville's friend, Harry Morrow, as a third partner. Their show would be known as The Great W. J. & M. Circus. As the date for the big show approached, sixteen-year-old Wilbur Wright, who had been taking great interest in the preparations, asked Orville what he had done about advance notices in the newspapers.

Orville had to admit that he had done nothing. Wilbur appeared to be shocked that no one had taken steps fully to prepare the public mind for the coming event, and offered to write a suitable reading notice about the street parade. This, he said, should be placed in the Richmond *Evening Item*. He had absorbed the method of expression used in circus bills and his forecast of the parade was a masterpiece. There was nothing amateurish about the way he introduced such words as "mammoth," "colossal," and "stupendous," nor about his use of impressively large figures—"thousands of strange birds from all parts of the world" that would positively be in the menagerie.

It was announced that the proprietors of the big show would personally lead the parade on "iron horses" and that Davy Crockett would positively appear with a grizzly bear. At the end of the notice, in professional manner, was the exact route of the parade, that the populace might not miss the great free exhibition of wonders. The notice also gave the prices of admission to the big show—three cents for children under three years, others, five cents. Wilbur gave the piece of publicity to Orville to take to the *Item* office. There was a little box just inside a door to a stairway leading to the editorial rooms, and the boys knew it was intended for news items. But they walked up and down the street in front of the newspaper office for a long time before they had the courage to enter the stairway. What if someone should see them! Finally, when they thought no one was looking, one of them ran up to the box and in desperate haste deposited their piece of publicity. Then both ran up the street at a speed that could have attracted attention. The editor of the *Item* evidently had a good news sense and recognized the mysterious "press release" as a local item worth printing. He had no way of knowing *who* "W. J. & M." were, but felt sure the account of that forthcoming parade had plenty of reader interest. It came about, therefore, that Wilbur's advance notice had a prominent position in the *Item* of September 10, 1883, under a heading that asked, "WHAT ARE THE BOYS UP TO?" Though some of Wilbur's figures about the number of rare birds and wild animals may have been a bit overdrawn, to conform to circus bill standards, he had not exaggerated the amazing nature of the parade. Two of the proprietors, Wright and Johnston, actually appeared at the head of the parade on their "iron horses." These were high wheel bicycles, one of them having wooden spokes.

The third associate proprietor of the big show, Harry Morrow, was unavoidably absent, because his parents had gone on a vacation trip to Michigan, and had insisted, much against his wishes, on taking him with them. A principal "parade wagon" was the running gear of an old buggy, with no body but only a few planks to make a platform on which were some of the "thousands of rare birds," and also the great, frightful grizzly bear held in leash by Davy Crockett. Though no horses were hitched to this "wagon," plenty of boys had volunteered their services as "slaves" to pull it through the streets. At the last minute, "Corky" Johnston, nine-year-old brother of one of the proprietors, got into a fight with the circus bosses, and they felt compelled to deny him the privilege of participating in the parade.

This created a problem, for he had been cast for the role of Davy Crockett, wearing his father's hunting togs, including high boots. The circus chiefs got around that, the best they could, by assigning the Davy Crockett part to Corky's younger brother, Griswold, not yet five years old. He was almost overwhelmed by the hunting suit, but in the rush of getting the parade started he was the best Davy Crockett available. Wilbur's advance notice was more successful than he had hoped for. It had aroused so much curiosity that when the parade reached that part of the announced line of march in the business section, the streets were lined with people—almost as many, in fact, as if the circus had been Barnum's. Messieurs W. & J., astounded by the unexpected attention the parade was attracting, began to feel much too conspicuous. They hastily decided that their route must be changed, and the parade turned up an alley! So many customers came that not all who clamored for admission to the Johnston barn could be accommodated, and it was decided to repeat the show. But while those who got into the barn were viewing the "menagerie," the boy who had been denied the privilege of appearing as Davy Crockett saw an opportunity to get his revenge. He got up on the barn roof and addressed the multitude, telling them they might as well disperse and seek their homes, because, he said, there would be no other performance. The crowd took him at his word. Orville Wright had previously organized another circus, in partnership with a neighbor boy named Miller, who had a Shetland pony. For this show the admission was only one cent. Though the gross receipts were not vast, the show was a great success, partly in consequence of the profound impression it had made on the Miller boy's father.

At the close of the performance, he announced that the show people would be guests of honor at a reception, to which the spectators also were cordially invited. Lemonade, ice cream, and cake were served in lavish quantities, and every boy felt that, taking the afternoon as a whole, he had, had his money's worth. But of all the enterprises in which the Wright brothers showed their initiative in Richmond, the Great W. J. & M. Circus probably caused the most talk. People thought the boy who had organized that show would doubtless amount to something.

Many ventured the opinion, too, that the youngster, whoever he was, who had prepared that notice for the newspaper about the parade, would surely be "heard from."

☐☐☐☐☐☐☐☐☐☐

Certain traits that were to show in Wilbur and Orville Wright—the pioneering urge, the gift for original thinking, and mechanical aptitude—were all in their ancestry. Take, for example, their grandfather, John G. Koerner. Native of a German village, near Schleiz, he became so bitterly opposed to German militarism and autocracy that he determined to migrate to the United States. He sailed from Bremen to Baltimore early in 1818 and went to live in Virginia. Besides gaining recognition in the United States for his mechanical ability and for the superior quality of farm wagons and carriages he manufactured, he became known, too, as a person who did his own thinking. He did not accept all that he heard or read. Indeed, he seems to have been a "character." It was his habit to read newspapers aloud to his family, and when, as invariably happened, he came to something that interested him because of approval, disapproval, or for any other reason, he would interpolate comment without changing his tone or rate of utterance. It was impossible for a listener to tell just how much that he seemed to be reading was actually in the paper and which ideas were his own.

One by one, members of his family would study the paper afterward to see if various surprising statements were really there. No matter how commonplace a newspaper article may have been, it was never colorless as he read it. His wife, the former Catherine Fry, American born, also came of pioneer ancestry, from the German language section of Switzerland.

Their daughter, Susan Catherine Koerner, was born April 30, 1831, when they lived at Hillsboro, Loudoun County, Virginia, but the family moved to Union County, Indiana, shortly after that—at a time when there was still pioneering life in the Hoosier country. The Koerner farm became a rather impressive one for those times. There were finally a dozen or fourteen buildings, including the carriage shop, all conspicuous for their workmanlike construction and orderliness. John Koerner lived to the age of eighty-six. Perhaps the most interesting pioneer of all in the Wright brothers's ancestry was Catharine Benham Van Cleve, the first white woman to set foot in Dayton. Her husband, John Van Cleve, whom she had married in New Jersey, was a descendant of a Van Cleve who had come from Holland to Long Island before 1650. When he proposed, a few years after their marriage that they should settle in the almost unexplored virgin forest region of Ohio, she liked the adventurous idea. They migrated to Cincinnati—then called Losantiville—in 1790. Within two years after their arrival, John Van Cleve was killed by Indians. His widow married Samuel Thompson and, in April, 1796, they decided to try their luck at a settlement about to be established, fifty miles to the north. The place had just been named in honor of Jonathan Dayton, a Revolutionary soldier. Three groups of people arranged to make the trip at about the same time. So unsettled was the country, and so nearly nonexistent were the wagon trails, that the party which included Catharine Benham Van Cleve Thompson preferred to travel in a flat-bottomed boat on the Miami River. The others went by land. Though the boat trip took about ten days, that group was the first to arrive. Among those in the boat were some of the Van Cleve children—another of them was in one of the overland parties. A Van Cleve son, Benjamin, became the first postmaster at Dayton, the first schoolteacher, and also the first county clerk. His marriage at Dayton in August, 1800, to Mary Whitten, was the first recorded in Montgomery County.

Margaret Van Cleve, a sister of Benjamin, had stayed in Cincinnati, because she was about to be married—to George Reeder, later an innkeeper. They had a daughter, Catharine, who became the wife of Dan Wright (not named Daniel, but plain Dan, as was also his father), who had come to Centerville, Ohio, near Dayton, in 1811. It was of this union that Milton Wright, father of Wilbur and Orville, was born—in a log cabin in Rush County, Indiana, November 17, 1828. Dan Wright's ancestry could be traced back to one John Wright, known to have bought Kelvedon Hall, in Essex County, England, in 1538. A less remote ancestor, Samuel Wright, had migrated to America in 1636, and settled at Springfield, Massachusetts. At the time of his marriage, Dan Wright was employed in a distillery. But he evidently did not feel comfortable over his occupation and quit the distillery job to devote his whole attention to farming. Moreover, he "got religion" and would no longer even sell his corn to distillers.

Perhaps it was because of the strong religious feeling of Dan Wright that his son, Milton, at the age of eighteen, had joined the United Brethren Church. Milton Wright attended a small college in nearby Hartsville, Indiana, and at the age of twenty-two he received from the United Brethren Church his certificate entitling him to preach. But he did not at once actively enter the ministry. The pioneer urge was in him and he went to the Willamette Valley, in Oregon, where for two years he was a teacher in a small college conducted under the auspices of the church. It was three or four years after finishing his course at Hartsville that he met the young woman, a student there, who was to become his wife. Mutual friends had spoken to him of Susan Catherine Koerner, of how charming, how "smart" she was, and when he found an opportunity to be introduced to her, he was by no means disinclined to make her acquaintance. They were married on November 24, 1859, a week after his thirty-first birthday. During the first few years after their marriage, the Milton Wrights lived at several different places in Indiana.

Their first child, Reuchlin, was born in March, 1861, on a farm near Fairmount, and Lorin, the second son, a year and a half later, in Fayette County, at the home of his grandparents. When Wilbur was born, April 16, 1867, the family was living on a small farm the father had bought near the village of Millville, eight miles east of New Castle. Wilbur was named for Wilbur Fiske, a churchman whom the father admired, but his name did not include the Fiske. None of the Wright children ever had a middle name. For a year, the Reverend Milton Wright was minister of a church at Hartsville, and also taught in the college he had attended there. Then, in June, 1869, he became editor of the *Religious Telescope*, a United Brethren weekly, at Dayton, the home of those pioneer ancestors. A year or more after their arrival for their first stay in Dayton, the Wright family bought, while it was still under construction, a modest seven room house at 7 Hawthorne Street. This was on the West Side, across the Miami River, and about a mile from the main business section.

Here Orville Wright—named for Orville Dewey, a Unitarian minister—was born on August 19, 1871, and his sister, Katharine, three years later to the day. During the family's absence in Cedar Rapids and Richmond, the Hawthorne Street house was rented, but the Wright family was once again to live there, for in June, 1884, the Reverend Milton Wright's work brought him from Richmond back to Dayton. When, sixteen months later, the tenant's lease expired and they were settled again at 7 Hawthorne Street, all the family felt that they were where they "belonged." The family's return to Dayton was a few days before Wilbur would have been graduated from high school at Richmond. With the final year of the course so nearly completed, he would have received his diploma if he had been present with his class on commencement day. But Wilbur did not consider the mere diploma itself important enough to justify a trip back to Richmond, even though the distance was less than fifty miles. His decision was a subject for family talks and all agreed that Wilbur should do as he thought best. The father felt, as did the others, that receiving a diploma was ceremonial and less important than the actual education gained. Wilbur decided to take a special course at the high school in Dayton the next year. He wished especially to continue the study of Greek, and to learn trigonometry. Orville had been in the sixth grade at Richmond, but a week or two before the end of the year he got into a bit of mischief that caused his teacher, Miss Bond, to dismiss him. She said he could not return to school until either his father or mother came with him to guarantee that his deportment would improve. But his father was away from home at the time, and his mother was too busy packing for the move to Dayton to take time for consultation with that teacher. Orville simply stayed out of school for the rest of the year. When he entered school in Dayton the next September, with no certificate to show that he had completed the sixth grade, it looked as if he might have to be in that grade for another year. But Orville was so violent and uncompromising in his protests that the school authorities said he might try the seventh grade until they could see how well he got along. At the end of the year he passed into the eighth grade with the highest mark in arithmetic in the city.

When Orville entered the eighth grade, Miss Jennings, who taught grammar, evidently thought she detected something mischievous about him and assigned him to a front seat in her class. The next year, the same teacher had been promoted to the high school, as a teacher of algebra, and again she put Orville up in front where she could keep an eye on him. Orville's front seats became a subject for family jests. Later on in his high school course, Orville was demonstrating a problem in geometry on the blackboard, when his teacher, Miss Wilson, pointed out that though he had the correct answer, he evidently had not followed the textbook. "*I got it out of another book*—'Wentworth's Geometry,'" Orville explained. And he added, "*I get a lot of good stuff from* 'Wentworth.'" Instead of complimenting him on having enough interest in the subject to consult another source, the teacher chided him for referring to what she called "a beautiful science" as "stuff." Orville had no compunction about telling at meal time of such episodes. He knew he wouldn't be scolded.

It was simply good conversational material and would provoke sympathetic laughter. The family was interested, too, in the inventiveness of the boys. Lorin had once invented an improvement on a hay baling machine. Wilbur had designed and built a practical device for folding paper. This was while he had the contract for folding the entire weekly issue of an eight-page church paper. He had found the handwork tedious and got up a machine that could be worked by a foot treadle. For a long time the mechanical ability that had aroused the most family admiration, though, was in the mother. Susan Koerner Wright was more than ordinarily resourceful in adapting household tools or utensils to unexpected uses. She was clever at designing clothes, too, and once she had built a sled for the two older boys. As her family used to say, she "*could mend anything.*" The mother, however, was not long to be spared to her family. On July 4, 1889, or less than four years after the return to Hawthorne Street, she died. During the latter years of her life, Wilbur was much with his mother, and devoted himself almost constantly to her care, for he too at that time was an invalid, unable to engage in much outdoor activity. Wilbur's illness was in consequence of an accident. While playing a game of shinny, on skates, he was hit in the face with a shinny club. The blow knocked out all his upper front teeth. He began to suffer from a heart disorder from which he did not completely recover for several years. After the death of the mother, and the departure of the two older brothers to establish homes of their own, the other members of the Wright family were all the more drawn together. Whatever one of them was doing interested all. And all—especially Wilbur—did much reading. Two groups of books were in the home, one in Bishop Wright's study upstairs, and another, used by the family, downstairs in the living room. Nearly all the books in the father's library were "very serious," but Wilbur often dipped into them, though the father made no effort to direct or control anyone's reading. Downstairs, however, were the books that both Wilbur and Orville liked best. These included a set of Washington Irving's works, both *Grimm's* and *Andersen's* fairy tales, Plutarch's *Lives*, a set of the *Spectator*, a set of Addison's *Essays*, Boswell's *Life of Johnson*, a set of Sir Walter Scott, Gibbon's *Decline and Fall of the Roman Empire*, Green's *History of England*, Guizot's *France*, an incomplete set of Nathaniel Hawthorne, and a set in which was Marey's *Animal Mechanism*. Here also were a set of the *Encyclopedia Britannica* and *Chambers's Encyclopedia*. The *Britannica* was an edition of the late 1870s and the *Chambers's Encyclopedia* was an earlier edition. Though Wilbur was the great reader, Orville was not far behind him. He was fascinated by scientific articles in the encyclopedia almost from the time he learned to read. Wilbur and Orville from time to time contributed to the family comfort in a substantial way. They built a spacious front porch, and all the lathe work for the posts they did themselves. Then they remodeled the interior of the house, changing the arrangement of the rooms. Other members of the family felt as much pride in such handiwork as if they had done it themselves. More than their sturdy, intelligent, pioneer ancestry, it was probably the kind of home they lived in that had most to do with what the younger brothers were later to achieve.

Orville expressed that with deep conviction many years afterward. A friend of his had remarked to him, "Even though what you accomplished was without the idea of making money, the fact remains that the Wright brothers will always be favorite examples of how American lads with no special advantages can get ahead." "But," said Orville seriously, "that isn't true. Because, you see, we did have special advantages." "What special advantages do you mean?" "Simply that we were lucky enough to grow up in a home environment where there was always much encouragement to children to pursue intellectual interests, to investigate whatever aroused curiosity. In a different kind of environment our curiosity might have been nipped long before it could have borne fruit."

☐☐☐☐☐☐☐☐☐☐

At the age of twelve, while living in Richmond, Indiana, Orville Wright became interested in wood engravings. His curiosity had been stirred by seeing some woodcuts by Timothy Cole and T. Johnson in the *Century* magazine. Wondering how the cuts were made he began to search the encyclopedia and one or two other books that told a little about the technique used. He then decided that he might be able to make some woodcuts himself if he had a suitable tool—and he went ahead to fashion such a tool from the spring of an old pocketknife. (The next Christmas, Wilbur gave him a set of engraving tools.)

After trying his hand at his first few woodcuts, Orville naturally wished to make prints from them, and for this purpose he used a press his father had for copying letters. Today seldom seen, the old-fashioned letterpress consisted of two horizontal metal plates that could be forced close together by turning a little circular handle at the top of a threaded rod attached to the upper plate. One's letter was moistened and placed next to a thin tissue sheet in a record book which went between the plates of the press. Under pressure, a copy of the letter was transferred to the tissue. Such a press was a fascinating device for a boy to play with. Indeed, Orville had used it for other purposes than that for which it was intended. It had also served him as a vise. And now it worked fairly well for making proofs from his woodcuts. It was at about this time that the Wright family returned to Dayton from Richmond, and Orville renewed close relations with his old chum, Ed Sines. To his delight he found that young Sines was already interested in printing. He had a small press, obtained by trading a file, covering more than a year, of a boys's magazine called *Golden Days*. This press was little more than a toy, capable of printing only one narrow line at a time, and the boys were never able to make much use of it. But, nevertheless, they immediately formed the printing firm of Sines and Wright. At the beginning of the partnership of Sines and Wright, their printing establishment was in a corner of the Sines kitchen. Ed's mother summed up the situation there when one day she noticed an envelope addressed to "Messieurs Sines and Wright," from a type foundry. "*It must be for you,*" she said to the partners, "*for you certainly are a pair of messieurs.*" Interested as they were in printing, Ed Sines and Orville had time for other hobbies. One of these was a telegraph line they rigged up between their homes. For years Wilbur Wright referred to it as "the first wireless telegraph," because the boys used to shout the messages back and forth to verify whatever they clicked out on the keys. It soon became evident that Orville had printers ink in his blood. This printing hobby was more than a passing fancy. His father was impressed by the boy's persistence in trying to use inadequate equipment. The father knew that two of his older sons, Wilbur and Lorin, had recently had a chance to trade a boat they had made, now seldom used, for a small printing press. If they would make that trade, he suggested, and donate the press to Orville—then he would buy for the youngster twenty-five pounds of brevier type. This deal was made.

  The new press would print anything up to 3 by 4½ inches. As the Sines kitchen was not quite the ideal location for their printing plant, Orville arranged for quarters in a "summer kitchen," not often used, at the Wright home. It now occurred to Messieurs Sines and Wright that it might be a good idea to print a newspaper for the benefit of their eighth grade classmates. They called it *The Midget*. Because of the limited capacity of their press, the paper was necessarily small, two narrow columns wide and four and one-half inches long. Most of the items in it were put directly into type, as they thought of them, and not from previously prepared copy. They found that the four pages they had planned entailed a surprising amount of work and to reduce this they put nothing on page three except "Sines and Wright," twice, diagonally across the page, in script type. After they had printed about one hundred copies for distribution, Orville's father saw one of these and immediately placed a ban on the whole issue. He insisted that the boys had not done themselves justice in slighting that third page. Readers of the paper, he said, might get the impression that the publishers were lazy or shiftless.

In a way, this suppression of the issue came almost as a relief, for the publishers had begun to feel misgivings about one somewhat daring item they had taken the liberty of printing. It was about their teacher, Miss Jennings, who was a strict disciplinarian. The item read, "*Next week we propose to publish one of Miss Jennings's famous lectures before the pupils of the Intermediate School on the Inherent Wickedness of School Children.*" Maybe, they reflected, it was just as well that *The Midget* was not to be distributed. Miss Jennings might take the item as good clean fun, but, on the other hand, she might raise a rumpus. Before long the partners had an opportunity to buy a quantity of display type for $2, and then they began trying to establish themselves in the job printing business. They set up their headquarters in the Wright barn, though on cold days they were likely to do their typesetting on a table in the Wright dining room. Neighborhood storekeepers gave them a few orders for printing, and the firm began to take on airs. They employed Forrest Whitfield, a neighbor boy, as printer's devil. He commanded a weekly wage of fifteen cents. All was going well until one day they received an order from a man who wished to pay for his printing not in money but in popcorn. He assured them that this popcorn, on the cob, was worth more than the $2 the printing would have cost. But before deciding if they should accept the popcorn in payment, the partners prudently went to a grocer to get an estimate of its value. Sure enough, it was worth $2, and the grocer offered to buy it from them at that price. Now Orville saw greater opportunities opening before them. With a liquid capital of $2, they could buy more type, do a greater variety of printing, and thus have more fun. But Ed Sines thought there was such a thing as overextension of plant and equipment. Why not just divide their popcorn and *eat* it? Each was so uncompromising in his convictions that there was only one thing to do, one must buy out the other and they would dissolve the partnership. Inasmuch as Orville already owned the press they were using and most of the type, it seemed logical that he should be the buyer. By paying his share of the popcorn he was able to take over his partner's interest without much cash outlay.

Thenceforth, when they worked together, as from time to time they continued to do, Ed Sines was no longer co-proprietor but an employee. At about this time, something set Orville to thinking of how interesting it would be to print circus bills. He wished some of his friends would organize a circus. Then he could do their printing. The idea seemed worth promoting. He went to the Truxell boys, and Fred LaRue, neighbors up the street, and convinced them that they had just the kind of abilities to organize and present a wonderful circus—one that would make a great hit with all the kids. The result of this talk was the Great Truxell Brothers and LaRue Show. Orville refused to accept any payment for printing the handbills and tickets of admission to the big show. The fun of doing it was all the reward he wanted.

Mrs. Wright had cleared out an upstairs room for Orville's printing activities and that was his base for some time. He began to feel the need for a larger printing press and he determined to build one. The bed for the new press was an old gravestone he got from a marble dealer. This press would print a sheet eleven by sixteen inches. Orville could now undertake larger printing projects. One order required more type than he had on hand. But that didn't stop him. After he had used up all his type, with the job only half done, he recalled having heard of stereotype plates. He looked up in an encyclopedia a description of how such plates were cast from the impression of the original type in wet cardboard. And he contrived to make such a plate from the type already set. Then he redistributed that type for use in setting the rest of the job. Ambitious to be a really good printer, Orville took employment during two summer vacations with a printing establishment in Dayton, and worked there sixty hours a week. But he felt that the most fun and satisfaction in connection with printing had been from building his own press. Along in the spring of 1888, when he was nearly seventeen years old, he started to build another press, bigger than any he had used before.

He didn't know exactly what he would do with it, but that question did not yet give him much concern. He would have the fun of building it. In the family woodshed was a pile of firewood cut in four-foot lengths. From these he made much of the framework, though he had to buy at a lumber yard a few longer pieces. From nearby junk yards he collected odds and ends of iron or steel that could be used. A difficult problem was to find a means of forcing the type against the printing surface, always with the same pressure, just enough and not too much. Orville searched the Wright barn and tool shed for something that could be adapted, but without success until his eye happened to alight on the old family buggy. The buggy had a folding top, held firmly in place, when raised, by steel bars hinged in the middle. They were designed to force the top just so far and no farther. Exactly what he needed! The job turned out to be much more difficult than Orville had expected, and Wilbur Wright, observing his kid brother at a tough job, offered to help him build the press.

Some of the suggestions Wilbur made for moving parts of that press were peculiar in that they seemed to violate all mechanical rules and could not possibly be expected to work. Yet they did. Sometime later, a well-dressed stranger entered the shop where Orville, merrily whistling, was feeding paper into his press, and asked if he might look at that "homemade printing outfit." He had heard about it while visiting in Dayton. What at once astonished Orville and two or three boys in the shop was that the visitor, with complete disregard for his good clothes, lay right down flat on his back on the floor to study the press in operation. After he had observed it for several minutes, he got up, brushed himself off, and remarked, "*It works all right, but I still don't understand why it works.*" Before leaving he laid his card on a table. He was the foreman of the pressroom of a newspaper in Denver. Now that he had his new press, Orville wished he could put it to some purpose to make full use of the greatly increased printing capacity. The press was big enough and fast enough to print a newspaper. Why not start a neighborhood weekly? He had hardly more than thought of this before he decided to do so. It was probably the first time a paper was ever started just to use a press. Orville now rented a room on West Third Street, near Broadway. The first issue of the paper—four three-column pages—appeared on March 1, 1889. In his salutatory, Orville said, "This week we issue the first number of the West Side News, a paper to be published in the interests of the people and business institutions of the West Side. Whatever tends to their advancement, moral, mental, and financial, will receive our closest attention." There were seventeen advertisements. A leading feature was a story about Abraham Lincoln and General Sherman, from the *Youth's Companion* and there was an article about Benjamin Franklin. The range of the publisher's reading was indicated by a number of short paragraphs on foreign affairs, and about the approaching inauguration of President-elect Benjamin Harrison. Altogether it was a creditable job.

No boyish "boners" or typographical errors were to be found. All copies of the first issue were distributed free, as samples, but the paper was soon a fairly profitable enterprise. After the first few numbers, it was enlarged from three columns wide to four columns. Ed Sines devoted himself to rounding up advertisements and news items. From time to time Wilbur Wright helped to fill space by writing humorous essays, and after a few weeks his name was added to the paper's masthead as "editor," along with Orville's as publisher. Another contributor to the *West Side News* was a young Negro lad, a friend of Orville since grammar grades, Paul Laurence Dunbar, whose poetry afterward made him famous. Dunbar, in 1890, started a paper, *The Tattler*, for Negro readers, and Orville did the printing. By the time the *West Side News* had been running a year, Orville had completed his course in high school. He thought the final year, devoted in the regular course largely to review, would hardly justify the time. Instead, having it in mind that he might decide to go to college and would need additional credits for college entrance requirements, he was a special student in Latin during that fourth year, attending high school an hour or two a day. The two elder Wright brothers had attended college in Iowa and Indiana, and later their sister Katharine took a degree at Oberlin, but both Wilbur and Orville gave up the idea of going to college, and neither ever received a diploma from high school. It may be added, however, that Orville in later years never agreed with those who suggested that *"college might have ruined the Wright brothers."* More than once he said they doubtless could have done their scientific work more easily if they had, had the advantage of college education. Having decided, partly because of interest in the job at hand, not to go to college, Orville, in April, 1890, with Wilbur as partner, converted the *West Side News* from a weekly to a four-page, five-column daily, called the *Evening Item*. This venture, though it showed no loss, was never profitable. At that time the Perfecting Press was coming into use and Dayton newspapers were issuing big, thick editions that proved to be increasingly keen competition for a small neighborhood sheet. After about four months the paper was suspended. But, as late as 1894, Orville and Wilbur published for a time a little two-column weekly called *Snapshots*, devoted to vigorous comments on current local events. After the first issue or two these were usually written by Wilbur. Both Orville and Wilbur now became absorbed in one more new interest. Orville had owned in Richmond an old high wheel bicycle for which he had paid $3—borrowed from Wilbur. Now, a new European type of bicycle with wheels about the same size, and called a "safety," had begun to be popular. In 1892, Orville bought one of these, a Columbia. It had pneumatic tires and cost $160. Six months later, Wilbur got a bicycle. His was an Eagle and he was able to get it at an auction for $80. Orville promptly became interested in track racing and began to enter his name in various local racing events. Wilbur, though he had been a great athlete—a wonderful fancy skater and the best performer in Dayton on a horizontal bar—never went in for racing, because not yet completely recovered from the effects of his skating accident. Within a few weeks or months from the time they bought their bicycles, these Wright brothers decided to go into the bicycle business—to sell certain well-known makes. Then they soon found that they would have to add a repair shop.

Their first sales room was at 1005 West Third Street. They rented it in December, 1892, to be ready for business when the bicycle season began in the early spring of 1893. For a while Orville divided his time between the bicycle shop and the job printing business across the street in which Ed Sines was still employed. (Sines continued to work there until 1898 when an accident to a lame knee forced him to seek another kind of work and a few months later the shop was sold.) The brothers soon had to move their bicycle business to larger quarters, at 1034 West Third Street. They were successful both in selling new machines and general repairing. Among the bicycles they sold at one time or another were the Coventry Cross, Halladay-Temple, Warwick, Reading, Smalley, Envoy and Fleetwing. By 1895 increased business had caused them to move once more, to 22 South Williams Street, and soon they began to manufacture bicycles. The first "custom made" model was called the Van Cleve—after their pioneer ancestors. A later and lower-priced model was the St. Clair, and finally they made a still lower-priced machine called the Wright Special. It sold for as low as $18. Before they were through with the business they had put out under their own brand several hundred bicycles. Many of these were built in the last building the brothers occupied, a remodeled dwelling house at 1127 West Third Street—the building afterward preserved as a museum at Henry Ford's Greenfield Village in Dearborn, Michigan. Much of their work when building new bicycles was done in winter, when selling was slack, in rooms upstairs over the shop, and from time to time the brothers were interrupted by the necessity of going down to attend to wants of customers. Sometimes they went down to meet a caller who wished only to borrow their air pump to inflate a tire. They had no pressure tank but kept a large hand pump on the wall near the front door.

To avoid needless trips downstairs, the Wrights contrived mechanical means by which they could tell if a caller's wants required their attention. They took an old two-tone bell, intended to be fastened to a bicycle handlebar, and attached it to the wall in their upstairs workrooms. By means of wires and other mechanism, the opening of the downstairs door yanked the thumb lever on the bell in one direction, producing one tone, and shutting the door pulled the little lever in an opposite direction to cause the other tone. The hook on which the air pump hung was also connected by a wire and a spring to a pointer upstairs. Thus it was possible to have secret knowledge upstairs if the caller might be a real customer or if he "only wanted air." If he promptly helped himself to the pump, there probably was no need for anyone to go down. Then when the pointer showed that the pump was back on the hook and the bell signaled the closing of the door, on the caller's departure, the brothers could feel sure they had not missed a sale of any kind by sticking to their work.

Throughout the time they were repairing, selling, and building bicycles, the Wrights continued to make various experiments, just for the fun of it. They made in 1893 what was doubtless the first pair of "balloon" tires ever installed on a vehicle. It was necessary to build a special "front fork" and widen the frame at the rear to make room for the over-sized pneumatics. Orville even found time during this period for experiments having nothing to do with bicycles. Along about 1895, he made a new kind of calculating machine for multiplying as well as for adding. He worked also on a typewriter more simplified than any in existence. Occasionally the brothers took in trade an old high wheel. They had two of these, about the same size that they couldn't sell for much, and the only way to get any benefit from them was to use them in a new way for sport. Why not, they asked themselves, convert them into a tandem? No one had ever heard of two high wheels operated as a unit, and though riding such an outfit might be dangerous, it also would be exciting. They put a swivel in the steel tube connecting the two wheels to prevent it from twisting and breaking. Then they began to practice, to learn the special technique the man on the rear seat had to know. It was a little different from any a bicyclist had needed before—a little like that of a man steering the rear end of a long fire truck. Though it looked fairly easy, only one person besides the Wrights ever succeeded in staying mounted.

Indeed, riding even on the front seat was perilous enough. One afternoon Orville took the rear seat with a boy named Tom Thorne in front. As they tried to steer around a hole in the muddy street, the handlebar caught the leg of the lad in front, which prevented his turning far enough. Of course there was a spill. Orville from the rear seat managed to land on his feet, but Tom Thorne, with one leg pinioned, was hurled headfirst to the street. When he came up for air none of his features was to be seen, so thoroughly was he plastered with mud. He looked so frightful that none of the boys who saw the mishap showed any amusement. They were afraid he had ruined his face. But Orville at once realized that the soft mud had prevented any injury and his young friend's appearance struck him as the funniest thing he had ever seen. For some moments he was doubled up with mirth, unable to control himself, while the other rider, not exactly indignant but unable to enter into the hilarity, stood trying to gouge the mud out of his eyes with his thumbs. It happened that Tom Thorne had an intimate acquaintance with a family living nearby and he went there, accompanied by Orville, to ask permission to wash up, but the girl who opened the door, though a lifelong friend was unwilling to believe the strange looking creature was anyone she knew. Tom asked her to call her mother. The mother had known him almost from the day of his birth, but she showed no sign of recognition now. She did finally identify him by his voice, however, and told him he might wash at the pump. He was able to remove some of the larger chunks of mud. Then he and Orville took the machine back to the shop. The episode was not one of the Wright triumphs. But neighbors who heard about it smiled and wondered what will those Wright boys be doing next? As boys and girls of high school age were potential customers for bicycles, Wilbur Wright thought there should be an effective way to stir their interest in the "makes" of bicycles sold by the Wright Cycle Company and he hit on a plan that showed him to have latent genius as an advertising man. He got a copy of a high school examination paper and had printed what appeared to be a set of examination questions—using the same kind of paper and the same typography. Then he arranged with one or two students to distribute these sheets at the high schools. At first glance a student would think he had got hold of an advance copy of an examination paper. But all the questions related to bicycles on sale by the Wrights. A chum of the Wrights, Cordy Ruse, in 1896 had built the first horseless buggy ever run over the streets of Dayton. The Wrights and others used to sit and talk with him about some of his problems. They had many jokes about the difficulties of hitting upon a suitable ignition system, a workable differential, and other seeming "insurmountables."

Another problem, caused by the vibration of a horseless carriage, had impressed Wilbur most of all. One day when the Wrights and several others were chatting with Cordy Ruse, Wilbur suddenly slapped his thigh and said, "*I've just thought of a wonderful invention! I'll have it patented. It's simple enough. All there is to it is a bed sheet to be fastened beneath an automobile to catch all the bolts, nuts, and other parts that'll keep dropping off.*" Orville thought that crude as horseless carriages were—they were probably the coming thing, and that eventually they might even hurt the bicycle trade. In 1897 he suggested to Wilbur that perhaps they might well give thought to the idea of going into the business of building automobiles. No, insisted Wilbur, shaking his head, they would never be practical. "*To try to build one that would be any account,*" declared Wilbur, "*you'd be tackling the impossible. Why, it would be easier to build a flying machine!*"

◻◻◻◻◻◻◻◻◻◻◻

Ever since the Wright brothers had played with their Penaud toy helicopter in Cedar Rapids, Iowa, their interest in whatever they chanced to read about flying machines was probably greater than if the seed had not been planted in childhood. Along in the early 1890s, both Wilbur and Orville were likely to read any article they saw on a scientific subject, and to talk about it. Occasionally an article in a magazine that came to the Wright home dealt with attempts of man to fly. As time went on, such articles interested the brothers more and more. In 1895, both were impressed—perhaps more than they then realized—by a brief item they had come upon about the glider experiments, in Germany, by Otto Lilienthal. He had been gliding through the air, down the side of a hill, on a machine he had built. That, the brothers thought, must be the king of sports, to go soaring through the air on a gliding machine. They wished they knew more about Lilienthal and his work. All the reports they could find about him were meager enough, but what little they did learn increased their enthusiasm. Lilienthal, "the father of gliding flights," was to have a tremendous influence on them.

Their interest in anything relating to Lilienthal was still strong in the summer of the next year, 1896, when Orville was taken ill—typhoid fever. Then, at a time when Orville was still delirious from the fever, Wilbur read that Lilienthal had been killed in a crash of his glider. After Orville was well-enough to hear about Lilienthal's fatal accident, both he and Wilbur felt a greater eagerness than ever to learn more about what Lilienthal had accomplished, as well as of what had been tried by others, toward human flight. Books dealing with attempts of man to fly appeared to be scarce, but the brothers got whatever was available in the Dayton library, besides looking up articles on the subject in the encyclopedia. All they read, however, during the next two or three years did not satisfy their craving for a better understanding of the whole problem of flight. Knowing that the Smithsonian Institution, at Washington, was interested in the subject of human flight, they decided to send a letter to the Smithsonian asking for suggestions as to reading material. The reply, received early in June, 1899, suggested, Octave Chanute's *Progress in Flying Machines,* Professor [Samuel Pierpont] Langley's *Experiments in Aerodynamics,* and the *Aeronautical Annuals* of 1895, 1896, and 1897, edited by James Means, which contained reprints of accounts of various experiments, clear back to the time of Leonardo da Vinci. Besides this list of suggested reading, the Smithsonian sent also some pamphlets, reprints of material extracted from their own annual reports, among which were [Louis Pierre] Mouillard's *Empire of the Air*, Langley's *Story of Experiments in Mechanical Flight*, and a paper by Lilienthal on the *Problem of Flying and Practical Experiments in Soaring*.

    This reading material arrived from Washington at a time when Katharine Wright had just returned from Oberlin College, accompanied by a young woman classmate. She had assumed that her brothers would help to entertain this guest, but, to her vexation, Wilbur and Orville had become too absorbed in their reading to have much time for girls. It was now evident to the brothers that though the previous ten years had been a period of unusual activity, the results had not been encouraging. [Hiram] Maxim, after spending one hundred thousand dollars, had abandoned his work, the [Clement] Ader machine, built at the expense of the French government, had been a failure, Lilienthal in Germany, and [Percy Sinclair] Pilcher, a marine engineer, in England, had been killed while trying to glide. Octave Chanute, too, after making some experiments in gliding, had quit. Since Lilienthal had already aroused the brothers's admiration, they were especially interested in what he had done. With hundreds of short flights, he had had more flying practice than anyone else, even though he had been in the air a total of only five hours in five years. Lilienthal became the Wrights's hero. They decided that he, by his experiments, had made more advance in the flying art than had anyone else up to that time—an opinion, it may be added, that they never changed. Their reading now gave the Wrights a good idea of how earlier experimenters had attempted to solve the problem of equilibrium. Some experimenters had placed the center of gravity far below the wings, on the theory that the weight would seek to remain at the lowest point. But it had been proved that the wings would then oscillate about the center of gravity in a manner destructive to stability. Others had arranged the wings in the shape of a broad V, to form a dihedral angle, with the center low and the wing tips elevated. This, too, tended to make the machine oscillate from side to side except in calm air. Penaud, in his models propelled by rubber bands, had used wings that formed a dihedral angle, and a rear stabilizer set with its forward edge lower than the rear edge. This produced inherent stability in both lateral and longitudinal directions.

Lilienthal, Chanute, and some of the others had used the Penaud system in their gliders, but in addition to that system they counted on shifting the weight of their bodies to help maintain equilibrium. All this reading, while adding to their store of knowledge, also gave the Wrights much misinformation.

One wrong idea they got was that men already knew how to design wings and propellers of such efficiency that motors then available could easily sustain the machine in the air, another, that the greatest problem was to maintain equilibrium. They also were misled into thinking that fore and aft control of a flying machine would be much more difficult than lateral control. That neither Lilienthal nor any other experimenter had ever tried anymore adequate method to insure lateral balance struck Orville as surprising. Why, he asked himself, wouldn't it be possible for the operator to vary the inclination of sections of the wings at the tips and thus obtain force for restoring balance from the difference in the lifts of the two opposite wing tips? That seems today an obvious enough idea, but no one had ever done anything about it before. Orville had hit on a fundamental principle. [Indeed, this principle later became the basic claim of the original Wright patent, and the claim was sustained, as covering the idea of the aileron control, in all countries where the Wright patents were adjudicated.] Orville made a rough sketch of a wing, showing a stationary section at the center, consisting of approximately one-third of the wing, measured from tip to tip, with two adjustable sections, one at either side. These sections were carried on shafts interconnected by cogs mounted on the center section and extending toward the wing tips.

The movement of a lever attached to one of the shafts would cause one wing section to rotate in one direction while the other wing would turn in the opposite direction. Thus a greater lift could be obtained on whichever side it was needed. The Wrights soon saw, however, that for two reasons this particular design did not provide a good structure for a gliding machine. First, with two-thirds of the entire weight of the machine and operator carried by the two shafts, the structure would be weak, and, second, with the ends of the wings free to turn about the shafts, there would not be enough rigidity for a machine that would have to be toted about. Then one night, some five or six weeks later, Wilbur came home from the bicycle shop, to tell Orville enthusiastically of an idea he had hit upon. A customer had dropped in to buy an inner tube for a tire. Wilbur had taken the tube from the pasteboard box it came in and was toying with the box while talking to the customer. As he twisted the box he observed that though the vertical sides were rigid endwise, the top and bottom sides could be twisted to have different angles at the opposite ends. Why, he thought, couldn't the wings of a gliding machine be warped from one end to the other in this same way? Thus the wings could be put at a greater angle at one side than at the other, without structural weakness. That plan seemed so satisfactory that the Wrights did not look for or consider any other method. A few weeks later, in August, 1899, the brothers built a biplane kite, and Wilbur, with a group of small boys as spectators, flew it on a common at the edge of town.

    This kite had wing surfaces five feet from tip to tip by thirteen inches wide. The warping of these surfaces could be accomplished by the use of four cords reaching from the kite to the ground. Two of the cords were attached to the forward corners of the right wing tips, one to the upper and one to the lower, the other ends of the cords, at the ground, were tied to opposite ends of a short stick to be held in the operator's hand. The cords tied to the left wing were arranged in the same way. With a stick in each hand, the operator could move the wings as he desired. The upper wing could be moved farther forward or farther backward than the lower wing, according to the direction in which the two sticks were simultaneously inclined, by movement of the wrists. By inclining the two sticks in opposite directions it was possible to draw one upper wing tip farther forward than the lower at that end, while at the other end of the kite the lower wing tip would be the one farther forward. This moving of the wing tips in opposite directions caused a twisting or warping of the wings. Then the wing at one end would be presented to the wind at a different angle from that at the other end. If one end of the kite started to sink, sidewise balance could be restored by exposing the wing at that end at a greater angle, thus getting more lift. Balance from front to rear was to be maintained by inclining the two sticks in the operator's hands in the same direction—to move the upper wing either forward or backward over the lower wing, to change the center of lift. But in addition to this moving of the wings forward and backward, the Wrights added an "elevator" at the rear. It was held by a pair of wooden rods attached at right angles to the uprights that connected the wings. When the upper wing was pulled forward, to turn the kite upward in front, the elevator met the air at its top side and was pressed downward, which helped to turn the wings upward—as the rear elevator does on planes today. Though their interest did not lag, the Wrights did nothing more for some time about kite experiments, except to seek information in regard to wind velocity in different parts of the country. They wrote to the Weather Bureau at Washington, in December, 1899, and Willis Moore, chief of that Bureau, sent them a number of government bulletins that included statistics on wind velocities at various places. They looked these over, but at that time made no further investigation of any of the places mentioned. In May, 1900, Wilbur Wright wrote a letter to Octave Chanute, living in Chicago, who had written *Progress in Flying Machines*. Though Chanute was better known in engineering circles by his work for certain western railroads, as well as for having built the Kansas City Bridge and the Chicago stockyards, his book, a reprint of his articles published from 1891 to 1893, had made him probably the best authority on the history of aeronautics. Thinking Chanute would be interested, Wilbur told him in his letter of a plan he had for experimenting with a man-carrying kite by means of which, Wilbur thought, one would be able to get hours of practice in operating a machine in the air. He proposed the use of a high tower from the top of which a cable would lead [attach] to the man-carrying kite. He described to Chanute, in his letter, the system of control to be used in the kite—the warping of wings for lateral control, and the shifting of the upper surface backward and forward for longitudinal control—the same system used in the five-foot kite tested the previous August. Then he asked Chanute if he had any information as to locations where winds suitable for carrying on such experiments might be found. [This letter from Wilbur marked the beginning of an acquaintance and correspondence with Chanute that lasted for a number of years.] Chanute suggested San Diego, California, and St. James City (Pine Island), Florida, to be considered because of the steady sea breezes. But, on the other hand, he pointed out that, since those places were deficient in sand hills, perhaps even better locations could be found on the Atlantic coast of South Carolina or Georgia. When the rush of the spring trade in bicycles began to subside, giving them more time for other interests, the Wrights again took up with enthusiasm the study of equilibrium. Each day they proposed and discussed new devices. Orville thought the shifting of the upper surface backward and forward over the lower one, for longitudinal equilibrium, though successful in their kite, would not be practical for a man-carrying glider, which would start and land on the ground. He suggested that the wing surfaces be fixed one above the other, and that an elevator be placed some distance in front of the wings, instead of at the rear. In this position there would be less danger of the elevator touching the ground in starting, and if from any cause the elevator were disabled it would be discovered before the machine got into the air. Wilbur then proposed that, since curved surfaces were more efficient than flat planes, the front rudder, or elevator, should be made flexible. Then it could be bent to present a concave surface on whichever side a pressure was desired, but would be flat when moving edgewise through the air.

  The Wrights did not at first think an elevator in front would provide inherent stability—that is, it would not give the machine the desired tendency to restore its own balance just from the arrangement of its fixed parts. But Wilbur shortly afterward developed a theory that led him to believe the machine would have that quality. Having read that the center of pressure moves toward the front edge of the wings whenever the wings are turned more nearly horizontal in flight, he thought inherent longitudinal stability could be obtained if the front elevator were set at a negative angle—that is, with its front edge lower than its rear edge. With such an arrangement of wings and elevator, every time the wings became more nearly horizontal in flight and met the air at a smaller angle on their under sides, the elevator would meet the air at a greater angle on its upper side. So, he reasoned, whenever, by becoming more nearly horizontal, the wings caused the center of pressure to move forward, tending to turn the machine upward in front, the front elevator would receive a greater downward pressure on its upper side and so counteract the disturbing pressure on the wings. Actual tests later proved that the negative angle of the front elevator did not provide the inherent stability expected. The explanation was that the center of pressure on cambered wings traveled in the opposite direction from that which Wilbur's reading had led him to expect. The Wrights later were to discover that Wilbur's reasoning was correct, but because the travel of the center of pressure was rearward instead of forward the elevator had to be set at a positive instead of at a negative angle. The Wrights's elevator possessed three features not found in the gliders of any of the earlier experimenters. It was in front of the wings, where it was less liable to damage by striking the ground in takeoff and landing, it was operable, instead of fixed as in other machines, and it flexed to present a convex surface to the air, instead of a flat surface. At this early stage of their work the Wrights considered this front elevator their most important invention, because, from their reading, they thought it was solving a problem more difficult than that of lateral control. Though the Wrights's reasons for placing the elevator in front of the wings were at first those just mentioned, they afterward found that this arrangement had much greater importance for two reasons not at first discovered. One of these was that it eliminated all danger of a nose dive when the plane got into what is known as a "stall"—when the speed became too slow. The other reason was that the elevator in front, set at a positive angle with the pressure on its under side, not only produced inherent stability, but also carried part of the load, and so relieved the wings to that extent. [An elevator in the rear, set at a negative angle to provide inherent stability, carries a pressure on its upper side, which adds just that much to the load the wings must carry.] Around the first of August, 1900, the brothers decided to build a man-carrying glider on which to try out their inventions. To get practice in operating it they would first fly it as a kite. For such kite flying, flat open country would be needed, and for the gliding, sand hills free from trees or shrubs. Once again they examined the reports they had received from the Weather Bureau at Washington.

Several of the places where winds might be suitable were in the Far West, but one in the East, much nearer to Dayton, was a place with an odd name, Kitty Hawk, North Carolina. They decided to write at once to Kitty Hawk for further information.

Wilbur Wright addressed a letter to the chief of the Kitty Hawk weather bureau station, asking for various details about the locality, explaining that he might wish to go there shortly to conduct experiments with a man-carrying kite. He inquired, too, if it would be possible for him and his brother to obtain board and lodging in the vicinity until they could get themselves established in a camp. Joseph J. Dosher, in charge of the Kitty Hawk station, who received the letter, replied briefly, on August 16, giving the direction of the prevailing winds, and he described the nature of the land for many miles. After writing his reply, Dosher handed Wilbur Wright's letter to a neighbor, William J. Tate, with the request that he also make a reply. "Bill" Tate (later known as Captain Tate) was probably the best-educated man in that locality. He lived about a mile inland from the weather station, in the hamlet or settlement of Kitty Hawk, where he had formerly been the postmaster. For all practical purposes he still was the postmaster, though the office was in his wife's name. Endowed with a gift for expressing himself readily in either speech or writing, Tate did a creditable job when he wrote to Wilbur Wright on August 18. Not only did he tell about the suitability of the Kitty Hawk region, because of the prevailing high winds, for the kind of experiments Wilbur had mentioned, but he went into details about the treeless sand hills and the general terrain. And he said arrangements could undoubtedly be made for the Wrights to obtain board for as long as desired. The letters from Dosher and Tate—particularly the one from Tate—convinced the Wrights that Kitty Hawk was the place for their experiments.

Almost immediately they decided they would go to Kitty Hawk as soon as they could build their glider. The work at Dayton, getting parts and material ready for the glider, required only a few weeks. Only the cutting and sewing of the cloth covering for the wings, the bending of the ash ribs into shape, and making the metal connections, took much time. The cost of the whole machine in actual money outlay was trifling, probably not more than $15. It was arranged that Orville should stay in Dayton, to look after the bicycle shop until Wilbur got settled at Kitty Hawk, and then join him there. Wilbur set out on a September day, taking with him parts of the glider and all material needed to assemble it except some spruce lumber he expected to obtain nearer his destination. The journey proved to be more of an undertaking than Wilbur expected.

❑❑❑❑❑❑❑❑❑❑❑

One must look at a map of North Carolina to get an idea of the isolation of the long strip of sandy beach that separates the Atlantic Ocean from Albemarle, Pamlico, and Roanoke Sounds. At the time the Wrights went there, no bridges connected this beach with any part of the North Carolina mainland or even with nearby Roanoke Island, seat of Sir Walter Raleigh's "Lost Colony." At one point on the beach was the Kitty Hawk Life-Saving Station, and alongside of it a government weather bureau.

About a mile back from the ocean was the hamlet of Kitty Hawk which, though it had a post office, was little more than a settlement—with only about a score of dwelling houses, most of them as widely scattered as in an ordinary farming community. Four miles south was the Kill Devil Hills Life-Saving Station. It was not surprising that when Wilbur Wright, on September 9, 1900, reached Elizabeth City, North Carolina, the nearest railroad point to his destination, the first persons he chanced to ask about Kitty Hawk had never heard of the place. Then he learned that a boat made weekly trips to Roanoke Island, but it had gone the day before. Not liking delay, he went to the waterfront to inquire if another boat might be available. There he met one Israel Perry, formerly a resident of Kitty Hawk, who lived the year round on his little flat-bottomed schooner. As no other boatman showed any interest in making the trip, Wilbur booked passage with "Captain" Perry, despite the boat's dirty, forbidding appearance. After loading parts of the glider and other goods that had been shipped from Dayton he set out with Perry on the morning of September 10 for the forty-mile voyage to Kitty Hawk. Wilbur noticed that the small boat they used to go from the wharf out to where the schooner was anchored was leaking badly and he asked if it was safe. "*Oh,*" Perry assured him, "*it's safer than the big boat.*" That didn't inspire too much confidence in what was in store, and Wilbur soon learned that any misgivings he felt were amply justified. Toward the middle of the afternoon they met a strong head wind that forced them to seek a smooth water haven in North River where they anchored to await better weather. By that time Wilbur had worked up a good appetite, but he discovered that neither the food nor the kitchen met even minimum standards of cleanliness and he made excuses, as politely as he could, for not eating. All he had with him against hunger was a small jar of jelly his sister Katharine had slipped into his suitcase. The weather was not favorable for continuing the voyage until the afternoon of the second day, and the boat reached a wharf, where there was a small store, on Kitty Hawk Bay, at about nine o'clock that night. Not knowing where else to go, Wilbur stayed aboard until the next morning. A small boy named [Elijah] Baum agreed to guide him to the home of William

J. Tate, about a quarter of a mile away. By the time Wilbur arrived there, on that morning of September 12, it was just forty-eight hours since he had tasted food other than his little supply of jelly. After introducing himself, and in response to "Bill" Tate's inquiries about how he enjoyed his trip, Wilbur spoke of his back being sore from lying on deck and of how his arm ached from holding on when the boat rolled. Then it came out that he had been unable to bring himself to eat the food provided on the Perry schooner. "*You mean to tell me*," asked "Bill" Tate, greatly concerned, "*that you've eaten no victuals for two days?*" Here was a situation that called for quick action in a hospitable home. It was after the Tates's breakfast hour, but Mrs. Tate soon had a fire in the kitchen stove and prepared a great platter of ham and eggs that the guest seemed to relish. Then Wilbur inquired if it would be possible for him to obtain board and lodging there for the week or more until his brother "Orv" arrived. Tate went into an adjoining room to ask his wife. As the door was ajar, Wilbur could hear what was said. Mrs. Tate was a bit alarmed. Here was a man able to devote time and money for weeks at a time to sport. Doubtless he must be a person of great wealth, accustomed to every luxury. Would he be satisfied with the best they could offer? Wilbur stepped to the door, explaining that he could not help overhearing their conversation, and said it must be understood that if he were accepted as a paying guest he would not expect any extra frills, but would greatly appreciate the courtesy. "*This fellow's a real gentleman*," thought Tate, and by way of settling the question, without waiting to hear anymore from his wife, he said to Wilbur, "*You must be tired. Why don't you come into our spare bedroom and take a nap?*" By the next day Wilbur was at work. The cloth covering for the glider—white French sateen of extra good quality—had already been shaped and sewed at Dayton, except at the ends, to permit fitting it over the framework. But now he had to make changes in the covering, because the glider was going to be smaller than originally planned. The longest timbers, for the wing spars, that he had been able to find in either Norfolk or Elizabeth City were only sixteen feet long instead of the eighteen-foot length he desired. Thus it was necessary to cut out strips from the middle of the lengths of cloth for both upper and lower wings. For resewing the cloth where necessary, Wilbur borrowed Mrs. Tate's machine. But all the rest of the work of assembling the glider was done at a tent Wilbur set up, about half a mile from the Tate home, at a spot where there were a few trees and a view of the bay.

He dragged the crates, containing various parts and tools, to the tent and hoped to have everything in readiness when Orville arrived. But the heat was intense—the job of carrying water to the camp used up much energy—and when Orville got there, on September 28, Wilbur told him regretfully that much work on the glider was still to be done. Orville's trip had been uneventful. Indeed, though he came on a better boat than Israel Perry's, he had struck such a calm sea that his voyage from Elizabeth City took two days, the same as Wilbur's. For the first five days after Orville's arrival, both brothers stayed at the Tate home. Then they established themselves in camp. One end of their tent, twelve by twenty-two feet, was tied to a tree for anchorage. The tree was headquarters for a mockingbird that sometimes joined in the harmony when Orville twanged at a mandolin he had brought from home. Not many visitors came to the camp from nearby Kitty Hawk. One reason for this was that the camp was considered dangerous after news got about that the Wrights used a gasoline stove. "Bill" Tate was favorably impressed, though, with an acetylene lamp, intended for a bicycle that the Wrights used for lighting. He said he had a notion to install such a system of gas lighting in his house.

It was necessary to carry water about one thousand feet over the sand. Orville volunteered to do the cooking—and he continued to do so during all their experiments at Kitty Hawk.

But he always felt that he had the better of the bargain, for the dishwashing job was Wilbur's. As it was impossible to obtain fresh bread, Orville learned to make biscuits, and without use of milk. They were good biscuits, too—better, his father afterward insisted, than anyone else could make. To simplify operations, Orville always mixed at one time enough flour and other dry ingredients to last for several days, as biscuits had to be baked three times daily. Working together, the brothers soon had the glider assembled. When completed, it weighed about fifty two pounds. Though the main spars were only sixteen feet long, the "bows" at the ends of each wing surface brought the total span to nearly seventeen and one-half feet. The total lifting area was 165 square feet instead of 200 as intended. A space eighteen inches wide at the center of the lower surface where the operator would lie, with feet over the rear spar, was left free of covering. The apparatus had no rear vanes or tail of any kind, but it had two important features never used by previous experimenters. One was the front rudder, or "elevator," the rear edge of which was about thirty inches from the nearest edge of the wings—the other was the wing warping. By an ingenious arrangement of the trussing, the wings could be twisted into a helicoidal warp from one end to the other, thus exposing one wing to the air at a greater angle than the other. This was to be used for bringing the machine back to the level after it was tipped up sidewise by a gust of wind. The Wrights's first surprise at Kitty Hawk was that the winds there were not what they had counted on. United States Weather Bureau reports had led them to think they would have winds of about fifteen miles an hour almost every day.

But now it dawned on them that, fifteen miles an hour was simply the daily average for a month. Sometimes the wind was sixty miles an hour, and the next day it would be entirely calm. It now began to look as if they might frequently have to wait a few days for suitable conditions, which meant that their experiments would require more time than they had expected. Almost as soon as they began their trials of the glider, the brothers got another surprise. According to the Lilienthal tables of air pressures, their machine of 165 square feet needed a wind of only from seventeen to twenty-one miles an hour to support it as a kite with a pilot aboard. But they found that much stronger winds were needed to lift it. Since suitable winds would not be plentiful, their plan of practicing by the hour aboard the glider while flying it as a kite would have to be postponed. Instead, they flew it as a kite, loaded with about fifty pounds of chain, but with no man aboard. They held it with two ropes, and operated the balancing system by cords from the ground. Though the results were promising, inspiring confidence in the system of maintaining equilibrium, the brothers knew that only by actual gliding experience could they confirm what the kite experiments had indicated as being true. One thing that puzzled them was that the machine appeared to be greatly deficient in lifting power as compared with calculated lift of curved surfaces of its size.

In wondering what might be the cause of this wide discrepancy between expected and actual lifts, the Wrights considered the possibility that it might be because the curvature of the wings was less than that used by Lilienthal. Or could it be that the cloth covering was too porous and permitted some of the lifting power of the wind to be lost? They wondered, too, if the Lilienthal tables they had followed, relating to air pressure on wing surfaces, could be in error. They next determined to try gliding on the side of a hill. That meant toting their machine four miles south of their camp to a great sand dune about one hundred feet high, called Kill Devil Hill. On their first day at the hill, the wind was about twenty-five miles an hour. As they lacked previous experience at gliding they decided to wait for less of a blow for their first attempt. The next day the wind had subsided to fourteen miles an hour, and they made about a dozen glides. "Bill" Tate was there and assisted them. In making these glides, the machine was usually only two or three feet from the soft, sandy ground, and though the brothers repeatedly made landings while moving at a speed of twenty miles an hour—neither operator nor machine was harmed. The slope of the hill toward the northeast was about 9½ degrees—or a drop of approximately one foot in six. After moving at a rate of about twenty-five to thirty miles an hour with reference to the wind, or ten to fifteen miles over the ground, the machine, while keeping its course parallel to the slope, increased its speed, thus indicating that it could glide on a slope less steep. Their control of the machine was even better than they had dared to expect. They got quick response to the slightest movement of the front elevator, which promised to be satisfactory in maintaining fore and aft balance. At first, they fastened the warping mechanism, to make it inoperable, and had only the elevator to manipulate, for they feared that, inexperienced as they were, if they tried to use both, then they might be unsuccessful with either. But even without the use of the warping mechanism it was possible to make glides of from five to ten seconds before the sidewise tilt of the machine forced a landing. Before making the last three or four flights, the Wrights loosened the warping wires to permit the sidewise control to be used. When these experiments of 1900 ended, instead of the hours of practice in the air the Wrights had hoped to have, they had flown the machine as a kite with a man aboard barely ten minutes, and had had only two minutes of actual gliding. Now that the experiments for that year were ended and they had no further use for the glider, the brothers weighted the machine with sand and left it on the hill. When "Bill" Tate saw that they were through with the glider he asked if he might have it, and they gladly gave it to him. Mrs. Tate used the sateen that covered the wings to make dresses for her two small daughters. She noted that it appeared to be unusually good fabric, more closely woven and better than she had seen in the stores.

    Some of her neighbors, when they saw the dresses she made of it, remarked that it seemed too bad to use such excellent material on a kite. Though the amount of practice was less than they had expected—all the Wrights had learned in that season of 1900 seemed to confirm the correctness of certain opinions held at the beginning. Their method of warping or twisting the wings to maintain lateral balance was better than dependence on either the dihedral angle or shifting the weight of the operator, better than any method yet tried. And their front elevator had been highly satisfactory as a means for directing the machine up and down. Before leaving Kitty Hawk they decided that their next experiments would be with a glider large enough to be flown as a kite, with an operator aboard, in winds ordinarily to be counted on. When the brothers set to work on their glider for the experiments of 1901, they decided to make it of the same general design as the first one, and with the same system of control. But they carried out their plan to give it considerably more area, to provide greater lifting power. Another change they made was to increase the curvature of the wings to conform to the shape on which Lilienthal had based his tables of air pressures. It had wings of about seven-foot chord (the straight line distance between the front and rear edges) with a total span of twenty-two feet, and weighed ninety-eight pounds. After a section twenty inches wide had been removed from the middle of the lower wing, and the rear corners of the wings rounded off, the total lifting area was 290 square feet, as compared with 165 in the previous glider. The front elevator, with its rear edge about two and one half feet away from the front edge of the wings, had a four-and-one-half foot chord and an area of eighteen square feet. This was a much larger machine than anyone had ever tried to fly.

The Wrights knew it could not be controlled simply by shifting the pilot's weight, as others had done, but they had faith in their own operable front elevator and believed they could manage it. If their calculations were correct, it would be supported in a wind of seventeen miles an hour, with the wing surfaces at an "angle of incidence" of only three degrees. ["Angle of incidence," now more often called "angle of attack," has been defined as the angle at which the plane presents itself to the air in advancing against it.] As it would be impractical to keep so large a machine with them in the tent, as they had done with the smaller glider, the brothers built near Kill Devil Hill, a rough frame shed, twenty-five feet long, sixteen feet wide, and seven feet high at the eaves. Both ends of the building except the gable parts were made into doors, hinged above. When open, the doors provided an awning at each end of the building. For living quarters they still used a tent. By driving a pipe ten or twelve feet into the sand they got a water supply. Though the great stretch of sandy waste seemed too desolate for anyone to bother about owning, yet it was all under the ownership of one person or another and the

Wrights took the precaution to obtain permission to erect their buildings. This year they were to have company in camp. Octave Chanute, with whom they had been in correspondence for about a year stopped in Dayton in June, 1901, at their invitation, to get better acquainted. When he learned that the Wrights had carried on their experiments in 1900 without the presence of a doctor in camp, and were intending to do so again, he told them he thought that was too risky, considering the kind of work and the isolation of the experiment ground. He said he knew a young man in Coatesville, Pennsylvania, George A. Spratt, "an amateur" in aeronautics, who had had some medical training. Spratt had never seen any gliding experiments, and Chanute thought he would be eager for the opportunity. If the Wrights would board him at camp, Chanute said, he would be glad to pay Spratt's traveling expenses to Kitty Hawk and would consider himself "*compensated by the pleasure given to him.*" Chanute also proposed that they have in camp with them Edward C. Huffaker, of Chuckey City, Tennessee, who was building a glider that Chanute was financing and the Wrights consented. Thus there were four regularly in camp that season, and for a time Chanute himself was with them as a guest. The new machine was completed and ready for trial on the afternoon of July 27.

Since it was designed to be flown in a wind of seventeen miles, and there was but thirteen miles of wind on that day, the brothers took the machine to the big Kill Devil Hill for its first trial. After five or six short tuning-up flights they made a glide of 315 feet in nineteen seconds. Although several flights on this first day of experiments in 1901 exceeded the best made the year before, yet it was soon evident that in several respects the machine was not as good as the first one. It was found that the wings, with a camber of one to twelve—the camber recommended by Lilienthal, and used by Chanute and others—was not so good as the camber of one to twenty-two, used by the Wrights in 1900. [Camber of one to twenty-two means that the length of the chord, the straight-line distance between the front and rear edges of the wings, is twenty-two times the distance *from* the chord to the deepest part of the wing curve.] This was demonstrated by the fact that the 1901 machine could not glide on a slope as nearly level as had the earlier machine. The Wrights found, too, that a machine with wings of one to twelve camber was not so easily controlled fore and aft as when the wings were of one to twenty-two camber. They decided therefore to reduce the camber of the wings to make them more like those of the earlier machine. When they resumed their gliding, after the camber had been reduced (one to eighteen), the control of the machine appeared to be as good as it was the year before, and they then made flights in winds of twenty-two to twenty-seven miles an hour, without accident. Though in most of these flights the lateral control was highly effective, in a few others—under conditions seemingly the same—the wing warping appeared to have no effect at all. The Wrights now made the discovery that in free flight, when the wing on one side of the machine was presented to the wind at a greater angle than that on the other side, the wing with the greater angle, instead of rising as it was expected to do—sometimes descended. The explanation was that the greater angle of the wing at one side gave more resistance to forward motion and thus reduced the speed on that side. This decrease in speed more than counter-balanced the effect of the larger angle of the wing in producing lift. [The Wrights had not discovered this when flying the glider as a kite, because, when held by ropes, the wings always maintained equal air speeds, even when their resistances were unbalanced.] It was evident to the brothers that their present method of controlling equilibrium was not yet complete. Something was needed to maintain equal speeds at the two wing tips. The idea occurred to them that the addition of a vertical fin attached to the machine at some distance in the rear of the wings might be the solution of the problem. But the test of such a fin had to be left until another season. The behavior of the glider in these various flights forced the Wrights to give thought to another scientific problem, that regarding the center of air pressure on curved surfaces. Contrary to the teachings of scientific books on the subject, it was becoming more and more evident that the travel of the center of pressure on a cambered surface is not always in the same direction as the travel on a plane surface. When the angle of attack on a plane surface is decreased, the center of pressure moves toward the front edge, but on a cambered surface this is true only when larger angles are being decreased. When the angle of attack on a cambered surface is decreased from, say, thirty degrees to twenty-five degrees, the center of pressure moves forward, as it does on a plane surface, but when a certain angle (between twelve and fifteen degrees) is reached, then the movement of the center of pressure is reversed. From there on, the center of pressure moves toward the rear so long as any further decrease is made in the angle of attack. The Wrights proved this by a series of experiments with a single surface from their plane. Knowledge of the phenomenon of this reversal of center of pressure was of great importance to them in their later work of designing aeroplanes. Scientific problems were not the only ones to perplex the Wrights. A sore trial were the mosquitoes and sand fleas, particularly numerous and aggressive in that summer of 1901. As Orville Wright recalled in later years, there were times when, he thought, while fighting mosquitoes through the night, that if he could just survive until morning he would pack up and return home. Those mosquitoes might have caused a long postponement of the conquest of the air.

By the time they left Kitty Hawk on August 20, the brothers had satisfied themselves that a glider of large surfaces could be controlled almost as easily as a smaller one, provided the control is by manipulation of the surfaces themselves instead of by movements of the operator's body. So far as they knew, judging from figures previously published, they had broken all records for distance in gliding. Chanute, who had witnessed part of the 1901 experiments, insisted that the results were better than had ever been attained before. All that was encouraging, but, on the other hand, if most of the supposedly scientific information available was worthless, then their task was even more formidable than they had expected. With no dependable previous knowledge to guide them, who were they to determine how man should fly? Wilbur seemed much discouraged. Possibly he had entertained hopes of actually flying, though he had always disclaimed having such an idea. He was ready to drop the experiments altogether. On the way home, Wilbur declared his belief "*Not within a thousand years would man ever fly!*"

Chanute urged the brothers not to drop their experiments, arguing that if they did it would be a long time before anyone else would come as near to understanding the problem or how to work toward its solution. Without knowing it, Chanute made a great contribution to aviation history, for the Wrights heeded his repeated admonitions against ceasing their efforts. Without the prodding of Chanute they might not have gone on. Chanute performed another great service for aeronautics when he, as president of the Western Society of Engineers, invited Wilbur Wright to address that body at a meeting in Chicago, September 18, 1901, on the subject "Some Aeronautical Experiments."

Wilbur shrank from the idea of making such a talk and would hardly have done so except to oblige his friend. He cautioned Chanute, though, not to make the speech a prominent feature of the program, because, he said, he made no pretense of being a public speaker. Chanute did nevertheless plan to use the announcement of the talk as a means to help make the meeting a big success. He wanted to know if it would be all right to make the occasion "Ladies Night." Wilbur decided that he would already be as badly scarred as a man could be and the presence of women would not make the situation much worse. But he insisted on one thing, that he must not be expected to appear in formal evening dress. In this speech Wilbur boldly declared that the best sets of figures obtainable regarding air pressure against airplane surfaces appeared to contain many serious errors.

Orville, at the shop in Dayton, was a little alarmed about that part of the speech. What if something about their own work had been wrong and the figures compiled by various scientists should finally be proved correct? Certainly it was no small responsibility for anyone so little known as Wilbur or he to denounce publicly the work of eminent scientists, dignified by preservation in books long regarded as authoritative. It would be both presumptuous and risky to brand supposedly established facts as untrue unless the person doing so could be unassailably sure of his ground. In this cautious state of mind Orville rigged up a little wind tunnel for the purpose of making a series of tests. This tunnel consisted simply of what appeared to be an old starch box, not more than eighteen inches long, that was lying in the shop. In it he placed a hastily constructed apparatus, a main part of which was simply a metal rod pivoted in the manner of a weather vane. Without attempting to give technical details of the method used, it may be said that a curved surface was balanced against a plane surface in an air current passing through the box. As Orville had provided the box with a glass top he could measure the angles to the wind at which the curved surface and the plane surface of equal area produced equal pressures. The experiments with this crude apparatus lasted only one day. They were conclusive enough so far as they went, indicating errors in published figures relating to air pressure on curved surfaces.

But as Orville was later to learn, the published errors were greatest in regard to wing surfaces set at small angles, such as would be used in flying, and he had tested thus far only larger angles. With the tests thus incomplete, Orville and Wilbur decided, on the latter's return from Chicago that it might be prudent to stay on the safe side and omit from the published record of Wilbur's speech the more severe part of his criticism of available figures. They would wait until further wind tunnel experiments could give more detailed knowledge. Consequently, when Wilbur's speech appeared in the December, 1901, issue of the *Journal of the Western Society of Engineers*, it was a bit less startling than the one he had actually delivered—though, even after the deletions, there still remained strong hints that accepted tables of figures might be wrong. And the record of the speech was treated as of great importance. It has probably been reprinted and quoted as often as any other article ever written on the subject of flying. The Wrights were not sure they would ever build another glider. But their curiosity, their passion for getting at truth, had now been too much aroused for them to quit studying the problem of air pressures. They decided to build another wind tunnel less crude than the one Orville had hastily used, and continue their experiments. The new tunnel consisted of an open-ended wooden box about sixteen inches square on the inside by six feet long. Into one end would come a current of air and the draft thus created would be "straightened," as well as made uniform, by having to pass through a set of small pigeon holes. It would have been a great convenience to use an electric fan for sending the air into the tunnel. But the Wrights had no electric current in their shop—still lighted by gas—and the fan was driven by a one-cylinder gas engine they had previously made. They attached the fan to a spindle that had held an emery wheel. A new measuring device, or balance, was built of wire intended for bicycle spokes, and pieces of hacksaw blades. These experiments were now done with much more refinement than at first, and the measurements were for both "lift" and "drift."

But as each curved surface measured was balanced against the pressure on a square plane, exposed at ninety degrees to the same air current, it was not necessary to know the precise speed of the air current. During that autumn and early winter of 1901, the brothers tested in the wind tunnel more than two hundred types of wing surfaces. They set these at different angles, starting with the angle at which the surface begins to lift, and then at 2½ degree intervals, up to twenty, and at five degree intervals up to forty-five degrees. They measured monoplane, biplane, and triplane models, also models in which one wing followed the other, as used by Langley in his experiments.

They measured the lift produced by different "aspect ratios"—that is, the ratio of the span of the wing to its chord. They found that the greater the span in proportion to the chord the more easily the wing may be supported. They measured thick and thin surfaces. One surface had a thickness of nearly one-sixth of its chord. Among other things, these experiments proved the fallacy of the sharp edge at the front of an airplane wing and the inefficiency of deeply cambered wings as then generally advocated by others. Sometimes they got a result so unexpected that they could hardly believe their own measurements—as, for example, when they discovered that, contrary to all previously published figures by students of the subject, a square plane gave a greater pressure when set at thirty degrees than at forty-five degrees. These wind tunnel experiments in the bicycle shop were carried on for only a little more than two months, and were ended before Christmas, 1901. The Wrights discontinued them with great reluctance, but, after all, they were still in the bicycle business, still obliged to give thought to their means for earning a living, and with no idea that this scientific research could ever be financially profitable. In those few weeks, however, they had accomplished something of almost incalculable importance.

They had not only made the first wind tunnel in which miniature wings were accurately tested, but were the first men in all the world to compile tables of figures from which one might design an airplane that could fly. Even today, in wind tunnels used in various aeronautical laboratories, equipped with the most elaborate and delicate instruments modern science can provide, the refinements obtained over the Wrights's figures for the same shapes of surfaces are surprisingly small. But it is doubtful if the difficulties and full value of the Wrights's scientific researches within their bicycle shop are yet appreciated. The world knows they were the first to build a machine capable of sustained flight and the first actually to fly, but it is not fully aware of all the tedious, grueling scientific laboratory work they had to do before flight was possible. Important as was the system of control with which the Wrights's name has been connected, it would not have given them success without their wind tunnel work which enabled them to design a machine that would lift itself. The Wrights had a double reason for making sure of their figures. With little money to spend on a hobby, it was much cheaper to rectify mistakes on paper than after the idea was put into material form. They knew that if they should decide to go on to further gliding attempts, they could not afford to spend much more money on apparatus built according to unreliable data. After compiling their own tables of figures, the Wrights gave copies of them to their friend Chanute and others interested in the problem of aerodynamics. Chanute well knew that the Wrights now had knowledge of aeronautics far beyond that of anyone else in the world, and he felt that for them to go on with their experiments was almost a duty. He much regretted, in the interest of science, he said, that they had reached a stopping place, for he was sure further experiments on their part promised "important results." Chanute might well have felt pride in the effectiveness of his insistence that the Wrights should go on experimenting, as well as in the results of his invitation to Wilbur to make that Chicago speech. Except for that speech and its daring statements that Orville thought needed more confirmation, there probably would have been no wind tunnel tests, and without the kind of knowledge then obtained, neither the Wrights nor anyone else could have built a practical flying machine. Those wind tunnel experiments marked one of the great turning points in the long history of attempts at human flight. It still remained for the Wrights to put their new knowledge to actual test in gliding, and they set out on August 25, 1902, for their third stay at Kitty Hawk. But not until September 8 were they able to begin the work of assembling their new glider, for the camp, battered by winter gales, needed much repairing, and they decided to build an addition to it for living quarters.

They did not have their machine ready for its first trial until September 19. This new glider was of not much greater lifting area than that of the previous year, though the wing span had been increased from twenty-two to thirty-two feet.

But since the wind tunnel experiments had demonstrated the importance of the "aspect ratio," the total span was now about six times the chord instead of three. One minor change also may be noted. In the earlier gliders, the wing-warping mechanism had been worked by movement of the operator's feet, but now in this 1902 glider it was done by sidewise movement of one's hips resting on a "cradle." The most noticeable change was the addition of a tail, consisting of fixed twin vertical vanes, with a total area of a trifle less than twelve square feet. Its purpose was to correct certain difficulties encountered in some of the flights with the 1901 machine. When the wing surfaces at the right and left sides were warped to present different angles toward the wind, the wing that had the greater angle, and therefore the more resistance, tended to lag behind, and then the slower speed offset what otherwise would have been the greater lifting power of that wing. The tail was expected to counter balance that difference in resistance of the wing tips. If the wing on one side tended to swerve forward, on a vertical axis, then the tail, more exposed to the wind on that same side, should—it was thought—stop the machine from further turning. Entirely apart from any advantages to be gained from the use of the tail, the first trials of the new machine were highly encouraging for another reason. It was soon evident that by disregarding all tables of air pressures used by their predecessors and building according to the figures obtained from their wind-tunnel experiments, the Wrights had made a big advance toward flight. Because of the knowledge they now had, not possessed by any previous experimenter, of how the wings should be shaped, this 1902 machine was of just about twice the "dynamic efficiency" of any other glider ever built, it could have been flown with probably less than half the power required for any other glider. Altogether the Wrights made more than one thousand gliding flights in September and October, 1902.

Several glides were of more than six hundred feet, and a number of them were against a thirty-six-mile-an-hour wind.

No previous experimenter had ever dared to try gliding in so stiff a wind. That the Wrights were successful at such feats gave proof of the effectiveness of their devices for control. Some of their flights lasted more than a minute and at times it was possible to soar in one spot without any descent. So impressive were such exhibitions that Bill Tate's brother, Dan, solemnly offered the opinion, "*All she needs is a coat of feathers to make her light and she will stay in the air indefinitely.*" About one time in fifty, however, the machine behaved in a manner quite mysterious. It would turn up sidewise and come sliding to the ground in spite of all the warp the operator could give to the wing tips. At one trial the lateral control would work perfectly and then the next time, under conditions that seemed to be about the same, it was impossible to prevent one wing end from striking the sand with a kind of spinning movement that the brothers called "well digging." This new problem that had not occurred in their previous gliders came from the fact that the machine had a tail. Those "well digging" accidents were tailspins—though that term did not come into use until several years afterward. But even after it was evident that the tail had something to do with the machine's peculiar behavior, neither brother was prepared to explain *why*. Then one night Orville drank more than his customary amount of coffee. Instead of going to sleep as usual the moment he got into bed, he lay awake for several hours. Those extra cups of coffee may have been important for the future of practical flight for, as he tossed about, he figured out the explanation of the phenomenon caused by the tail.

Here it is, as he eagerly gave it to Wilbur, and to their brother Lorin, who was visiting them, at breakfast the next morning, "*When the machine became tilted laterally it began to slide sidewise while advancing, just as a sled slides downhill or a ball rolls down an inclined plane, the speed increasing in an accelerated ratio. If the tilt happened to be a little worse than usual, or if the operator were a little slow in getting the balance corrected, the machine slid sidewise so fast that this movement caused the vertical vanes to strike the wind on the side toward the low wing instead of on the side toward the high wing, as it was expected to do. In this state of affairs the vertical vanes did not counteract the turning of the machine about a vertical axis, caused by the difference of resistance of the warped wings on the right and left sides, on the contrary, the vanes assisted in the turning movement, and the result was worse than if there were no fixed vertical tail.*" If his explanation was sound, as Orville felt sure it was, then, he said, it would be necessary to make the vertical tail movable, to permit the operator to bring pressure to bear on the side toward the higher wing. [This is the form of the Wright system of control generally used today—the independent control of aileron and rudder.] Wilbur promptly saw that the explanation was probably correct and nodded approvingly. And he immediately made a suggestion. A particular relation existed, he said, in the desired pressures on the tail, no matter whether the trouble was due to difference of resistance of the wing tips or on account of sliding.

Whatever the reason, it was desirable to get rid of the pressure on the side toward the low wing, to which a greater angle of incidence must be imparted in restoring lateral balance, and bring pressure on the side of the tail toward the high wing where there must be a reduced angle. So why not have the mechanism that controlled the wing warping and that which moved the tail operated in conjunction? Then the pilot, instead of having to control three things at once, would need to attend only to the front elevator and the wing-warping device. The brothers at once attached the wires controlling the tail to those that warped the wings—and they also changed the tail from two vertical fins to a single vertical rudder. After the changes in the 1902 glider, the Wrights had their machine in about the form pictured and described in the drawings and specifications of their patent, applied for on the 23rd of the next March. With their accurate data for making calculations, and a system of balance effective in winds as well as in calms, the brothers believed that they now could build a successful power flyer.

□□□□□□□□□□

Immediately on their return to Dayton after the 1902 glider flights, the Wrights set to work to carry out plans, already begun at Kitty Hawk, for a power machine. The satisfactory performance of the glider had demonstrated the accuracy of the laboratory work on which its design was based, and they now felt sure they could calculate in advance the performance of any machine they built with a degree of accuracy not possible with the data available to their predecessors. Early in their preparations, they took steps to obtain a suitable engine. They knew that a steam engine might do well enough for their purpose, but a gasoline engine would be simpler and better. Some time previously they had built an air-cooled, one-cylinder gas engine for operating the machinery of their small workshop, but they did not feel experienced enough to build the kind they now needed and preferred to buy one. They wanted a motor to produce at least eight horsepower and to weigh, without accessories, not more than twenty pounds per horsepower. It seemed doubtful if such a motor as they required was then being manufactured, but perhaps one of the automobile companies could build one light enough by reducing the weight of the flywheel and using more aluminum than in the regular output. On December 3, 1902, they sent letters to a number of automobile companies, and to gasoline motor manufacturers—altogether, to nearly a dozen, asking if they could furnish a motor that would develop eight brake horsepower and weigh not more than 200 pounds. Orville Wright was not sure in after years whether he and Wilbur revealed in their letters the use they planned for the motor they were seeking, but most of the companies replied that they were too busy with their regular business to undertake such a special order. There is reason to suspect the companies may have got wind of the purpose to which the motor would be put and were afraid to become implicated in the project. If a company provided a motor for a so-called flying machine, and this fact should leak out, it could hurt their business prestige, because it might look as if they considered human flight a possibility. One company replied, however, that they had motors, rated at eight horsepower, according to the French system of ratings, which weighed only 135 pounds, and if the Wrights thought this would develop enough power for their purpose, they could buy one.

    After an examination of the particulars of this motor, from which they learned that it had but a single cylinder, of four inch bore and five inch stroke, the Wrights decided that its power was probably much overrated. Finally the brothers decided that they would have to build their motor themselves. They estimated that they could make one of four cylinders, of four inch bore and four inch stroke, weighing not more than two hundred pounds, with accessories included. Their mechanic, Charlie Taylor, gave them enthusiastic help. In its final form, the bare engine, without magneto, weighed 152 pounds, with accessories, 170 pounds.

At 1,200 revolutions per minute, it developed sixteen horsepower—but only for the first fifteen seconds after starting, after a minute or two it did not give more than about twelve horsepower. Since, however, they had not counted on more than eight horsepower, for a machine of a total weight of 600 pounds, now they could add 150 pounds for strengthening wings and other parts. Not yet knowing how much power an engine of that size ought to have developed, the Wrights were much pleased with its performance. Long afterward they found out that the engine should have provided about twice as much power as it did. The trouble, as they later said, was their "Jack of experience in building gasoline motors." The wings of this new power machine had a total span of a few inches more than forty feet, and the upper and lower wing surfaces were six feet apart. To reduce the danger of the engine ever falling on the pilot, it was placed on the lower wing a little to right of center. The pilot would ride lying flat, as on the glider, but to the left of center, to balance the weight. To guard against the machine rolling over in landing, the sled-like runners were extended farther out in front of the main surfaces than on the glider. These two runners were four feet, eight inches apart. The tail of the machine had twin movable vanes instead of a single vane as in the 1902 glider.

The Wrights left the designing of the propellers until the last, because they felt sure that part of the job would be easy enough. Their tables of air pressures, derived from wind tunnel experiments, would enable them, they thought, to calculate exactly the thrust necessary to sustain the machine in flight. But to design a propeller that would give the needed amount of thrust, with the power at their command, was a problem they had not yet considered. No data on air propellers were available, but the Wrights had always understood that it was not difficult to obtain an efficiency of fifty percent with marine propellers. All that should be necessary would be to learn the theory of the operation of propellers from books on marine engineering and then substitute air pressures for water pressures. What could be simpler or easier? Accordingly, the brothers got several such books from the Dayton Public Library. But when they began to read those books, they discovered to their surprise that much less was known about propellers than they had supposed. All the formulae on propellers in the books were found to be based on experiment and observation rather than on theory. The marine engineers, when they saw that a propeller would not move a boat fast enough, had then tried one larger, or of a different pitch, until they got one that would serve their purpose. But they could not design a propeller on paper and foresee exactly what its performance on a certain type of motor boat would be. Exact knowledge of the action of the screw propeller, though it had been in use for a century, was still lacking. The Wrights knew that rough estimates, which might be near enough for a motor boat, would not do for an airplane. On a boat a propeller having only a fraction of one percent of the desired efficiency could move the boat a little, but on an airplane, unless the propeller had the full amount of thrust needed, it would be worthless, for it couldn't lift the plane into the air at all! In short, the Wrights had to have a propeller that would do exactly what was expected of it. And they had neither the time nor money to carry on a long series of experiments with different kinds of propellers until they could hit on one suitable. They couldn't afford to make mistakes except on paper. They must somehow learn enough about how propellers acted, and why, to enable them to make accurate calculations. It was apparent to the Wrights that a propeller was simply an airfoil traveling in a spiral course. As they could calculate the effect of an airfoil traveling in a straight course, why should they not be able to calculate the effect in a spiral course? At first thought that did not seem too difficult, but they soon found that they had let themselves into a tough job. Since nothing about a propeller, or the medium in which it acts, would be standing still, it was not easy to find even a point from which to make a start. The more they studied it, the more complex the problem became. "The thrust depends upon the speed and the angle at which the blade strikes the air, the angle at which the blade strikes the air depends upon the speed at which the propeller is turning, the speed the machine is traveling forward, and the speed at which the air is slipping backward, the slip of the air backward depends upon the thrust exerted by the propeller, and the amount of air acted upon." It was not exactly as simple as some of the problems in the school arithmetic—to determine how many sheep a man had or how many leaps a hound must make to overtake a hare. In trying to work out a theory about the action of screw propellers, Wilbur and Orville got into many arguments. Right here it may be noted that this habit the brothers had of arguing technical points was one of the reasons why they were able to accomplish all they finally did in a relatively short time. Neither was a "yes" man to the other. But in their arguments about propellers a peculiar thing happened. "*Often,*" Orville later reported, "*after an hour or so of heated argument, we would discover that we were as far from agreement as when we started, but that each had changed to the other's original position.*" Many months passed before the intricacies of the problem began to untangle themselves.

    The Wrights finally got a better understanding of the action of screw propellers than anyone had ever had before. The time came when they felt sure of their ability to design propellers of exactly the right diameter, pitch, and area for their needs.

    A calculation indicated that 305 revolutions of the propeller would be required to produce 100 pounds thrust. Later, actual measurement showed that only 302 instead of 305 propeller turns were required, or just under one percent of the calculated amount. The propellers delivered in useful work 66 percent of the power expended. That was about one-third more than either Hiram Maxim or Professor Langley in their attempts at flying had ever been able to attain. For two reasons the Wrights decided to use two propellers. First, they could in that way obtain a reaction against a greater quantity of air, and at the same time use a larger pitch angle, and, by having the propellers run in opposite directions, the gyroscopic action of one would neutralize that of the other. The propellers were on tubular shafts about ten feet apart, both driven by chains running over sprockets, somewhat as on a bicycle. Lucius M. Wainwright, president of the Diamond Chain Company, of Indianapolis, became interested in the Wrights's transmission problem, and gave them valuable advice. The Wrights found that the chains would have to be run through guides to prevent slapping and to overcome undue stresses on the machine. They adopted tubular guides and found that they could cross one of the chains in a figure eight and thus have the propellers running in opposite directions. Not until September 23 was all in readiness for the Wrights to set out for Kitty Hawk. They were able to make good connections with a boat and arrived at camp two days later, on a Friday. Discussing en route what they hoped to accomplish, neither had the slightest doubt about the fulfillment of their dreams. Besides being full of confidence they also felt the exuberance of excellent physical condition. Orville was now thirty-two years old and Wilbur thirty-six. Five foot ten and a quarter inches in height, Wilbur was the taller of the two by a little more than an inch and a half. Orville weighed 145 pounds, about five more than Wilbur. Each of them had grayish-blue eyes and they might have been recognized as brothers, though in their own family Wilbur at that time was considered "more of a Wright" in his facial conformation. Orville looked a little more like his mother. Both were suitably built for bird men. Plenty of annoyances, difficulties, and delays were still to be faced.

When they reached their camp near Kill Devil Hill, the Wrights found that a storm had blown it from its foundation posts. They repaired the shed and also built a new one. With two sheds they had enough space for housing both the 1902 glider and the power machine, and also for a better workshop. Just as the new building was nearing completion, the Kitty Hawk region had one of the worst storms in years. It came without warning, soon blowing forty miles an hour, and increased during the night until the next day the wind was more than seventy-five miles an hour. Orville risked climbing to the roof to nail down some of the more exposed parts. But by the time he got to the roof edge, the wind had blown his coat about him in a manner to pinion his arms and leave him helpless. Wilbur rushed to his assistance and held down his coat, but the wind was so strong that it was almost impossible to swing a hammer accurately enough to hit a nail. Three weeks were needed for assembling the new machine. From time to time, also, they took out the 1902 glider, still in fairly good condition in the shed where they had left it, and got practice. After the first few trials each brother was able to make a new world's record by gliding for more than a minute. It was hoped to have the power machine ready for its first trial early in November. But at the first run of the motor on the completed machine, an unexpected strain from backfiring twisted one of the propeller shafts and tore loose the cross-arm to which the propeller was fastened. Both shafts were then sent back to the bicycle shop at Dayton to be made stronger. Dr. Spratt had arrived on October 23 to witness tests of the new machine, but the weather had become so wintry that he started home on November 5, taking with him as far as Norfolk the shafts for shipment to Dayton. Octave Chanute came, on invitation, the next day, but he too found it difficult to be comfortable with the weather increasingly wintry and he stayed less than a week.

  Before leaving camp, Chanute had unintentionally given them something else to worry about. He had remarked that at least twenty percent usually must be allowed in chain transmission for loss in power. As the Wrights had allowed only five percent, they felt considerable alarm. Since Chanute was a capable and famous engineer, it seemed prudent to find out whose estimates were more nearly correct. After Chanute had gone, the brothers suspended one of the drive chains over a sprocket and hung a bag of sand at each end of the chain. By measuring the amount of weight on one side needed to lift that on the other, they calculated the loss in transmission. As nearly as they could tell, this loss was even less than the five percent they had estimated. The shafts, made of larger and heavier tubing, arrived from Dayton on November 20. When they were tested again, a new difficulty appeared. The sprockets, which were screwed to the shafts and locked with nuts of opposite thread, kept coming loose. This was a small problem, and yet the brothers did not at once see any way to solve it. They went to bed discouraged. The next day, however, they tried, as they often did, something they had learned in the bicycle business. They had found a great variety of uses for the kind of cement intended for fastening tires to rims. Once they had used it successfully in fastening the hands of a stopwatch that several watchsmiths had said was beyond repair. Why not try tire cement on those sprockets? They heated the propeller shafts and sprockets, poured melted cement into the threads and screwed them together. There were no more loose sprockets. Just as the machine was ready for test—bad weather set in. There was rain or snow for several days and a wind of twenty-five to thirty miles an hour from the north. But while being delayed by the weather the Wrights were not idle. They busied themselves contriving a mechanism to measure automatically the duration of a flight from the time the machine started to move forward to the time it stopped, the distance traveled through the air in that time, and the number of revolutions made by the motor and propeller.

A stopwatch took the time, an anemometer measured the air traveled through, and a counter took the number of revolutions made by the motor. The watch, anemometer, and revolution counter were all automatically started and stopped simultaneously. During this time, the Wrights occupied themselves also in making tests of the strength of the wings, as well as many satisfactory tests of the engine. During a test of the engine, on November 28, they discovered that one of the recently strengthened tubular shafts had developed a flaw and cracked.

With winter almost upon them, there was no time to trust to express service in getting the shafts to Dayton. Orville decided he would go there at once. Instead of tubular shafts, they would use solid tool steel, necessary, it seemed, to take up the shock of premature or missed explosions of the engine. Not until Friday, December 11, did Orville get back to camp. [En route, he had read in a newspaper of the last unsuccessful attempt to fly the Langley machine over the Potomac at Washington.] It didn't take long to install the new propeller shafts and the next afternoon, Saturday, the machine was again ready for trial. But the wind was so light that a start could not have been made from the level ground with a run of only sixty feet permitted by the monorail track to be used. Nor was there enough time before dark to take the machine to one of the nearby hills, where, by placing the track on the steep incline, enough speed could be promptly attained for starting in calm air. All day Sunday the Wrights just sat at the camp and read, hoping for suitable weather the next day.

They were now particularly eager to avoid delay because of their boyish craving to be at home by Christmas. If there should be a spell of bad wintry weather they might have to stay at Kitty Hawk for another two, or three weeks. Monday, December 14, dawned beautifully clear, but cold, and there was not enough wind to permit a start from level ground near the camp. The Wrights therefore decided to attempt a flight from the side of Kill Devil Hill. With a relatively light wind it should be all the easier to handle the machine. The pilot, whichever one of them it should be, ought to be able not only to fly successfully but to go on down far beyond the Kitty Hawk Life-Saving Station, nearly five miles away, before contrary to reports of secretiveness, the Wrights, naturally desiring witnesses, had extended a general invitation to people living within five or six miles to come and see their first attempt at flight. But it was impossible for them to send word or give a signal as to the exact time the attempt would be made. They had arranged, however, to put a signal on one of the sheds that could be seen from the Kill Devil Life-Saving Station only a little more than a mile away. Members of the life saving crew were on the lookout for the signal. Soon after the signal was hung against the wall of the shed, the Wrights were joined by John T. Daniels, Robert Westcott, Thomas Beacham, William S. Dough, and "Uncle Benny" O'Neal. All helped to get the machine to the place selected, a quarter of a mile away, on the hillside. It would not have been easy to drag the 750 pound machine that distance and the Wrights used a characteristic bit of ingenuity. They set the machine on the monorail track they were going to use for the takeoff, slid it along to the end of the sixty-foot wooden rail, then took up a rear section of the track and added it to the front end. By thus re-laying the track over and over, they were able to have the machine run on wheels all the way. The sled-like skids that were the landing gear of the machine rested on a truck—a plank about six feet long, laid across a much smaller piece of wood to which were attached two small wheels, one in front of the other. Each was kept on the track by two vertical guides. These little wheels had ball bearings. They were modified hubs from wheels of a bicycle. The rail itself was two by four inches, set on edge, with the upper surface covered by a thin strip of metal. As soon as they reached the hill, the Wrights prepared for the test.

Each was eager for the chance to make the first trial, and they tossed a coin to determine which of them it should be. Wilbur won the toss. After the machine had been fastened to the track by wire to prevent its moving until released by the operator, one of the Wrights started the motor and let it run for a few minutes to make sure it was working properly. Then Wilbur took his place on the machine. Two small boys, with a dog, who had come to see what was going on, were scared away by the noise of the motor. Here is Orville Wright's own account of what then happened, "*I took a position at one of the wings, intending to help balance the machine as it ran down the track. But when the restraining wire was slipped, the machine started off so quickly I could stay with it only a few feet. After a 35 to 40 foot run, it lifted from the rail. But it was allowed to turn up too much. It climbed a few feet, stalled, and then settled to the ground near the foot of the hill, 105 feet below. My stopwatch showed that it had been in the air just 3½ seconds. In landing, the left wing touched first. The machine swung around, dug the skids into the sand and broke one of them. Several other parts were also broken, but the damage to the machine was not serious. While the tests had shown nothing as* to whether the power of the motor was sufficient to keep the machine up, since the landing was made many feet below the starting point, the experiment had demonstrated that the method adopted for launching the machine was a safe and practical one. On the whole, we were much pleased. Two days were consumed in making repairs, and the machine was not ready again till late in the afternoon of the 16th. While we had it out on the track in front of the building, making the final adjustments, a stranger came along. After looking at the machine a few seconds he inquired what it was. When we told him it was a flying machine he asked whether we intended to fly it. We said we did, as soon as we had a suitable wind. He looked at it several minutes longer and then, wishing to be courteous, remarked that it looked as if it would fly, if it had a 'suitable wind.' We were much amused, for, no doubt, he had in mind the recent 75-mile gale when he repeated our words, 'a suitable wind.' During the night of December 16th a strong cold wind blew from the north. When we arose on the morning of the 17th, the puddles of water, which had been standing about the camp since the recent rains, were covered with ice. The wind had a velocity of 10 to 12 meters per second (22 to 27 miles an hour). We thought it would die down before long, and so remained indoors the early part of the morning. But when ten o'clock arrived, and the wind was as brisk as ever, we decided that we had better get the machine out and attempt a flight. We hung out the signal for the men of the Life-Saving Station. We thought that by facing the flyer into a strong wind, there ought to be no trouble in launching it from the level ground about camp. We realized the difficulties of flying in so high a wind, but estimated that the added dangers in flight would be partly compensated for by the slower speed in landing. We laid the track on a smooth stretch of ground about one hundred feet west of the new building. The biting cold wind made work difficult, and we had to warm up frequently in our living room, where we had a good fire in an improvised stove made of a large carbide can. By the time all was ready, J. T. Daniels, W. S. Dough and A. D. Etheridge, members of the Kill Devil Life-Saving Station, W. C. Brinkley of Manteo, and Johnny Moore, a boy from Nags

Head, had arrived. We had a 'Richard' hand anemometer with which we measured the velocity of the wind. Measurements made just before starting the first flight showed velocities of 11 to 12 meters per second, or 24 to 27 miles per hour. Measurements made just before the last flight gave between 9 and 10 meters per second. One made just afterward showed a little over 8 meters. The records of the Government Weather Bureau at Kitty Hawk gave the velocity of the wind between the hours of 10:30 and 12 o'clock, the time during which the four flights were made, as averaging 27 miles at the time of the first flight and 24 miles at the time of the last. With all the knowledge and skill acquired in thousands of flights in the last ten years, I would hardly think today of making my first flight on a strange machine in a twenty-seven-mile wind, even if I knew that the machine had already been flown and was safe. After these years of experience, I look with amazement upon our audacity in attempting flights with a new and untried machine under such circumstances. Yet faith in our calculations and the design of the first machine, based upon our tables of air pressures, obtained by months of careful laboratory work, and confidence in our system of control developed by three years of actual experiences in balancing gliders in the air, had convinced us that the machine was capable of lifting and maintaining itself in the air, and that, with a little practice, it could be safely flown. Wilbur having used his turn in the unsuccessful attempt on the 14th, the right to the first trial now belonged to me. After running the motor a few minutes to heat it up, I released the wire that held the machine to the track, and the machine started forward into the wind. Wilbur ran at the side of the machine, holding the wing to balance it on the track. Unlike the start on the 14th made in a calm—the machine—facing a 27-mile wind, started very slowly. Wilbur was able to stay with it till it lifted from the track after a forty-foot run. One of the [Kill Devil Hills] Life-Saving [Station] men snapped the camera for us, taking a picture just as the machine had reached the end of the track and had risen to a height of about two feet. The slow forward speed of the machine over the ground is clearly shown in the picture by Wilbur's attitude. He stayed along beside the machine without any effort. The course of the flight up and down was exceedingly erratic, partly due to the irregularity of the air and partly to lack of experience in handling this machine. The control of the front rudder was difficult on account of its being balanced too near the center. This gave it a tendency to turn itself when started, so that it turned too far on one side and then too far on the other. As a result, the machine would rise suddenly to about ten feet, and then as suddenly dart for the ground. A sudden dart when a little over a hundred feet from the end of the track, or a little over 120 feet from the point at which it rose into the air, ended the flight. As the velocity of the wind was over 35 feet per second and the speed of the machine over the ground against this wind ten feet per second, the speed of the machine relative to the air was over 45 feet per second, and the length of the flight was equivalent to a flight of 540 feet made in calm air. This flight lasted only 12 seconds, but it was nevertheless the first in the history of the world in which a machine carrying a man had raised itself by its own power into the air in full flight, had sailed forward without reduction of speed, and had finally landed at a point as high as that from which it started. With the assistance of our visitors we carried the machine back to the track and prepared for another flight. The wind, however, had chilled us all through, so that before attempting a second flight, we all went to the building again to warm up. Johnny Moore, seeing under the table a box filled with eggs, asked one of the Station men where we got so many of them. The people of the neighborhood eke out a bare existence by catching fish during the short fishing season, and their supplies of other articles of food are limited. He probably never had seen so many eggs at one time in his whole life. The one addressed jokingly asked him whether he hadn't noticed the small hen running about the outside of the building. 'That chicken lays eight to ten eggs a day!' Moore, having just seen a piece of machinery lift itself from the ground and fly, a thing at that time considered as impossible as perpetual motion, was ready to believe nearly anything. But after going out and having a good look at the wonderful fowl, he returned with the remark, 'It's only a common-looking chicken!' At twenty minutes after eleven Wilbur started on the second flight. The course of this flight was much like that of the first, very much up and down. The speed over the ground was somewhat faster than that of the first flight, due to the lesser wind. The duration of the flight was less than a second longer than the first, but the distance covered was about seventy-five feet greater. Twenty minutes later, the third flight started. This one was steadier than the first one an hour before. I was proceeding along pretty well when a sudden gust from the right lifted the machine up twelve to fifteen feet and turned it up sidewise in an alarming manner. It began a lively sidling off to the left. I warped the wings to try to recover the lateral balance and at the same time pointed the machine down to reach the ground as quickly as possible. The lateral control was more effective than I had imagined and before I reached the ground the right wing was lower than the left and struck first. The time of this flight was fifteen seconds and the distance over the ground a little over 200 feet. Wilbur started the fourth and last flight at just 12 o'clock. The first few hundred feet were up and down, as before, but by the time three hundred feet had been covered, the machine was under much better control. The course for the next four or five hundred feet had but little undulation. However, when out about eight hundred feet the machine began pitching again, and, in one of its darts downward, struck the ground. The distance over the ground was measured and found to be 852 feet, the time of the flight 59 seconds. The frame supporting the front rudder was badly broken, but the main part of the machine was not injured at all. We estimated that the machine could be put in condition for flight again in a day or two. While we were standing about discussing this last flight, a sudden strong gust of wind struck the machine and began to turn it over. Everybody made a rush for it. Wilbur, who was at one end, seized it in front. Mr. Daniels and I, who were behind, tried to stop it by holding to the rear uprights. All our efforts were in vain. The machine rolled over and over. Daniels, who had retained his grip, was carried along with it, and was thrown about, head over heels, inside of the machine. Fortunately he was not seriously injured, though badly bruised in falling about against the motor, chain guides, etc. The ribs in the surfaces of the machine were broken, the motor injured and the chain guides badly bent, so that all possibility of further flights with it for that year were at an end." It is unlikely that any of the five spectators who had seen these flights sensed their scientific importance. But some of them felt interested, from one point of view, because they would have the laugh on a number of natives thereabouts who had insisted that these Wright brothers must be a pair of harmless cranks. A common argument had been, "*God didn't intend man to fly. If he did, he would have given him a set of wings.*" It was the regret of his life to the Wrights's friend, "Bill" Tate, that he missed witnessing that first flight. He had decided that "*no one but a crazy man would attempt to fly in such a wind,*" and made no effort to be there. After preparing and eating their lunch, and then washing their dishes, Wilbur and Orville set out, about two o'clock that afternoon, to walk over to the Kitty Hawk Weather Station, four or five miles away, to send a telegram to their father. It must have been about three o'clock when they reached the station. So few telegrams were sent from this locality that no regular commercial office existed and it was permitted to send them over this government wire as far as Norfolk where they would be relayed by phone from the weather bureau to the office of one of the telegraph companies. Orville wrote out the following message to their father, "*Success four flights Thursday morning all against twenty-one-mile wind started from level with engine power alone average speed through air thirty-one miles longest 59 seconds, inform press, home Christmas. Orville Wright.*" What Orville meant when he wrote "against twenty-one mile wind" was that the wind was at least twenty-one miles an hour during each of the flights. At the time of the first flight it was, as already noted, between twenty-four and twenty-seven miles an hour—probably about twenty-six miles. After handing the message to Joseph J. Dosher, the weather bureau operator, Orville joined Wilbur over in a corner of the room to examine the record on an instrument that recorded the wind velocity.

Dosher got an almost instantaneous connection with Norfolk, and while the Wrights were still looking at the wind record, he said, "*The operator in Norfolk wants to know if it is all right to give the news to a reporter friend.*" But the Wrights replied, "*Absolutely no!*" They preferred to have the first news of the event come from Dayton. Dosher clicked out the refusal. The operator at Norfolk, however, did not heed the warning. When they left the weather bureau after sending their message, the Wrights went over to the Kitty Hawk Life-Saving Station, a few steps away, and chatted with members of the crew there. Captain S. J. Payne, in charge of the station, declared that he had seen one of the flights with the aid of a pair of binoculars. Then the Wrights walked to the post office at Kitty Hawk, and before returning to camp they stopped for a farewell visit at the home of Captain James Hobbs, who had often done hauling and other work for them. Meanwhile, the telegraph operator at Norfolk, disregarding the Wrights's adverse response to his request, had promptly gone ahead and given a tip about the flights to a young friend, H. P. Moore, of the Norfolk *Virginian-Pilot*. Moore was connected with the circulation department of the paper but was breaking in as a reporter and was in the habit of calling at the weather bureau. He made a desperate effort to reach by telephone over the government line someone at Kitty Hawk or elsewhere along the coast who could furnish details about what the flying machine looked like, and about this Mr. Wright who was supposed to have operated it. Whatever information he got did not come from eyewitnesses of the flights, or from anyone who had ever seen the machine, and the account published the next morning was about ninety-nine percent inaccurate. It described a flight of *three miles* by Wilbur and told of Orville then running about yelling "Eureka." The machine had one six-blade propeller beneath it, to elevate it, so the story ran, and another propeller at the rear to shove it forward. "*Very little can be learned here about the Wrights,*" the story said. "*They are supposed by the natives of Kitty Hawk to be people of means and are always well dressed.*" [When Moore met Orville, years later, and asked him what he thought of the account, Orville good-naturedly replied, "*It was an amazing piece of work. Though ninety-nine percent wrong, it did contain one fact that was correct. *There* had *been a flight.*" Then Moore wrote that Orville had corroborated his story.] One must give the *Virginian-Pilot* editors credit for treating the news as important. The headline over the flight story the next morning extended clear across the top of the first page. Moore sent brief "queries" outlining the story, to twenty-one other newspapers over the country, including several in Ohio, one of them the Dayton *Journal*. But nearly all the telegraph editors resented having a correspondent suggest that a human being could fly by machinery. Of the twenty-one newspapers to whom it was offered, only five ordered the story [for print]. They were the New York *American*, the Washington DC *Post*, the Chicago *Record-Herald*, the Philadelphia *Record*, and the Cincinnati *Enquirer*. But not all five papers that received the story published it the next morning. The Chicago *Record-Herald* and the Washington *Post* delayed using it, and the Philadelphia *Record* did not print it at all. Thus only three newspapers in the United States had a report of the great event at Kitty Hawk the next morning. The Cincinnati *Enquirer* was the only one besides the *Virginian-Pilot* that gave space to the account on the front page. As the *Associated Press* is a cooperative news gathering agency and the *Virginian-Pilot* was a member, the story was available to the *AP* at Norfolk, but the *AP* was not yet interested in it.

One might have thought the news would especially interest the Dayton *Journal* but Frank Tunison, the telegraph editor there (who also handled outgoing news for the *Associated Press*) was a man who took pride in not being easily fooled, and he paid no attention to the query from Norfolk. Orville's telegram to his father did not reach Dayton until 5:25 that evening. In transmission, errors had got into the message, fifty-nine seconds had become fifty-seven, and the sender's name was spelled "Orevelle." Katharine Wright immediately sent a message to Octave Chanute that the "boys" had reported four successful flights. Bishop Wright asked his son Lorin to prepare a brief statement with a copy of the message and give it to the *Associated Press*. After he had finished his dinner, Lorin went to the office of the *Journal* and inquired if the *Associated Press* representative was there. He was referred to Frank Tunison. Whether Tunison had already received the query from Moore at Norfolk is not certain. But he seemed annoyed over being expected to accept such a tale. Without looking up from his work, he yawned and said to Lorin, "*Fifty-seven seconds, hey? If it had been fifty-seven minutes then it might have been a news item.*"

Nothing about the Wrights's feat appeared in the Dayton *Journal* the next morning. But news considered important enough to be displayed on the first page of that same issue included items about a routine weekly meeting of the local united trades and labor council, a colored man named Charles Brown, who admitted pocketbook thefts, the pardoning of a robber from Joliet prison, in Illinois. On the page opposite the editorial page, the biggest, blackest headline was, "*Stores are Filled with Christmas Shoppers.*" Dayton afternoon papers on that December 18 did print accounts of the receipt of the telegram by Bishop Wright, as well as other "facts" about the flight. The Dayton *Herald* article appeared to be a rehash of the dispatch from Norfolk in the Cincinnati *Enquirer*. Over the article in the Dayton *Daily News*, on an inside page, alongside of so-called "country correspondence" from nearby towns, the heading was, "Dayton Boys Emulate Great Santos-Dumont." Santos-Dumont had flown in an airship, and now the Wrights had flown in something or other. Therefore the Wrights must be imitators of Alberto Santos-Dumont! Lacking scientific knowledge, the editors failed to distinguish between a flying machine, heavier-than-air, and an airship consisting of a gas bag equipped with a propeller.

Indeed, from then on, nearly all who had heard of the reported flights, editors included, were in one or the other of two groups of disbelievers, (1) those who refused to believe the flights had taken place at all, and (2) those who thought that even if they had been made they were not of great importance. The *Associated Press*, that had declined to accept news of the flights at either Norfolk or Dayton the day before, now sent out for afternoon papers on December 18, a brief report, less than 350 words, from Norfolk. This appeared to be simply a condensation of the article in the *Virginian-Pilot* that morning and contained most of the same inaccuracies. Not more than two or three sentences in the *AP* dispatch were correct. "*The machine flew for three miles,*" the report said, "*and gracefully descended to the earth at the spot selected by the man in the navigator's car as a suitable landing place. Preparatory to its flight the machine was placed upon a platform—on a high sand hill and when all was in readiness the fastenings to the machine were released and it started down an incline. The navigator, Wilbur Wright, then started a small gasoline engine which worked the propellers. When the end of the incline was reached the machine gradually arose until it obtained an altitude of 60 feet. In the center is the navigator's car and suspended just below the bottom plane is a small gasoline engine, which furnishes the motive power for the propelling and elevating wheels. There are two 6-blade propellers,*" the dispatch said, "*one arranged just below the frame so as to exert an upward force when in motion and the other extends horizontally from the rear to the center of the car furnishing forward impetus. Protruding from the center of the car is a huge fan-shaped rudder of canvas, stretched upon a frame of wood. This rudder is controlled by the navigator and may be moved to each side, raised or lowered.*"

Not all the *Associated Press* papers printed the brief dispatch in full—in fact, many did not use it at all. With the first reports "confirmed" by the *Associated Press*, two papers, the Washington *Post* and Chicago *Record-Herald*, that had withheld the story bought from Mr. Moore at Norfolk, finally printed the Moore dispatch on the morning of December 19. The Washington *Post* even used it on the front page, but cautiously inserted qualifying phrases, saying "it is reported" that a flight was made. And the Chicago *Record-Herald* on December 20 had an editorial about the flights, or about "the" flight. But as the editorial restated many of the inaccuracies contained in the news report, it only added to the general misinformation. [A few newspaper editors are still touchy about the inadequate reporting of the Wrights's first flights. As recently as January 29, 1941, the

Chicago *Daily News* had an editorial of nearly half a column defending the merit of the hopelessly inaccurate *Associated Press* dispatch from Norfolk on December 18, 1903. And shortly afterward, on February 12, 1941, in connection with a letter from a reader who sought to give the historic facts, the *Daily News* editor, still unwilling to accept the truth, added a note insisting once again that there was "nothing fantastic" about that *AP* report from Norfolk.] At a meeting of the American Association for the Advancement of Science, in St. Louis, December 28 to January 2, Octave Chanute made an address on the subject of Aerial Navigation in which he referred to the Wrights's flights. But little was said about the Chanute speech in the newspapers. [Chanute used that address as the basis for an article in the March, 1904, issue of *Popular Science Monthly* in which he said, "*Now that an initial success has been achieved with a flying machine, we can discern some of the uses of such apparatus and also some of its limitations. Its first application will probably be military.*" He said, too, that "*it may even carry mails in special cases, but the useful loads carried will be very small. The machines will eventually be fast, they will be used in sport, but they are not to be thought of as commercial carriers.*" He did not think it would ever be practical to carry loads "*such as a store of explosives, or big guns to shoot them.*"] Almost as surprising as the lack of effort by the usually painstaking *Associated Press* to get the facts about the Kitty Hawk event, was the failure of the *Associated Press*, or any other press association, or any newspaper, to rush a staff man to Dayton in an effort to obtain the whole amazing story of what the Wrights had done. Desiring to correct the misinformation that had been printed, the Wrights prepared a statement about their recent flights, and gave this to the *Associated Press* with the request that it be published. This appeared, at least in part, in probably a majority of the *Associated Press* newspapers, on January 6, but the initiative, it should be noted, did not come from the press association, but from the Wrights themselves.

A few editorial "paragraphers" made derisive comments on one sentence of the statement which suggested that "*the day of flying had arrived.*" Exactly one month after the Kitty Hawk flights, on Sunday, January 17, the New York *Herald*, in its magazine section, had an article headed, "The Machine That Flies." Despite the time that had elapsed, affording opportunity to get the facts, this article not only contained a mass of preposterous misstatements but even quoted Wilbur Wright for many of them. The article was accompanied by a drawing, an artist's conception of the machine in flight, and a diagram, showing the two "six-bladed propellers," one behind the machine and the other beneath it, to give it elevation.

□□□□□□□□□□

The Wrights felt a glow of pride and satisfaction in having both invented and demonstrated the device that had baffled the ablest scientists through the centuries. But still they did not expect to make their fortunes. True, they had applied, on March 23, 1903, or nearly nine months before they flew, for basic patents (not issued until May 22, 1906), but that was by way of establishing an authentic record. Thus far they hadn't even employed a patent lawyer. Long afterward, Orville Wright was asked what he and Wilbur would have taken for all their secrets of aviation, for all patent rights *for the entire world*, if someone had come along to talk terms just after those first flights. He wasn't sure, but he had an idea that if they had received an offer of ten thousand dollars they might have accepted it. Since the airplane was not yet developed into a type for practical use, ten thousand dollars might have been considered a fair return for their time, effort, and outlay. They had, had all the fun and satisfaction and their expenses had been surprisingly small. Their cash outlay for building and flying their power plane was less than $1,000, and that included their railroad fares to and from Kitty Hawk.

Of course, the greater part of their expenses would have been for mechanical labor, much of which they did themselves. But skilled labor was low-priced at that time, one could hire a better than average mechanic for as little as $16 a week. Even if the Wrights had charged themselves with the cost of their own work, their total expenses on the power plane would still have been less than $2,000. Many fanciful stories have been told about the sacrifices the Wright family made to enable the brothers to fly, and of how they were financed by this person or that. More than one man of wealth in Dayton has encouraged the belief that *he* financed them. One persistent story is that they raised money for their experiments by the sale of an Iowa farm in which they had an interest. The truth is that this farm, which had been deeded by their father to the *four* Wright brothers, was sold early in 1902 before Wilbur and Orville had even begun work on their power plane or spent much on their experiments. The sale was made at the request of their brother Reuchlin, and had no relation whatsoever to aviation. Nor is it true that the Wright home was mortgaged during the time of the brothers's experiments.

Another story was that their sister Katharine had furnished the money they needed out of her salary as schoolteacher. Katharine Wright was always amused over that tale, for she was never a hoarder of money, nor a financier, and could hardly have provided funds even if this had been necessary. Any rumor that her brothers could have borrowed money from her, rather than lending money to her, as they sometimes did, was almost as funny to Katharine as another report—that her brothers had relied on her for mathematical assistance in their calculations. The simple fact is that no one ever financed the Wrights's work except Wilbur and Orville themselves. Their bicycle business had been giving them a decent income and at the end of the year 1903 they still had a few thousand dollars savings in a local building and loan association.

Whatever financial scrimping was necessary *came* after they had flown—after they knew they had made a great discovery. But the Wrights's belief that they had achieved something of great importance was not bolstered by the attitude of the general public. Not only were there no receptions, brass bands, or parades in their honor, but most people paid less attention to the history-making feat than if the "boys" had simply been on vacation and caught a big fish, or shot a bear. Before the flights some of the neighbors had been puzzled by reports that the Wrights were working on a flying machine. One man in business near the Wright shop had become acquainted with an inventor who thought he was about to perfect a perpetual motion machine, and this businessman promptly sent the inventor to the Wrights, assuming that he would find them kindred spirits. John G. Feight, living next door to the Wright home, had remarked, just before the brothers went to Kitty Hawk, "*Flying and perpetual motion will come at the same time.*" Now that flights had been made, neighbors didn't doubt the truth of the reports—though one of them had his own explanation. Mr. Webbert, father of the man from whom the Wrights rented their shop, said, "*I have known those boys ever since they were small children, and if they say they flew I know they did, but I think there must be special conditions down in North Carolina that would enable them to fly by the power of a motor. There is only one thing that could lift a machine like that in this part of the country—spirit power.*" Webbert was a spiritualist. He had *seen* tables and pianos lifted at seances. But even if the boys *had* flown—what of it?

Men were flying in Europe, weren't they? Hadn't [Alberto] Santos-Dumont flown some kind of self-propelled balloon? The one person who had almost unbounded enthusiasm for what the brothers had accomplished was their father. They found it difficult to keep a complete file of the photographs they had made showing different phases of their experiments, because the moment their father's eye fell on one of these pictures he would pick it up and mail it to some relative along with a letter telling with pride what the boys had done. Two brothers in Boston sensed, however, that, if the scant reports about the Kitty Hawk event were based on truth, then something of great significance had happened. These men were Samuel and Godfrey Lowell Cabot, wealthy and influential members of a famous family.

Both of them, particularly Samuel, had long been interested in whatever progress was being made in aeronautics. On December 19, the day after the first news of the flights was published—Samuel Cabot sent to the Wrights a telegram of congratulations. Two days later, his brother Godfrey wrote them a letter. In that letter Godfrey Cabot wanted to know if they thought their machine could be used for carrying freight. He was financially interested in an industrial operation in West Virginia, he said, where conditions would justify a rate of $10 a ton for transporting goods by air only sixteen miles. One reason why nearly everyone in the United States was disinclined to swallow the reports about flying with a machine heavier than air was that important scientists had already explained in the public prints why the thing was impossible. When a man of the profound scientific wisdom of Simon Newcomb, for example, had demonstrated with unassailable logic why man couldn't fly, why should the public be fooled by silly stories about two obscure bicycle repairmen who hadn't even been to college?

Professor Newcomb was so distinguished an astronomer that he was the only American since Benjamin Franklin to be made an associate of the Institute of France. It was widely assumed that what he didn't know about laws of physics simply wasn't in books, and that when he said flying couldn't be done, there was no need to inquire any further. More than once Professor Newcomb had written that flight without gas bags would require the discovery of some new metal or a new unsuspected force in nature. Then, in an article in the *Independent*—October 22, 1903—while the Wrights were at Kitty Hawk assembling their power machine—he not only proved that trying to fly was nonsense, but went further and showed that even if a man did fly, he wouldn't dare to stop. "*Once he slackens his speed, down he begins to fall. Once he stops, he falls [in] a dead mass. How shall he reach the ground without destroying his delicate machinery? I do not think that even the most imaginative inventor has yet put on paper a demonstrative, successful way of meeting this difficulty.*" In all his statements, Professor Newcomb had the support of other eminent authorities, including Rear Admiral George W. Melville, then chief engineer for the United States Navy, who, a year or two previously, in the *North American Review*, had set forth convincingly the absurdity of attempts to fly. The most recent Newcomb article was all the more impressive as a forecast from the fact that it appeared only fifteen days after one of Professor [Samuel Pierpont] Langley's unsuccessful attempts at flight. That is, Langley's attempt seemed to show that flight was beyond human possibility, and then Newcomb's article explained why it was impossible.

Though these pooh-poohing statements by Newcomb and other scientists were probably read by relatively few people, they were seen by editors, editorial writers, and others who could have much influence on public opinion. Naturally, no editor who "knew" a thing couldn't be done would permit his paper to record the fact that it had been done. Oddly enough, one of the first public announcements by word of mouth about the Wrights's Kitty Hawk flights was in a Sunday school. A. I. Root, founder of a still prosperous business for the sale of honey and beekeepers supplies at Medina, Ohio, taught a Sunday school class.

One morning shortly before the dismissal bell, observing that the boys in the class were restless, he sought to restore order by catching their interest. Perhaps he wished to show, too, that miracles as wonderful as any in the Bible were still possible. "*Do you know, friends,*" he said, "*that two Ohio boys, or young men rather, have outstripped the world in demonstrating that a flying machine can be constructed without the aid of a balloon?*" He had read a brief item about the Wrights in an Akron paper. The class became attentive and Root went on, "*During the past two months these two boys have made a machine that actually flew through the air for more than half a mile, carrying one of the boys with it. This young man is not only a credit to our state but to the whole country and to the world.*" Though this was several weeks after the Wrights had first flown, no one in the class had ever heard about it, and incredulously they fired questions at the teacher. "*Where do the boys live? What are their names? When and where did their machine fly?*" Root described, not too accurately, the Kitty Hawk flights, and added, "*When they make their next trial I am going to try to be on hand to see the experiment.*" An important part of Root's business was publication of the still widely circulated magazine, *Gleanings in Bee Culture*, and in his issue of March 1, 1904, he told of the episode in the Sunday school. By printing that story, the Medina bee man may possibly have been the first editor of a scientific publication in the United States to report that man could fly. [*Popular Science Monthly* in its issue of March, 1904, had an article by Octave Chanute in which the flights were mentioned.] Root a little later even predicted, "*Possibly we may be able to fly over the North Pole.*" The Wrights were more amused than disturbed by the lack of general recognition that flying was now possible. They inwardly chuckled when they heard people still using the old expression, "*Why, a person could no more do that than he could fly!*" But they knew they had only begun to learn about handling a flying machine.

❏❏❏❏❏❏❏❏❏❏

In all their work on their power plane the Wrights's main incentive had been to gain the distinction of being the first of mankind to fly. They had not designed the machine for practical use. Now, however, even though they did not yet foresee many of the uses for which the airplane was destined, they began to think it could be developed into a machine useful for scouting in warfare, for carrying mail to isolated places, for exploration, and that it would appeal to those who could afford it for sport. If their machine was capable, as they had demonstrated, of flying by its own power for 852 feet against a 20 mile wind, there was no reason why it shouldn't go many times that far. But if the machine was to be practical, many improvements would be necessary, and they would need more experience in flying. Much practice would be required, and that would mean more expense in proportion to income, for they would have less time for building and repairing bicycles. But they decided to devote to aviation whatever amount of time seemed necessary. A number of bicycles at their shop were in various stages of completion. But no new ones were started after the Wrights's return from Kitty Hawk—though some of those on hand were completed and sold. The brothers now began to turn over to Charlie Taylor, their chief mechanic, most of the routine work of the shop. In January, 1904, the brothers began building a new plane. It was similar to the one flown at Kitty Hawk, but there were a number of changes, including more sturdy construction throughout. The weight exceeded that of the original plane by about eighty pounds. [In flight, the weight, including the pilot, and 70 pounds of iron bars carried on the framework under the front elevator, was 900 pounds.] The wing camber was changed from 1-20 to 1-25—that is, the curvature was decreased, and the ribs were tapered from front to rear spar instead of being of uniform depth, as in the earlier model. An entirely new engine went into the 1904 machine. In fact, the Wrights started to build three new engines. One of these had four cylinders of $4\frac{1}{8}$ inch bore, another, four cylinders of only 4 inch bore, as the one used at Kitty Hawk, and the third was a V-type, of eight cylinders. The $4\frac{1}{8}$ inch bore was the one installed in the 1904 plane and gave a satisfactory amount of power—but not so much as the Wrights later developed in the other four-cylinder motor of only four-inch bore. That motor they kept in their shop and used for a kind of guinea pig, trying various improvements and refinements until it produced as much power as they had expected from the V-type motor of eight cylinders and twice as much as the original motor used at Kitty Hawk. They then gave up the idea of completing the V-type motor. Another change in the 1904 machine was using white pine instead of spruce for the front and rear spars in the wings. Spruce was not available in Dayton at that time, and tests the Wrights made at their shop, in the manner usually employed for ascertaining the strength of woods, indicated that the two woods were about equally strong. [But in actual use, when stresses came suddenly, as in landing, the white pine spars snapped "like taffy under a hammer blow," though spruce had always withstood such shocks. The brothers rebuilt the wings, with all spars of spruce.] To obtain practice, their first need was a suitable field, not too far from home. They found a cow pasture, fairly level, handy to an Interurban railway, at Simms Station, eight miles from Dayton, toward Springfield. This field, often called the Huffman Prairie, was part of a farm belonging to a Dayton bank president, Torrence Huffman. Compared with a modern flying field the area of sixty-eight acres they wanted to use was not quite ideal. It contained a number of trees, besides being near power wires and poles. But it was as good as they could find and without delay the Wrights introduced themselves to Mr. Huffman to ask if they might rent his pasture for their experiments. He granted the request and told them they were welcome to use the field free of charge. But he said he hoped they would drive his cows to a safe place and not run over them. By April 15, 1904, the Wrights had built a rough wooden shed at the Huffman Pasture, in preparation for their experiments.

Even if they had tried, the Wrights could hardly have kept secret what they were doing here at the Huffman Prairie, with an Interurban car line and two highways passing the field they were using. But they took special precautions against being thought secretive, for they knew that the best way to avoid being bothered by newspaper people or others was to make no mystery of what they were doing. Before they had attempted even one trial flight at the Huffman Pasture they wrote letters to each of the Dayton papers, as well as to each of the Cincinnati papers, that on May 23 they would attempt to fly and would be glad to have any newspaper representative who felt interested come and watch them. Their only request was that no pictures be taken, and that the reports should not be sensational. This latter stipulation was to avoid attracting crowds, but as it turned out there was no need to be concerned about curiosity seekers.

About a dozen newspapermen showed up. Also on hand were a number of friends and neighbors of the Wright family. Altogether perhaps thirty-five persons were present—all by invitation. The Wrights dragged their machine out of the shed to wait for a suitable wind before launching the machine from the short stretch of wooden track. As it happened, the wind was unusually high that day, about twenty-five miles an hour—and the Wrights said they would wait for it to die down a little. When the high wind did cease, it went suddenly to an almost complete calm, and a wind of at least eleven miles an hour was needed to take off from so short a track. The Wrights said they would try a flight if the wind picked up. But the wind failed to do so. The crowd waited and two or three of the reporters—too experienced to be easily fooled—began to make comments to one another. They hadn't wanted to come in the first place. Why had they been asked to waste time on such an assignment? Most of the guests, though, had only sympathy for the brothers. They actually seemed sincere in thinking they *could* fly. Though sorry to disappoint the spectators, the Wrights showed no signs of embarrassment. They had learned to take events as they came. Finally, after the day had dragged on with no sign of a more favorable wind, one of the brothers announced, "*We can't fly today, but since you've taken the trouble to come and wait so long, we'll let the machine skim along the track and you'll get an idea of what it's supposed to do. With so short a track, we may not get off the ground, but you'll see how it operates.*" Then the engine misbehaved. It worked all right in the warming-up period, but began to skip explosions as soon as the machine started down the track. This was caused, the Wrights soon learned, by the flow of air over the mouth of the intake pipe—a trouble never experienced with the engine used at Kitty Hawk. After running the length of the track, the machine slid off the end without rising into the air at all. That wasn't much of a story for the reporters.

  Their assumption that they had been sent on a wild goose chase seemed to be confirmed. Would there be a flight the next day? The Wrights couldn't be sure. First of all they must find out what ailed that engine. They might be able to do that overnight, or it might take longer. However, all who wished to return the next day would be welcome. Indeed, the Wrights said, any newspaper representative would be welcome at *any* time. Two or three of the newspapermen did return the next day. The engine still sulked, but the wind was a bit more favorable and the Wrights decided to show the reporters what they could. This time the machine rose five or six feet from the ground and went through the air for nearly sixty feet before it came down. An electric contact point in one of the engine cylinders had worked loose, and only three cylinders were hitting. The few reporters present, though now convinced that the age of flying had not yet come, wrote friendly articles and made the most of what they had seen. The versions differed widely. One report had the machine rising to a height of seventy-five feet. In the Cincinnati *Enquirer* account was a comment that the machine "*is more substantially constructed than other machines of its kind.*" None of those newspapermen ever returned. During all their experiments that year and the next, the Wrights had about all the privacy they needed. They used to smile over a comment by Octave Chanute, "*It is a marvel to me that the newspapers haven't spotted you.*" Having disposed of the reporters, the inventors resumed their work. Almost as soon as the new trials began, the brothers encountered a new difficulty. A track 60 feet long had been adequate for launching the machine in the wind at Kitty Hawk, but a track of 160 feet, or even one of 240 feet, was not long enough for use at Huffman Field where the winds were usually light. The Huffman Field was covered with hummocks from six inches to a foot high. Only a few spots free from hummocks were suitable for a 240 foot track. And landing wheels, such as were used later, would have been impractical on that uneven ground.

Laying 240 feet of track, after finding enough ground space free from hummocks, was a considerable job. But frequently, after the track was laid, the wind would change its direction, and then all the work had to be done over. After a few times, the brothers gave up trying to use so long a track, and ordinarily used one of only 160 feet. As steady winds of eleven miles an hour, the least that would do for starting from a 160 foot track, were not frequent, the Wrights had to be in readiness to take advantage of occasional gusts of strong wind. With their machine on the track, they waited until they could "see" a flurry of wind coming—that is, until they could see weeds being agitated by the wind in the distance. Then they would start the motor and run the machine down the track to meet the wind gust when it reached the end of the rail. In that way they sometimes succeeded in making a start on a day generally calm. But one such start ended disastrously, and Orville, who was piloting the machine, had one of his narrowest escapes. When the machine first met the flurry of wind, it rose rapidly, but a second later it was on the ground with the wings pointing vertically into the air. It had dived at a steep angle, throwing Orville forward to the ground. The upper wing spar came down across the middle of his back. But luckily, a section about two feet wide, just wide enough to miss hitting him, was broken out. No other damage was done to the spar, and the Wrights could never account for the seemingly miraculous breakage that provided a space for safety over the very place where Orville lay on the ground. After that accident, Charlie Taylor, who had seen other narrow escapes, gloomily told the neighbors across the road that every time he saw one of the brothers's start on a flight he felt that he was seeing him alive for the last time. Early in July the Wrights made alterations in the machine which located the center of gravity farther toward the rear than it had been before. In the first trial after those alterations, the machine, after leaving the track, kept turning up more and more and looked as if it were going to loop the loop. The center of gravity was so far back that the front elevator, even when turned to its limit, could not check the upward turn. While pointing vertically upward, the machine came to a stop and then began to slide backward. By the time it reached the ground it was once more so nearly level that if the skids had, had a slight upward bend at their rear ends, the landing might have been made without damage. As it was, the rear ends of the skids dug into the ground, but the damage was slight. Before their experiments had progressed far in 1904 the Wrights saw that a better method of launching the machine was needed. They decided that a derrick with a falling weight would be the simplest and cheapest device. A 1,600 pound weight, falling a distance of 16½ feet, was so geared with ropes and pulleys that it produced a 350 pound pull on the machine through a distance of 49½ feet. By this arrangement the machine could be put into the air after a run of only 50 feet, even in a dead calm. Shifting the track was now seldom necessary. Up to the time the derrick catapult was ready for its first trial on September 7, less than forty starts had been made and many of them failed for lack of speed. But now the length of the flights increased rapidly. The shorter flights had been in almost a straight line, but as the lengths of the flights increased it was necessary to make turns to stay within the field. Then a new trouble—or rather an old one that supposedly had been overcome at Kitty Hawk—began to bother the Wrights. Often in making a short turn they suddenly found themselves in a tailspin which ended in a crash requiring days, or even weeks, for repairs. They soon learned what it was in making the turn that caused the tailspin, but they found it difficult to avoid, because they had no way of knowing at what angle the air was striking the machine. This led to the "invention" of the first instrument for guidance of a pilot in flying. They simply attached a short piece of string to the crossbar beneath the front elevator. When the machine traveled directly forward the string trailed straight backward, but when the machine slipped to either side the string blew to one side or the other and indicated approximately the amount of the side slip.

By close observance of this string it was possible to avoid entirely the danger of tailspins, but the pilot learning to fly had so many things to attend to, so it seemed to him, that he sometimes neglected to watch the string closely enough. After it was found that the derrick permitted the plane to be launched at any time, the Wrights often let the machine stand on the track during the day with the weights raised, ready to start at a moment's notice. One day in early November, while idly strolling in front of the track, Orville thought he saw a slight movement of the plane on the track. A more careful look did not confirm his first impression—nevertheless he turned and leisurely walked towards the plane. When within a few steps of it he saw that it actually *was* in motion. The wire that held it against the pull of the 1,600 pound weight was attached to a stake driven into the soft ground several feet. That stake was slowly coming out of the ground! By leaping upon one of the skids, Orville reached the elevator control lever in time to prevent the machine from rising as it rushed down the track. A strained shoulder was the principal damage, though the machine suffered a few slight breakages. Not until the 51st flight in 1904, when the machine stayed in the air one minute and one second, did the Wrights beat their best Kitty Hawk record of 59 seconds. The first complete circle was not made until September 20. But toward the end of the 1904 experiments, there were two five-minute flights. In each of these the machine circled the field four or five times without stopping. The total flying time during 1904 was only 45 minutes. But the knowledge and experience gained from that three quarters of an hour were of almost inestimable importance. Toward the end of May, 1905, the Wrights began assembling a machine all new with the exception of the motor and the propeller-driving mechanism. Strengthening of the structure at places where the previous machine had been too weak in making landings added about 25 pounds more weight. The principal changes, however, were in wing design, addition of some new features not in the earlier machines, and in making the wing-warping and operation of the tail rudder independent of each other. The camber of the wings was changed from 1-25, used in 1904, back to 1-20 as used in 1903 at Kitty Hawk. This change was to enable the machine to get off at a slower speed. The most radical change was the addition of two semicircular vanes, called "blinkers," between the two surfaces of the front elevator. This device was later patented by the Wrights. The purpose of the "blinkers" was to assist the rear rudder in overcoming the unequal resistances of the two wings when they were warped while making a turn. Gliding experiments in 1902 had shown that the pressure on a fixed vane in the rear of the wings tended to speed the higher wing when the machine slipped in the direction of the lower wing, and caused a tailspin. The vane had to be made movable to relieve this pressure.

It now occurred to the Wrights that if a fixed vane were placed in front of the wings, instead of behind them, its effect would be the reverse of that when the vane was in the rear, and that there would be less need of operating the rear rudder to overcome the unbalanced resistance of the two wings. Moreover, when the machine slipped inward while "banking" a turn, the speed of the low wing would be increased and a tailspin avoided. The operation of the rear rudder could now be made independent of the wing warp without danger. It was found that the "blinkers" entirely removed the danger of tail spinning but that they added to the difficulty of steering, both when flying straight and when making turns. Consequently they were not used in all the flights. [In modern planes the effect of the "blinkers" is gained by extending the fuselage far out in front of the wings.] Though tailspins could be avoided without use of "blinkers," by carefully observing the little piece of string that indicated side slip, yet they sometimes occurred. In one flight, in September, 1905, when the "blinkers" were not on the machine, Orville suddenly discovered he was in a tailspin and that he was about to come down in the top of a forty-foot thorn tree. The thorns were several inches long, and the idea of falling through them to the ground was not alluring. Orville quickly turned the machine into an almost vertical dive while turning in a circle 50 to 100 feet in diameter. The inner wing of the machine hit a branch of the tree, imbedding a thorn in an upright, and tore off the branch. In the dive, the higher wing, because of much greater speed, soon passed the lower wing in the downward plunge and itself became the low wing. The machine thus was in a steep bank with the high side toward the tree, just the opposite from what it had been before. When Orville turned the elevator to avoid striking the ground, the machine turned suddenly and unexpectedly away from the tree, because, in this steeply banked condition, the elevator exerted more pressure laterally than it did vertically. [When an aeroplane is banked to 45 degrees the elevator serves just as much for a rudder as for an elevator, and the rudder just as much for an elevator as for a rudder.] Though the machine lightly touched the ground, Orville flew it on back to the hangar, where the branch of the tree was found still clinging to the upright. It had been the practice of the Wrights to dive the machine to recover speed in a stall, but this quick recovery was from an entirely different cause—the great difference in the speeds of the two wings. An amusing flight by Orville in 1905 was made after some weeks of inactivity in flying and after the machine had undergone a number of changes since his last flight.

When the machine left the starting rail it began pitching like a bucking broncho. Orville wanted to stop, but at every plunge the plane came down so steeply he did not dare attempt a landing. As soon as he got control of the machine, after going three or four hundred feet, he did land safely. Wilbur rushed up to inquire why he had stopped just when he had really got going. Orville explained that he would have landed even sooner, but had taken the first opportunity to stop without smashing the machine to pieces. Though the rudder and wing-warp were entirely independent of each other in all the flights of 1905, the Wrights several years later resumed having the two controls interconnected, to operate together, but with an arrangement needed for modifying their relationship when making turns. Another change that improved control of the 1905 machine was in giving the wings considerably less angle at the tips than in the central part. By this arrangement, the tips stalled later than other parts of the wings and some lateral control remained even after the central part of the wings were in a stalled condition. After the Wrights had made the blades of their propellers much wider and thinner than the original ones, they discovered that the performance of the propellers in flight did not agree closely with their calculations, as in the earlier propellers. They could see only one reason for this, and that was that the propeller blades twisted from their normal shape under pressure in flight. To find out quickly if this was the real reason, they fastened to each blade a small surface, like an elevator, out behind the blades, set at an angle to balance the pressures that were distorting the blades. They called the surfaces "little jokers." When they found that the "little jokers" cured the trouble, they dispensed with them and began to give the blades a backward sweep, which served the same purpose. In the flying season of 1905, the control of the machine was much improved by increasing the area of the front rudder from 50 to 85 square feet, and by moving it to nearly twice the distance from the wings. This added distance made response to the movement of the rudder slower, and control of the machine much easier. The lateral control also was improved by enlarging the rear rudder from 20 to 34 square feet, and by moving it to a position three feet farther back of the wings.

On account of frequent rains, the soggy condition of the field, and other weather conditions, only nine attempts to fly were made in the first two months of experiments in 1905, and only three of these lasted for as much as ten seconds. But after the first of September progress was rapid. During all this time, the newspapers had continued to let the Wrights alone. Indeed, the failure of the newspapers in Dayton and elsewhere to say much about the history-making experiments at Huffman Field was often used as an argument to prove that there couldn't be any truth in the rumors that men had actually contrived a successful flying machine. "*You couldn't have kept a thing like that secret. Some reporter surely would have heard about it!*" Dan Kumler, who was city editor of James M. Cox's *Daily News*, in Dayton, during those early years of flying, recalled in 1940, not long before his death, that many people who had been on Interurban cars passing the Huffman Field and seen the Wrights in the air used to come to the *Daily News* office to inquire why there was nothing in the paper about the flights. "*Such callers,*" said Kumler, "*got to be a nuisance.*" "And why wasn't there anything in the paper?" Kumler was asked. "*We just didn't believe it,*" he said. "*Of course you remember that the Wrights at that time were terribly secretive.*" "You mean they were secretive about the fact that they were flying over an open field?" "*I guess,*" said Kumler, grinning, after a moment's reflection, "*the truth is that we were just plain dumb.*" James M. Cox, owner of the *Daily News*, has likewise confessed that "*none of us believed the reports*" of flights. One fact that kept the earlier flights relatively inconspicuous was that much of the time the plane was within 10 or 15 feet of the ground. Only occasionally was it up as high as 50 feet. There were no flights beyond the field itself, because if necessary to make a forced landing elsewhere, dragging the machine back to its shed might not have been easy. The Wrights had aimed at first to avoid being in the air when an Interurban car was passing. But that precaution soon proved to be unnecessary. Few people ever paid any attention to the flights. One day, though, the general manager of the Interurban [rail] line was on a passing car when the plane was in the air and he ordered the car stopped—he and the chief engineer of the line who was with him got off and stayed a while to look at the incredible sight.

Across the Springfield pike from the field lived the Beard family, tenants on the Torrence Huffman farm. Whenever the plane landed abruptly Mrs. Beard was likely to dash across the road with a bottle of arnica, feeling sure it would be needed, as sometimes it was. But there were few other visitors.

Two somewhat mysterious visitors did come, however. The Wrights saw two men wandering about nearby fields during most of one day and thought they must be hunters, though there was not much game thereabouts. Again the next day the two strangers were seen, and finally they came across the field to where the Wrights were adjusting their machine. One of them carried a camera. They asked if visitors were permitted.

"*Yes, only we'd rather you didn't take any pictures*," one of the brothers courteously replied. The man with the camera set it down off to one side—twenty feet away—as if to make it plain that he was not trying to sneak any shots. Then he inquired if it was all right to look into the shed. The brothers told him to make himself right at home. Was he a newspaperman? No, he said, he was not a newspaperman, though he sometimes did writing for publication. That was as near as he came to introducing himself. After the callers had gone, Charlie Taylor, the Wrights's mechanic, said, "*That fellow's no writer. At least he's no ordinary writer. When he looked at the different parts of the machine he called them all by their right names.*" Later the Wrights learned the identity of the visitor. Orville chanced to see a picture of him in a New York newspaper. His identity was confirmed some time afterward when he and Orville were formally introduced to each other—though neither referred to their previous meeting. The man had been chief engineer for Professor Langley of the Smithsonian Institution. Toward the end of September, the Wrights were able greatly to increase their distances. On September 26, there was an uninterrupted flight of 11⅛ miles in 18 minutes and 9 seconds, and on September 29, one of 12 miles in 19 minutes 55 seconds. Then, on October 3, there was a new record of 15¼ miles in 25 minutes 5 seconds, another, on October 4, of 20¾ miles in 33 minutes 17 seconds, and finally, on October 5, 24⅕ miles in 38 minutes 3 seconds. The flights of October 3 and 4 would have been longer except that certain bearings had become overheated. By October 5 the inventors had added more grease cups where needed and also installed a larger gas tank. But the tank was not full when that final test began and the flight ended because the fuel was exhausted. It was the intention of the Wrights to make one more test and put the record at more than an hour, but now for the first time the miracle of flight actually began to attract more spectators and the brothers decided it might be prudent to quit for the season before details of the machine's construction became public knowledge.

However, there was one more short flight—just one circle of the field—on October 16. After the close of the 1905 experiments, a test of the engine showed that it produced more power than when first put into use. This gain was attributed to the increased smoothness of the cylinders and pistons produced by wear. Looking back over their experiments, the Wrights noted that "*in 1903, 62 pounds per horsepower were carried at a speed of 30 miles an hour, in 1904, 53 pounds at 34 miles an hour, and in 1905, 46 pounds at 38 miles an hour.*" Thus the weight carried per horsepower was in inverse ratio to the speed—the smaller the weight carried per horsepower, the higher the speed.

That seems obvious enough now, but at the time the Wrights were making these experiments many scientists still accepted the "Langley Law," that the greater the speed, the less horsepower necessary. The Wrights now knew that the airplane would have practical use—though they did not foresee how safely trans-Atlantic flights would be made—and not even in their wildest dreams did they think of anyone ever flying at night.

☐☐☐☐☐☐☐☐☐☐

Though Dayton newspapermen had not besieged the Huffman Pasture for details of the great news story lurking there during 1904-1905, one of their number had occasionally been in contact with the Wrights. That was Luther Beard—no kin to the other Beards mentioned—managing editor of the Dayton *Journal*. Besides being a newspaper editor, Beard also taught school at Fairfield, about two miles from the Huffman Farm, and went back and forth by the Interurban car line that passed the field where the Wrights were making history. It sometimes happened that on the trip to Dayton he was on the same car with one or both of the Wright brothers, returning from their flights. "*I used to chat with them in a friendly way and was always polite to them,*" Beard recalled, years afterward, chuckling over the joke on himself, "*because I sort of felt sorry for them. They seemed like well meaning, decent enough young men. Yet there they were, neglecting their business to waste their time day after day on that ridiculous flying machine. I had an idea that it must worry their father.*" In these conversations, neither the Wrights nor Beard was likely to bring up the subject of aviation. The Wrights showed no eagerness to talk about what they were doing, and Beard kept to subjects he considered more sensible. But one day, in the autumn of 1904, several of the schoolchildren told him they had seen the Wrights flying all around the field. Maybe, thought Beard—that might make a little local item for the paper. When he next saw Orville Wright on the car, a day or two afterward, Beard asked him if it was true that they had been flying all the way around the field. Oh, yes, Orville admitted, they often did that. Then Orville began to talk about something else. Evidently, Beard decided, the fact that an airplane could be flown under perfect control in circles didn't amount to anything after all. Orville Wright himself didn't seem to think it was unusual or important. There was no use putting it in the paper. One more reason perhaps for not printing much in the *Journal* about what the poor, misguided Wrights were doing was that such items were annoying to Frank Tunison, another of the editors—the same Tunison who had turned down the story of the first flight at Kitty Hawk. Having decided that the Wrights were not news, he was naturally irritated to see any reference to them, even on an inside page. "*Why do we print such stuff?*" he would ask. However, Beard said to Orville, as they rode along on the car, "*If you ever do something unusual be sure and let us know.*" From time to time he went or telephoned to the Wright home to find out if by remote chance the brothers had done anything worth mentioning. "*Done anything of special interest lately?*" he asked Orville Wright one evening. "*Oh, nothing much,*" replied Orville. "*Today one of us flew for nearly five minutes.*" "*Where did you go?*" asked Beard. "*Around the field.*" "*Oh! Just around the field. I see. Well, we'll keep in touch with you.*" Doubtless, reflected the newspaperman, the Wrights's circling of Mr. Huffman's pasture for five minutes was pretty good for two local boys. But it was hardly a thing to take up space in the paper. Hadn't Santos-Dumont circled the Eiffel Tower, and flown all around Paris? One more newspaper writer, like hundreds of others, had failed to distinguish between an airship with a gas bag and a flying machine heavier than air.

[At the time of the thirty-eight-minute flight in 1905, however, Luther Beard was among the spectators at the field.]

Another bright young newspaperman in that vicinity didn't grasp quite the full significance of what the Wrights were doing. The Dayton *Journal* had a branch office at Xenia, about eleven miles from where the Wrights did their flying. The reporter in charge of that branch office was an enterprising lad, just out of college, who answered to the name of Fred C. Kelly. His eagle eye spotted an item about the Wrights and their flying machine in a country weekly, the Osborn *Local*, published in a village a mile or two from the Huffman Field. Did he investigate the story? No, he didn't need to investigate it to feel sure it must be nonsense. The fact of human flight was still unacceptable and ridiculous even to professional humorists. The humorous weekly, *Puck*, in its issue of October 19, 1904—nearly a month after that first circular flight—published a joke, inspired presumably by absurd reports about two young men at Dayton, "When," inquired the friend, "*will you wing your first flight?*" "*Just as soon,*" replied the flying machine inventor, "*as I can get the laws of gravitation repealed.*" The significance of the first complete circular flight, on September 20, 1904, was not overlooked, however, by one man who witnessed it. That was Amos Ives Root, the Medina bee man. He had traveled by automobile the day before to Xenia, where he had a relative, and then went to the Huffman Field, only a few miles away, to become better acquainted with the Wrights.

His trip of 175 miles from Medina without serious difficulty with his machine was then almost a feat in itself. He had not needed any repairs until he reached Xenia. [Incidentally, he had remonstrated with the repairman he dealt with there, Mr. Baldner, for his frequent use of profanity, and he was impressed by the fact that no matter how puzzling or discouraging the problem, the Wrights never uttered a profane word.] After going to Huffman Field, Root became more than ever interested in the Wrights and as he wished to see all he could of their work for a few days, he arranged for board and lodging at the Beard home across the road. [A little later he even offered to pay the Wrights $100 for material he had obtained from them for articles about their work—but they refused to accept any payment.] Root knew that the circular flight he had just witnessed was of prime importance, for it demonstrated that the airplane would have practical use. He wrote an eyewitness account of what the Wrights had done for the January 1 (1905) issue of his magazine, *Gleanings in Bee Culture*, and sent a marked copy to the editor of the *Scientific American*, with a letter telling the editor he was free to reprint the article. The editor wrote back that he had not received the marked copy. So Root sent another. But when the editor of the *Scientific American* saw what Root had printed he paid no attention to it. Root continued to print articles about the Wrights in his magazine. In December, 1905, he published the fact that a great number of long flights had been made during the previous season, "one of 24 miles in 38 minutes," probably the first publication of that event in the United States. At about the same time, in its issue of December 16, 1905, the *Scientific American* said, in an editorial headed "Retrospect for the Year" "*The most promising results (with the airplane) to date were those obtained last year by the Wright brothers, one of whom made a flight of over half a mile in a power-propelled machine.*"

Previously in the same editorial, though, was the assertion, "*the only successful 'flying' that has been done this year—must be credited to the balloon type.*" By that time, the Wrights's total flying distance was about 160 miles. In its issue of January 13, 1906, in an article headed "*The Wright Aeroplane and Its Fabled Performances,*" the *Scientific American* commented skeptically on a letter written by the Wright brothers which had been published in a Paris automobile journal. In that letter the Wrights had given details of the long flights of late September and early October, 1905. In expressing its disbelief in the "alleged" flights described in the Wright letter, the *Scientific American* said, "*If such sensational and tremendously important experiments are being conducted in a not very remote part of the country, on a subject in which almost everybody feels the most profound interest, is it possible to believe that the enterprising American reporter, who, it is well-known, comes down the chimney when the door is locked in his face—even if he has to scale a fifteen story skyscraper to do so—would not have ascertained all about them and published them broadcast long ago?*" A few weeks later, in February, 1906, the editor of the *Scientific American* wrote to the Wrights to inquire if there was any truth in reports that they were negotiating with the French Government. He enclosed in his letter a clipping of "*The Wright Aeroplane and its Fabled Performances.*" The Wrights wrote in reply that since the *Scientific American* obtained the data of what it termed "alleged experiments" directly from a published letter signed by the Wright brothers, and since it did not discredit the authenticity of the letter, but only the truthfulness of the statements, they were at a loss to understand why the editor should desire further statements from such a source. They did not answer the inquiry about the negotiations with the French Government. Most of the long flights in late September and early October, 1905, had been seen by Amos Stauffer, a farmer working in an adjoining field. But he went right ahead husking corn. Another witness, however, was more of a gossip. At one of the October flights, William Fouts, a Dayton druggist, was present, and the Wrights cautioned him not to say anything about what he had seen. But Fouts must have taken a few people into his confidence. In the afternoon of October 5, the Dayton *Daily News* had an article saying the Wrights were making sensational flights every day.

The Dayton correspondent for the *Cincinnati Post* reported this to his paper which printed it the next day. A fairly good-sized crowd then went to the Huffman Pasture. But when they found nothing going on there most of them decided that the reports must have been much exaggerated. Nothing more was said about the Wrights in Ohio papers for some time. John Tomlinson, a reporter on the Dayton *Journal*, and correspondent for out-of-town papers, offered $50 to Henry Webbert, friend of the Wrights, to let him know the date of their next flight. There was one more short flight on October 16, but no newspapermen or other onlookers were at the field. On March 12, 1906, the Wrights had sent to the Aero Club of America the following list of names of reputable men who had seen one or more of their flights, E. W. Ellis, assistant city auditor, Torrence Huffman, bank president, C. S. Billman, secretary, and W. H. Shank, treasurer of the West Side Building and Loan Association, William, Henry, and Charles Webbert, in the plumbing business, Frank Hamburger, hardware dealer, Howard M. Myers, post office employee, William Fouts and Reuben Schindler, druggists, William Weber, plumber, Bernard H. Lambers, of Dayton Malleable Iron Works. Besides those living in Dayton, were, O. F. Jamieson, traveling salesman, of East Germantown, Ohio, David Beard and Amos Stauffer, of Osborn, and Theodore Waddell, of the Census Bureau at Washington. The Wrights had a list of about sixty persons who had witnessed flights. Those witnesses named in the published list got requests for confirmatory letters from the *Scientific American* whose editor finally had decided that reports of what the Wrights had done might be worth looking into. Then, in the issue of April 7, 1906, the magazine reported the long flights of the previous autumn and quoted in full a letter from one of the witnesses. More than six months later, on November 21, 1906, the Aero Club itself wrote to the various persons named in the list received from the Wrights, asking for letters about the flights they had seen. As late as October, 1906, the *Scientific American* had devoted more than a column to a letter from J. C. Press, of South Norwalk, Connecticut, who presented arguments to justify his belief that "*man may fly within a few years.*" But, on the other hand, the letter writer quoted the editor of *Collier's Weekly* as expressing "*disbelief in even the ultimate possibility of flight.*"

At last, however, in the issue of December 15, 1906, or nearly three years after the Wrights's first flights, the *Scientific American* printed an editorial which indicated that the editor was now becoming aware of the facts [of the stated flights]. The editorial said, "*In all the history of invention, there is probably no parallel to the unostentatious manner in which the Wright brothers of Dayton, Ohio, ushered into the world their epoch-making invention of the first successful aeroplane flying machine.*"

☐☐☐☐☐☐☐☐☐☐

From the time that they knew their invention was practical, the Wrights wished to offer to their own government a world monopoly on all their patents and, still more important, all their secrets relating to the airplane. They thought it might be useful to the Army for scouting purposes. But as they had greater interest at first in learning more about flying and improving their machine than in making money out of it, they did not at once attempt negotiations with government officials at Washington. When they did make such an effort they received a rude shock. The United States Army not only didn't believe there was any such device in existence as a practical flying machine, but was not disposed to investigate. At least one foreign government showed more awareness and more curiosity. In the autumn of 1904, the Wrights got a letter from Lieutenant Colonel John Edward Capper, of the Royal Aircraft Factory [a government experimental laboratory dealing with aeronautics] at Aldershot.

He wrote on shipboard en route to the United States, and enclosed a note of introduction from another Englishman whom the Wrights knew—Patrick Young Alexander—member of the Aeronautical Society of Great Britain. [Alexander had called upon the Wrights at Dayton in 1902, with a letter of introduction from Octave Chanute.] Colonel Capper wanted to know if he might see the Wrights in Dayton when he returned eastward from a visit to the St. Louis Exposition. They told him they would be glad to see him and he came to Dayton, accompanied by his wife, in November. Soon after his arrival, Colonel Capper frankly said that he was there at the request of his government. The Wrights told him of what they had accomplished during that previous season of 1904 at the Huffman Field. Before leaving, Colonel Capper asked them to make his government some kind of proposal.

The Wrights made no haste about submitting a proposal to the British, but, on January 10, 1905, about two months after the Capper visit, they wrote to him asking if he was sure his government was receptive to an offer. In this letter they suggested that a government in possession of such a machine as they now could furnish, and the knowledge and instruction they could impart might have a lead of several years over governments which waited to buy a perfected machine before making a start in this line. The letter was signed, Wright Cycle Company. Whatever the British Government might desire, the Wrights did not intend to take any steps that could prevent the United States Government from having opportunity to control all rights in their invention for the entire world, and before having any further word from the British it seemed wise to learn from Washington just what our own government might want. They wrote, on January 18, 1905, to their member of Congress from the Dayton district, Robert M. Nevin, as follows, "*The series of aeronautical experiments upon which we have been engaged for* the past five years has ended in the production of a flying machine of a type fitted for practical use. It not only flies through the air at high speed, but it also lands without being wrecked. During the year 1904 one hundred and five flights were made at our experimenting station, on the Huffman Prairie, east of the city, and though our experience in handling the machine has been too short to give any high degree of skill, we nevertheless succeeded, toward the end of the season, in making two flights of five minutes each, in which we sailed round and round the field until a distance of about three miles had been covered, at a speed of thirty-five miles an hour. The first of these record flights was made on November 9th, in celebration of the phenomenal political victory of the preceding day, and the second, on December 1st, in honor of the one hundredth flight of the season. The numerous flights in straight lines, in circles, and over "S" shaped courses, in calms and in winds, have made it quite certain that flying has been brought to a point where it can be made of great practical use in various ways, one of which is that of scouting and carrying messages in time of war. If the latter features are of interest to our own government, we shall be pleased to take up the matter either on a basis of providing machines of agreed specification, at a contract price, or of furnishing all the scientific and practical information we have accumulated in these years of experimenting, together with a license to use our patents, thus putting the government in a position to operate on its own account. If you can find it convenient to ascertain whether this is a subject of interest to our own government, it would oblige us greatly, as early information on this point will aid us in making our plans for the future, respectfully yours, Wilbur and Orville Wright." Mr. Nevin forwarded the letter to the Secretary of War who turned it over to the Board of Ordnance and Fortification. That Board evidently regarded the letter simply as something for their "crank file."

They had received many proposals in the past from inventors of perpetual motion machines and flying machines and had stock paragraphs to use in reply. Their response to Nevin, signed by Major General George Lewis Gillespie, of the General Staff, the President of the Board of Ordnance and Fortification said, "*I have the honor to inform you that, as many requests have been made for financial assistance in the development of designs for flying machines, the Board has found it necessary to decline to make allotments for the experimental development of devices for mechanical flight, and has determined that, before suggestions with that object in view will be considered, the device must have been brought to the stage of practical operation without expense to the United States. It appears from the letter of Messieurs Wilbur and Orville Wright that their machine has not yet been brought to the stage of practical operation, but as soon as it shall have been perfected, this Board would be pleased to receive further representations from them in regard to it.*" It will be noted, of course, that what the letter said bore almost no relation to anything the Wrights had written. Having thus been brushed aside by their own government, the Wrights now might have been conscience clear to do as they saw fit with a foreign government. But nevertheless they determined that, no matter how public officials at Washington behaved, they would take no steps which could shut off their own government from use of the airplane if Army people ever got around to understanding the machine's potential importance. On February 11, 1905, the Wrights received a letter from the British War Office, asking them to submit terms, and March 1, without giving formal terms, they outlined in a general way what they were willing to do. "*Although we consider it advisable,*" they wrote to the British War Office, "*that any agreement which may be made at present be based upon a single machine and necessary instruction in its use, we would be willing, if desired, to insert in the contract, an option on the purchase of all that we know concerning the subject of aviation. We are ready to enter into a contract with the British Government to construct and deliver to it an aerial scouting machine of the aeroplane type.*" Specifications included these, The machine to be capable of carrying two men of average weight, and supplies of fuel for a flight of not less than fifty miles, its speed, when flying in still air, to be not less than thirty miles an hour, the machine to be of substantial enough construction to make landings without being broken, when operated with a reasonable degree of skill. Another provision was that the purchase price should be determined by the maximum distance covered in one of the trial flights, £500, or about $2,500 for each mile. If none of the trial flights was of at least ten miles, then the British Government would not be obligated to accept the machine.

There were further exchanges of letters between the Wrights and the British (altogether twenty-four letters in the years 1905-1906), but the brothers began to suspect that the British were mainly interested in prolonging the negotiations as a means of keeping in touch and knowing what progress was being made in aviation. Probably, thought the Wrights, the British shrewdly foresaw that the flying machine would not add to the isolation of the British Isles, and did not wish to hasten its development. But they doubtless wished to be well-informed about whatever was happening in the conquest of the air. The British War Office wrote on May 13, 1905, that they were asking Colonel H. Foster, their military attache, in Washington, to call upon the Wrights at their "works"—meaning, presumably, at their shop—and to see their machine in flight. The brothers were urged by their friend Octave Chanute on one of his visits to Dayton, to make another offer of their machine to the United States Army. Because of the treatment they had received from the War Department, the Wrights were naturally reluctant to expose themselves to further rebuffs, but Chanute was insistent that such behavior by Army people surely would not occur again. Thus prodded by Chanute, the Wrights, on October 9, 1905, wrote to the Secretary of War, "*Some months ago we made an informal offer to furnish to the War Department practical flying machines suitable for scouting purposes. The matter was referred to the Board of Ordnance and Fortification, which seems to have given it scant consideration. We do not wish to take this invention abroad, unless we find it necessary to do so and therefore write again, renewing the offer. We are prepared to furnish a machine on contract, to be accepted only after trial trips in which the conditions of the contract have been fulfilled, the machine to carry an operator* and supplies of fuel, etc., sufficient for a flight of one hundred miles, the price of the machine to be regulated according to a sliding scale based on the performance of the machine in the trial trips, the minimum performance to be a flight of at least twenty-five miles at a speed of not less than thirty miles an hour. We are also willing to take contracts to build machines carrying more than one man, respectfully yours, Wilbur and Orville Wright." Once again the Secretary of War referred their letter to the Board of Ordnance and Fortification. Major General John Coalter Bates, member of the General Staff, had become president of the Board since the previous correspondence, and he signed the reply. The Wrights blinked at the familiar phrases in the opening paragraph, "*I have the honor to inform you,*" said the Major General, "*that, as many requests have been made for financial assistance in the development of designs for flying machines, the Board has found it necessary to decline to make allotments for the experimental development of devices for mechanical flight, and has determined that, before suggestions with that object in view will be considered, the device must have been brought to the stage of practical operation without expense to the United States.*" The letter went on, "*Before the question of making a contract with you for the furnishing of a flying machine is considered it will be necessary for you to furnish this Board with the approximate cost of the completed machine, the date upon which it would be delivered, and with such drawings and descriptions thereof as are necessary to enable its construction to be understood and a definite conclusion as to its practicability to be arrived at. Upon receipt of this information, the matter will receive the careful consideration of the Board.*" In other words, the Board would have to see drawings and descriptions to determine if the machine the Wrights had been flying could fly. Regardless of whatever irritation they felt, the Wrights wrote to the Ordnance Board on October 19. In that letter they said, "*We have no thought of asking financial assistance from the government. We propose to sell the results of experiments finished at our own expense. In order that we may submit a proposition conforming as nearly as possible to the ideas of your* board, it is desirable that we be informed what conditions you would wish to lay down as to the performance of the machine in the official trials, prior to the acceptance of the machine. We cannot well fix a price, or a time for delivery, till we have your idea of the qualifications necessary to such a machine. We ought also to know whether you would wish to reserve a monopoly on the use of the invention, or whether you would permit us to accept orders for similar machines from other governments, and give public exhibitions, etc. Proof of our ability to execute an undertaking of the nature proposed will be furnished whenever desired." Here is what Captain T. C. Dickson, Recorder of the Board, wrote in reply, "*The Board of Ordnance and Fortification at its meeting October 24, 1905, took the following action, the Board then considered a letter, dated October 19, 1905, from Wilbur and Orville Wright requesting the requirements prescribed by the Board that a flying machine would have to fulfill before it would be accepted. It is recommended the Messieurs Wright be informed that the Board does not care to formulate any requirements for the performance of a flying machine or take any further action on the subject until a machine is produced which by actual operation is shown to be able to produce horizontal flight and to carry an operator.*" Such letters did not encourage the Wrights to press their offer further. As Wilbur expressed it, they had taken pains to see that "*opportunity gave a good clear knock on the War Department door.*" It had always been their business practice, he said, to sell to those who wished to buy instead of trying to force goods upon people who did not want them. And now if the American Government had decided to spend no more money on flying machines until their practical use should be demonstrated abroad, the Wrights felt that there wasn't much they could do about it. Chanute, too, was now convinced that the seeming stupidity of War Department officials was not accidental. His comment was, "*Those fellows are a bunch of asses.*" On that same day, October 19, when they wrote to the Ordnance Board, the Wrights had sent a letter also to the British War Office amending their earlier proposal. They said that recent events justified them in making the acceptance of their machine dependent upon a trial flight of at least fifty miles, instead of only ten miles as in the original offer. Shortly afterward, on November 22, 1905, the Wrights received a letter from Colonel Foster, the British military attache in Washington, asking if it would be possible for him to see the Wright machine in flight. Experiments for that year had been completed, but, the Wrights replied, if Colonel Foster came to Dayton he could meet and talk with many persons who had witnessed flights. That didn't satisfy Colonel Foster. He wrote again on November 29 that the War Office had had many descriptions of airplane flights by persons supposed to have witnessed them. What the War Office wanted, he said, was for him to *see* a flight. The Wrights made it plain to the Colonel that they saw no point to making a demonstration of their machine unless negotiations had reached a point where a deal could be closed if the machine's performance was as represented. They reminded him that it wasn't necessary for the British War Office to put up any money in advance—only to sign an agreement that a deal would be closed after the Wrights had shown what their machine could do. Communications continued to pass between the Wrights and the British. Colonel Foster was succeeded as British military attache at Washington by Colonel Gleichen and the latter made a trip to Dayton. But nothing came of the negotiations. In December, 1906, the British finally wrote to the Wrights that they had decided not to buy an airplane.

Meanwhile, in the spring of 1906, the War Department at Washington heard once more about the Wrights in consequence of an exchange of letters between the Wrights and Godfrey Lowell Cabot, of Boston, who, it will be remembered, had written to them just after the Kitty Hawk flights in 1903. Cabot had seen a bulletin published by the Aero Club of America, on March 12, 1906, that told about the progress the Wrights had made during the season of 1905 at Huffman Field. He had learned also, from his brother Samuel, a little about the Wrights's offer to the US War Department. Samuel Cabot got the news, presumably, from Chanute, with whom he from time to time exchanged letters. [He had written to Chanute asking if the Wrights needed any financial assistance for carrying on their experiments, and Chanute told him they did not.] Godfrey Cabot wrote to the brothers [in April, 1906] saying that he supposed they had offered their machine to the US Army "with negative results," but that if they ever decided to form a company to exploit the machine's commercial possibilities, he wished they would send him a prospectus. In their reply to Cabot (May 19), the Wrights confirmed the reports about their correspondence with the Ordnance Board. Cabot was so astounded over the treatment they had received that he promptly sent the facts to his relative, Henry Cabot Lodge, United States Senator from Massachusetts. Lodge forwarded Cabot's letter, along with one of his own, to the Secretary of War—who sent it to the Board of Ordnance and Fortification. Brigadier General William Crozier, president of the Ordnance Board, wrote to Senator Lodge, on May 26, acknowledging his letter to the Secretary of War, and stating that "*if those in control of the flying machine invented by the Wright brothers will place themselves in communication with the Board of Ordnance and Fortification, War Department, Washington, DC, any proposition they may have to make will be given consideration by the Board.*" Shortly afterward, Godfrey Cabot called upon General Crozier in Washington and showed him copies of the Aero Club *Bulletin* which told about the Wrights flying twenty-four miles in 1905. Since this was convincing evidence that the Wrights's machine was capable of horizontal flight, General Crozier may have been somewhat embarrassed. He said the Ordnance Board would be glad to receive a proposition from the Wrights. He said, too, that he might send a representative to see the Wrights in Dayton. In reply to a letter from Cabot reporting his talk with Crozier, the Wrights (on June 21) wrote, "*If General Crozier should decide to send a representative to Dayton we would be glad to furnish him convincing proof that a machine has been produced which by actual operation has been shown to be able to produce horizontal flight and to carry an operator.*" This letter also said, "*We are ready to negotiate whenever the Board is ready, but as the former correspondence closed with a strong intimation that the Board did* not wish to be bothered with our offers, we naturally have no intention of taking the initiative again." General Crozier did not send any representative to Dayton. Several months later, in November, 1906, newspapers got wind of the fact that there had been some kind of correspondence between the Wrights and the War Department. On November 29, many newspapers carried a dispatch from Washington which said, "*While General Crozier will not discuss negotiations with the Wrights, he said today, 'You may simply say it is now up to the Wright brothers to say whether the government shall take their invention. They know the government's attitude and have its offer.'* " There had been no Government offer. The last communication the Wrights had received from the War Department was the one, more than a year before, in which the Ordnance Board said it did not wish to take any further action. The Wrights felt sure that the War Department no longer doubted the existence of a successful flying machine. It appeared, though, that certain Army officers still were unwilling frankly to admit their blundering behavior and come down from their high horse. There was reason to believe that the Ordnance Board would welcome a face-saving opportunity and hoped the Wrights would once again take the initiative by making a new proposal. But the Wrights were not ready to do so. Their advances had too often been spurned. The next move, they thought, should come from the War Department. In that frame of mind, early in the spring of 1907, the inventors evolved a plan for bringing their machine to the attention of the War Department in a manner quite dramatic. An exposition was going to be held on the Virginia coast that year to celebrate the three hundredth anniversary of the founding of the first English colony, at Jamestown. In connection with this Jamestown Exposition there would be a great naval review, April 26, at Hampton Roads.

President Theodore Roosevelt and other important government people, including Army and Navy officers, would be present. What would be the matter, the Wrights asked themselves, with appearing there unexpectedly in their flying machine? They could equip their machine with hydroplanes and pontoons for starting and landing on water, take it to Kitty Hawk, and then fly it, over Currituck Sound and beyond, to the scene of the naval review. After circling a few hundred feet above the battleships, the machine would disappear as suddenly and as mysteriously as it had come. No newspaper people or anyone else would know where it came from or how to get in touch with those who knew about it and the mystery would grow.

Officers of the Army and Navy would be asked embarrassing questions. Had they arranged for the flying machine to appear, and had it been adopted for use in time of war? Those who still "knew" there was no practical flying machine would be set to wondering. The Wrights had many a quiet chuckle at the thought of the effect of their practical joke if it could be carried out. It was not too dangerous a project. Much of the flight could be made over shallow water in Currituck Sound. It would easily be possible to fly as far as the scene of the naval review and out of sight on the return trip before coming down. They put an engine, with propellers attached to it, on pontoons, and placed this experimental outfit on the river at Dayton for preliminary trials. After a day or so of these tests it was evident that the plan of mounting their machine on hydroplanes and pontoons and taking off from the water was practical. But the inventors took aboard a passenger who tried to be helpful. In his efforts to throw his weight where he thought it would help the balance, he succeeded only in tilting the machine so steeply that it dived below the surface. The propellers were damaged. Before repairs could be made, something broke the dam in the river. The Wrights had to abandon their plans for a prank that might have been a national sensation. Only a short time after the Wrights were planning their surprise flight, in that spring of 1907, Herbert Parsons, a member of Congress from New York, sent to President Roosevelt a clipping from the *Scientific American*—whose editor now knew about the Wrights. Roosevelt sent the clipping, with a note signed by his secretary, to Secretary of War [William Howard] Taft. The note suggested a talk with Representative Parsons to discuss the idea of experimenting with the Wright flying machine. Taft sent the clipping and White House note to the Ordnance Board, with a note signed by his own secretary and headed "Endorsement." The personnel of the Ordnance Board had changed, at least partly, since the earlier correspondence with the Wrights. But the same attitude of aloofness regarding flying machines still existed. The Board could not, however, ignore a letter from the office of the President of the United States, Commander-in-Chief of the Army and Navy, with an endorsement from the Secretary of War. It might have been expected that the Board members would feel bound to investigate the reported flying machine. But they couldn't bring themselves to go that far. All they did was to send, on May 11, a brief letter to the Wrights, signed by Major Samson M. Fuller, Recorder of the Board. The letter said, "*I am directed by the President of the Board to enclose copies of two letters referring to your aeroplane, for your information, and to say that the Board has before it several propositions for the construction and test of aeroplanes, and if you desire to take any action in the matter, will be glad to hear from you on the subject.*" Accompanying the letter were copies of the notes from the White House and the office of the Secretary of War. The Wrights believed they knew why those copies were sent. It was to let them know that the Ordnance Board was writing only because of orders from higher up.

Though the letter from the Board was standoffs enough, yet it did not imply, as some of the earlier letters did, that the Wrights were a pair of beggars, or cranks, seeking funds. The Wrights thought the letter had been forced and that it really was a mere gesture, but nevertheless they treated it as if the Ordnance Board might now be seriously interested. In their reply, May 17, the Wrights said they had some flying machines under construction and would be glad to make a formal proposal to sell one or more of them to the Government if the War Department was interested. They said the machine would carry two men and a supply of fuel for a flight of 200 kilometers, that a trial flight of at least 50 kilometers, at a speed not less than 50 kilometers an hour, would be made before representatives of the Government before any part of the purchase price was paid. They suggested a conference for the purpose of discussing the matter in detail. And they said they were willing to submit a formal proposition, if that was preferred. In the next letter from the Ordnance Board, dated May 22, 1907, nothing was said about the Wrights's suggestion for a conference, but the Wrights were requested to make a formal proposal incorporating the specifications and conditions contained in their letter to the Board, dated May 17.

The Wrights sent a formal proposal on May 31. In this proposal they repeated all the specifications and conditions mentioned in their letter of the 17th, and in addition agreed to the following, to teach an operator to fly the machine, to return to the starting point in the 50 kilometer test flight, and to land without any damage that would prevent the machine being started immediately upon another flight. The price stated was $100,000 for the first machine, others to be furnished at a reasonable margin above the cost of manufacture. They added that they were willing to make the contract speed 40 miles an hour, provided an additional sum would be allowed for each mile in excess of that speed in the trial flight, with a forfeit of an equal amount for every mile below. Again the Wrights made it plain that nothing was to be paid to them until after a trial flight had met all contract requirements. The next letter from the Ordnance Board dated June 8 said that $100,000 was more than the Board had available, and that such an amount could not be obtained without a special appropriation by Congress at its next session. Then the letter went on to ask what the price would include, whether the United States would be granted exclusive use, or whether the Wrights contemplated commercial exploitation of their machine, or negotiations with foreign governments. The Wrights wrote in reply explaining just what was included in the price. They said it did not include any period during which the use of the invention would belong exclusively to the United States, since a recent contract precluded such an offer, and that it was their intention to furnish machines for military use before entering the commercial field. The letter repeated what the

Wrights had said before, that when a contract had been signed they would produce a machine at their own expense and make flights as specified in the contract in the presence of representatives of the War Department before any money whatever was paid to them. That was the last letter to pass between the Ordnance Board and the Wrights for some time. But while the Wrights were in Europe, the Board undoubtedly began to hear from military attaches and others about the brothers's negotiations abroad. At any rate, the Board began to show signs of uneasiness and they wrote a letter, signed by Major Fuller, October 5—received by the Wrights in Europe—to say that the Wright proposal of June 15 had again been given consideration by the Board at its meeting of October 3, 1907, but that nothing definite could be done before a meeting of Congress, as Congressional action would be necessary to accept the proposition, since the funds at the Board's disposal were insufficient. The Wrights's reply, from London, on October 30, made it clear that if the price was the only thing in the way—that could probably be satisfactorily adjusted. Wilbur Wright started home from Europe ahead of Orville, but before he left, it was agreed between the brothers that their price for an airplane to the United States Government would be $25,000.

◻◻◻◻◻◻◻◻◻◻◻

Though the importance of the Wrights's achievements was unrecognized in the United States until long after their first power flights, reports about their gliding prior to those flights had aroused much interest abroad. In the spring of 1903, the Wrights's Chicago friend, Octave Chanute, had gone to his native France in the interest of the St. Louis Exposition to be held the next year. One purpose of his visit was to arrange with Alberto Santos-Dumont, the Brazilian aeronaut, who lived in Paris, to make flights at St. Louis with his dirigible balloon. While in Paris, Chanute was invited by the Aero Club to give a talk regarding aviation in the United States. In this talk, on April 2, he told of his own gliding experiments in 1896 and of those of the Wright brothers in 1901 and 1902, illustrated by photographs. Then in the August, 1903, issue of *L'Aerophile* Chanute published an article on the same subject, with photographic illustrations, scale drawings, and structural details of the Wright 1902 glider. In the *Revue des Sciences* of November, 1903, he again published photographs and description of that machine. This 1902 glider far surpassed any that had ever been built before, and in it the problem of equilibrium had practically been solved. That glider was the basis of the specifications in the Wright patent.

Chanute's revelations therefore were sensational. And they did not fall on deaf ears. Until this time, about the only man in France who was showing any interest in aviation was Captain Louis Ferdinand Ferber of the French army, who himself had made gliding experiments as a hobby while serving in an Alpine artillery corps. As early as 1901 he had begun an exchange of letters with Chanute, after having read in the *Illustrierte Aeronautische Mitteilungen*, a German magazine devoted mainly to ballooning, a brief article, supplied by Wilbur Wright, about the 1900 experiments at Kitty Hawk. A little later he wrote for information to the Wrights themselves. But now after the Chanute speech, Ferber was no longer alone among Frenchmen in thinking the Wrights's experiments might be significant.

Though belief in the possibility of a successful flying machine had been at lowest ebb in France, the information now made available by Chanute caused a greatly revived interest. Heretofore the Aero Club had devoted its attention almost entirely to balloons and dirigibles, but it considered the French as leaders in every line pertaining to aeronautics. Immediately following the Chanute address telling of the Wrights's gliding experiments in America, several members of the Aero Club, led by Ernest Archdeacon, decided to organize a special committee on aviation. Archdeacon also made a warm appeal in favor of organizing contests for gliders to show that the French did not intend to allow anyone to surpass them in any branch of aeronautics. He subscribed three thousand francs for the organization of such contests and for prizes. *L'Aerophile*, official organ of the Club, which up to this time had published little about aviation, now suddenly began to carry many articles and items of news concerning projected experiments in gliding. But it was some months before the French actually passed from the "talking" to the "doing" stage in gliding. In the meantime a brief dispatch about the Wrights's power flights on December 17, 1903, had appeared in French and other European daily papers. Though the reports of these power flights were received with considerable skepticism, nevertheless they created such a furor in French aeronautical circles that before the end of January, 1904, no less than six gliders of the Wright 1902 type were being built in France from data furnished by Chanute. Ernest Archdeacon, of the Aero Club, placed an order with M. Dargent, a model maker of Chalais-Meudon, to build a copy of the Wright 1902 glider. Early in 1904 (January 28), Captain Ferber delivered a lecture at Lyon on the subject of gliding experiments, and a young man named Gabriel Voisin, just finishing his course in a technical school, came to him to ask advice about how to get into the field of aviation. He said he wished to "consecrate his life" to aviation. Ferber suggested that he should go to see Archdeacon. Voisin did so, and Archdeacon employed him to test the glider built by Dargent. Ferber gave Voisin his instructions in gliding. Then Archdeacon employed Voisin to build still another glider like the Wright machine. That contact with Archdeacon gave Voisin his start toward becoming a famous airplane manufacturer. And it was from that glider "*du type de Wright*," as the French papers called it, tested by Voisin, that grew the first Voisin machines, soon to be followed by those of other copyists. Here was the real beginning of French—indeed of European—aviation.

Articles about the Wright power flights were appearing in the French, English and German aeronautical magazines. A longer article about the Kitty Hawk event was printed in the March, 1904, issue of *Illustrierte Aeronautische Mitteilungen* from Carl Dienstbach, a musician in New York, who as a sideline was the magazine's correspondent. One copyist after another began to use devices and technical knowledge invented or discovered by the Wrights. When Ferber received a letter from the American publication, the *Scientific American*, asking for an account of his own gliding experiments, he wrote to them that he was simply a "disciple of the Wright Brothers." But these copyists were not content to follow the Chanute revelations and build gliders just like that of the Wrights. Instead, they tried to improve upon the Wrights's work. The "improvements" were not successful, because the builders did not have the Wrights's knowledge and wind tunnel data, except that used in the 1902 glider, to guide them. So great were their difficulties that some of the experimenters began to place blame on Chanute.

They thought Chanute must have misrepresented what the Wrights had done—maybe purposely. That was the only way they could account for their failure to get the good results obtained by the Wrights. Robert Esnault-Pelterie, a member of the Aero Club, pointed out that they had not put to a fair test the information on the Wright glider that Chanute had given them, because, he said, in building their gliders they had not strictly adhered to Chanute's description and specifications. Since they had all the data needed to reproduce the glider that Chanute had reported as having been so successful, Esnault-Pelterie said, the way to determine the value of the information was to build a Wright glider exactly like Chanute had described and then test it to see how it performed. He himself then built such a machine, in 1904, and reported that he got the same performance as had the Wrights. While the French were carrying on these experiments with copies of the 1902 Wright glider, the Wrights themselves were busy with their power machine with which they made more than 100 starts in 1904. It was not until late October, 1906, or nearly three years after the Wrights's first power flights, that a French power machine was flown. [This machine, piloted by [Alberto] Santos-Dumont, was reported to have made a hop of 200 feet, about ten feet above the ground.] Before long, Archdeacon and another member of the Aero Club, Henri Deutsch de la Meurthe, were offering aviation prizes, and doing all they could to encourage someone to try to build a successful power plane. But as Captain Ferber later made clear to Georges Besancon, editor of *L'Aerophile*, in a letter Besancon published in his issue of June, 1907, this revival of interest in aviation in France, and whatever was accomplished, was all a direct outgrowth of information about what the Wrights had done in America. In October, 1905, reports about the long flights accomplished that year by the Wrights with their power machine were received in France. They created an even greater stir in French aeronautical circles than had the earlier reports. Just at the time these reports reached France an organization was formed there to be known as the Federation Aeronautique Internationale (FAI), the purpose of which was to verify and record the truth about reported aeronautical flights. The Aero Club of America, formed at about the same time, was made the official representative of the FAI in America. No flight had as yet been made in France with a motor plane. Long afterward, many uninformed persons, even in the United States, declared that the flights by the Wrights prior to 1908 really should not count, as they had not been officially witnessed by any representative of the FAI—the organization that came into being after the flights had been made.

As the tempo of interest increased, the Wrights were kept fairly busy writing letters to France in reply to requests for information. At the time of the first reports of the 1903 flights at Kitty Hawk, probably the only person in France inclined to believe them was Captain Ferber. Knowing what he did, from correspondence with Chanute, and with the Wrights themselves, he was not too incredulous. If he had said at first that he believed human flight might have occurred, he doubtless would have been laughed at—especially by those who had been most busily experimenting. But as early as May, 1905, Captain Ferber had written to the Wrights, asking if they would sell a power plane and at what price. They were not ready to discuss such a project at that time and, though Ferber wrote a second letter prodding them, they did not reply until October 9, four days after they had completed their most important flying experiments for that year. In that letter, after telling of their recent long flights, the Wrights said they were prepared to furnish machines on contract, to be accepted only after trial trips of at least forty kilometers, the machine to carry an operator and enough supplies of fuel for a flight of 160 kilometers. They said they would be willing to make contracts in which the minimum distance of the trial trip would be more than forty kilometers, but that the price of the machine would then be greater. They were also ready, the letter added, to build machines carrying more than one man. No figures as to price were given. Hoping to have the French War Department buy a plane, Ferber went to his chief, Colonel Bertrand, director of the laboratory of research pertaining to military aeronautics.

But Colonel Bertrand told him the French Government could not commit itself to pay a sum "probably enormous" for an invention not yet authenticated. All that it was possible to do said Bertrand was to appoint and send a commission to see the Wrights. Again Ferber wrote to the Wrights, on October 21, asking what the price for a machine would be. He said he didn't think his government would any longer be interested in paying so great a sum as it had been when he had first asked for a price. The Wrights replied, on November 4, saying they would consent to reduce their price to the French Government to one million francs—$200,000—the money to be paid only after the genuine value of their discoveries had been demonstrated by a flight of one of their machines in the presence of French Government representatives. Ferber had not told in his letter what the French Government had been willing to pay and the Wrights did not say what the price of one million francs was reduced *from*.

The price was to include a complete machine, and instruction in the Wright discoveries relating to the scientific principles of the art, formulas for the designing of machines of other sizes and speeds, and personal instruction of operators in the use of the machine. At the time Captain Ferber was thus dickering for the possible purchase of a Wright flying machine, others in France who were interested in aeronautics still doubted if such a machine existed. About the middle of October, Frank S. Lahm, a member of the Aero Club of France, had a chance meeting with his friend Patrick Y. Alexander, of the Aeronautical Society of Great Britain, who had visited the Wrights as recently as the previous April. Alexander expressed to Lahm his strong belief that the Wrights had actually been making power flights in America. Lahm was an American. After going to France from Mansfield, Ohio, many years before, he had introduced the Remington typewriter to Europe. As a hobby he had taken up ballooning and held a pilot's license. It was of more than casual interest to him that Alexander believed successful flights had been made in America. Lahm then made an effort to learn the facts from a source right in Dayton, Ohio. He wrote to Nelson Bierce, a manufacturer there whom he knew, asking what sort of people the Wrights were and what was known about their reported experiments. Bierce didn't make any investigation, but wrote to Lahm, late in November, that the Wrights were considered men of good character, and that they were said to be carrying on some kind of flying experiments near Dayton, but, he said, no one seemed to know much about the nature of these experiments. Before there was time for Bierce's letter to reach him, Lahm got other news about the Wrights. A letter they had sent on November 17, to Besancon, editor of *L'Aerophile*, giving a detailed account of their most recent experiments, had been published on November 30 in *L'Auto*, a Paris daily dealing with sports. Besancon had given the letter to *L'Auto* because his own next monthly issue would not go to press for a week or more and he was afraid a rival German publication might print, before he could, similar information from the Wrights. That letter to Besancon, containing much specific information, created a sensation. There was much animated talk about its contents that night of November 30 at the Aero Club. Indeed, that date is noteworthy in aeronautical history, for publication of the letter to Besancon led to several important investigations.

    News about the Wrights's recent flights that the letter revealed was taken up by one or two of the wire services and cabled back to the United States where it reached various newspapers, including those in Dayton. But Dayton editors couldn't understand why the Wrights should have stirred up so much excitement in France. One investigation was started by Lahm, now determined to get the facts. He had a brother-in-law in Mansfield, Ohio, Henry M. Weaver, (a manufacturer of cash carriers for department stores), and Weaver had a son, Henry, Jr., perhaps not too busy to go to Dayton and find out all about the Wrights. Immediately after leaving his friends at the Aero Club, Lahm sent this cable to the younger Weaver, "*Verify what Wright brothers claim, necessary go Dayton today, prompt answer cable.*" The young man in Mansfield, never having heard of the Wrights, supposed the message must be for his father, then away on a business trip, and he forwarded it to him at the Grand Pacific Hotel in Chicago. It was received by the father on December 1, shortly after he had retired for the night. Weaver, Sr., didn't at once recall ever having heard of the Wrights, but if they had a "claim" against his brother-in-law, he would see what could be done about settling it. As the question must be important he sent a wire to Dayton that very night. Having no street address for them, he addressed it simply to "Wright Brothers." This message was not clear to the Wrights and their reply the next morning was as puzzling to Weaver as his had been to them. To get down to dots and make sure he was addressing the people he sought, Weaver then sent another telegram asking the Wrights if they knew F. S. Lahm, of Paris. The Wrights didn't know Lahm but they knew *of* him and replied, "*Yes, Lahm, French aeronaut.*"

When he noted that word "aeronaut," Weaver began to remember vaguely having heard some years previously about two brothers who had experimented with a glider somewhere in the Carolinas. The mystery seemed to be lifting. Doubtless the Wrights had made a glider for Lahm and now there was some misunderstanding about the price. He immediately telegraphed again to the Wrights, saying he would arrive in Dayton the next morning (Sunday), and asking the Wrights to meet him at the Algonquin Hotel. When he reached the hotel in Dayton, Weaver discovered that there was no firm of Wright Brothers in the telephone book or city directory. The hotel clerk had never heard of them. Others whom he asked if they knew of anyone in Dayton having a flying machine looked at him blankly and shook their heads. Well, these Wrights must be somewhere, Weaver reflected, for they had replied to his two earlier telegrams. He may have feared that their place of business was closed for the weekend before they could have received his telegram asking them to meet him. At any rate, he went to the office of the telegraph company. There he met the messenger boy who had delivered his message. The boy explained that the brothers had their office at the Wright Cycle Company but that, since it was Sunday, they could not be reached except at their home. Weaver then returned to his hotel. There he found Orville Wright waiting for him. As soon as they began to talk, Weaver said, "*You made a glider, I believe, for Mr. Lahm, in Paris.*" Orville, of course, shook his head. No, he said, they had never made a glider for Mr. Lahm. "*Then,*" asked Weaver, even more puzzled, "*what in the world can be the meaning of this cable?*" And he handed to Orville the message from Paris. Orville then understood. Evidently, he said, Lahm, a member of the Aero Club of France, wished to find out if the report of their flights sent to the Aero Club by the Wright brothers was true. As Weaver later reported in a letter to Lahm, he was already impressed by this younger Wright brother. "*His very appearance would disarm any suspicion—with a face more of a poet than an inventor or promoter. In contour, head and face resemble Edgar Allan Poe—very modest in alluding to the marvels they have accomplished.*" Orville, somewhat amused, said if an investigation was desired, they might as well get right at it.

It was too late in the season for flying, and the machine had been taken apart, but he could introduce the visitor to many responsible people who had seen them fly. Orville took him to the home of C. S. Billman, of the West Side Savings and Loan Company. The Billmans were a fairly large family and nearly all had seen the Wrights fly. When the callers were taken into the sitting room the first member of the family to appear was a four year old boy. "*Son,*" asked Weaver jokingly, "*have you ever seen a flying machine?*" He wasn't expecting to get evidence just yet, but the boy began to run around the room, trying to imitate with his hands the motion of a propeller and to make a noise like the machine. Turning to Orville, Weaver laughingly observed, "*I'm about convinced already. That boy couldn't be a bribed witness.*" They also went, by Interurban car, to talk with the Beard family, across from the flying field, and with Amos Stauffer, the nearest farmer up the road. As Weaver reported, "*On October 5, he [Stauffer] was cutting corn in the next field east, which is higher ground. When he noticed the aeroplane had started on its flight he remarked to his helper, 'Well, the boys are at it again,' and kept on cutting corn, at the same time keeping an eye on the great white form rushing about its course. 'I just kept on shocking corn,' he continued, 'until I got down to the fence, and the darned thing was still going round. I thought it would never stop.' I asked him how long he thought the flight continued, and he replied it seemed to him it was in the air for half an hour.*" Then Orville and Weaver returned to Dayton and called on William Fouts, West Side druggist, who had witnessed the long flight on October 5.

Later they went to the Wright home. Of that visit Weaver wrote, "*The elder brother, Wilbur, I found even quieter and less demonstrative than the younger. He looked the scholar and recluse. Neither is married. As Mr. Wright expressed it, they had not the means to support 'a wife and a flying machine too.'* " Weaver was completely convinced before he left Dayton, and on December 3, cabled to Lahm, "*Claims completely verified.*" A few days later, on December 6, back at his home in Mansfield, he rushed a letter to Lahm giving his evidence of what the Wrights had done. In a little more than a week after Weaver's visit to Dayton, another investigator appeared there, Robert Coquelle, representing *L'Auto*, of Paris. He had been in New York attending the six-day bicycle races and arrived in Dayton on December 12.

Since his paper and *Les Sports* had taken opposite sides regarding the possibility that the Wrights had flown, and *L'Auto* had been pro-Wright, Coquelle wished to report on these "*deux marchands de cycles*" in a way to make a sensation. The imaginative tale he wrote about how "mysterious" were the

Wrights was almost worthy of his compatriot, Dumas. The Wrights gave him names of people who had witnessed flights but it is believed he didn't bother to consult many of them, evidently feeling sure he could invent a better story than they could tell him. However, Coquelle was convinced that the reports about the Wrights's flights were not exaggerated and he cabled a preliminary dispatch to his paper, "*Wright brothers refuse to show their machine but I have seen some witnesses it is impossible to doubt.*" On December 13, the day after Coquelle's visit to Dayton, the Wrights sent another letter to Georges Besancon, editor of *L'Aerophile*, in reply to questions of his, and gave him details of their recent flights, distances, height at which they flew, size of field, and so on. Incidentally the closing paragraph of that letter contained a statement in contradiction of a myth, still widely accepted, "*The claim often made in the 19th century that the lack of sufficiently light motors alone prohibited man from the empire of the air was quite unfounded. At the speeds which birds usually employ, a well-designed flyer can in actual practice sustain a gross weight of 30 kilograms for each horsepower of the motor, which gives ample margin for such motors as might easily have been built 50 years ago.*" Before Besancon could have received this letter, with its details of recent flights, Robert Coquelle arrived in Paris, having taken a boat from New York only a day or two after his stay in Dayton, and his sensational story was published.

Much of this report seemed so incredible that one member of the Aero Club said it almost made him wonder if the Wright brothers existed at all. What Weaver had written in his letter seemed convincing enough to Lahm and he prepared a French translation of it to read to the aviation committee of the Aero Club of France at a meeting on the night of December 29, 1905. That meeting, as Lahm later told about it to friends, and in an article he gave to the Mansfield (Ohio) *News*, published October 24, 1908, was a memorable one. The skeptical members of the committee, greatly in the majority, having heard of Weaver's telegram, assumed the more elaborate report would be favorable to the Wrights, and were prepared to combat it.

Characteristic of the French, there was almost ceremonious politeness at the beginning of the meeting because everyone supposed there might be less politeness as the discussions went on. By the time Lahm had finished reading the letter, everyone began to talk at once. Archdeacon, who presided, was famous for a high-pitched staccato voice and it could be heard calling for order as he also rapped on the table before him with a flat metal ruler. One member observed that they had seen nothing about the Wrights's flights in American newspapers, recognized as enterprising. He found himself incapable of believing, he said, that all the journalists in America would permit so important a piece of news to escape them. Another remarked that they had heard the Wright brothers were of modest enough wealth. Who, he asked, is their financier? It would be interesting to talk with him. Lahm was hard put to it to explain the lack of news about the flights in the American papers. He himself didn't understand that. But he tried to explain that since the brothers did most of the mechanical work on their machine themselves they did not require financial assistance. His voice, however, was drowned in the hubbub. As the discussion continued, so vehement were the contradictions of the Weaver letter that Lahm, Ferber, Besancon, and Coquelle, the only ones present who seemed to believe it, hardly dared express themselves at all. Someone turned to Coquelle and asked him if he really accepted the stories of the Wrights's flights. "I do," he said—but in a low voice. All conceded that Lahm's friend Weaver had doubtless been sincere in what he wrote but they insisted that he had somehow been fooled. They "knew" flight was impossible with a motor of only twelve horsepower. Indeed, many had decided that power flight would always be an impossibility. This belief was all the stronger because a number present had personally done enough in attempts to fly to know the difficulties. One member after another strolled into an adjoining room where they could argue without being called to order. Finally Archdeacon found himself nearly alone. When, long after midnight, the meeting finally broke up the one thing all were agreed upon was that human flight, if true, was of vast consequence. When the Wrights learned how great the incredulity at the Aero Club in France was they were only amused that the stories seemed to the French too wonderful to be true. On December 31 the Weaver letter to Lahm was published in full in *L'Auto*. The next day it appeared in the Paris edition of the New York *Herald* and also in *Les Sports*, competitor of *L'Auto*. Though the Aero Club did not yet know it, Captain Ferber in November had started still another investigation. He had written to the Wrights on November 15, asking permission to send an "official" commission to see them. The Wrights answered on December 5 that they thought it highly advisable that the French Government send a commission to make a thorough investigation of their claims, and that it should be done at once. Eight days later the Wrights received a cable from Ferber saying, "*Friend with full powers for stating terms of contract will sail next Saturday.*" Ferber also sent a letter, a copy of which, he said, would be carried by Arnold Fordyce as his means of identification, but this letter did not reach the Wrights until after the visitor had arrived.

As Ferber only a few weeks before had asked permission to send a military commission, the brothers supposed the man en route to Dayton represented the War Ministry. Arnold Fordyce, the French emissary, arrived in New York on the *Lorraine*, and reached Dayton shortly after Christmas, 1905. He was about thirty-five years old, formerly an actor, of characteristic French politeness, and he spoke English. His first meeting with the Wrights was in their office over the old bicycle shop. To the Wrights's surprise he told them, in reply to a question, that he had no connection with the French War Ministry. He had come, he said, on behalf of a syndicate of wealthy men who wished to buy a flying machine and to present it to the French Government for the national defense. He said he was secretary to Henri Letellier, member of the syndicate and owner and editor of the Paris newspaper, *Le Journal*. He went on to explain that Letellier and his associates in the syndicate were presenting the plane to the Government with the hope they might receive decorations of the Legion of Honor. His story seemed to the Wrights a bit fishy. They thought it more probable that he was really representing the French War Ministry, but that the War Ministry did not wish to appear directly in negotiations for a flying machine. The Wrights went ahead, though, to give him the information he sought. First of all, he wished to make sure that they really had a machine that would fly. They arranged for him to meet a number of trustworthy persons who had witnessed flights, among them bankers, other prominent businessmen, and county officials.

Fordyce was soon convinced that the machine would do all that had been claimed for it, and he wanted a contract to take back with him to his principals. Though Ferber's cable had stated that Fordyce was coming with "full powers" he did not have a power-of-attorney to represent his principals. Still believing that Fordyce's true mission was in the interest of the French War Ministry, the Wrights had no objection to entering into a contract with him granting an option for a short period. They made it clear, however, that they reserved the right to deal with their own Government at any time, even though the United States War Department had not seemed appreciative of their former offers of exclusive rights to the aeroplane. They also made it clear that Letellier and his associates in the "syndicate" would have no rights whatever in the machine, except the right to pay for it. The machine would be delivered only to the French Government. The Fordyce option was for the purchase of one flying machine at a price of 1,000,000 francs, or $200,000, the price the Wrights already had set in a letter to Captain Ferber. The option was to become void if the holder failed by February 5, 1906, to deposit in escrow with J. P. Morgan and Company, New York, 25,000 francs ($5,000) to the joint credit of the Wright brothers and Arnold Fordyce. It was provided that the contract would become null and void if the holder failed to make a further deposit in escrow with J. P. Morgan and Company by April 5, 1906, to bring the total to 1,000,000 francs. But if the holder failed to deposit altogether 1,000,000 francs, as stipulated, then the first deposit of 25,000 francs would belong to the Wright brothers. If on the other hand the Wrights failed to carry out any part of their own obligations under the contract they would receive nothing. On February 5, 1906, the date stated in the option for the first deposit, the Wrights received a telegram from Morgan, Harjes and Company, Paris, stating that 25,000 francs had been deposited with them in escrow to the joint credit of the Wright Brothers and Arnold Fordyce. This seemed to confirm the suspicion held by the Wrights that Fordyce represented the French Ministry of War and not a syndicate. But this suspicion later proved to be false.

Sometime after the Wrights had given this option they heard an entirely different story about the nature of Fordyce's mission. According to this story, Captain Ferber, unable to persuade his superior officers in the War Ministry to send an official investigator to Dayton—had hit on the idea of having an investigation made by a Paris newspaper. He then went to see Letellier, owner of *Le Journal*. Letellier saw the possibilities of prestige for his paper by being able to print the facts about the Wrights. If they really had flown, that would be of great interest, and if they were only "bluffers," as many in France thought they were, the truth about them would still be worth publishing. Letellier could well have afforded the gamble of sending an investigator to Dayton. Aside from his ownership of *Le Journal*, he was a man of considerable wealth, having made his money as a contractor. He had built the main fortresses at Liege. Whatever the truth may have been, if Letellier had intended to publish what Fordyce learned about the Wrights, he did not at once do so.

He took the Fordyce option and presented it to the War Ministry and he received in return a letter from the Minister of War stating that if a Wright plane were acquired by the Ministry the purchase would be made through *Le Journal*. Thus *Le Journal* not only would have a big "scoop" on news of the purchase, but would receive credit and acclaim for a big patriotic act. Perhaps the owner of the paper would be decorated. For some time war clouds had been gathering over Morocco and it looked as if there might be trouble between France and Germany. If war should come, a flying machine for scouting purposes would be of great value. But in spite of the fact that a Frenchman, Fordyce, had been to see the Wrights and reported favorably about them, the French war chiefs couldn't bring themselves to accept as a certainty the existence of a practical flying machine. The story seemed too incredible. There must be a "catch" somewhere. Still, the War Ministry was willing to risk making the down payment of 25,000 francs. But when [Eugene] Etienne sent the down payment of 25,000 francs to Morgan, Harjes and Company, the Paris branch of the banking firm of J. P. Morgan and Company, on the last day of the allotted time, he nearly lost the option, for an unexpected reason. Morgan, Harjes and Company did not wish to accept the money. Though the bank was under American control, French procedure prevailed, and its officers were reluctant to hold money in escrow. They feared there might be a dispute as to whether it finally would belong to the War Ministry that deposited it, or to the Wrights. It required eight hours of perspiring persuasion on the part of a War Ministry representative before the bankers agreed to accept the money and the option became binding. After the option was in force, but before the date set in the contract for the final payment, the French War Ministry sent a commission to Dayton for the purpose of obtaining some amendments to the contract, pertaining to the test flights. This commission, which sailed from Cherbourg on the *Saint Paul*, was headed by Commandant Bonel, of the Army Engineer Corps. Another member was Arnold Fordyce.

They reached New York on March 18, 1906. The other two members were Captain Fournier, military attache of the French Embassy at Washington, and Walter Van Rensselaer Berry, an American subject, who was legal counselor to that embassy. Though Fordyce was by now zealously pro-Wright, the men at the War Ministry had no fear of his exerting too much influence on the others, because of the presence of Commandant Bonel, who was outspokenly skeptical. He had witnessed tests by the French Government of the unsuccessful machine designed by Clement Ader, a few years previously, and was convinced that no heavier-than-air machine had ever flown or ever could. Bonel would hardly let the commission make a fool of itself. Since he was the only one of the four who spoke no English, he would need to have everything explained to him—all the more reason why he would not be easily imposed upon. Before the French quartet had been in Dayton long, however, Bonel was the most enthusiastic convert of all. The visitors met dependable witnesses of flights who had previously talked to Fordyce, and photographs of the machine in flight could hardly be fakes. Most of all, they were impressed by the obviously high character of the Wrights themselves. In cables to France they strongly recommended that the deal be closed. But while the commission was still in Dayton, the European war crisis had subsided. Even before the formal settlement of the dispute, at the close of the conference at Algeciras, Spain, on April 7, it was known that France would still have a favored position in Morocco, and the need for a scouting plane by the French Army became less pressing. The War Ministry now began to demand more and more in airplane performance. They would cable asking if the plane could fly at an altitude of at least 1,000 feet, if the speed could be greater than hitherto mentioned. Then the next day there would be a request for greater weight-carrying capacity. The Wrights, slow as always to make rash promises, said frankly that they had never flown much higher than 100 feet, but that the plane could fly at much more than 1,000 feet, though they would probably need additional practice before making a demonstration. They could increase either the speed or the weight-carrying capacity, too, but it would not be easy to do both in the same machine—no more than one could produce a draft horse and a race horse in the same animal. The demonstrations of the machine the Wrights agreed to make were already stiff enough, and if they failed on any one of them, within the allotted time, even if only on account of delay caused by accident, their contract would be broken, but they felt sure of what they could do and were willing to take the chance. When the time limit for the deposit of the rest of the 1,000,000 francs with J. P. Morgan expired, on April 5, the commission was recalled. Before leaving Dayton the visitors expressed their own vexation over the rejection by the Paris officials of their recommendations. The members of the commission still believed, though, that when Bonel and Fordyce were back in Paris and presented all the facts to the War Ministry, there would be an extension of time and the deal carried out. But it never was. The French Minister of War agreed, however, that the Wrights were entitled to receive the forfeit money of 25,000 francs held in escrow by J. P. Morgan and Company.

Before leaving Dayton, the Frenchmen said they believed they knew what was back of the failure to close the deal. They said frankly that it was probably the present attitude of Captain Ferber, the man who had been instrumental in starting the negotiations. Ferber, they thought, with the Moroccan question no longer pressing, had now decided that with his knowledge of the Wright plane he could build one himself, and so become the French pioneer in aviation—a greater honor than being merely the instrument of introducing the aeroplane into France. During the time the Frenchmen were at their hotel in Dayton, it might have been expected that their presence would become known to local newspapermen and that the world would have learned of what was going on. To avoid attracting attention they had taken the precaution to avoid the Hotel Algonquin where Fordyce had stayed on his earlier visit, and were at the Beckel House. They were unmolested there until an employee of one of the telegraph offices "tipped off" a reporter friend. The telegrapher had noticed various cables in code going to France and felt sure the Frenchmen must be carrying on an important deal. A reporter nabbed Fordyce and Bonel one evening in the hotel lobby on their return from a theater. As Bonel spoke no English, Fordyce parried the reporter's questions. He thought a plausible explanation of their presence would be that they were studying the water system of a typical American city. But what he said was that they were studying Dayton's "water pipes." That satisfied as well as amused the reporter and nothing about the French commission got into the papers. The local newspapermen had failed to note that, after Fordyce's previous visit, the New York

Herald of January 4 had printed a brief item about his having seen the Wrights to discuss a contract. It never occurred to anyone in Dayton that the Wright brothers could have attracted visitors from across the Atlantic, for the Wrights still were not "news." If the Frenchmen had made a statement that they were there dickering with the Wrights for a $200,000 contract, it is possible that the local papers would not have printed it. They might not have believed such a tale. Only a few days after the French commission had left Dayton, another foreign visitor dropped in on the Wrights—the Englishman, Patrick Y. Alexander. After some casual talk, he inquired with seeming innocence, as if just to make conversation, "*Is the French commission still here?*" The Wrights were startled. So great had been the secrecy about the visit of the Frenchmen that not many even in the French Government were permitted to know about their trip to Dayton. How did this mysterious "Britisher" know about it? The Wrights assumed that he must have been a volunteer worker in the British secret service. It was now obvious that he had crossed the Atlantic for no other purpose than to call on the Wrights and had hoped to burst in upon them while the Frenchmen were still there. After a stay of only one day in Dayton he hastened back to New York to sail on the next boat. His call made it all the more clear that the British were then more interested in what other European governments were doing about planes than in acquiring an air fleet of their own. Incredulity about the Wrights's power flights continued at the Aero Club and in newspaper circles in France. In November, 1906, the Wrights received a visitor in Dayton, Sherman Morse, representing the New York *Herald*. His introduction was a cabled message to his managing editor from the owner of the paper, James Gordon Bennett Jr., in Paris. The message said, "*Send one of your best reporters to Dayton to get truth about Wright brothers reported flights.*" The reporter got the truth and wrote intelligent articles that appeared in the New York *Herald*. These included reports of men who had witnessed flights. Parts of the Morse articles appeared in the *Herald*'s Paris edition on November 22 and 23. But evidently those in charge of the

Paris *Herald* still were not convinced by the reports from Dayton by their own man. On November 28, the Paris *Herald* had an editorial about the Wrights which included the statement that in Europe curiosity about their machine was "*clouded with skepticism owing to the fact that information regarding the invention is so small while the results which its inventors claim to have achieved are so colossal.*" And the next day, the Paris *Herald* gave space to a news item in which Santos-Dumont was reported as saying that he "*did not find any evidence of their [the Wrights] having done anything at all.*" Late in 1906, Frank S. Lahm, who had [previously] cabled his brother-in-law, Weaver, to make an investigation, was in the United States, and he, accompanied by [Henry] Weaver, went on November 22 to see the Wrights in Dayton. He was convinced, of course, that their statements could be relied upon, but he made further investigation of his own, interviewing witnesses not previously seen by Weaver. After his return to Paris, he prepared a long letter to the Paris *Herald*, in which he expressed his belief in the reported flights.

The newspaper devoted a column to the Lahm letter on February 10, 1907. But having distrusted what their own representative had written, it was not to be expected that the editors would give full belief to what Lahm now told them.

In the same issue as his letter, was an editorial heading of "*Flyers or Liars.*" "*The Wrights have flown or they have not flown,*" the paper profoundly stated [with doubt]. "*They possess a machine or they do not possess one. They are in fact either flyers or liars. It is difficult to fly. It is easy to say 'we have flown.'*"

☐☐☐☐☐☐☐☐☐☐☐

The Wrights were at work in 1906 developing a new engine having vertical instead of horizontal cylinders. Though they were doing no flying, brief references to them occasionally appeared in newspapers. These caught the attention of a New York businessman, U. S. Eddy, who thought the Wrights and their Patents might be of interest to Charles R. Flint and Company, New York bankers and promoters. Eddy was a former partner of

Flint in a shipping line and knew that they were constantly on the lookout for new inventions worthy of their consideration. Partly to do a favor for an old friend and associate, he decided to go to Dayton for a talk with the Wrights. Eddy arrived in Dayton on Thanksgiving Day and saw the Wrights the next day. They did not discuss business at this meeting. Eddy simply got acquainted with them, and satisfied himself that any statements they made about their invention could be depended upon, but he did tell them he felt sure the Flint firm would be much interested in helping them to develop the machine's financial possibilities. The Wrights left Dayton on December 5 for New York, to attend an exhibit to be given by the newly formed Aero Club of America. Before leaving New York they went with Eddy to meet Frank R. Cordley, a member of the Flint firm. At this time Flint was in Europe, but the Wrights met him in New York not long afterward. Flint was often over-enthusiastic about new projects, and Cordley was the more cautious member of the firm. His job was to hold Flint in check. But he, as well as Flint and other associates, was favorably impressed by the Wrights, and they began to talk business.

On December 26, 1906, George H. Nolte, an employee of the firm, went to Dayton to work out preliminary details. At first the Flints spoke of the possibility of buying all European rights to the airplane, but the deal finally made was that the Flints should be the Wrights's business representatives, on a twenty percent commission basis, in all countries except the United States. A year or two later it was agreed that the Wrights should manage their own affairs also in Great Britain and its colonies. The Flints proposed that they would have the Czar of Russia, and certain other crowned heads, request private demonstrations of the flying machine. But the Wrights were not impressed by such suggestions and in a letter to the Flints said they thought it would be better for them to "*look the ground over first before making arrangements with the Czar.*" The Flints had an associate in Europe, Hart O. Berg, who, in 1899, had helped to introduce American electric automobiles on the continent. He had acted, too, for Simon Lake, inventor of the submarine, in dealing with

Russia and other foreign governments. They thought Berg might be able to start negotiations for forming a European Wright company. But Berg, not knowing the Wrights, and feeling scant confidence in what they were reported to have done, was less than lukewarm over the idea. Flint suggested that it would be well for at least one of the Wrights to go to Europe, with expenses paid, to discuss their invention with Berg and give him more faith in it. The Wrights themselves, said Flint, could do more than anyone else to implant in Berg the wholehearted enthusiasm he would need to convince possible buyers. On May 15, 1907, a telegram came from the Flint office urging that one of the Wrights should start to Europe at once. Wilbur "grabbed a few things" and prepared to go to New York the next day, to sail on the *Campania*. As he planned to tarry abroad only a short time—only long enough to convince Berg—his baggage consisted of one suitcase. He would stop first in England for a brief stay before going to Paris. Wilbur was to land in Liverpool on a Saturday. Berg, eager to see one of the Wrights face to face and settle in his own mind if these inventors were really dependable, went to London to meet him. "*I knew him the minute he stepped from the train,*" said Berg long afterward. "*To begin with, it is always easy to spot an American among Englishmen, and I saw no other American coming down the platform. But even if there had been other Americans I'm sure I would have known which one was Wilbur Wright. There was a modest self-assurance about him that tallied with his character as I had heard about it.*" After the first greetings, Berg said, "*Now let's see about picking up the rest of your luggage.*" But Wilbur smilingly explained that the one suitcase was all he had brought. On the way to the hotel, Wilbur decided that it might be advisable for him to buy a suit of evening clothes and they went at once to a tailor shop on the Strand.

It didn't take Berg long to convince himself that Wilbur Wright was no slicker, but decidedly on the level, and that if he said his machine would fly, then it must be true. A day after their first meeting, Berg and Wilbur were joined by Frank R. Cordley, of the Flint firm, in Europe on a vacation trip, and the three went to

Paris together. They "descended," as the French say, at the Hotel Meurice, on the Rue de Rivoli. It was still broad daylight when they arrived and Berg almost immediately led Wilbur across the street into the Tuileries Gardens. They strolled to the Place de la Concorde and looked up the length of the magnificent Avenue des Champs Elysees to the Arc de Triomphe. The horse chestnut trees were still in blossom, and Berg, a resident of Paris during most of his life, was feeling happy over the opportunity to show this stranger his first glimpse of the most beautiful city on earth at its loveliest season. Before he had been long in Paris, Wilbur attended a balloon meet at St. Cloud, and a few days later made his first trip in a balloon. A Paris *Herald* reporter, who talked with Wilbur at St. Cloud, was impressed by his reticence and made this statement, "*Mr. Wright talked carefully, as if all was mapped out in advance. It was obvious that he feared to be caught in a trap concerning his remarkable machine and what he wants to do with it. At the end of each question his clean-shaven face relapsed into a broad, sphinx-like smile.*" It now seemed wise to try to form a company to buy European rights to the airplane, or to sell the rights to a private financier, rather than to deal with the Government, through politicians, and a wealthy man had become interested, Henri Deutsch de la Meurthe, an oil magnate, who had also been a patron of ballooning. When Wilbur Wright met Deutsch de la Meurthe, the latter, a cautious trader, said that before investing any money he wanted to make sure the French Government would be interested in buying airplanes.

    Wilbur then decided that it would be both discourteous and imprudent not to have a talk with Letellier or Fordyce, with whom there had been previous negotiations, and let them know what was going on—particularly since Deutsch de la Meurthe was known to have close relations with *Le Matin*, a rival of Letellier's newspaper, *Le Journal*. He got in touch with Fordyce, and told him a little of the current situation. Shortly afterward, Letellier invited Wilbur to lunch. Letellier seemed indignant that the Wrights had not resumed negotiations with him. Wilbur told him he could doubtless be included if a company should be formed.

But that didn't suit Letellier. He didn't care to join a company organized by Deutsch de la Meurthe—if a company was formed he wanted to be the prime mover in it himself. He said nothing, however, about interfering with efforts being made to form a company—possibly because he thought they would not be successful. Deutsch de la Meurthe now went to call upon the Minister of Marine, with whom he was well-acquainted, and was escorted by him to meet the Minister of War, General Picquart, a hero of the [Alfred] Dreyfus case. General [Georges] Picquart was not familiar with what had previously been done regarding the possible purchase of a Wright machine, as the negotiations had been carried on during the regime of his predecessor. But he had Commandant Bonel bring the records to him and when he looked them over was impressed by the fact that the Wrights's invention had been considered seriously. No less impressed was Deutsch de la Meurthe. General Picquart said he realized the importance of the Wright invention and was disposed to take favorable action toward buying planes, provided the Wrights would guarantee that their machine could fly at a height of 300 meters.

That was enough encouragement for Deutsch de la Meurthe. In fact, he became highly enthusiastic over the outlook. He had not before appreciated the seriousness of the previous negotiations. Now he began to talk about details of the articles of incorporation of a proposed company. Commandant Bonel was elated over the news that his government might at last be buying Wright airplanes. His pride and prestige had been hurt by the failure of his recommendations to be accepted. Moreover, for patriotic reasons, he wanted the French Army to be the first to adopt what he regarded as an epoch-making new invention. Now that the outlook was once again more favorable, he was in a communicative mood when he chanced to meet Fordyce, with whom he had traveled to Dayton. Fordyce showed his surprise at what Bonel told him. He went at once to tell this news to his employer, Henri Letellier. Now Letellier expressed great indignation. He had an agreement in writing, he said, that if the War Ministry bought any Wright airplanes the purchase should be made through *Le Journal*, and any departure from that plan he must construe as an unfriendly and illegal act. Immediately he went to the office of the Minister of War where with great politeness he showed to General Picquart a letter obtained from his predecessor. Since the option the Wrights had given to Fordyce had expired, the agreement between the War Ministry and Letellier was no longer in force. But General Picquart, if he understood that, after a hasty examination of the records, did not argue the point. Possibly he was too practical a politician to enter a controversy with an influential publisher. At any rate, he asked Deutsch de la Meurthe to withdraw from the negotiations. It was Deutsch de la Meurthe's turn to be indignant. He believed at first that the Wrights had simply used him for a tool. But later, when he understood the facts and saw that the Wrights were not to blame for what had happened, he once more was friendly with them. The Wrights saw that their most promising opportunity for an immediate contract was through Letellier and *Le Journal*. Consequently, Fordyce, representing that newspaper, came back into the picture. Within a day or two after negotiations were thus resumed, Fordyce came to Berg in an apologetic mood, showing deep embarrassment. He said he had been asked to submit a proposal that it hardly seemed worthwhile to discuss at all, and yet he had no choice but to convey a message, as had been requested of him, by a man high in government circles. The deal might go through at once, said Fordyce, but there would have to be a little re-wording of the contract. The Wrights must not ask 1,000,000 francs but 1,250,000 francs. Then they would receive their million francs. Berg knew well enough what would happen when he told this to Wilbur. There would be no objection to having the contract call for more money than the Wrights were to receive, said Wilbur calmly, *but* the contract must give the name of the man who would receive that additional sum. Berg went to the office of the man who had communicated, by way of Fordyce, the astounding suggestion. He hoped there had been some misunderstanding. But to Berg's astonishment and disgust, the man said with shocking candor that he would indeed expect

250,000 francs ($50,000) as his reward for putting through the deal. Before indignantly walking out of the man's office, Berg told him the Wrights would never be a party to such financial irregularity and that the negotiations with the Minister of War would have to be carried on without the cooperation of anyone in the Government who expected to be paid for his efforts. [After the First World War that same man was tried for treason.] Meanwhile, Wilbur had cabled to Orville to join him in Paris. And with the prospect that it might be necessary to make a demonstration of what the Wright machine could do, a plane was crated and shipped from Dayton to France. Orville arrived in Paris around the first of August, and the Wright's chief mechanic, Charlie Taylor, came about a week later. While crossing the Atlantic, Orville had a talk with another passenger that illustrates his possession of a freakish kind of memory. An Englishman had been introduced to him and, after a few moments of conversation, Orville asked if they had not met before. No, the Englishman said, they had not. He had no recollection of any previous meeting, and he was sure if there had been one he would remember it. The man's face was not familiar, but there was something about his voice and gestures that somehow stirred in Orville old memories. Finally, Orville inquired, "*Were you by any chance at the World's Fair in Chicago back in 1893?*" The Englishman nodded. "*And*," asked Orville, "*did you ever have occasion to explain to a bystander some kind of device at one of the exhibits?*" Yes, that also might have happened. "*There*," said Orville, much relieved that his memory had not played him tricks, "*must have been where I saw you. I felt sure I couldn't be mistaken about your voice.*" After Orville had joined Wilbur at the Hotel Meurice, the brothers did not find their business affairs too pressing to do a lot of sightseeing. Neither one spoke French, but Orville had acquired a fair reading knowledge of it.

Oddly enough, Wilbur, who had learned Greek and Latin easily, made no effort to learn French. He jokingly said it was a convenience not to know it, as it saved him from a lot of talking. As they went about their sightseeing, Wilbur, always a reader of history was especially fascinated by all places of historic interest. Orville found himself spending much time each day in the Louvre. Those days gave him an appreciation of good paintings that he never lost. Negotiations with the French Government dragged on. For weeks the Wrights were kept in uncertainty. They never saw any of the people they were dealing with. Their only contact with anyone at the War Ministry was through Fordyce, and they had no way of knowing, except from what he told them, whether any progress was being made. Nothing came of the long negotiations. The Wrights were not alone in being disappointed. Commandant Bonel, not long afterward, perhaps as a consequence of the failure of his recommendations to be accepted, resigned from the Army. Late in the summer of 1907, the Wrights left Paris. Orville went first to London, at the suggestion of Flint and Company to have a talk with the receiver of the Barnum and Bailey Circus and the Buffalo Bill Wild West Show, then in bankruptcy. The receiver wondered if the Wright plane could be flown within an enclosure where an admission fee could be charged. Wilbur Wright had set out with Berg for St. Petersburg. They changed their minds about going to Russia, however, and, instead, stopped at Berlin where Orville shortly afterward joined them. As the train on which Wilbur and Berg traveled was passing through Belgium, Wilbur noticed a sign indicating that they were in the little town of Jemappes. Then he recalled that a great battle took place there back in 1792. He began to discuss the battle with an exact knowledge of details that astounded Berg. Wilbur had read about it in his youth.

Over and over again, Berg and others who dealt with Wilbur Wright—were similarly impressed not only by the range of his reading but by the fact that no knowledge he had once acquired ever seemed to grow dim. In Berlin, the brothers were able to gain direct contact with top flight men—with the minister of the Kaiser's war department, and also with the minister of the department of transportation. These German officials were highly intelligent and not slow about recognizing the tremendous importance of the Wright machine if it would perform as the brothers said it could. The Wrights had proposed a contract in which they would agree to furnish a machine capable of carrying, at a speed of forty miles an hour, two men and a supply of fuel for a flight of 125 miles, and to make a demonstration flight of one hour fulfilling every requirement of the contract before one pfennig should be paid to them. The German officials could not deny the fairness of this offer, and could see no reason why the Wrights should have made it unless they could carry it out. Besides, they were not altogether unacquainted with the earlier work of the Wright brothers, accounts of whose glider and power flights had been appearing for five or six years in German technical publications. But in spite of all this the officials were in a quandary. They could not bring themselves to believe that what the Wrights now offered could be possible. They were afraid to sign their names to a contract that generally would be considered as foolish as a contract for a perpetual motion machine. They might become the laughingstock of the world. On the other hand, these officials did not want to let an invention of such potentialities, if it really existed, slip through their fingers. They therefore gave, instead of a signed contract, their solemn verbal promise that if the Wrights would make a flight before them, such as had been offered in the proposed written contract, they would buy planes on the terms the Wrights had offered.

The Wrights felt that these officials, being at the head of important departments, could be relied upon, and they were willing to take their verbal guarantee to buy planes upon the successful demonstration of the machine. When they left Germany, they fully expected to return the next March to make such a demonstration. [They could not foresee that they would have too many other engagements in definite contracts elsewhere before another four months had passed.] Wilbur Wright returned from Europe in November of 1907. But Orville remained a little longer to attend to having a number of engines built in Paris by the firm of Barriquand and Marre. The Wrights wanted to have in reserve duplicates of their American engine, at that time in customs, at Le Havre, for use the next year.

Barriquand and Marre were manufacturers of precision instruments and had built light motors. They doubted if the Wright motor gave as much power as was claimed for it, but they felt sure that if it did, the copies they made of it—on account of more careful workmanship—would give considerably more power than the original. But as later events showed, they gave less.

At that time it was not known that when one motor is made as an exact copy, to the thousandth of an inch, of another motor, of supposedly the same steels and other metals, but from different foundries and mills, months of experiment are required before the new motor can be made to work properly.

□□□□□□□□□□

While in Paris, in 1907, the Wrights naturally had visits with Frank S. Lahm, who had arranged with his brother-in-law, Henry Weaver, of Mansfield, to investigate the reports from America of human flight. Lahm invited the inventors to his home and there they met his son, Lieutenant Frank P. Lahm, who was recuperating from an attack of typhoid fever. The younger Lahm, a former instructor at West Point, had recently spent a year at the French Cavalry School at Saumur. He, as well as his father, was much interested in aeronautics. The previous October he had won the James Gordon Bennett Balloon Race by starting at Paris and landing in England. Probably the only American Army officer who recognized that the airplane should now be taken seriously, he was delighted to meet the Wright brothers, with whom he now began a lasting friendship. After he had learned a little about their negotiations in France, he began to urge the United States War Department to take more interest in the airplane. It so happened, that, in September, 1907, only a few weeks after this meeting, Lieutenant Lahm was transferred by the War Department from the Cavalry to the Signal Corps, to be stationed at Washington. His first assignment was to make a tour of Europe, before returning to Washington, and report on the situation regarding dirigible aircraft in several countries. Soon afterward he returned to Washington. The presence of a man in the War Department there who felt enthusiasm for the airplane's possibilities, and who had strong faith in the Wrights, may have had its effect on his associates. At any rate, there was now in the War Department a man who believed in the Wrights. When Wilbur stopped in Washington shortly before Thanksgiving, 1907, en route to Dayton, on his return from France, he had a talk with General Crozier and Major Fuller of the Ordnance Department, and with General Allen, head of the Signal Corps—the organization that would conduct tests of the airplane and use it if the Ordnance Board sanctioned and provided funds for its purchase. At this meeting Wilbur stated the price the Wrights would accept ($25,000) and the performance of the machine that they were willing to guarantee. These terms, agreed upon between the brothers before Wilbur left France, were stiff enough, it was thought, to bar any competition. The Ordnance Board was to have a meeting on December 5, and Wilbur was invited to appear before it. He did so, but the meeting did not inspire him with confidence that an early contract could be obtained at the price of $25,000. The Wrights were not willing to accept less, because they thought they had better prospects abroad. However, the Signal Corps soon began drawing up specifications, and, on December 23, advertised for bids.

    Inasmuch as the Wright machine was the only one in existence that could meet these requirements, and the price was understood in advance, advertising for bids may have been superfluous, but it was considered necessary to meet demands of red tape. Among specifications set forth in the advertisement for bids were these, the plane must be tested in the presence of Army officers, it must be able to carry for one hour a passenger besides the pilot, the two weighing not less than 350 pounds, it must show an average speed of forty miles an hour, in a ten-mile test, and carry enough fuel for 125 miles. Also, the machine must have "demountability," that is, it should be built in such a way that it could be taken apart, and later reassembled, without too much difficulty, when necessary to transport it on an army truck from one place to another. Almost from the day the advertisements for bids appeared, the War Department was subject to editorial attacks—not because it had been so slow about interesting itself in the airplane, but because it had done so at all. The New York *Globe* said, "*One might be inclined to assume from the following announcement, 'the United States Army is asking bids for a military airship,' that the era of practical human flight had arrived, or at least that the government had seriously taken up the problem of developing this means of travel. A very brief examination of the conditions imposed and the reward offered for successful bidders suffices, however, to prove this assumption a delusion. A machine such as is described in the Signal Corps's specifications would record the solution of all the difficulties in the way of the heavier-than-air airship, and, in fact, finally give mankind almost as complete control of the air as it now has of the land and the water. It would be worth to the world almost any number of millions of dollars, would certainly revolutionize warfare and possibly the transportation of passengers, would open to easy access regions hitherto inaccessible except to the most daring pioneers and would, in short, be probably the most epoch-making invention in the history of civilization. Nothing in any way approaching such a machine has ever been constructed (the Wright brothers's claims still await public confirmation), and the man who has achieved such a success would have, or at least should have, no need of competing in a contest where the successful bidder might be given his trial because his offer was a few hundred or thousand dollars lower than that of someone else. If there is any possibility that such an airship is within measurable distance of perfection any government could well afford to provide its inventor with unlimited resources and promise him a prize, in case of success, running into the millions.*" The *American Magazine of Aeronautics* (later called *Aeronautics*) devoted its opening article in the issue of January, 1908, to pointing out the absurdity of what the War Department was trying to do. "*There is not a known flying machine in the world which could fulfill these specifications at the present moment,*" [declared the editorial]. "*Had an inventor such a machine as required would he not be in a position to ask almost any reasonable* sum from the government for its use? Would not the government, instead of the inventor, be a bidder? Perhaps the Signal Corps has been too much influenced by the 'hot air' of theorizers, in which aeronautics unfortunately abounds, who have fathomed the entire problem without ever accomplishing anything, talk is their stock in trade and models or machines are beneath them because beyond their impractical nature. Why is not the experience with Professor Langley a good guide? We doubt very much if the government receives any bids at all possible to be accepted." To the surprise of nearly everyone, forty-one proposals were received. Most of the bidders were the same kind of cranks the Ordnance Board had at first supposed the Wrights to be, and their bids were rejected when they failed to put up a required ten percent of the proposed price of the plane, as a sign of good faith. Two other bidders besides the Wrights did make a ten percent deposit. One of these, J. F. Scott, of Chicago, had made a bid of $1,000, and promised delivery of a plane in 185 days. Another was Augustus Moore Herring. His price was $20,000, delivery to be in 180 days. The Wrights's bid was $25,000, with delivery promised in 200 days. Receipt of these unexpected bids created a problem.

Everyone assumed that none of the bidders except the Wrights had anything practical to offer, and yet the government would be expected to accept the lowest bid and let the winner show what he could do. No matter how dismally he failed to meet requirements, dealing with him would take up time and cause delays. General Allen, of the Signal Corps, went to Secretary of War [William Howard] Taft to inquire how the War Department might get around the difficulty. Taft said they could accept all legal bids and as only the Wrights could meet the requirements, the others would be eliminated. The only difficulty was that even if no money would ever be paid to the other bidders, yet it would be illegal to accept the bids unless enough money to pay for whatever was ordered was known to be available. However, Taft suggested a way around that. He knew that the President had at his disposal an emergency fund to do with as he saw fit. If the President wished to he could guarantee that all bidders would be paid if they met the tests. General Allen, accompanied by Captain Charles deForest Chandler and Lieutenant F. P. Lahm, Signal Corps officers, called upon President Roosevelt who promptly agreed with Taft's suggestion. He told them to accept all bids and that he would place funds at their disposal to meet legal technicalities. The Signal Corps then agreed to buy planes from all three bidders if they met the necessary requirements. One of those bidders soon eliminated himself by asking the Government to return his ten percent deposit. Though the government was not obliged to return the deposit, it nevertheless did so. Herring, the only remaining legal bidder besides the Wrights, hung on a while longer. What Augustus Moore Herring had in mind was simply to obtain the contract in consequence of his lower price and then try to sublet it to the Wrights. He even had the effrontery to go to Dayton to see the Wrights and make such a proposal. Naturally, they were not interested. The Wrights's bid was accepted on February 8, 1908. As it happened, this was not the only important contract the Wrights entered into at about that time. On March 3, three weeks after the Signal Corps had accepted their bid, they closed a contract with Lazare Weiller, a wealthy Frenchman, to form a syndicate to buy the rights to manufacture, sell, or license the use of the Wright plane in France. Upon completion of certain tests of the machine, the Wrights were to receive a substantial amount in cash, a block of stock, and provision for royalties. The French company would be known as La Compagnie Generale de Navigation Aerienne.

    A member of the syndicate was [Henri] Deutsch de la Meurthe who had taken steps toward forming a French company some time previously. One provision of the US War Department contract was that the Government could deduct ten percent of the purchase price for each mile per hour that the machine fell short of the forty-mile goal. That is, if it went only thirty-nine miles an hour, the Wrights would be docked ten percent, if only thirty-eight miles, another ten percent, and so on. If the machine did not do at least thirty-six miles an hour, then the Government didn't have to accept it at all. On the other hand, the Wrights would receive a ten percent bonus for each mile per hour they attained above forty. It was the intention of the Signal Corps, and the Wrights so understood it, that these reduced or additional payments would be for either a mile or a fraction of a mile. But a Government legal department made a surprising interpretation of that part of the contract. If at the time of the tests the plane went $40^{99}/_{100}$ miles, the Wrights would not be paid for more than 40, but if the plane fell short of 40 miles an hour by only $1/_{100}$ of a mile, or even less, then they would be docked for a full mile.

[Orville did not learn of that astounding example of the legal mind at work until after he arrived at Washington to prepare for the tests and it was then too late to build a faster plane. But in the final tests the next year, he had a plane that he knew would give the buyer no opportunity to take advantage of what he regarded as a one-sided interpretation of the contract.] Though the Wrights had done no flying since October, 1905, they had done much work on improving both plane and engine. Their newest engine, capable of producing about thirty-five horsepower continuously, was also so much better as to reliability that now long flights could be made without danger of failure of the motive power. During all their experiments at the Huffman Pasture they had continued to ride "belly-buster," as a boy usually does when coasting on a sled. Lying flat in that way and controlling the mechanism partly by swinging the hips from one side to the other was good enough for the experimental stages of aviation, but the Wrights knew that if a plane was to have practical use the pilot must be able to take an ordinary sitting position and do the controlling and guiding with his hands and feet as in an automobile. It was not all fun lying flat for an hour at a time with head raised to be on the lookout for possible obstacles. "*I used to think,*" said Orville in later years, "*the back of my neck would break if I endured one more turn around the field.*" The brothers therefore had adopted a different arrangement of the control levers, for use in a sitting position, and a seat for a passenger. Moreover, the machine could be steered from either seat and thus was suitable for training other pilots if occasion should arise. The plane sent to France for possible trials in 1907 was thus equipped. They revamped the machine they had used at the Huffman Pasture in 1905, and installed their later improvements. It now had an engine with vertical instead of horizontal cylinders. With this machine they would go to Kitty Hawk and gain needed practice in handling their new arrangement of the control levers. The United States Government tests would be made at Fort Myer, Virginia, near Washington. Delivery of the machine had to be made by August 28, and the tests themselves were to begin shortly afterward, in September. But at about that same time, one of the brothers would make a demonstration in France. They had not yet decided which of them would fly at Fort Myer and which should go to France. But both had to be well-prepared and there was no time to lose. They must be established at Kitty Hawk as soon as possible. Wilbur Wright set out for Kitty Hawk ahead of Orville and arrived there April 9, 1908. He was joined within a week by a mechanic from Dayton, Charles W. Furnas. First of all, it was necessary to do much rebuilding of the camp. The buildings had not only suffered from storms, but had been stripped of much timber by persons who supposed the Wrights had permanently abandoned them. The plane was shipped in crates from Dayton April 11, but had to be left for some time in a freight depot at Elizabeth City until the new shed was completed at Kitty Hawk.

Both Orville and the plane reached there on April 25. It might have been expected that with at least two governments now showing interest in the Wright plane, each of the brothers would have been besieged en route by reporters and others. But the general public, including reporters, still seemed disinclined to believe in human flight. At about the same time that the Wrights were preparing to go to Kitty Hawk, a publisher brought out a new novel by H. G. Wells, *Tono Bungay*, in which the leading character built a gliding machine "along the lines of the Wright brothers's airplane," and finally a flying machine. That stirred one or two American book reviewers to chide the author for putting such fantastic material into a tale otherwise plausible. Because of the persistence of that kind of incredulity, the Wrights did not expect many sightseers, least of all newspapermen, at Kitty Hawk during their preparations for government tests. Therefore they did not think it necessary to keep their plans secret. Though they weren't seeking reporters, neither were they trying to avoid them. They simply went ahead without giving any thought to newspapermen one way or another. But the Wrights were about to be discovered. Not until May 6 did either of the brothers make a flight. But the newspapers, instead of ignoring what the Wrights had done, now began to report what they had *not* done. On May 1, the *Virginian-Pilot*, of Norfolk (the same paper that had reported, not too accurately, the first flight of an airplane), carried a wild tale that one of the Wright brothers had flown the day before ten miles out over the ocean. Practically the same story was widely published the next day. Katharine Wright on May 2 telegraphed her brothers that "the newspapers" had reported a flight. As the Wrights later learned, the *B. Z. Mittag*, in Berlin, carried a dispatch from Paris, "*From America comes the news that the Wright brothers for the first time have made in public a controlled flight. The flight was made on April 30, at Norfolk, Virginia, before a US Government Commission.*" That same story must have reached London, for the Wrights received a cablegram from Patrick Alexander, "*Very hearty congratulations.*"

Joseph Dosher, who had been the Weather Bureau man at Kitty Hawk in 1903, but was now stationed 30 miles north of Kitty Hawk, telephoned to the Kill Devil Hills Life-Saving crew, on May 2, seeking information about the Wrights, presumably at the request of some newspaper. That same day, the Greensboro (North Carolina) *News* published a telegram from Elizabeth City, dated May 1, saying that the Wright brothers "of airship fame" were at Nags Head with their "famous flying machine." On May 1, the New York *Herald* had wired to the Weather Bureau operator at Manteo, on Roanoke Island, for information. And on May 2, the *Herald* published an item with a Norfolk dateline, that the Wrights were reported to have flown "over the ocean." This dispatch appeared also in the *Herald*'s Paris edition. Just below the report in the Paris edition was an editorial comment that if the Wrights had actually flown two miles, then they had broken the records of [Ferdinand Marie Leon] Delagrange and [Henri and Maurice] Farman in France. The *Herald* editor evidently was still unaware that long before Delagrange, Farman, or other Wright copyists abroad had even left the ground in flight, the Wright brothers had flown twenty-four miles. Inasmuch as the Wrights had not yet begun their flights of 1908, it was not easy for the New York *Herald* to obtain confirmation or more details about the imaginary flight out over the ocean. No regularly employed newspaperman at Norfolk wanted to go to Kitty Hawk on what might be a wild goose chase. But D. Bruce Salley, a freelance reporter at Norfolk, was willing to make the trip. Salley reached Manteo on May 4, and the Wright brothers's records show that he came to their camp the next day. He told the brothers he had been asked by a New York paper to investigate the story of their flight over the ocean. The day after Salley's visit, the Wrights did make their first flight of the season, and though Salley did not see it, he learned about it by phone from one of the men at the Kill Devil Hills Life-Saving Station. His informant told him that one of the Wrights had flown at least 1,000 feet, at about sixty feet above the ground. Salley immediately sent a query from Manteo, giving briefly the gist of the story, to a list of papers he hoped would be interested. Most of the papers ignored the message, but the telegraph editor of the Cleveland (Ohio) *Leader* not only wasn't interested but was indignant that his intelligence should be insulted by the offer of so improbable a tale. He declined to pay the telegraph toll for the short message, even though at the night press rate of only one-third of a cent a word the cost could hardly have been more than a dime. His only reply to Salley was an admonition to "cut out the wildcat stuff." Salley, now equally indignant, wired back offering to give names of well-known persons who could testify to his reliability, but the Cleveland editor paid no further attention. When Salley's query reached the office of the New York *Herald*, it put the editors in a quandary. Though they had printed the brief report about a flight that hadn't occurred—now they were beginning to wonder if all the reports about the Wrights weren't fakes. Yet they knew that the owner of the newspaper, James Gordon Bennett, living in Paris, would almost certainly discharge any editor responsible for omitting the story if it *were* true. They decided, with misgivings, to print the story and it appeared the next morning on the first page of the *Herald*, though not in the most prominent position. Then the editors determined to send a staff man to Kitty Hawk for the facts. They picked for this job their star reporter, brilliant, lovable Byron Rufus Newton—later to become Assistant Secretary of the Treasury, and afterward Collector of Customs in New York—one of the ablest newspapermen of his time.

If the Wrights proved to be fakers no one could do a better job than "By" Newton at exposing them. Other editors, too, decided that the time had come to get the "lowdown" on the Wright brothers. By the time Newton reached the little boarding place, the Tranquil House, in Manteo, he had been joined by two other correspondents, William Hoster, of the New York *American*, and P. H. McGowan, of the London *Daily Mail*. The next day two others arrived [on the scene], Arthur Ruhl, writer, and James H. Hare, photographer, for *Collier's Weekly*. The newly arrived correspondents, noting the desolate isolation of Kitty Hawk, thought it probable enough that the Wrights must prefer to be let alone. Perhaps, they thought, if intruders came, the Wrights wouldn't fly at all. They decided that if the Wrights were secretive, they themselves would be no less so. They would hide in the pine woods, as near as possible to the Wright camp, and observe with field glasses what happened. That meant a short walk to a wharf on Roanoke Island, five miles by sailing boat to Haman's Bay, across the sound, and then a walk of a mile or so over the sand to the place where they should secrete themselves. They made a dicker with a boatman to take them all back and forth each day and act as their guide. Provided with food and water, field glasses, and cameras, they set out about 4 o'clock each morning from May 11 to May 14 to keep their vigil. Hour after hour they fought mosquitoes and wood ticks and sometimes were drenched by rain. But to their astonishment they several times witnessed human flight. The first flight any of them witnessed was early in the morning of May 11. *"For some minutes,"* wrote Newton, *"the propeller blades continued to flash in the sun, and then the machine rose obliquely into the air. At first it came directly toward us, so that we could not tell how fast it was going except that it appeared to increase rapidly in size as it approached. In the excitement of this first flight, men trained to observe details under all sorts of distractions forgot their cameras, forgot their watches, forgot everything but this aerial monster chattering over our heads."* However, "Jimmy" Hare got a good photograph of that flight. On May 14, the correspondents saw what no person on earth had ever seen before—a flying machine under complete control carrying *two* men. First Wilbur made a short flight with Charles W. Furnas as passenger, and then Orville flew with Furnas for nearly three minutes. Newton predicted in his diary just after that, *"Someday Congress will erect a monument here to these Wrights."* [A Monument was dedicated in November 1932.] The last flight on May 14, made by Wilbur Wright, ended in an accident. Wilbur had pulled a wrong lever. Repairs would have taken a week, and as the time the brothers could spare had elapsed, the experiments stopped. But after removing the engine and other machinery for shipment to Dayton, the Wrights left the plane in the shed at Kitty Hawk, thinking they might return. The ending of these trials brought no grief to the correspondents who had been getting up before daylight each morning, and returning to Manteo late each afternoon, footsore and tired, with their dispatches still to be written. One night's dispatches had brought unexpected trouble for "By" Newton. Though his report had been filed ahead of McGowan's, in plenty of time to be relayed from his paper's New York office to Paris and appear in the next morning's issue of the Paris edition, a needless delay occurred in New York. In consequence, Newton, through no fault of his own, was "scooped" by McGowan the next day in the continental edition of the London *Daily Mail*. When James Gordon Bennett, proprietor of the New York *Herald*, observed that his Paris *Herald* failed to have any account of the sensational flights at Kitty Hawk the day before, as reported in the rival *Daily Mail*, he was furious.

During the two seasons when the Wrights had flown a total of 160 miles at Huffman Prairie, Bennett, with scores of reporters at his disposal, had failed to learn the truth of what the Wrights had done. But now when he thought a reporter had missed a story about them, he did not wait to make inquiries but promptly sent a cable to New York ordering Newton suspended from the staff. Under Bennett's way of conducting his papers, suspension usually was a preliminary to permanent discharge. Though he was reinstated after he had sent to Bennett a review of the facts, along with some affidavits, Newton, all the rest of his life, felt a grievance against Bennett and the *Herald*. Incidentally, McGowan's "scoop" in the continental edition of the *Daily Mail* which had so disturbed Bennett, was not accepted as truth by everyone who read it. Charles A. Bertrand, in one of the Paris papers, May 15, published this comment, "*He [McGowan] depicts the flight in a manner that does honor to his imagination. If the Wrights hadn't been seen in Europe, one would be justified in believing their very existence as uncertain as their apparatus.*" During the several days the correspondents were at Kitty Hawk, the Wrights knew they were being observed. From time to time they caught glimpses of men's heads over the hilltop in the distance. Moreover, they heard each day, from members of a life saving crew, just how many visitors had come. But they simply thought it was a good joke on the mysterious observers, whoever they were. Arthur Ruhl, of *Collier's*, had met the Wrights in Dayton about a year before. On May 14, before the final flight, he came over to the camp. But he said nothing about being a member of the group that had been observing the flights. The Wrights invited Ruhl to stay for lunch. But he declined. He seemed to the Wrights ill at ease and anxious to get away. At a meeting with him some time afterward they learned why. He had come against the wishes of the other correspondents and was afraid he might give away the fact that they were in the nearby woods. On May 15, the day after the crash, when it was evident that there would be no more flights, McGowan, of the *Daily Mail*, went to the camp, accompanied by still another correspondent who had just arrived, Gilson Gardner, of the Washington office of the Newspaper Enterprise Association. McGowan remarked that he had once visited Octave Chanute's camp at Dune Park, near Chicago, in 1897 for the Chicago *Tribune*. Another visitor at the camp, a day or two before that, was a young man named J. C. Burkhardt, dressed in a brand new outfit of hunting togs. He was a college boy who had come all the way from Ithaca just to satisfy his curiosity. "*What would you have done,*" Orville Wright was asked, afterward, "*if all those correspondents had come right to your camp each day and sat there to watch you?*" "*We'd have had to go ahead just as if they weren't there,*" he replied. "*We couldn't have delayed our work. There was too much to do and our time was short.*" That the Wrights would have treated the correspondents politely enough was indicated in a letter from Orville Wright to Byron Newton, dated June 7, 1908. Immediately after his return to New York, Newton had written graciously to the Wrights, enclosing clippings of his dispatches to the *Herald*, and expressing his admiration for them and their achievements. "*We were aware of the presence of newspapermen in the woods,*" wrote Orville in reply, "*at least we had often been told that they were there. Their presence, however, did not bother us in the least, and I am only sorry that you did not come over to see us at our camp. The display of a white flag would have disposed of the rifles and shotguns with which the machine is reported to have been guarded.*" After publication of many dispatches from these eyewitnesses at Kitty Hawk and front page headlines, it might have been expected that the fact of human flight would now be generally accepted. As Newton had written to his paper, there was "*no longer any ground for questioning the performance of these men and their wonderful machine.*" Ruhl in *Collier's* had told how the correspondents had informed the world that "*it was all right, the rumors true—that man could fly.*" Yet even such reports by leading journalists still did not convince the general public. People began to concede that perhaps there might be something in it, but many newspapers still did not publish the news. When Newton sent an article, some weeks later, on what he had seen at Kitty Hawk, to a leading magazine, it came back to him with the editor's comment, "While your manuscript has been read with much interest, it does not seem to qualify either as fact or fiction."

☐☐☐☐☐☐☐☐☐☐☐

The Wrights decided that Wilbur should go to France to make the demonstrations there. Orville would stay in America to build the machine for the United States Government and test it at Fort Myer, near Washington. Wilbur did not return to Dayton from Kitty Hawk but went to New York where he sailed for Europe on May 21. Orville arrived at Fort Myer in August. Two mechanics, Taylor and Furnas, who were to assist him, had reached there a few days earlier. Army officers designated a shed on the Fort Myer grounds for use in assembling and housing the plane. Orville's first flight was on September 3, 1908. He went from the Cosmos Club, where he was staying, to Fort Myer by streetcar. It is doubtful if any of the others on that car suspected that this fellow passenger was on his way to perform a miracle. When he reached Fort Myer, Orville got the impression that not all the Army officers present thought he would succeed in meeting the tests required by the contract. The area from which the flights would be made was only about 700 by 1,000 feet.

Neither of the Wrights had ever before made flights within so small a space. Considering that this was an opportunity to see the outstanding wonder of the century, the crowd that strung about the parade ground was small. Theodore Roosevelt Jr., estimated it for his father, then President, at less than one thousand. Indeed, it was probably much less than that. Orville circled the field one and one-half times on that first test and was in the air only one minute, eleven seconds, but the crowd "went crazy." "When the plane first rose," said Roosevelt Jr., in describing the event, years afterward, "the crowd's gasp of astonishment was not alone at the wonder of it, but because it was so unexpected. I'll never forget the impression the sound from the *crowd made on me. It was a sound of complete surprise.*" When he landed after this flight it was Orville's turn to be astonished. Three or four supposedly "hardboiled" newspapermen who rushed up to interview him had been so stirred by witnessing the "impossible" that each of them had tears streaming down his cheeks. [Those who witnessed this flight might have been prepared for what they saw and less surprised, since Wilbur Wright for more than a month had been making flights in France—told about in a later chapter—and some of these were reported in the newspapers. But the brief newspaper accounts of Wilbur's flights seldom if ever had first page display and were not treated as important news. On August 9, the day after Wilbur's first flight, the New York *Times* had no mention of the event, though it gave first page space to a dispatch from Canton, Ohio, about a balloon trip, and to a dispatch from Berlin about the German Kaiser contributing to a fund for building another Zeppelin airship.] Nor did newspapers show too much excitement about this great public demonstration of practical aviation. It was not considered front page news even by Washington papers.

The New York *World* account was on page five and most of the report was not about the wonder of the flying machine, but about the behavior of the crowd, described as in fear of being hit by what the *World* called "the vessel." Many thousands were present on the second day of the tests when Orville flew about three miles in four minutes, fifteen seconds. After one of these flights, a reporter, it was said, got in touch with Professor Simon Newcomb who, a few years before, had so irrefutably explained why flying was impossible. The reporter wanted to know if Professor Newcomb thought passenger planes would be the next step. "No," Newcomb was reported to have replied, "*because no plane could ever carry the weight of anyone besides the pilot.*" It might have been expected that by this time Professor Newcomb would have become more cautious! Orville made a short flight on September 7, and two flights the next day, one of eleven minutes, ten seconds, the other of seven minutes, thirty-four seconds. On the morning of September 9, he circled the field fifty-seven times in fifty-seven minutes, twenty-five seconds. Later in the day, he circled the field fifty-five times in one hour, two and one-quarter minutes. Then he surprised and delighted his friend, Lieutenant Frank P. Lahm, by inviting him to go with him for a flight. They were in the air six minutes, twenty-four seconds, and circled the field six and one-half times. All three of these flights on the ninth established new world endurance records, two of them for flights with pilot alone, and the third for pilot with passenger. Orville made a flight of one hour, five minutes, fifty-two seconds on September 10, rising to a height of 200 feet and exceeding the world endurance record made by himself the day before. On the next day he again broke the one-man endurance record by flying for one hour, ten minutes, and twenty-four seconds, while circling the field fifty-seven times and describing two figure eights.

On the twelfth, he increased the two-man endurance record by taking with him Major George O. Squier, Acting Chief Signal Officer, for a flight of nine minutes, six seconds. Immediately after that, Orville made a flight alone. He circled the field seventy-one times in one hour and fifteen minutes—again breaking the endurance record for one-man flight. It was estimated that he reached a height of 300 feet. The next and final flight, September 17, ended in tragedy. Lieutenant Thomas Selfridge, a twenty-six-year-old West Point graduate, from San Francisco, had been assigned at his own request to go along as passenger. Before they had been in the air more than three or four minutes, and while in the fourth round at a height of about 125 feet over the field, Orville heard, or felt, a light tapping in the rear part of the machine. He thought it was in the chain drive. A hurried glance revealed nothing wrong there, but he decided to shut off the power and descend. Hardly had he reached this decision when two big thumps, which shook the machine violently, followed by the machine swerving to the right, showed that something had gone wrong. He immediately shut off the motor. Directly ahead was a gulley filled with small trees—a dangerous landing spot. He decided on a half-circle to the left, to land on the parade grounds, and it was then that he discovered that the tail was inoperative. By twisting the wings to give the greatest possible resistance to the left one, he did succeed in turning the machine until it faced directly into the field. In this maneuver the machine had descended about one-third of the way toward the ground without any indication of serious trouble. Orville moved the lever to straighten the wing tips, to proceed straight ahead. Then the machine suddenly turned down in front. For fifty feet it was headed almost directly toward the ground, although the front elevator was turned to its limit. When about twenty-five feet from the ground the machine began to right itself, and if there had been another twenty feet to go, or possibly even ten feet, it might have landed safely. But the recovery of control came too late. The machine hit the ground with such impact that Lieutenant Selfridge was fatally injured and died a few hours later. His skull had been fractured by a blow against one of the wooden uprights of the framework. Orville, though at first believed to be perhaps fatally hurt, had miraculously, escaped with what then appeared to be only a fractured left leg and four broken ribs. He never lost consciousness and his first concern was about Selfridge. [Not until twelve years later, after suffering severe pains, did Orville learn, from a careful X-ray examination in a famous medical clinic, that the Fort Myer accident had also caused three fractures in the hip bones, besides a dislocation of one of them.] Now that an airplane passenger had been killed, the Fort Myer demonstrations at last reached the front pages of newspapers. The day after the accident, the mechanics, Taylor and Furnas, brought the broken propeller and some of the other broken parts to Orville's bedside. From these parts he was able to determine the cause of the accident.

A new pair of propellers, several inches longer than any previously used, had been installed just before the flight. The trouble started when a longitudinal crack developed in one blade of the right propeller. This crack permitted the blade to flatten and lose much of its thrust, with the result that the pressures on the two blades became unequal, causing a severe vibration of the propeller shaft housing. The vibration loosened one of the stay wires that held in position the tube in which the propeller shaft turned. Then the propeller began to swing sidewise and forward until a blade hit and tore loose the stay wire to the vertical tail, permitting the tail to take a nearly horizontal position. A pressure on the tail's underside lifted the rear of the machine, thus causing it to dart for the ground. While Orville was recovering from his injuries, an acquaintance, Carl H. Claudy, visited him and asked, "*Has it got your nerve?*" "*Nerve?*" repeated Orville, not quite understanding. "*Oh, you mean will I be afraid to fly again? The only thing I'm afraid of is that I can't get well soon enough to finish those tests next year.*" The cost had been high, but one result of those incomplete tests was that widespread incredulity in the United States about the Wrights's achievements now finally ceased. At last, everyone, including even the most skeptical scientists, was convinced that a practical flying machine was a reality.

☐☐☐☐☐☐☐☐☐☐

Wilbur Wright reached France in May, 1908, to fly the Wright machine that for a year had been in its crate at the customs warehouse in Le Havre. If he accomplished what he expected, final details of the Wrights's business arrangement with the recently formed French syndicate would be carried out. As during the previous stay, when both the Wright brothers were in Europe, Wilbur kept in close touch with Hart O. Berg, European associate of Charles R. Flint and Company, the Wrights's business representatives in all except the English-speaking countries. One of the first questions to be settled was where the actual demonstration of the Wright plane should take place. Naturally, there were not yet any areas in Europe designated as flying fields. The locality for the flights was determined in consequence of the courtesies of Leon Bollee, an automobile manufacturer, who had a factory at Le Mans, about 125 miles from Paris. When Bollee learned that Wilbur Wright was in France and looking for a suitable field, he sent a message to Wilbur suggesting that a satisfactory place could doubtless be found near Le Mans where there was a great stretch of level country. He added that Wilbur would be welcome to use a wing of the Bollee factory for assembling his plane. Wilbur Wright and Hart O. Berg took a train to Le Mans where they spent several hours "looking for a good pasture." The most nearly ideal field for their purpose was a large open area at Auvours, about five miles from Le Mans, used by the French war department for testing artillery, but it was not then available. Another place they noticed was the Hunaudieres racetrack. The oval field within the track appeared to be large enough for their needs. There were a few trees, but Wilbur said he could easily steer clear of them. The next day, in Paris, Mr. Nicolai, president of the Jockey Club and principal owner of the Hunaudieres racetrack, agreed to the use of the field, at a monthly rental, for as long as needed. Now the crated Wright plane was shipped from Le Havre to the Bollee factory and, late in June, Wilbur set to work there. He assembled the working parts and put the motor and cooling system to a series of rigid tests.

On July 4 Wilbur met with a painful accident. A rubber connection in the cooling system burst and he was badly scalded on his left arm by hot water. This was one of several unavoidable delays that made many skeptics think it would be a long time before Wilbur would attempt a public demonstration. One Paris newspaper said, "*le bluff continue.*" Wilbur had been quoted as saying that the tests would be "child's play," and "*jeu d'enfant*" was often repeated, with sarcasm, by the incredulous. Painful as his burns were, Wilbur saw a funny side to the accident and sent home a hilarious letter about the French doctor who came "with a keg of oil" to apply to the blisters. Shortly afterward, Wilbur wanted a coiled wire spring to insert in a hose used in the cooling system, to prevent the hose from collapsing from suction.

A French mechanic who had been assisting him went with him to a nearby factory to have the coil made. Not knowing any French, Wilbur could not follow the long conversation he overheard, but they came away without the coil. It seemed strange to Wilbur that the kind of wire needed should not have been easily obtainable and he spoke of this to the man who had been his interpreter. But, said the Frenchman, the wire *was* available. "*Then,*" asked Wilbur, in surprise, "*why didn't we get it?*" Oh, explained the Frenchman, because when he and the man at the factory talked it over it didn't seem to them that using a coiled wire spring in the way Wilbur had in mind was a sound idea. While working on his machine at the Bollee factory, Wilbur did something, probably just because it seemed the natural thing to do, with no thought of the impression it would make, that delighted the hearts of the factory employees. He kept the same hours that the others did and his whole behavior was as if he were simply one more workman. When the whistle blew for the noon hour, he knocked off along with the others, and went, in overalls, to lunch. This lack of any sign of aloofness caused much favorable comment. Wilbur's greatest admirer, however, was Leon Bollee himself. Though they had no common language, they managed to exchange ideas and formed a warm friendship. Bollee, a jolly rotund man with a saucy little beard, was ever ready to be of any service. Incidentally, though Bollee had no thought of personal gain when he generously offered the use of space in his factory, the fact that Wilbur worked on his plane there did not hurt the sale of Bollee cars. But the work was soon transferred from the Bollee factory to the field at Hunaudieres where a hastily constructed hangar had been built. Another item of preparation was the setting up of a launching derrick, similar to the one the Wrights had first used in their experiments at the Huffman Pasture. Huge weights were attached at one end of a rope which ran over pulleys and had a metal ring at the other end to be caught on a hook at the front of the plane. When the plane shot forward, the rope automatically dropped away.

    As at previous trials, the plane when ready to take off rested on a small truck having two flanged wheels that ran on a single rail, iron shod, wooden track, about sixty feet long. Not until August 8, did Wilbur attempt his first flight. A good-sized crowd was present, the majority from Le Mans and the nearby countryside, but it included many members of the Aero Club of France and various newspaper representatives from Paris. In describing the scene, years afterward, Hart O. Berg said, "*Wilbur*

Wright's quiet self-confidence was reassuring. One thing that, to me at least, made his appearance all the more dramatic, was that he was not dressed as if about to do something daring or unusual. He, of course, had no special pilot's helmet or jacket, since no such garb yet existed, but appeared in the ordinary gray suit he usually wore, and a cap. And he had on, as he nearly always did when not in overalls, a high, starched collar." At least one man among the spectators felt certain the flight would not be a success. That was Ernest Archdeacon, prominent in the Aero Club. So sure was Archdeacon that Wilbur Wright would be deflated that, as the time set for the flight approached, he was explaining to those near him in the grandstand just what was "wrong" about the design of the Wright machine, and why it could not be expected to fly well. Wilbur's immediate preparations had been made with great care. First of all, the starting rail had been set precisely in the direction of and against the wind. The engine was started by two men, each pulling down a blade of the two propellers and the plane was held back by a wire attached to a hook and releasing trigger near the pilot's seat. After the engine was warmed up, Fleury, Berg's chauffeur, took hold of the right wing. Wilbur released the trigger and the plane was pulled forward by the falling weights. Fleury kept it in balance until the accelerating speed left him behind. By the time it had reached the end of the rail, the plane left the track with enough speed to sustain itself and climb. At some distance, directly in front of Wilbur as he started to rise, were tall trees, but they gave him no concern. He bore off easily to the left and went ahead in a curve that brought him back almost over the starting point. Then he swung to the right and made another great turn. Most of the time, he was thirty or thirty-five feet above the ground. He was in the air only one minute and forty-five seconds, but he had made history. The crowd knew well they had "seen something" and behaved accordingly. In the excited babble of voices one or two phrases could be heard again and again. "*Cet homme a conquis l'air!*" "*Il nest pas bluffeur!*" Yes, truly Wilbur had conquered the air, and he was no bluffer. That American word "bluffer" had been much used during the time that reports from the United States about the Wrights had been stirring controversy in France. Now "*bluffeur*" became, more than ever, a part of the French language. "*To think that one would call the Wrights 'bluffeurs!'* " lamented the French press over and over again. For the next few minutes after Wilbur landed, Berg was kept busy laughingly warding off agitated Frenchmen who sought to bestow a formal accolade by kissing Wilbur in the French manner on both cheeks. He suspected that Wilbur might consider that carrying enthusiasm too far. One of the skeptical members of the Aero Club, Edouard Surcouf, a balloonist, had arrived at the field late, barely in time to see Wilbur in the air. Now he was about the most enthusiastic of all. He rushed up to Berg, exclaiming, "*C'est le plus grand erreur du siecle!*" Disbelieving the claims of the Wrights may not have been the biggest error of the century, but obviously it *had* at least been a mistake. The only person who offered criticism or minimized the brilliance of his feat was Wilbur Wright.

When asked by a reporter for the Paris edition of the New York *Herald* if he was satisfied with the exhibition, he replied, according to that paper, "*Not altogether. When in the air I made no less than ten mistakes owing to the fact that I have been laying off from flying so long, but I corrected them rapidly, so I don't suppose anyone watching really knew I had made any mistake at all. I was very pleased at the way my first flight in France was received.*" A crowd of Aero Club members and other admirers were insistent that Wilbur should go back to Paris with them to celebrate the achievement at the best dinner to be obtained in that center of inspired cooking. But Wilbur just thanked them and said he wished to give his machine a little going over. Early that evening, so the newspapers reported, "*he was asleep at the side of his creation.*" The French press the next day not only treated the flight as the biggest news, but was unsparing in its praise, as were various rivals in the field of aviation who were quoted. All admitted that there was a world of difference between the best French planes yet produced, and the one Wilbur Wright had just demonstrated. The *Figaro* said, "*It was not merely a success but a* triumph, a conclusive trial and a decisive victory for aviation, the news of which will revolutionize scientific circles throughout the world." Le Journal observed that, "*It was the first trial of the Wright airplane, whose qualities have long been regarded with doubt, and it was perfect.*" Louis Bleriot, member of the Aero Club, wealthy manufacturer of automobile headlights, and himself a flyer, was quoted in *Le Matin* as saying, "*The Wright machine is indeed superior to our airplanes.*" As early as May, 1908, when the Wrights were still at Kitty Hawk, the Frenchman, Henri Farman, had issued a challenge to them to participate in a flying contest, for $5,000—later raised to $10,000. But the challenge, made only in public prints, was never sent directly to the Wrights. It may have been simply what today would be called a "publicity stunt." [Farman's best straightaway flight of about a mile and a quarter had been made at Issy, France, on March 21, 1908.] Nothing more was heard of the Farman challenge now. A French paper commented that the Farman plane and also that of Leon Delagrange were approximate copies of the Wright plane but that the Wright machine "*seems more solid, more controllable, and more scientific.*" Two days after that first demonstration, on August 10, Wilbur made two more short flights, the first one a figure eight, and the other, three complete circles. He flew on August 11 for 3 minutes 43 seconds, the next day, 6 minutes 56 seconds, and on August 13, 8 minutes 13.2 seconds. This time he did seven wide "*orbes*," as the French described them. In landing that day Wilbur broke the left wing of his plane and repairs kept him from flying until August 21. He took time out on August 24 to attend an agricultural fair where reporters observed that he seemed much interested in pigs and cattle and, as one paper expressed it, "*talked much more freely about them than about aviation.*" After those first few flights, the army officer in charge of the artillery testing grounds at Auvours let it be known that the military people at Paris would be proud to have Wilbur Wright's further demonstrations carried on there. As the military field was larger than that at Hunaudieres, Wilbur was glad to make the change. The Hunaudieres hangar—which Wilbur persisted in calling the "shed"—was torn down and rebuilt within twenty-four hours at Auvours. As the two fields were only about ten miles apart, Wilbur could have flown the plane to the new location, but with so much at stake he was taking no chances. The plane was placed longitudinally on two wheels fastened behind Leon Bollee's automobile and towed to the Auvours field without removing the wings. Within a month after setting up operations at Auvours, Wilbur was flying many times the distance between the two fields. All parts of France were now flooded with souvenir postcards bearing pictures of Wilbur or of his plane in flight. And the French people gave him all the hero worship of which they were capable. There was talk of a public subscription for a testimonial to him. When the French ambassador to the United States reached New York a short time later he declared that Wilbur Wright was accepted as the biggest man in France. It wasn't alone his achievements in the air that won the people, but also his modesty, decency, and intelligence. The French papers made enthusiastic comment on the fact that in conversation he seemed to be exceptionally well-informed not only about scientific work, but also on art, literature, medicine, and affairs of the world. Newspapermen liked Wilbur because he always made it plain that they were welcome. They probably liked him all the more because, as a joke, he usually put them at manual work, to fetch tools, or help drag the plane in and out of the hangar. Those who had access to the hangar were impressed by the orderliness of the place. Wilbur's canvas cot was hauled up by ropes toward the roof during the day, and the space where he slept was divided from another section of the building by a low partition made of wood from packing cases. Wilbur explained that one room was his bedroom, the other his dining room. Another trait that appealed to the French was Wilbur's punctuality at all appointments. No one ever had to wait even a minute on him.

Nothing Wilbur was overheard to say by French journalists seemed too trivial to be recorded. One day he said "fine" to an assistant, by way of commendation, and the next day a Paris paper explained that Wilbur meant *"C'est beau."* *"Boys, let's fix these ropes*" was promptly translated as "*Allons, jeunes gens, allez disposer les cordes.*" Wilbur was flooded with letters of all kinds. Some were from scientists seeking information, and hundreds came from women who desired to make his acquaintance. He tried his best to answer all sensible questions from scientists—the others went into the stove. He was equally considerate of scientific-minded people—including those who might be considered rivals in aviation—who came in person. To all who had real interest he patiently explained any detail of his machine. But he was capable of quiet sarcasm toward the ill-informed who started to "enlighten" him about aerodynamics. It now became the fashionable thing for Parisians to take a train down to Le Mans and drive from there to the Champ d'Auvours to see Wilbur fly. Amusing episodes grew out of that. Since the flights were not often announced in advance, those who made the sightseeing trip had to take their chances. But some of the callers felt almost a personal affront if Wilbur made no flight on the day they happened to be there. One American society woman living in Paris was bitterly resentful when she was told that Monsieur Wright was taking a nap and therefore would not fly that afternoon. "*The idea,*" said she, petulantly, "*of his being asleep when I came all the way down here to see him in the air!*"

Cabmen at Le Mans found the sudden influx of visitors so profitable that they tried to make the most of it and encouraged people who had been disappointed to come again the next day. They would always say, "*He is sure to fly tomorrow. We have it on good authority.*" So grateful to Wilbur were members of the "Le Mans-Auvours Aeroplane Bus Service" for the profitable trade he had created, that they wanted to give a banquet in his honor. News of Wilbur's flights at Le Mans naturally caused talk in England. Members of the Aeronautical Society of Great Britain, one after another, went to Le Mans in doubt about the flights being as wonderful as reported, but returned convinced that the age of practical flying machines had come. One of the first to go from England to investigate was Griffith Brewer, who had been making balloon ascensions since 1891. Half apologetically, lest he be thought overcredulous, he confided to an old associate of his in ballooning, Charles S. Rolls, founder of the Rolls Royce motor car firm, that he was going to France to see Wilbur Wright fly. Rolls laughed and said he had just returned from seeing him fly. On his arrival at Le Mans, Brewer walked to the shed at the edge of the field. Opposite the shed, in the middle of the field, was Wilbur Wright tuning up his machine. As a crowd was about Wilbur, Brewer hesitated to add to it, but sat down by the shed to smoke his pipe. When a mechanic came from the machine over to the shed for a tool, Brewer handed him a calling card with the request that he give it to Wilbur Wright. Wilbur glanced at the card, nodded to Brewer, and went on with his work.

There was no flight, but it was some time before Wilbur returned to the shed—and as he stayed inside for what seemed a long time, Brewer began to think there might be an indefinite wait. Then Wilbur came out, putting on his coat, and said, "*Now, Mr. Brewer, we'll go and have some dinner.*" They went to Madame Pollet's Inn nearby for a simple meal and Brewer, eager though he was to discuss aviation, wondered if the inventor might not appreciate a rest from the subject of flying. He therefore talked to him of affairs in America. Wilbur liked that, and they formed a friendship. On September 12, Wilbur was guest of honor at a dinner in Paris given by the Aero Club of the Sarthe (the governmental department in which Le Mans was located). It was understood that he would not be expected to make a speech, but Baron d'Estournelles, member of the Senate from Le Mans, who presided, did nevertheless call upon him. Wilbur then, in justification of his unwillingness to say much, made a remark that became famous. "*I know of only one bird, the parrot, that talks,*" he was quoted as saying, "*and it can't fly very high.*" For the first time in France, Wilbur, on September 16, took up a passenger, a young French balloonist, Ernest Zens. Two days later, in the early morning of September 18, as he was about to make a flight, Wilbur got word about the tragic accident at Fort Myer the day before, when Lieutenant Selfridge was killed and Orville Wright injured, it was not yet known how seriously. Within a few hours cables brought word that Orville would recover, and Wilbur was able to fly again the next day. Two days later, on September 21, he flew about forty miles, in 1 hour 31 minutes 25.4 seconds. News of that proved to be better medicine for Orville, in Washington, than anything the attending physician could do. Many passengers now made short flights with Wilbur. They included, on October 3, [George] Dickin of the Paris edition of the New York *Herald*, and Frantz Reichel of the Paris *Figaro*.

Reichel was so enthusiastic over his flight of nearly an hour, that on landing he threw his arms about Wilbur. Leon Bollee had his first flight on October 5, and the next day Arnold Fordyce flew with Wilbur for 1 hour 4 minutes and 26 seconds, the longest flight yet made in an airplane with a passenger. Now that Wilbur was carrying much weight and on longer flights, the Paris edition of the New York *Herald* became impressed with future possibilities for carrying mail by plane. It predicted that the time might come when there would be special stamps for "aeroplane delivery." A witness to several of these flights in early October was Major [Bader Fletcher Smyth] Baden-Powell, President of the Aeronautical Society of Great Britain (and a brother of the founder of the Boy Scouts). He was so impressed by what he saw that he sounded a warning to his fellow countrymen. Major Baden-Powell was quoted as follows in the Paris edition of the New York *Herald* on October 6, 1908, "*If only some of our people in England could see or imagine what Mr. Wright is now doing I am certain it would give them a terrible shock. A conquest of the air by any nation means more than the average man is willing to admit or even think about. That Wilbur Wright is in possession of a power which controls the fate of nations is beyond dispute.*" Hart O. Berg, on October 7, went for a flight, his first, lasting three minutes and twenty-four seconds. Immediately afterward Wilbur took Mrs. Berg for a flight, of two minutes, three seconds, the first ever made anywhere in the world by a woman. [One or two women were reported to have been in planes that made short hops, but Mrs. Berg was certainly the first woman to participate in a real flight.] Berg tied a rope about the lower part of his wife's skirt to keep it from blowing. A Paris dressmaker who was among the spectators, noted that Mrs. Berg could hardly walk, after landing, with that rope above her ankles. There, thought the *couturiere*, was a suggestion for something fashionable. A costume with skirt thus drawn between the ankles and the knees to make natural locomotion difficult should appeal to any customers who happened to be both stupid and rich. Thus was born the "hobble skirt" which, for a short time, was considered "smart." The next day, October 8, her royal highness, Margherita of Savoy, the dowager queen of Italy, who was touring France, came to see a flight. "*You have let me witness the most astonishing spectacle I have ever seen,*" was her comment to Wilbur Wright. On that same October 8, Griffith Brewer, making his second visit to Le Mans, won the distinction of being the first Englishman ever to fly. He was followed almost immediately by three other British Aeronautical Society members, [Charles] S. Rolls, [Frank Hedges] Butler, and Major Baden-Powell.

One of the Englishmen remarked, "*How decent it is of Wilbur Wright never to accept a fee for any of these flights, when there are scores of persons who would gladly pay hundreds of pounds for the privilege.*" Wilbur continued until the end of the year to take up passengers at Auvours. Among them, on October 10, was [Paul] Painleve, of the French Institute. As they were taking off, Painleve gaily waved his hand at the crowd and in so doing accidentally pulled a rope overhead that Wilbur used for stopping the engine. After another start, the flight lasted one hour, nine minutes, forty-five seconds, and covered forty-six miles, a world record for both duration and distance for an airplane carrying two persons. Two other women besides Mrs. Berg had short flights—Mesdames Leon Bollee and Lazare Weiller. A passenger on October 24 was Dr. Pirelli, leading tire manufacturer in Italy. Later, in November, F. S. Lahm, one of the first in Europe to believe the Wrights had flown, had his first ride in a plane. Among the distinguished people who made passenger flights were two destined to die by assassins's bullets, Paul Doumer, member of the French parliament, afterward President of France, and Louis Barthou, Minister of Public Works and Aerial Communications, afterward premier. Under the terms of the contract between the Wrights and the newly formed French company, one of the Wright brothers was to train three pilots.

Wilbur began this training at Auvours. The students were Count Charles de Lambert, Paul Tissandier, and Captain Lucas de Girardville. Both Tissandier and de Lambert had made flights as passengers on September 28, but did not begin their training until later. Captain Lucas de Girardville went up as a passenger for the first time on October 12. The first to receive a lesson at piloting was Count de Lambert on October 28. The Aero Club of France had offered a prize of 2,500 francs for an altitude of twenty-five meters. But there was a "catch" to that offer. A little clique in the Aero Club, a bit over-chauvinistic, wanted a native experimenter to win, and that was why the altitude to be attained was fairly low. It was stipulated that anyone competing for the prize must start without use of derrick or catapult. The French experimenters had wheels on their machines and could get as long a start as necessary before leaving the ground. But the Wright machine, designed for the rough, sandy ground at Kitty Hawk, and the somewhat bumpy Huffman Field, still had skids instead of wheels. Thus the rules for the contest seemed to be aimed to prevent Wilbur Wright from winning the prize. Members of the Aero Club of the Sarthe thought their compatriots in the Aero Club of France were being unsportsmanlike, and they offered a prize of 1,000 francs for an altitude record of thirty meters. Wilbur won it on November 13. In doing so he went three times as high as required, reaching an altitude of ninety meters. Then Wilbur decided that he might as well win the prize of the Aero Club of France, and do so on their own terms. He arranged for a longer starting track than usual, and, five days after taking the prize for thirty meters, he started without the use of derrick or catapult and won the prize for twenty-five meters. To the delight of his friends in the Aero Club of the Sarthe, he purposely did not throw in much altitude for good measure, and went only high enough to clear safely the captive balloon that showed the height required. On December 16, Wilbur astounded the spectators by shutting off the motor at an altitude of about 200 feet and volplaning slowly down. And on December 18, he flew for 1 hour 54 minutes 53.4 seconds. Later that same day he won another prize offered by the Aero Club of the Sarthe for an altitude of a hundred meters. Wilbur went ten meters higher than required. This was a new world's record for altitude. Then on December 31, the last day he ever flew at Auvours, he made what was then an almost incredible record of staying continuously in the air 2 hours 20 minutes 23.2 seconds. For this feat he won the Michelin award of $4,000, or 20,000 francs. As the weather at Le Mans was no longer ideal for flying, it was necessary to seek a warmer climate, and at the suggestion of Paul Tissandier, Wilbur decided to go to Pau, a beautiful winter resort city of 35,000, at the edge of the Pyrenees. The city of Pau provided a field and a hangar. At about the same time, Orville Wright, now rapidly recuperating from his injuries at Fort Myer, arrived in Paris with their sister, Katharine, for a reunion with Wilbur. Then Wilbur went on down to Pau, and his brother and sister joined him there a week or two later. En route to Pau, their train met with an accident near the town of Dax, in which two persons were killed. The Wrights escaped injury, but Orville was a bit startled for another reason. When the crash came, his mattress tipped up on one side at the same time that his watch, pocketbook and other articles slid off a stand or shelf beside the bed. His valuables thus got themselves hid beneath the mattress and, until he chanced to find them, it looked as if he had been robbed. As at Le Mans, Wilbur lived at the hangar, where he had a French cook the hospitable Mayor de Lassence, of Pau, had selected. His brother and sister lived at the Hotel Gassion, not far from the famous old chateau where Henry IV was born, and within a short stroll from the place near the center of the city that affords what Lamartine has called the finest land view in all the world. The Wrights were not long in discovering that life here should be ideal. Wilbur's French cook proved to be competent enough at preparing regional and other choice dishes—though Katharine Wright did not think he had quite the best technique with a broom for keeping the quarters clean. A London newspaper photographer gave Orville a photograph of his sister demonstrating to that Frenchman how to handle a broom. By coming to Pau the Wrights had unintentionally played a joke on James Gordon Bennett, owner of the New York *Herald* and Paris *Herald*.

A few years previously, when Bennett was spending the winter there, he had a tally-ho party and someone in the party had attracted the attention of the police. The episode was reported in local newspapers. Bennett was so indignant that he laid down a rule for both his papers to say as little as possible about Pau. But now, with Wilbur Wright flying there, the town could hardly be ignored. Pau datelines were again frequent in the Bennett papers. Wilbur did not attempt any new records at Pau, but devoted most of his time to teaching the young pilots for the French Wright company. Count Charles de Lambert continued his training, and his wife, almost equally enthusiastic over aviation, made a passenger flight. Another woman to make a flight at Pau was Katharine Wright herself. It was her first trip in a plane, though, as she laughingly remarked, she had *heard* plenty about aviation. An American multi-millionaire from Philadelphia, spending some time at Pau, announced, with the self-confidence money sometimes gives, that he intended to make a flight with Wilbur. When told that Wilbur was not taking up any passengers, he replied, "*Oh, I daresay that can be arranged.*" "*I'd like to be around when you do the arranging, just to see how it's done,*" observed Lord Northcliffe, owner of the London *Daily Mail*, who had recently arrived and become acquainted with the Wrights. The American went away without having had his ride.

In February, King Alfonso of Spain came to Pau with his entourage, and the Wrights were formally presented to him at the field. "*An honor and a pleasure to meet you,*" said the king. Alfonso showed more boyish enthusiasm about the plane than almost anyone. He was eager to fly, but both his queen and his cabinet had exacted a promise that he would not. However, he climbed aboard the plane and sat there for a long time fascinated while Wilbur painstakingly explained every detail. A little later, on March 17, still another king arrived. Edward VII of England came by automobile with his suite from nearby Biarritz. The presentation of the brothers and their sister was made at the field and Edward showed his customary graciousness. He did not seek any technical details about the machine, but was much interested in seeing the flights themselves and in meeting the Wrights. It was during the stay of King Edward that Katharine Wright made her second trip in an airplane. Other famous personages continued to come to Pau, among them Lord Arthur Balfour, former Prime Minister of England. Sometimes when Wilbur was preparing for a flight, visitors would pull on the rope that raised the weights on the launching derrick. Balfour insisted that he must not be denied this privilege of "taking part in a miracle" and did his share of yanking at the rope. Another man who shared in handling the rope that day was a young English duke. "*I'm so glad that young man is helping with the rope,*" said Lord Northcliffe to Orville Wright, with a motion of his head toward the duke, "*for I'm sure it is the only useful thing he has ever done in his life.*"

Northcliffe, after his meeting with the Wrights at Pau, became one of their most enthusiastic supporters in England. Long afterward, he made this comment, "*I never knew more, unaffected people than Wilbur, Orville, and Katharine. After the Wrights had been in Europe a few weeks they became world heroes, and when they went to Pau their demonstrations were visited by thousands of people from all parts of Europe—by kings and lesser men—but I don't think the excitement and interest produced by their extraordinary feat had any effect on them at all.*"

☐☐☐☐☐☐☐☐☐☐

Shortly after they were established at Pau, the Wrights received a call from a German, Captain Alfred Hildebrandt. This was not the first time he had tried to see them. He had stopped in Dayton, on his way homeward after attending the international balloon races at St. Louis, in 1907, but on reaching Dayton he learned that the Wrights were in Europe. Captain Hildebrandt came to Pau on behalf of a newspaper publisher. His principal was Herr Scherl, owner of the *Lokal Anzeiger*, a leading paper in Berlin. Scherl thought it would be a great stroke of advertising for his paper if he could arrange for a big public demonstration of a Wright machine, with the general public invited to be the paper's guests. It was arranged that one of the Wrights should make a series of flights at Berlin, later that year, for a substantial fee.

The brothers later decided that the Berlin flights should be made by Orville. A move had been started in Italy to have demonstrations of the Wright plane in Rome. Dr. Pirelli, Italian tire manufacturer, who had flown with Wilbur Wright at Le Mans, was believed to have made the first suggestion that led to organizing an aviation club at Rome to buy a Wright plane. This "club" was supposed to be backed at least partly by the Italian Government, and the arrangement with the Wrights provided for the training of two lieutenants, one from the Navy, the other from the Army. Parts and material for six new planes had already been shipped to Europe from Dayton, and the parts for one of these were sent to Pau, where they were built into a complete machine. The machine was then taken down in sections and shipped to Rome. [The one used in the French flights became the personal property of Lazare Weiller, organizer of the French Wright company, and later it went to a museum in Paris.]

In April the Wrights returned from Pau to Paris, and after a brief stay there Wilbur went to Rome. He was joined there later by Orville and Katharine, who went to a hotel opposite the [Palazzo] Barberini Palace. Count and Countess di Celleri, of the Italian nobility, had a cottage adjoining their villa near the flying field at Centocelle, and they offered it to Wilbur. Countess di Celleri later felt more than repaid when she had a passenger flight in the Wright plane. When the machine shipped from Pau in sections arrived in Rome it was reassembled in an automobile factory, just outside the city limits, on the Flaminian Way. It was then moved across the city on a truck drawn by a magnificent team of gray horses to a military field in Centocelle. As the strange-looking machine was carried through Roman streets past ancient ruins, it is doubtful if amazed beholders had ever seen a greater contrast between old and new. Almost immediately after his arrival, Wilbur began the training of the Italian flyers, naval Lieutenant Calderara and Lieutenant Savoia, of the army engineering corps. [Calderara was afterward the air attache at the Italian Embassy in Washington, and Lieutenant Savoia became the head of the well-known Italian aviation company of that name.] King Victor Emmanuel came to witness flights. As he strolled about the field with a folding camera suspended from his shoulder, he might have been mistaken for just one more tourist. Other sightseers who came to the field were the elder [John Pierpont] Morgan and the famous railroader, James J. Hill.

Among those who made flights with Wilbur were Lloyd Griscom, the American Ambassador, and [Sidney Costantino] Sonnino, former premier of Italy. Soon after that, for the first time, an operator took a motion picture from an airplane in flight. While at Rome the Wrights established friendship with another German, Captain [Richard] von Kehler, whom they had already met in Berlin, and he played an important part in steps toward forming a Wright company in Germany. Captain von Kehler was managing director of the Studien Gesellschaft, an organization for the study of aeronautics that had been formed after a meeting between certain outstanding German industrialists and the Kaiser, back in 1906. The Kaiser had called the representatives of the Krupps and other powerful industrialists to Potsdam to give them a big banquet at the close of which he said he thought Germany should be looking into the possibilities of the development of the airship (lighter-than-air). Just what should be done he did not pretend to know. That problem, he said, he would turn over to them. They knew what he meant. They, as a patriotic duty, must provide money for research and experimentation in the lighter-than-air field or else lose standing with their Kaiser. Thus, did the Studien Gesellschaft come into being. The organization began experiments by building a dirigible known as the Parseval, named for its designer, Major [August von] Parseval. The Parseval turned out to be an expensive experiment. At the end of two years the subscribed funds were nearly exhausted and the project far from completion. The subscribers began to fear another invitation to dinner. Just at this time they began to hear reports about the aeroplane flights of the Wrights in France, and they became much interested. It occurred to them that experiments with the new flying machine would perhaps be less expensive than experiments with a dirigible, and that prospects for the aeroplane might be greater than for the dirigible. Captain von Kehler went to Rome to talk with the Wrights. He told them that some of the wealthy men in the Studien Gesellschaft would like to form a German Wright company. Before he left Rome, a preliminary contract was signed. Its terms provided that the brothers should receive cash, a block of stock in the company, and ten percent royalty on all planes sold. The final contract was closed in August, 1909. After leaving Rome the Wrights made a brief stay in Paris and went to Le Mans to receive a bronze art piece presented by the Aero Club of the Sarthe. The work in bronze, by Louis-Albert Carvin, showed the Wright brothers at the edge of a chasm gazing upon an eagle in flight. Above them was a winged figure—the spirit of aviation. From France the Wrights went to London. There they received gold medals from the Aeronautical Society of Great Britain and from the Aero Club of the United Kingdom at formal banquets. Before going to these dinners Griffith Brewer was describing to Wilbur some of the people he would meet.

Of one man he said, "*You'll readily recognize him, as he is the ugliest man in the Aeronautical Society.*" To which Wilbur replied, "*He'll lose that distinction on this occasion, because now there will be a pair of us.*" On their arrival in New York the Wrights attended a luncheon in their honor given by the Aero Club of America. The Aero Club had awarded medals to the Wrights and these were formally presented a month later by President Taft at the White House. After an absence of many months, the Wrights arrived in Dayton early in May. Five weeks later the city had a great celebration in their honor. Their hometown had now recognized the Wrights's importance. This "homecoming" for the

Wrights lasted two days, June 17 and 18. At 9 o'clock on that morning of June 17, they heard a deafening sound. It did not at once occur to them what it was. Every factory whistle in Dayton was blowing and every bell ringing—all in their honor. This continued for ten minutes. Bands were playing and cannons booming. At 10 o'clock the brothers rode in a carriage, escorted by bands, to the opening events. Ed Sines, boyhood chum of Orville, and Ed Ellis, long a friend of Wilbur, were in the carriage with them. Sines and Ellis, as a practical joke, gleefully shook hands, as if *they* were the heroes, with all who tried to greet the Wrights along the route, and few knew the difference. After reviewing a parade in their honor that afternoon, the Wrights returned to their shop. That night they had opportunity to see a display of fireworks that included their own profiles, eight feet high, entwined with an American flag. During these two days, practically all business in Dayton was suspended—except the sale of souvenir postal cards showing the Huffman Pasture, the Hawthorne Street home, the flying field at Le Mans, France, and the parade ground at Fort Myer. On the second day, the inventors's father, Bishop Wright, gave the invocation preceding the presentation of medals to his sons. One medal that had been ordered by act of Congress was presented by General James Allen, chief signal officer of the Army, another, by the Ohio legislature, was presented by Governor Harmon, and a third from the city of Dayton was presented by the Mayor. The Wrights were alongside of 2,500 schoolchildren, dressed in red, white and blue, to represent an immense American flag. Patriotic fervor ran high. The home folk knew now that the Wrights could fly, they knew, too, that international fame had not changed them. They were the same unassuming pair they had always been. Before the celebration was quite over, Wilbur and Orville took a train to Washington. The time for completing those Government trials at Fort Myer was approaching and there was much to be done. Orville made his first flight on June 28, and finished on July 30. One of the most memorable of the flights in this series was on that final day when Orville, with an Army officer, Lieutenant

Benjamin D. Foulois, for passenger, made the first cross country trip yet made in an airplane, a total distance of about ten miles to Alexandria and return—without any suitable landing spots if trouble had occurred. This was the speed test. The machine now used was capable of about four miles an hour greater speed than the one in the tests the previous year. The turning point in Alexandria was at Shuter's Hill, where a Masonic temple now stands. A captive balloon floated above the hill, and a telegraph line had been run to the top of the hill where an operator was stationed to give a signal when Orville had passed that point. But a strong wind that day blew down the telegraph line and also kept the balloon so close to the ground that Orville could not see the turning point in advance and covered more than the required distance. As the plane passed out of sight for a time on the return trip, the crowd feared the worst, but when it reappeared, headed back toward the parade ground, the honking of automobile horns and excited cheering indicated that everyone knew they had all seen an extraordinary event. The time for the ten miles was fourteen minutes, or just under forty-three miles an hour. Thus the Wrights got a bonus of $5,000 more than the basic price agreed upon—ten percent for each complete mile per hour more than forty—and they received $30,000 for the machine. Almost immediately after the Fort Myer trials and formal acceptance of the machine, on August 2, by the United States Government, Orville Wright, accompanied by his sister Katharine, set out for Berlin. Orville would start training a flyer for the German Wright company immediately after giving the exhibition arranged for by Captain Hildebrandt on behalf of the *Lokal Anzeiger*.

These first flights in Germany were to be made at Tempelhof Field, then a military parade ground, at the outskirts of Berlin. On the day set for the initial flight, there was a terrible wind and Captain Hildebrandt, who accompanied Orville to the field, was torn between his desire not to disappoint the crowd and his fear of seeing Orville take too great a risk. Orville said he would follow Hildebrandt's wishes. "*No*," said Hildebrandt, "*don't go up.*" The next day even more people were present. Orville made a flight of fifteen minutes. When he landed it was difficult to keep the crowd from almost smothering him with adulation. People clamored for a chance not only to look at him up close, but to *touch* him. Men, women, and children struggled to lay gentle hands on him, even to touch his sleeve or the hem of his coat. Evidently it was some kind of belief in the desirability of physical contact with a miracle man. After a later flight, when Orville stayed in the air fifty-five minutes, the crowd about him and Katharine, who were accompanied by Mr. and Mrs. Charles R. Flint, was so dense that Orville felt duty bound to move as fast as he could away from his party, to relieve the pressure on them. Thereafter a hollow square of German soldiers kept the crowd at a safe distance. The German Crown Prince, Frederick Wilhelm, sought to get in touch with Orville to ask the privilege of seeing a flight. He telephoned to the Wrights's suite at the Hotel Esplanade, and the call was answered by a young German woman whom Katharine Wright had employed as interpreter when shopping. When the girl discovered that the voice over the phone was that of a member of the royal family, she dropped the telephone receiver and almost fainted. Members of the hotel staff were not much less agitated when they learned that royalty might be calling on two of their guests. Orville Wright and his sister were invited by Kaiser Wilhelm himself to be present—the only civilian guests—on August 29, when Count von Zeppelin would make the first trip in his latest model airship from Friedrichshafen, and land at Tegel Field, Berlin. When he met Count von Zeppelin, Orville offered to take him for an airplane ride the next day. The Count, after expressing his appreciation, pleaded lack of time. But he invited Orville to accompany him in the airship on a trip, September 5, from Frankfort to Mannheim, and Orville accepted. In the course of that trip, Orville, by using a stopwatch in his pocket and counting telephone poles, was able to tell if the reported speed of the ship was correct. [When the Wrights were in Europe in 1907, they had seen flights by government-owned dirigibles in more than one country, and had noted that the German ship, *Der Gross*, was the only one that made the speed claimed for it. All they needed to learn was the length of the airship. Then by sighting on the corner of a building, while using a stopwatch, they could tell to the fraction of a second how long it took for the ship to travel its own length.]

On the airship's arrival at Mannheim, the crowd was so great that Orville soon became separated from Captain Hildebrandt, who had come along as his interpreter. Here he was, not knowing much German—supposed to be guest of honor at a luncheon—and he didn't even recall the name of the hotel where the affair was to be held. A member of the committee in charge of the luncheon decided that Orville would doubtless make his way to the center of the city, in search of the right hotel, and that there was just one way to locate him—to drive about the principal streets until he caught sight of him. This man had never met Orville but he felt sure he would recognize him from pictures he had seen. The plan, to Orville's immense relief, succeeded.

On September 16, Orville raised the world's altitude record from 100 to 172 meters. Two days later, he made a new world's record for a flight with a passenger. Accompanied by Captain Paul Englehardt, he flew for one hour, thirty-five minutes, forty-seven seconds. Toward the end of his stay in Germany, Orville's flights were at Bornstedt Field, near Potsdam. It was there that he trained two pilots for the German Wright company—Captain Englehardt and Herr Keidel. Since his first meeting with Orville, the German Crown Prince had made no secret of his eager desire to fly as a passenger. As early as September 9, Orville had made a special flight of fifteen minutes for the Crown Prince to witness. Though he was willing enough to oblige the Crown Prince by taking him for a passenger flight, he hesitated to do so, lest it might be disapproved by the Kaiser, and he made one excuse after another for delay. He had been warned that if he took the Crown Prince as passenger against the Kaiser's wishes, then he might immediately become *persona non grata*. The prudent thing to do, it seemed to Orville, was to give members of the royal family plenty of notification. Different members of the family came to Bornstedt Field from time to time, and when he met any of them Orville was sure to remark that he and the Crown Prince [Friedrich Wilhelm] were going to have a flight together before long. As no one made any objection, the German Crown Prince finally became, on October 2, the first member of a royal family ever to ride in an airplane.

On landing, the Crown Prince handed to Orville, as a token of appreciation, a jeweled stick pin—a crown set in rubies, with a "W" in diamonds. [The "W" was not for Wright, but for Wilhelm, the Crown Prince's name.] On that same day, Orville ascended 1,600 feet for a new—though unofficial—world's altitude record. Orville's farewell ascent in Germany was a twenty-five minute flight, October 15, for Kaiser Wilhelm to see. The Kaiser was enthusiastic and frankly so. He was outspoken in expressing his belief that the airplane might revolutionize warfare, and talked about the different military uses to which the machine could be put. One thing that impressed him was the maneuverability of the plane. Orville had made complete turns within a space not much more than 100 feet wide. Now, during the time that Orville was making these sensational demonstrations in Germany, Wilbur Wright, in America, had been doing his share to glorify the brotherly partnership.

On September 29, in connection with the Hudson-Fulton Celebration, Wilbur made spectacular flights witnessed by millions of people. Two of these were over Governors Island, and another was from Governors Island around the Statue of Liberty and back again. On October 4, Wilbur flew twenty-one miles from Governors Island up the Hudson River beyond Grant's Tomb and back to the starting point. It was one of the most daring flights yet made in an airplane, and Wilbur had taken the precaution to buy a red canoe which he roped to the lower part of the plane.

The part of the canoe ordinarily open was covered with canvas to make it watertight. Wilbur's idea was that if anything went wrong the canoe might possibly serve as a buoy, or pontoon, to keep the machine afloat. In going up the river he flew over ferry boats, and hot gases from the smokestacks did cause the plane to make what looked like dangerous plunges.

A second flight was planned for that afternoon, and everyone who could exert influence had applied for a pass to the military reservation on Governors Island. But they were disappointed, for the engine blew a cylinder and that brought the series of flights to a close. Almost immediately after his flights for the Hudson-Fulton Celebration, Wilbur began preparations to train two Army Signal Corps officers, as provided for in the contract for the sale of a plane to the United States Government. This was done at College Park, Maryland, near Washington. The men trained were Lieutenants Frank P. Lahm and Frederic E. Humphreys. Their instruction began on October 8 and was completed October 26. Lieutenant Lahm, who had been the first army officer ever to fly as a passenger in a plane, received the first lesson in pilotage. But Humphreys made the first solo flight, a few minutes before Lahm's. Wilbur also gave some lessons to Lieutenant Benjamin D. Foulois between October 23 and 27.

Orville and Katharine Wright sailed from Europe on the *Adriatic*, due in New York November 4. After leaving Germany, Orville had investigated the outlook of the recently formed French company. Already it appeared that this company would be a disappointment. Count de Lambert had given the company the best kind of advertising by flying a Wright plane over Paris, around and above the Eiffel Tower. But the French Wright company evidently was depending more on political influence and on entertaining important people than on sound salesmanship. The War Ministry hesitated to buy planes for fear of public criticism. General Picquart, the Army officer who had stood for justice in the [Alfred] Dreyfus case, had become Minister of War. He once inquired of the Wrights if it would be possible to buy their planes directly from them in the United States. That would have been against provisions of the contract with the company in France, but there was another reason why it could not be done. The Wrights were not yet organized to produce planes in great numbers. Though there were now two commercial companies for the manufacture of Wright planes in Europe, no such company yet existed in America.

After companies to manufacture the Wright brothers's invention had been organized in France and Germany, and a plane had been sold in Italy, it might have been expected that important business people in the United States would see commercial possibilities in the Wright patents. The inventors had, indeed, received offers. One proposal had come from two brothers, in Detroit, influential stockholders in the Packard Automobile Company, Russell A. and Frederick M. Alger—who some time before had been the first in the United States to order a Wright machine for private use. But the first American company to manufacture the plane was promoted by a mere youngster. That was Clinton R. Peterkin. He was barely twenty-four and looked even younger. Only a year or two previously he had been with J. P. Morgan and Company as "office boy"—a job he had taken at the age of fifteen. But he had intelligently made the most of his opportunities by spending all the time he could in the firm's inner rooms, and had learned something of how new business enterprises were started. Now, recently returned from a stay in the West because of ill health, Peterkin wished to be a promoter, and he wondered if the Wright brothers would agree to the formation of a flying machine company. By chance he learned that Wilbur Wright was spending a few days at the Park Avenue Hotel in New York, and in October, 1909, he went to see him. Wilbur was approachable enough and received Peterkin in a friendly way, though he didn't seem to set too much store by the young man's proposals. In reply to questions, Wilbur said that he and his brother would not care to have a company formed unless those in it were men of consequence. They would want names that carried weight. Then Peterkin spoke of knowing John Pierpont Morgan, whom he might be able to interest. Without making any kind of agreement or promise, Wilbur told him he could go ahead and see what he could do—doubtless assuming that he would soon become discouraged. But Peterkin saw J. P. Morgan who told him he would take stock and that he would subscribe also for his friend Judge Elbert H. Gary, head of the United States Steel Corporation. After seeing Morgan, Peterkin was enthusiastically telling of his project to a distant relative of his, a member of a law firm with offices in the financial district. The senior partner in that law firm, DeLancey Nicoll, chanced to overhear what Peterkin was saying and grew interested. He suggested that perhaps he might be of help. That was a good piece of luck for Peterkin. He could hardly have found a better ally, for DeLancey Nicoll had an exceptionally wide and intimate acquaintance among men in the world of finance.

All he needed to do to interest some of his friends was to call them on the telephone. In a surprisingly short time an impressive list of moneyed men were enrolled as subscribers in the proposed flying machine company. A number of them were prominent in the field of transportation. The list included Cornelius Vanderbilt, August Belmont, Howard Gould, Theodore P. Shonts, Allan A. Ryan, Mortimer F. Plant, Andrew Freedman, and [Edward Julius] Berwind. Shonts was president of the New York Interborough subway. Ryan, a son of Thomas F. Ryan, was a director of the Bethlehem Steel Corporation. Plant was chairman of the Board of Directors of the Southern Express Company, and Vice President of the Chicago, Indianapolis and Louisville Railroad. Berwind, as President of the Berwind-White Coal Mining Company, had accumulated a great fortune from coal contracts with big steamship lines. Freedman had made his money originally as a sports promoter and then in various financial operations. [He later provided funds for founding the Andrew Freedman Home in New York.] The Wrights wanted to have in the company their friends Robert J. Collier, publisher of *Collier's Weekly*, and the two Alger brothers of Detroit. Those names were promptly added. But the names of J. P. Morgan and [Elbert Henry] Gary were not in the final list of stockholders. The truth was that some of the others in the proposed company did not want Morgan with them because they believed—probably correctly—that he would dominate the company, that where he sat would be the head of the table. One of them phoned to

Morgan that the stock was oversubscribed. When he thus got strong hints that his participation was not too eagerly desired, Morgan promptly withdrew his offer to take stock for himself and Gary. On November 22, 1909, only about a month after Peterkin's first talk with Wilbur, the Wright Company was incorporated.

The capital stock represented a paid-in value of $200,000. In payment for all rights to their patents in the United States, the Wright brothers received stock and cash, besides a provision for ten percent royalty on all planes sold, and the Wright Company would thenceforth bear the expense of prosecuting all suits against patent infringers. From the Wright brothers point of view, the one fly in the ointment was that they now found themselves more involved than ever before in business affairs. It had been their dream to be entirely out of business and able to give their whole time to scientific research. The company opened impressive offices in the Night and Day Bank Building, 527 Fifth Avenue, New York, but the factory would be in Dayton.

In January, 1910, Frank Russell, a cousin of the Algers, who had been appointed factory manager, arrived in Dayton and went to see the Wrights at their office over the old bicycle shop. As the brothers had no desk space to offer him, they suggested a room at the rear of a plumbing shop down the street where he might make temporary headquarters. According to Russell, Wilbur Wright came there a day or two later carrying a basket filled with letters, directed to the Wright Company that had been accumulating. "*I don't know what you'll want to do about these,*" Russell has reported Wilbur as jokingly saying, "*maybe they should be opened. But of course if you open a letter, there's always the danger that you may decide to answer it, and then you're apt to find yourself involved in a long correspondence.*" At first the Wright Company rented floor space in a factory building, but almost immediately the company started to build a modern factory of its own, and it was ready for use by November, 1910. Within a short time after the company started operations in its rented space it had a force of employees at mechanical work and was able to produce about two airplanes a month. The Wrights well knew that the time was not yet for the company to operate profitably by selling planes for private use. Their main opportunity to show a good return on the capital invested would be from public exhibitions. Relatively few people in the United States had yet seen an airplane in flight and crowds would flock to behold this new miracle—still, in 1910, almost incredible. As soon as they decided to give public exhibitions, the Wrights got in touch with another pioneer of the air, [Augustus] Roy Knabenshue, a young man from Toledo, who had been making balloon flights since his early teens, and was the first in the United States to have piloted a steerable balloon. They had previously become acquainted with Knabenshue. Because of his curiosity over anything pertaining to aerial navigation, he had once subscribed to a press-clipping bureau which sent him anything found in the papers about aeronautics, and in this way he had been able to read an occasional news item about the two Dayton men said to have flown. With a fairly irresistible impish grin, Knabenshue never had much trouble making new acquaintances, and he decided to call upon the Wrights. That was before the Wright flights at Fort Myer and in France, and the brothers were not then interested when Knabenshue suggested that they sell him planes for exhibitions. "Well," he said, "*I have been making airship flights at the big state fairs, besides promoting public exhibitions, and I know how to make the proper contacts. You may have heard about my flights in a small dirigible at the St. Louis World's Fair. If you ever decide to give exhibitions, just let me know.*" Though exhibitions had been farthest from the Wrights's thoughts at the time of that first meeting with Knabenshue, now the situation was different. Roy Knabenshue would probably be the very man they needed. They sent a telegram to him and he received it at Los Angeles. He wired back that he would see them as soon as he returned to Ohio. This he did soon afterward. The result of their conversation was that Roy took charge of the work of arranging for public flights. He had need of a competent secretary and an intelligent young woman, Miss Mabel Beck, came to take the job. This was her first employment and she seemed a bit ill at ease, lest her work might not be satisfactory, but almost immediately she became an extraordinarily good assistant—so good, in fact, that Wilbur Wright afterward selected her to work with him in connection with suits against patent infringers, and after his death she became secretary to Orville Wright, in which position, at this writing, she still is. By the time Knabenshue had started planning for public exhibitions—Orville Wright had begun the training of pilots to handle the exhibition planes being built.

The weather was still too wintry for flying at Huffman Field, now leased by the Wright Company, and it was necessary to find a suitable place in a warmer climate. The field selected was at Montgomery, Alabama. [Today known as Maxwell Field, it is used by the United States Government.] Shortly after his arrival at Montgomery, early in 1910, Orville Wright had a new experience in the air. While at an altitude of about 1,500 feet he found himself unable to descend, even though the machine was pointed downward as much as seemed safe. Brought up to have faith in the force of gravity, he didn't know at first what to make of this. For nearly five minutes he stayed there, in a puzzled state of mind bordering on alarm. Later it occurred to him that the machine must have been in a whirlwind of rising air current of unusual diameter, and that doubtless he could have returned quickly to earth if he had first steered horizontally to get away from the rising current. The first pilot Orville trained was Walter Brookins of Dayton. "Brookie" was a logical candidate for that distinction, for since the age of four he had been a kind of "pet" of Orville's. After Orville had left Montgomery and returned to Dayton on May 8, Brookins himself became an instructor. He began, at Montgomery, the training of Arch Hoxsey, noted for his personal charm and his gay, immaculate clothes, and also that of Spencer C. Crane. On his return to Dayton, Orville opened a flying school at the same Huffman Field the Wright brothers had used for their experiments in 1904-1905. Here he trained A. L. Welsh and Duval LaChapelle. When Brookins arrived there from Montgomery, near the end of May, he took on the training of Ralph Johnstone and Frank T. Coffyn, besides completing the training of Hoxsey. Two others trained at the same field later in the year were [Philip Orin] Parmalee and [Clifford] Turpin.

Orville Wright continued to make frequent flights until 1915, personally testing every new device used on a Wright plane. [He did not make his final flight as a pilot until 1918.] More than one person who witnessed flights at the Huffman Field (or at Simms Station, as the place was better known) has made comment that it was never difficult to pick Orville Wright from the other flyers, whether he was on the ground or in a plane. Students, and instructors too, would be dressed to the teeth for flying, with special suits, goggles, helmets, gauntlets, and so on, but Orville always wore an ordinary business suit. He might put on a pair of automobile goggles and shift his cap backward, and on cold days he would turn up his coat collar, but otherwise he was dressed as for the street. When he was in the air anyone could recognize who it was—from the smoothness of his flying. And when he wished to test the control and stability of a plane, he would sometimes come down and make figure eights at steep angles with the wing tip maybe not more than a few feet from the grass. The public was no longer unaware of the significance of the flights at Huffman Field. Sightseers began to use every possible pretext to come as close to the planes as possible. One evening as Orville Wright was standing near the hangar, a bystander edged up to him. "*I flew with Orville Wright down at Montgomery,*" he declared, "*and he told me to make myself at home here.*"

Never before having seen Orville, he had mistaken him for an employee. Three flights at Huffman Field in May, 1910, were especially noteworthy. A short one by Wilbur—one minute twenty-nine seconds—on May 21—was the first he had made alone since his sensational feats starting from Governors Island. And it was the last flight as a pilot Wilbur ever made. But on May 25 he and Orville flew for a short time together—with Orville piloting—the only occasion when the Wright brothers were both in the air at the same time. Later that same day, Orville took his father, Bishop Milton Wright—then eighty-two years old, for his first trip in a flying machine. They flew for six minutes fifty-five seconds, most of the time at about 350 feet. The only thing that Bishop Wright said while in the air was a request to go "*higher, higher.*" The average charge by the Wright Company for a series of exhibition flights at a county fair or elsewhere was about $5,000 for each plane used. At Indianapolis, the scene of the first exhibition, five planes were used. The weather was not ideal for the Indianapolis event, but the crowd was much impressed.

Another early exhibition was at Atlantic City, where, for the first time, wheels were publicly used on a Wright machine for starting and landing. Roy Knabenshue knew from his experience in making public airship exhibitions, that it was not enough to go where a fair or carnival was to be held and suggest airplane flights as a feature. To get all the business possible for his company he must promote exhibition flights in places where no such big outdoor events were yet contemplated. He particularly desired to have flights made in large cities where newspaper reports of the event would attract attention over a large area and aid him in making further bookings. With this in mind he went to Chicago and started inquiries to learn whether public-spirited citizens there would be willing to underwrite a big public demonstration of aviation along the lake front. Several people told him the man he should see was Harold McCormick, one of the controlling stockholders in the wealthy International Harvester Company. He went at once to McCormick's offices in the Harvester Building. But when he reached the outer office, he discovered that it was not easy to get any farther. "*What was it you wished to see Mr. McCormick about?*" asked a secretary. "*I don't wish to sell him anything,*" Roy explained, smiling in a manner that should have won confidence, but didn't. "*Please, just say to him that there's a man here who has an important suggestion for him.*"

"*But if you'll tell me what the suggestion is,*" the secretary proposed, "*then he can let you know if he is interested.*" "*No, I'll tell you what you do,*" countered Roy. "*Please hand my card to him and let him decide if he wishes to see me.*" The secretary reluctantly took Roy's card which indicated that he represented the Wright Company of Dayton, Ohio. A moment later the secretary returned to say that Mr. McCormick was too busy to see anyone. Roy walked out of the building into Michigan Avenue, discouraged. "No matter how good an idea you've got," he reflected, "and no matter how much some of these big executives might be interested, you don't get a chance to tell them about it."

As he strolled along, his eye chanced to fall on a big sign that read, "THINK OF IT, THE RECORD-HERALD NOW ONE CENT." Then he remembered that the Chicago *Record-Herald*, rival of the *Tribune* in the morning field, had recently reduced its price and was making a big bid for increased circulation.

He also recalled that [Herman Henry] Kohlsaat, owner of the *Record-Herald*, had known his father. Using his father's name for an introduction, he had little difficulty, a half hour later, in gaining access to Kohlsaat's private office to tell him what was on his mind. The publisher grew interested. Yes, it might be a good idea to have some airplane flights along the lakefront and invite the public to see them as guests of the *Record-Herald*.

Before he left the office, Roy had the preliminary arrangements all made. On the opening day of the big event, when Walter Brookins, as pilot, was about to take off on the first flight, Knabenshue remarked to him, *"That corner window on the fourth floor of the Harvester Building is in the office of a man I hope will see what's going on."* The next day Knabenshue appeared once again at Harold McCormick's office in the Harvester Building and presented his business card to the same secretary he had met on his previous visit. After looking at the card, the secretary, without waiting to consult anyone, said, *"Oh, yes, you're with the Wright Company. I'm sure Mr. McCormick will wish to see you. Just step this way."* Roy had made this call partly as a kind of practical joke—for the satisfaction of entering an office where he had once been denied. But as a result of the talk he then had with McCormick, it was arranged that a committee of Chicago citizens should sponsor, the next year, another aviation meeting there, to be the biggest thing of the kind ever held. Meanwhile, on the final day of the 1910 exhibitions at Chicago, Brookins made the first long cross-country flight, 185 miles, to Springfield, Illinois. It was not, however, a nonstop flight. He made one landing in a cornfield, and it was necessary to obtain permission from the farm owner to cut a wide strip across the field to provide space for the plane to take off. In that same year, 1910, Dayton people saw the first flight over the city itself. Thousands had now seen flights at the Huffman Field, Simms Station, but no flight had ever been made nearer than eight miles to the hometown where successful flying was conceived. The Greater Dayton Association was holding, in September, an industrial exhibit, but it was operating at a loss. Those in charge of the exhibit saw that something would have to be done to arouse interest. Orville Wright was asked if he would start at Simms Station, fly to Dayton and circle over the city. He agreed and the newspapers announced the flight for the next day. It was stirring news—even to Katharine Wright. She had started to Oberlin to attend a college meeting, but, when on her arrival there she happened to see a newspaper item about Orville's flight scheduled for the next day, she hastened home at once. Another premier event in 1910 was when an airplane for the first time in the world was used for commercial express service. The Morehouse-Martin Company, a department store in Columbus, Ohio, arranged to have a bolt of silk brought from Huffman Field to a driving park beyond Columbus. The distance of more than sixty miles was covered at better than a mile a minute, then considered fast airplane speed, and the "express fee" was $5,000, or about $71.42 a pound. But within a day or two the store had a good profit on the transaction, for it sold small pieces of the silk for souvenirs, and the gross returns were more than $6,000. Then, at Belmont Park, New York, in late October, 1910, Wright planes participated in a great International Aviation Tournament. All other planes taking part were licensed by the Wright Company. Orville Wright now devoted his time mainly to supervision of engineering at the factory of the Wright Company. Wilbur was kept busy looking after the prosecution of suits against patent infringers and in March, 1911, he went to Europe in connection with suits brought by the Wright Company of France. From France he went to

Germany and while there called at the home of the widow of Otto Lilienthal to offer his homage to the memory of that pioneer in aviation whose work had been an inspiration to the Wrights.

After Wilbur's return to America, Orville spent several weeks in October, 1911, at Kitty Hawk, where he went to do some experimenting with an automatic control device and to make soaring flights with a glider. In camp with him were Alec Ogilvie of England, who flew a Wright plane, Orville's brother Lorin, and Lorin's ten-year-old boy, "Buster" [Horace Wright]. On account of the presence of a group of newspapermen who appeared and were at the camp each day during his entire stay at Kitty Hawk, Orville never tested the new automatic device, but before his soaring experiments were over he had made, on October 24, a new record, soaring for nine minutes forty-five seconds. [This was to remain the world's record until ten years later when it was exceeded in Germany.] That same year, 1911, the Wright Company benefited from another aviation record. [Calbraith Perry] Rodgers, who had received some of his flying training at the Wright School, made—between September 11 and November 5—the first transcontinental airplane trip, from New York to California. New as their line of business was, the Wright Company was profitable from the start—especially so during the first year or two when the sight of a flying machine was still a novelty and contracts for exhibition flights were numerous. [It might have been more profitable if the Wrights had not insisted that no contracts be made to include flights on Sunday.] But inevitably the exhibition part of the business began to taper off—and such profits as might still have come from it were reduced by the persistent illegal competition of patent infringers. More and more, the company's dealings were with the United States Army and Navy and with private buyers of planes. The first private plane sold had gone to Robert J. Collier, and others seeking the excitement or prestige of owning a plane had been making inquiries. The retail price of a plane was $5,000. With aviation thus becoming more practical, the Wrights were receiving from their invention a form of reward they had never expected. They would now have wealth, not vast, but enough to enable them to look forward to the time when they might retire and work happily together on scientific research. They were making plans too, for their new home on a seventeen-acre wooded tract they had named Hawthorn Hill, in the Dayton suburb of Oakwood. But tragic days were ahead. Early in May, shortly after visiting the new home site with other members of the family, Wilbur was taken ill. What at first was assumed to be a minor indisposition proved to be typhoid fever. Worn out from worries over protecting in patent litigation the rights he knew were his and his brother's, he was not in condition to combat the disease.

After an illness of three weeks, despite the best efforts of eminent specialists, early in the morning of Thursday, May 30, 1912, Wilbur Wright died. He was aged only forty-five years and forty-four days. Messages of condolence and expressions of the world's loss poured in from two hemispheres, among them those from heads of governments. Orville Wright succeeded his brother as president of the Wright Company. In June, 1913, Grover Loening, a young man who had become acquainted with Wilbur at the time of the Hudson-Fulton exhibition flights, came to the Wright Company as engineer, and then became factory manager. Loening had the distinction of being the first person in the United States to study aeronautical science in a university.

Business affairs had been complicated earlier that year by the fact that Dayton had the worst flood in its history. The Wright factory was not under water but not many of the employees could reach the building. Among the hundreds of houses under water was the Wright home on Hawthorne Street. To Orville a serious part of the loss there was the damage to photographic negatives showing his and Wilbur's progress toward flight. But the negative of the famous picture of the first power flight was not much harmed. Accompanied by his sister, Orville made his last trip to Europe in 1913, on business relating to a patent suit in Germany. At about the same time he sanctioned the forming of a Wright company in England. Before Wilbur's death, there had been opportunities for a company in England, but the brothers had held back because all the offers appeared to be purely stock promotions in which the names of members of the English nobility would appear as sponsors. The British company as finally organized did not make planes itself, but issued licenses for use of the patents. Within a year after it was formed the English company accepted from the British Government a flat payment for all claims against the government, for use of the Wright patents up to that time and during the remainder of the life of the basic patents. Though the amount paid was no trifling sum, the settlement was widely applauded by prominent Englishmen, among them Lord Northcliffe, as showing a generous attitude on the part of the patent owner—about as little as could have been compatible with full recognition of the priority of the Wrights's invention. By this time, the Wright Company had more applications to train student pilots than they could handle. Even a few young women wished to become pilots. Two capable students, of a somewhat earlier period, destined to go far in aviation, were Thomas D. Milling, later General Milling, of the United States Army Air Corps, and Henry H. Arnold, who during the Second World War was Lieutenant General Arnold, Commanding General of the Army Air Forces and Deputy Chief of Staff for Air. One unfortunate student pilot, who had begun his training at the Wright School in 1912, later got himself into much trouble. This man became one of the best flyers in the United States. As he had plenty of money he bought a plane of his own, and he used to give free exhibitions at his estate near Philadelphia. In one way or another he did much for aviation.

But in 1917, when the United States entered the First World War, that young pilot refused to register in the draft and became notorious as a draft evader. His name?—Grover Cleveland Bergdoll. The early Wright plane he had bought is today on exhibition at the Franklin Institute in Philadelphia. It is believed to be the only authentic Model B—the first model built by the Wright Company—in existence. In 1914, Orville Wright had bought the stock of all other shareholders in the Wright Company, except that of his friend, Robert J. Collier, who, for sentimental reason, wished to retain his interest. Orville's motive in acquiring almost complete ownership of the company had been as a step toward getting entirely out of business. Both he and Wilbur Wright had agreed to stay with the company for a period of years, not yet expired, and he could not honorably dispose of his own holdings so long as those with whom he had made the agreement were still in the company. But almost immediately after buying the shares of the others, he let it be known that he might be willing to sell his entire interest. To this, Collier, the only other shareholder, agreed. In 1915, Orville received an offer and gave an option to a small group of eastern capitalists that included William Boyce Thompson and Frank Manville, the latter president of the Johns-Manville Company. The deal was closed in October, 1915. Just after Orville had given his option to the eastern syndicate, Robert J. Collier came to tell him an important piece of news, and to urge him not to sell just yet. Collier had been having some talks with his friend, the wealthy Harry Payne Whitney, and had urged upon him the idea of doing what Collier thought would be a wonderful piece of philanthropy that would mean much for the future of aviation in the United States. What Collier wanted him to do was to buy the stock of the Wright Company, thus gaining ownership of the Wright patents, and then immediately make the patents free to anyone in the United States who wished to manufacture airplanes. Whitney was willing to carry out the Collier suggestion. To do so he was also ready to pay more for the stock of the Wright Company than the syndicate had offered.

But Orville explained to Collier that the option already given was legally drawn and the holders presumably wished to exercise it. Collier's daring idea and Whitney's generous acceptance of it had come just a little too late.

□□□□□□□□□□

The Wrights had found that patents covering the basic features of their invention were not enough protection against infringers. Indeed, having the technical details on file in the

Patent Office, where anyone who desired might see them, was, in a way, to the advantage of those who would help themselves to an inventor's work and ideas. Only a decision in the courts could determine the justice of an inventor's claims. But the courts work slowly and legal procedure is expensive. Except for their good fortune—never contemplated when they started—in realizing substantial sums from their invention, the brothers might not have been financially able to carry on the fight that finally gave them worldwide recognition as the first to contrive a successful flying machine. Altogether the brothers had active part in a dozen different suits in the United States against infringers—and there were suits in France and Germany in each of which about a dozen infringers were involved. Most of the suits in the United States did not go beyond the early stages, as the infringers were not disposed to continue after a preliminary injunction had been issued. But three suits were of special importance. One of these was against Louis Paulhan, French aviator, who was about to give exhibitions in the United States, using planes made in France.

Another was against Claude Grahame-White, English aviator, also about to give exhibitions in the United States with planes that infringed the Wright patents. The most important suit of all was against the Herring-Curtiss Company and Glenn H. Curtiss. This case was bitterly contested and was carried up to the US Court of Appeals. It was brought by the Wright brothers, late in 1909, but the Wright Company, formed shortly afterward, succeeded the brothers as complainants. Because of the importance of this suit in aviation history, it is worthwhile to examine the background of the relations between the Wrights and Glenn Curtiss. The Wrights's personal acquaintance with Curtiss began in May, 1906, when he wrote to them in regard to the light motors of which he was a manufacturer. Then in early September, 1906, Curtiss visited the Wright office and workshop. He was brought there by his friend, Captain Thomas S. Baldwin, a well-known aeronaut, who was giving exhibition flights in Dayton with his dirigible balloon on which he used a motor he had persuaded Curtiss to build for him. It was to make repairs on that motor that Curtiss had come to Dayton. After that meeting, the four men, Curtiss, Baldwin, and the Wrights, were together much of the time for several days. When in response to questions about their work, the Wrights showed a number of photographs of their flights made at the Huffman Pasture during the two previous years, Curtiss seemed much astonished. He remarked that it was the first time he had been able to believe anyone had actually been in the air with a flying machine. Long afterward, in an interview in the New York *Times* (February 28, 1914), Baldwin recalled the many talks he and Glenn Curtiss had with the Wrights in that fall of 1906. "*I sometimes suggested to Curtiss,*" Baldwin told the interviewer, "*that he was asking too many questions, but he kept right on. The Wrights had the frankness of schoolboys in it all and had a rare confidence in us. I am sure Curtiss at that time never thought of taking up flying.*" A year after the Wrights's first meetings with Curtiss, in October, 1907, the Aerial Experiment Association was formed by Alexander Graham Bell and others, with headquarters first in Nova Scotia and later at Hammondsport, New York, where Curtiss lived. He became "Director of Experiments." This was the first time Curtiss had been directly connected with aviation except as a manufacturer of motors, and three months later, a letter he wrote to the Wrights indicated that motors rather than aviation were still his chief interest. "*I just wish to keep in touch with you,*" he wrote, "*and let you know that we have been making considerable progress in engine construction.*" After listing and describing the various engines he was building, he proposed to furnish to the Wrights "gratis" one of his fifty-horsepower engines. But the offer was not accepted. The letter mentioned that Captain Baldwin was a "permanent fixture in this establishment"—a fact not without importance, considering information that Baldwin was later to reveal. Further on in the letter, Curtiss told of Dr. Bell's reading to the members of the Aerial Experiment Association the United States Government's specifications for the purchase of a flying machine, and added, "*You, of course, are the only persons who could come anywhere near doing what is required.*" About a fortnight after receipt of that letter from Curtiss, the Wrights got another letter dated January 15, 1908, written on Aerial Experiment Association stationery, and signed by Lieutenant T. Selfridge, whose name appeared on the letterhead as secretary of the association. [This was the same Selfridge who was killed a few months later in the tragic airplane accident at Fort Myer.]

In that letter, Selfridge, on behalf of the Experiment Association, said, "*I am taking the liberty of writing you and asking your advice on certain points connected with gliding experiments, or rather glider construction, which we started here last Monday. Will you kindly tell me what results you obtained on the travel of the center of pressure both on aerocurves and aeroplanes? Also, what is a good, efficient method of constructing the ribs of the surfaces so that they will be light and yet strong enough to maintain their curvature under ordinary conditions, and a good means of fastening them to the cloth and upper lateral cords of the frame? I hope I am not imposing too much by asking you these questions.*"

Supposing the information would be used only for scientific purposes, the Wrights obligingly replied at once as follows, "*You will find much of the information you desire in the addresses of our Mr. Wilbur Wright before the Western Society of Engineers, published in the* Journals *of the Society of December, 1901, and August, 1903. The travel of the center of pressure on aeroplanes is from the center at 90 degrees, toward the front edge as the angle becomes smaller. The center of pressure on a curved surface is approximately at its center at 90 degrees, moves forward as the angle is decreased until a critical angle is reached, after which it reverses, and moves toward the rear edge. The critical angle varies for different shaped curves, but is generally reached at some angle between 12 and 18 degrees. With the angles used in gliding flight the travel will be between the center of the surface and a point one-third back from the front edge. The methods of construction used in our gliders are fully described in an article by Mr. Chanute in the* Revue des Sciences *in 1903 (we do not remember the month) and in the specifications of our United States patent, Number 821.393. The ribs of our gliders were made of* second growth ash, steamed and bent to shape." Selfridge replied in a few days saying he had been able to obtain a copy of the patent and would endeavor to get the other references the Wrights had supplied. The data must have been useful to the Aerial Experiment Association for early the following summer, Glenn Curtiss, "Director of Experiments," had a power-driven airplane, called the "June Bug," in which he made a flight on July 4, 1908, at Hammondsport. That flight created the belief in the minds of many who were not fully informed that the Aerial Experiment Association must have done an amazing job of original research. This belief was encouraged by the fact that after the Aerial Experiment Association began building and experimenting with flying machines, using much information they had obtained from the Wrights, they neglected, in public statements about their work, to so much as mention the Wright brothers. Soon after the report of the flight of the "June Bug," there appeared in the press a statement that the Aerial Experiment Association was disbanding, and that Glenn H. Curtiss was going to engage in exhibition flying. That news led Orville Wright to send to Curtiss the following letter, "*I learn from the* Scientific American *that your "June Bug" has movable surfaces at the tips of the wings, adjustable to different angles on the right and left sides for maintaining the lateral balance. In our letter to Lieutenant Selfridge of January 18th, replying to his of the 15th, in which he asked for information on the construction of flyers, we referred him to several publications containing descriptions of the structural features of our machines, and to our US patent Number 821.393. We did not intend, of course, to give permission to use the patented features of our machine for exhibitions or in a commercial way. This patent broadly covers the combination of sustaining surfaces to the right and left of the center of a flying machine adjustable to different angles, with vertical surfaces adjustable to correct inequalities in the horizontal resistances of the differently adjusted wings. Claim 14 of our patent Number 821.393 specifically covers the combination which we are informed you are using. We believe it will be very difficult to develop a successful machine* without the use of some of the features covered in this patent. The commercial part of our business is taking so much of our time that we have not been able to undertake public exhibitions. If it is your desire to enter the exhibition business, we would be glad to take up the matter of a license to operate under our patents for that purpose." Curtiss replied that, contrary to newspaper reports, he did not expect to do anything in the way of exhibitions—that his flights had been in connection with the Aerial Experiment Association's work. The matter of the patents he had referred, he said, to the Secretary of the Association. A few weeks later, when Orville went to Washington in preparation for the Fort Myer tests of the Wright machine, Captain Baldwin was there teaching Army officers to operate a new dirigible balloon for which Curtiss had furnished the motor. In speaking of the experiments in aviation being carried on by Curtiss and other members of the Aerial Experiment Association at Hammondsport, Baldwin said warningly to Orville, "*I hear them talking.*" He went on to caution Orville that the work those men were doing would infringe the Wright patents. By the following year, Curtiss had formed a commercial company, the Herring-Curtiss Company, to make or exhibit airplanes. On January 3, 1910, Judge John R. Hazel, of the Federal Circuit Court, at Buffalo, New York, granted a temporary restraining order against the Herring-Curtiss Company and Glenn H. Curtiss to prevent them from infringement of the Wright patents. In handing down his decision, Judge Hazel said, "*It appears that the defendant Curtiss had notice of the success of the Wright machine, and that a patent had been issued in 1906. Indeed, no one interfered with the rights of the patentees by constructing machines similar to theirs until in July, 1908, when Curtiss exhibited a flying machine which he called the "June Bug." He was immediately notified by the patentees that such machine, with its movable surfaces at the tips, or wings, infringed the patent in suit, and he replied that he did not intend to publicly exhibit the machine for profit, but merely was engaged in exhibiting it for scientific purposes as a member of the Aerial Experiment Association. To this the patentees did not object. Subsequently, however, the machine* with supplementary planes placed midway between the upper and lower aeroplanes, was publicly exhibited by the defendant corporation, and used by Curtiss in aerial flights for prizes and emoluments. It further appears that the defendants now threaten to continue such use for gain and profit, and to engage in the manufacture and sale of such infringing machine, thereby becoming an active rival of complainant in the business of constructing flying machines embodying the claims in suit, but such use of the infringing machine it is the duty of this Court on the papers presented to enjoin." Then, in February, 1910, Judge Learned Hand, in the Federal Circuit Court, at New York, issued an injunction to prevent the French aviator, Louis Paulhan, from making exhibitions in the United States unless he would put up an indemnity to the amount of $25,000. The Court declared that both the Bleriot and Farman planes that the defendant was planning to use were infringements of the Wright patents.

Not until January 13, 1914, did the US Circuit Court of Appeals hand down its decision in the Wright suit against Curtiss. The decision was in favor of the Wright Company. In his interview in the New York *Times*, already quoted from, published in the New York *Times*, February 28, 1914, Captain Thomas S. Baldwin, though a close associate of Curtiss heartily endorsed the final decision in the Wright *vs.* Curtiss case. Referring to that decision he told the interviewer, "*It is high time for all the rest of us to step up and admit that not a one of us ever would have got off the ground in flight if the Wrights had not unlocked the secret for us. I want to go on record as saying that the Wrights are fully entitled to the decision they have at last received. Mr. Curtiss is a friend of mine today,*" said Baldwin, "*and I have served in his companies as a director. But it is due to the Wrights as a simple matter of justice to have the story of the actual genesis of flight fully established.*" By that time, Captain Baldwin had abandoned the dirigible balloon for the airplane, and thus he, too, had been an infringer of the Wright patent. But as his public statements indicated, he showed an attitude quite different from that of most other infringers. Glenn Martin was another, like Baldwin, who acknowledged indebtedness to the Wrights. After the Wrights had won their important suit against Curtiss in the Circuit Court of Appeals, Curtiss made no secret of the fact that he still hoped to find a possible loophole to get around the Wright patent.

Since the decision of the Court enjoined him from using two ailerons operating simultaneously in opposite directions, he thought perhaps he could escape penalty by using just one aileron at a time, while the other remained inoperative. This, however, was covered by Claim 1 of the Wright patent, if the claim were given a liberal interpretation, as the Court had said the Wright Patent was entitled to, on account of the Wrights being the pioneers in the art of flying. But Claim 1 had not been cited in the former suits, and so had not as yet been adjudicated. If Curtiss could just show, or seem to show, in some way that the Wrights were not exactly pioneers, that some other machine capable of flight antedated the Wright machine, then he would be in a stronger position to defend himself against Claim 1 if it should be cited against him. Anticipating a suit, Curtiss took astounding means to prepare for combating it—as will appear. But after all the evidence was taken in that case and just before the case was to come to trial, Orville Wright sold his interest in the Wright Company to New York capitalists. Curtiss then contrived to gain delay after delay by approaching the new owners with proposals of settlement. These negotiations dragged on until the United States entered the First World War, and the Manufacturers Aircraft Association was organized for cross-licensing manufacturers who were building machines for the United States Government. Through this cross-licensing agreement, the Wright Company received royalty on all planes manufactured for the Government. Consequently, this last case against Curtiss never came to trial. The Wrights won their patent suits, too, in the highest courts of both Germany and France.

The court in Germany made the comment in its oral decision that their discovery that a rear rudder was a balancing device rather than a steering device should entitle them to a basic patent. Without going into too much detail about the various patent suits, the important point is that the priority of the Wright patents was sustained by the courts in both the United States and Europe. Every airplane that flies, in any part of the world, even today, does so by use of devices and discoveries first made by the Wright brothers. These patent suits were a terrible ordeal for the attorneys and judges concerned, for aviation was so new that many of the technical terms were beyond the knowledge of nearly everyone. It was as if lawyers and judges had to learn a new language and take a course in the theoretical side of aeronautical engineering as they went along. In a case against a foreign aviator, Wilbur Wright was called upon in Court to explain the function and operation of a rudder when an aeroplane is making a circle. Wilbur got hold of a piece of string and a fragment of chalk and went to a blackboard, where he made it clear to the judge that when a machine is making a turn the pressure is on the opposite side of an aeroplane rudder from what it is on a ship's or a dirigible's rudder when they are making the same turn. After the judge had issued a temporary restraining order, at the end of the day's proceedings, Clarence J. Shearn, attorney for the defendant, gloomily remarked, "*If it hadn't been for Wright and that damned piece of string, we would have won.*" One bit of testimony in another case was in regard to the accuracy of observations of men who fly airplanes.

To show the inaccuracy of most people's observations on phenomena having to do with physical laws, Wilbur used for illustration what a man thinks happens when riding a bicycle. "*I have asked dozens of bicycle riders,*" said Wilbur, "*how they turn a bicycle to the left. I have never found a single person who stated all the facts correctly when first asked. They almost invariably said that, to turn to the left, they turned the handlebar to the left and as a result made a turn to the left. But on further questioning them, some would agree that they first turned the handlebar a little to the right, and then as the machine became inclined to the left, they turned the handlebar to the left and made the circle, inclining inwardly. To a scientific student it is very clear that without the preliminary movement of the handlebar to the right, a movement of* the handlebar to the left would cause the bicycle to run out from under the man, who would continue headlong in his original direction. Yet I have found many people who would deny having ever noticed the preliminary movement of the handlebar to the right. I have never found a non-scientific bicycle rider who had particularly noticed it and spoke of it from his own conscious observation and initiative. I found the same condition among aviators with whom I have flown. Some have almost no consciousness of whether the machine is rising a little or descending a little, or whether it is sliding somewhat to the right or to the left. The ability to notice these things, even in small degrees, is the main quality which distinguishes skilled aviators from novices and born flyers from men who will never be able to handle flying machines competently." Even though the Wrights won all their patent suits collecting royalties proved to be something else.

□□□□□□□□□□□

Why was the original Wright airplane, the first flying machine in the world capable of flight, deposited in the Science Museum at South Kensington, London, England, rather than in the United States National Museum, administered by the Smithsonian Institution, at Washington? Why should Exhibit A of one of the greatest of all American scientific achievements be in exile? For the answer to these questions, puzzling to a vast number of patriotic Americans, we must trace events back a number of years. It will be remembered that Dr. Samuel Pierpont Langley, while Director and Secretary of the Smithsonian, with a $50,000 government fund at his disposal for experiments (besides $20,000 from the Hodgkins Fund), had failed in his attempts to build a successful man-carrying flying machine.

At each trial, in 1903, his machine promptly fell from its launching platform into the Potomac. Doubtless Langley's failure was a bitter disappointment to him—all the more so because he was derided in the public press for having even tried what was commonly believed to be impossible. But when the Wrights flew only nine days after Langley's final unsuccessful trial, they in a measure saved the Langley reputation. No one could any longer say that he was a "crank." The Wrights had vindicated his belief that man could fly. Langley uttered no word to minimize the importance of the Wrights's feat. Nor was anything unfriendly toward Langley ever said by either of the Wrights. On the contrary, the Wrights more than once gave Langley credit for having been a source of inspiration to them, from the simple fact that he, an eminent scientist, considered human flight possible.

Indeed, the Wrights took advantage of an opportunity to save the Langley name from being made ridiculous. After Dr. Langley's death, the Smithsonian Regents ordered the erection in the Smithsonian building of a tablet in his memory. The plan was to inscribe on the tablet the "Langley Law," as Langley's chief contribution to aeronautical science. Dr. Charles D. Walcott, who succeeded Dr. Langley as Secretary of the Smithsonian, sent the proposed inscription to the Wrights for their opinion of it. Wilbur Wright replied that it would be both unwise and unfair to Langley to rest his reputation in aerodynamics especially on that so-called Langley Law or upon the computations which gave rise to it.

The Wrights knew at that time, as all aeronautical engineers know today, that the Langley Law was simply a mistake and not true. Because of what Wilbur Wright pointed out in his letter, the Langley Law was omitted from the memorial tablet. But, having eliminated the discredited Law that *was* Langley's, Dr. Walcott then put in its place on the tablet an inscription crediting Langley for a discovery that *wasn't* his! The inscription claimed for Langley that he had "discovered the relations of speed and angle of inclination to the lifting power of surfaces moving in the air." [His tables of air pressures had been antedated by both Duchemin and Lilienthal.] This tendency to claim for Langley what was not his was destined to show itself in a more pernicious form in later acts of Dr. Walcott. If Langley had lived, the relations between the Smithsonian and the Wrights would doubtless have continued to be marked by mutual respect and consideration. But after Dr. Langley's death, the attitude of the Smithsonian began to change. The Institution started a subtle campaign to belittle the Wrights, to try to take from them much of the credit for having both produced and demonstrated the first machine capable of flight, and for having done the original research that made the machine possible. Indeed, the Institution even went so far as to issue false and misleading statements. One of these was in connection with the first award of a Langley medal, publicly presented to the Wrights in February, 1910.

In referring to that presentation, the Annual Report for the year 1910, by the Secretary of the Institution, quoted Wilbur Wright as making a statement not made by him on that occasion at all, but used in a different connection at another time. The improper use of that quotation helped to create a false impression over the world that the Wrights had acknowledged indebtedness to Langley's scientific work. The truth was that Wilbur Wright had, in a private letter, mentioned indebtedness to Langley, not for scientific data but for the fact that it was encouraging to know that the head of a scientific institution believed human flight to be possible. [Langley's published work in the field of aerodynamics dealt with measurements of air pressures on flat surfaces only—and later experiments proved even that to be incorrect.] The Smithsonian has more than once mentioned the award of the Langley medal to the Wrights as a proof of the Institution's disposition to honor them. But the truth is that the Langley medal was established to honor Langley, not the Wrights. Neither in the award nor in the presentation of the medal to the Wright brothers was there any suggestion that the Wrights were the first to fly. In 1910, Dr. Walcott made it evident that the Institution actually did not want the original Wright plane of 1903 as an exhibit. This could be seen in letters he sent to Wilbur Wright in the spring of 1910. The first of these, dated March 7, said, "*The National Museum is endeavoring to enlarge its collections illustrating the progress of aviation and, in this connection, it has been suggested that you might be willing to deposit one of your machines, or a model thereof, for exhibition purposes. The great public interest manifested in this science and the numerous inquiries from visitors for the Wright machine make it* manifest that if one were placed on exhibition here it would form one of the most interesting specimens in the national collections. It is sincerely hoped that you may find it possible to accede to this request." Wilbur Wright replied as follows, "My dear Dr. Walcott, if you will inform us just what your preference would be in the matter of a flier for the National Museum we will see what would be possible in the way of meeting your wishes. At present nothing is in condition for such use. But there are three possibilities. We might construct a small model showing the general construction of the aeroplane, but with a dummy power plant. Or we can reconstruct the 1903 machine with which the first flights were made at Kitty Hawk. Most of the parts are still in existence. This machine would occupy a space 40 feet by 20 feet by 8 feet. Or a model showing the general design of the latter machine could be constructed." The peculiar attitude of the Smithsonian then began to appear. In his next letter to Wilbur Wright, dated April 11, 1910, Dr. Walcott wrote, "the matter of the representation of the Wright airplane has been very carefully considered by Mr. George C. Maynard, who has charge of the Division of Technology in the National Museum. I told him to indicate what he would like for the exhibit, in order that the matter might be placed clearly before you and your brother."

In his report he says, "The following objects illustrating the Wright inventions would make a very valuable addition to the aeronautical exhibits in the Museum. (1) A quarter-size model of the aeroplane used by Orville Wright at Fort Myer, Virginia, in September, 1908. Such a model equipped with a dummy power plant, as suggested by the Wrights, would be quite suitable. (2) If there are any radical differences between the machine referred to and the one used at Kitty Hawk, a second model of the latter machine would be very appropriate. (3) A full-sized Wright aeroplane. Inasmuch as the machine used at Fort Myer has attracted such worldwide interest, that machine, if it can be repaired or reconstructed, would seem most suitable. If, however, the Wright brothers think the Kitty Hawk machine would answer the purpose better, their judgment might decide the question. (4) If the Wright brothers have an engine of an early type used by them which could be placed in a floor case for close inspection that will be desirable. The engine of the Langley Aerodrome is now on exhibition in a glass case and the original full-size machine is soon to be hung in one of the large halls. The three Langley quarter-size models are on exhibition. The natural plan would be to install the different Wright machines along with the Langley machines, making the exhibit illustrate two very important steps in the history of the aeronautical art. The request of Mr. Maynard is rather a large one, but we will have to leave it to your discretion as to what you think it is practicable for you to do. Sincerely yours, Charles D. Walcott, Secretary." If Dr. Walcott's suggestions, that the Wrights provide a reproduction in model size of their 1908 plane and the 1908 plane itself, had been accepted, then the proposed exhibits in the National Museum of models and full-size machines by Langley and the Wrights could easily have been of a nature to give a wrong impression. Surely a good many uninformed visitors to the museum would hardly have known, or stopped to think, that it is one thing to build and fly a small model plane, but an altogether different problem to build and fly a plane, of the same design, large enough to carry a man. Small models of flying machines were flown by the Frenchman, Penaud, as early as 1871. But a larger machine of the same design could not be flown—as the Wrights themselves in early boyhood had found out.

Likewise, the fact that Langley flew a steam-driven model in 1896, and a gas-driven model in 1903, would not indicate to anyone who understands such matters that a full-size machine of the same design as either of the models could support itself in the air. Langley's own experiments had proved how great is the gap between success with a model and with a larger machine.

His full-size machine of 1903, of the same design as the model flown earlier that year, collapsed the moment it was launched. But suppose an uninformed visitor noticed, side by side, a Langley model plane of 1903, and a reproduction in model size of the Wright machine flown with a pilot in 1908. If he hadn't read the labels carefully, or if the labels didn't go into enough detail to make the facts clear, couldn't he easily have received the false impression that Langley had been at least five years ahead of the Wrights? And if the visitor didn't know that the Langley full-size machine of 1903 never flew, wouldn't the sight of it, alongside the Wright machine flown in 1908, have seemed to confirm the wrong impression? Perhaps, however, that was the impression Dr. Walcott wanted museum visitors to receive! The Walcott letter said, it may be noted, that if there were "any radical differences" between the first Wright machine and the one flown in 1908, then a "model" of the first machine might be appropriate. But since there were no radical differences between the 1903 and 1908 machines, not even a small-sized model of the first machine ever to be flown was being asked for. The Wrights took the letter to mean that the Smithsonian did not want an exhibit that would emphasize the fact of their having flown a successful, man-carrying machine as early as 1903. They thought it was significant that the letter did not say that the Wrights's own opinion would decide which machine was more suitable, but only that their judgment "might" decide the question. Because of their strong belief that the Smithsonian was showing a prejudiced attitude, they made no reply to the Walcott letter. There was no further correspondence on this subject between the Smithsonian and the Wrights until six years later. In 1916, the original Wright plane was exhibited at the dedication of the new buildings of the Massachusetts Institute of Technology. Dr. Alexander Graham Bell, a Regent of the Smithsonian Institution, saw the plane and expressed astonishment. It was the first he knew that it was still in existence. Shortly afterward, in a conversation with Orville Wright, he asked why the plane was not being exhibited by the Smithsonian. "*Because,*" replied Orville, "*the Smithsonian does not want it.*" "*Indeed the Smithsonian does want it!*" exclaimed Dr. Bell. He was sincere in thinking so and requested Dr. Walcott to get in touch with Orville Wright. Walcott on December 23, 1916, wrote what Orville considered a perfunctory letter saying, "*the importance of securing for the National Museum the Wright aeroplane which was exhibited at the opening of the new buildings of the Massachusetts Institute of Technology has been suggested to* me." Orville Wright replied that he would be glad to take up the question with Dr. Walcott in a personal interview. A few days later the two met in Washington, but it was soon evident to Orville that Dr. Walcott's attitude had not changed, that he did not want that original Wright machine which had flown exhibited beside the Langley machine which had failed to fly. When Orville found that Walcott's attitude had not changed in the six years since the former correspondence, he gave the question no further consideration. Meanwhile, in 1914, after the Federal courts had upheld the Wright patents in the suits against Glenn H. Curtiss and others, and recognized the Wrights as "pioneers" in the practical art of flying with heavier-than-air machines, an astounding thing happened. A few days after the final court decision had been delivered, Lincoln Beachey, a Curtiss stockholder, telegraphed to Secretary Walcott, of the Smithsonian, asking permission to attempt a flight with the original Langley machine. That proposal was not accepted, but two months later, when Glenn H. Curtiss himself said he would like to test the Langley machine, his request was granted.

The Smithsonian entered into a deal with Curtiss—in which he was to receive a payment of $2,000—and was permitted to take the original Langley plane from the Smithsonian to his shop at Hammondsport, New York. There he made numerous vital changes in the machine, using knowledge of aerodynamics discovered by the Wrights but never possessed by Langley.

No information is available to indicate that the Smithsonian offered any objection to these alterations being made. The Smithsonian's official observer, in connection with the tests of the machine, was Dr. [Alfred Francis] Zahm, who had been technical expert for Curtiss in the recent lawsuits and was to serve again in that capacity in another suit soon to follow.

No one officially representing any disinterested scientific body was present during the time the changes in the machine were made, nor during the time it was tested. It seems highly improbable that Dr. Walcott could have been so unintelligent or so uninformed as not to know about the recent decision of the US

Court of Appeals against Curtiss, and equally improbable that he could have been unaware of Zahm's relations with Curtiss as expert witness and adviser. One may well wonder, too, if Dr. Walcott could have failed to understand why Curtiss had recently become interested in testing the Langley plane. In hundreds of pages of direct testimony in the lawsuits, neither Curtiss nor Zahm had mentioned Langley's name, though they had more than once referred to Chanute, Maxim, Henson, Marriott, Boulton, Pilcher, Harte, and other pioneers. One may further wonder if Walcott could have been unaware when, in 1913, the Smithsonian awarded the Langley medal to Curtiss, that he had already been pronounced an infringer of the Wright patents by a Federal court, and that another decision in a higher court was pending. It almost looked as if there might have been an intent to try to influence that decision. Curtiss had a strong motive for wanting to make it appear that the Langley plane could have flown. The United States Court of Appeals had held that the Wrights were pioneers in the field of heavier-than-air flying machines, and that therefore their patent claims were entitled to a "liberal interpretation." If Curtiss could demonstrate, or seem to demonstrate, that a machine capable of flight had been built before the Wright machine, then he could weaken their claims, to his financial advantage, in a patent suit he expected to have to defend. In consequence of the important changes that were made, Curtiss finally was able to make several short hops, of less than five seconds, with the reconstructed machine, in May and June, 1914, over Lake Keuka, at Hammondsport, New York. Then the Smithsonian, in its annual report of the US National Museum for that year, falsely stated that the original Langley plane had been flown "without modification!" And the annual report of the Smithsonian Institution for 1914, with equally glaring falsity, said, *"It [the Langley machine] has demonstrated that with its original structure and power, it is capable of flying with a pilot and several hundred pounds of useful load. It is the first aeroplane in the history of the world of which this can truthfully be said."* The Institution's annual report for 1915 continued to repeat such untruths. *"The* tests thus far made have shown that former Secretary Langley had succeeded in building the first aeroplane capable of sustained free flight with a man." Similar misstatements were made in the Institution's reports for 1916, 1917, 1918, and afterward.

Altogether here had been something probably unique in scientific procedure. A test was made purporting to determine if the original Langley plane was capable of flight, but the test was not made with the machine as designed and built by Langley, nor with an exact copy of it. No disinterested official observer was present. Misstatements were published about the results, and no information was furnished, regarding the changes made, to enable anyone to learn the truth. To have made one more honest test of the Langley plane that had immediately crashed each time it was launched over the Potomac would have been permissible. But for a scientific institution officially to distort scientific facts, and in collaboration with a man who stood to gain financially by what he was doing, has been called worse than scandalous. After the Langley machine had been restored as nearly as possible to its original state, it was placed on exhibition by the Smithsonian. Soon afterward it bore a label that falsely proclaimed it to be "*the first man-carrying aeroplane in the history of the world capable of sustained free flight.*" But neither in connection with the exhibit of the Langley plane nor in any report of the Smithsonian Institution was there any hint of the fundamental changes made at Hammondsport, without which the plane could not possibly have carried its weight. One of these changes had to do with the supporting posts on the wings. Professor Langley had not known—indeed, no one knew until the Wrights's wind-tunnel experiments established the facts—where the center of the air pressure would be on a curved surface, and consequently he had failed to place his wing-trussing posts where they were most needed. In the attempts to fly the machine over the Potomac, in 1903, the wing that bore the greater part of the weight had each time collapsed at the moment the apparatus left the starting platform. [Lacking the knowledge about curved surfaces that later was available, those in charge of the 1903 trials had blamed the trouble on the launching apparatus.] At the Hammondsport tests, the trussing posts were moved thirty inches rearward.

This brought the guy posts almost exactly in the same plane with the center of pressure on the wings and thus eliminated the backward pull that had wrecked the machine in the 1903 tests. Three fundamental changes were made in the design of the wings themselves (1) the camber was greatly changed (2) the shape of the leading edge was entirely different (3) the aspect ratio—the ratio of span to chord—was increased. These three features are the most important characteristics in determining the efficiency of a wing. The change of the camber of itself may increase the efficiency of a wing by thirty percent. And not only were the wings changed as to design, but they were strengthened by various means of reinforcing and trussing not used by Langley. Even the cloth on the wings was improved by varnishing, to make the wings more efficient. Langley had not used varnish on the cloth. Numerous changes were made in other parts of the machine. The large fixed vertical keel surface, situated below the main frame in 1903, was entirely omitted in 1914. This omission improved the machine's stability. A different kind of rudder was used. The position of the "Penaud tail" used by Langley was raised about ten inches to increase the stability of the machine, and was connected to a modern steering post, to give better control. The forward corners of the original Langley propellers were cut off in the manner of the early Wright propellers to increase their efficiency. As the system of control Langley had used was not adequate, the aileron system, covered by Wright patents, a system unknown to Langley, was added. How did all these changes become known? Orville Wright called attention to them in an affidavit in 1915 in the Wright-Curtiss lawsuit. One way to learn most of the facts is astonishingly simple. All that is necessary to any observer who knows what to look for is to make careful comparisons of the Smithsonian photographs of the original Langley machine with Smithsonian photographs of the machine tested at Hammondsport. It was learned, too, that even the engine used by Langley was changed in several respects. A modern type carburetor, a new intake manifold, a magneto ignition, and a modern radiator were installed. Though all these changes and many others were made in the machine at Hammondsport, the Smithsonian published only a few of them—the less important. It did not tell of the fundamental changes. And the Institution made statements that, by implication, practically amounted to a denial that any changes of importance had been made. By omitting from its published reports at the time and for many years afterward, the facts about the changes in the Langley machine, the Smithsonian Institution succeeded in deluding the public. If the stories about these fake tests had been issued by Curtiss, who conducted them, or by an organization less well-known than the Smithsonian, they might not have been taken seriously. But when false and misleading announcements were backed by the prestige of a famous scientific institution, it was possible to have the fraudulent character of the experiments pass generally unsuspected.

When the reports of Secretary Walcott of the Smithsonian Institution said the "*original*" Langley machine had made "flights," and when the report of the National Museum said the Langley machine had been flown "without modification," such statements, untrue though they were, naturally carried weight. Indeed, the misstatements were so widely accepted as fact that they began to find their way into school textbooks and into encyclopedias. Griffith Brewer, the English aeronaut, delivered a lecture before the Royal Aeronautical Society in London, in October, 1921, and exposed the fraudulent nature of the Hammondsport tests. In this lecture he mentioned many of the vital changes made in the Langley plane before any attempt was made to fly it. Dr. Walcott made a statement in reply to Brewer. Up to this time Orville Wright had thought that Walcott could have been ignorant of those changes, but after reading the Walcott statement he was convinced that there was nothing accidental or unintentional about the misstatements published by the Smithsonian regarding the tests at Hammondsport. While the Kitty Hawk plane rested in its storage place, subject to possible fire hazards, officials of the Science Museum at South Kensington, London, England, had made requests to have the machine for exhibition there. After Orville Wright became convinced that none of the Members or Regents of the Smithsonian Institution or any other influential persons were enough interested in establishing the facts in controversy to go to the trouble of making an investigation, he reluctantly decided, in 1923, to accede to the requests from London. In reply to letters deploring this decision, he has expressed his reasons as follows, "*I believe my course in sending our Kitty Hawk machine to a foreign museum is the only way of correcting the history of the flying machine, which by false and misleading statements has been perverted by the Smithsonian Institution. In its campaign to discredit others in the flying art, the Smithsonian has issued scores of these false and misleading statements. They can be proved to be false and misleading from documents. But the people of today do not take the trouble to examine this evidence. With this machine in any American museum the national pride would be satisfied, nothing further would be done and the Smithsonian would continue its propaganda. In a foreign museum this machine will be a constant reminder of the reason of its being there, and after the people and petty jealousies of this day are gone, the historians of the future may examine impartially the evidence and make history accord with it. Your regret that this old machine must leave our country can hardly be so great as my own.*" Reluctant to carry out his intention to send the Kitty Hawk plane out of the country, Orville Wright in 1925 proposed that the controversy be settled through the investigations of an impartial committee. But the suggestion got no response. He wrote a letter, on May 14, 1925, to Chief Justice William Howard Taft, as Chancellor of the Smithsonian Institution, in the hope that it might yet be possible to have an impartial hearing. In this letter, after reviewing the relations of the Wrights and the Smithsonian, he said, "*It was not until 1921 that I became convinced that the officials of the Smithsonian, at least Dr. Walcott, were fully-acquainted with the character of the tests at Hammondsport. I had thought up to that* time that they might have been ignorant of the fundamental changes which had been incorporated in the machine before these tests were made, and that when these changes were pointed out to them they would hasten to correct their erroneous reports. They did not do this, but have continued to repeat their early statements. By these the public has been led to think that flights were made in 1914 with the original Langley machine, with no changes, excepting such as were necessary to attach floats for the new system of launching. When the proofs on both sides concerning these changes are shown, I do not think it will take you five minutes to make up your mind whether the changes were made and whether they were of importance. It seems to me possible that you as Chancellor of the Smithsonian Institution may wish me to present personally to you my evidence on these points and to have Dr. Walcott present at the same time to give his proofs to the contrary. It may be a way of cutting short a long and bitter controversy." Chief Justice Taft replied that his position as Chancellor and head of the Smithsonian was purely nominal, that his other duties were such that he did not have the time to give any real attention to questions that have to be settled by the Institution's Secretary.

A similar preference to stand aside was shown by others nominally in a position to exercise authority over the acts of the Smithsonian. That Institution has as its members the President of the United States, the Vice President, the Chief Justice of the Supreme Court, and members of the President's cabinet. Its Board of Regents is made up of the Chief Justice, the Vice President, three members of the Senate, three members of the House of Representatives, and six citizens appointed by joint resolution of Congress. Any one of these members of the Board of Regents could doubtless have forced an investigation of any reported injustice committed by the Smithsonian. But all had other duties to occupy their time and, like Chief Justice Taft, they were willing to let the Secretary of the Smithsonian act as he saw fit. Thus the Secretary of the Smithsonian, which administers several important government bureaus besides the National Museum, could exercise great influence. That is how it came about that the attempt to mislead the public regarding the epochal achievements of the Wrights went so long unchecked by official action. And as Orville Wright once said he had discovered, "*Silent truth cannot withstand error aided by continued propaganda.*" After the exchange of letters with Chief Justice Taft, Orville Wright still delayed sending the Kitty Hawk plane to England. There was nothing impetuous about what he did.

Not until early in 1928, or fourteen years after the fraudulent tests at Hammondsport, with the Smithsonian still showing no intention to correct its false record of those flights, did he send the machine to the Science Museum at South Kensington. The arrangement he made with the Science Museum was that the plane should stay there for not less than five years and permanently unless brought back to the United States within his lifetime. Early in 1928, a bill was introduced in Congress to ascertain which, was the first heavier-than-air flying machine.

Shortly afterward the Smithsonian adopted a resolution declaring that "*to the Wrights belongs the credit of making the first successful flight with a power-propelled heavier-than-air machine carrying a man.*" That resolution was, of course, superfluous, for there had never been any question, even by the Smithsonian, as to the first machine to make a sustained flight. But the Smithsonian continued to claim for Professor Langley credit for the *invention* of the first machine *capable* of flight. Dr. Charles G. Abbot became the Secretary and Director of the Smithsonian Institution in 1928, succeeding Dr. Walcott, who had died in 1927. Soon after he became the head of the Institution, Dr. Abbot invited Orville Wright to go to lunch with him at the Carlton Hotel in Washington. In the course of their talk Dr. Abbot expressed the wish that they might come to an agreement by which the Kitty Hawk plane could be returned to America and placed under the care of the Smithsonian in the National Museum. Orville Wright said that this could easily be done. All that he asked for, he said, was a correction in the Smithsonian publications of the false and misleading statements previously made in those publications. Dr. Abbot expressed a willingness to do so, provided this could be accomplished without injuring the reputation of his predecessor or the prestige of the Institution. But the painful fact was that the Smithsonian, however spotless its previous reputation, had committed a reprehensible act, and its reputation and prestige were bound to suffer when its guilt became known. Having committed a serious offense, one or the other of two courses were open to it, (1) to confess its guilt and make a full, frank correction, or (2) to try to keep the misdeed concealed.

Unfortunately, the Institution adopted, at the beginning, the latter course, evidently in the belief that its great prestige, acquired through an honorable past, could crush any imputation against it. Indeed, that course did prove successful up to the time Orville Wright sent the Kitty Hawk plane abroad. Dr. Abbot had not been responsible for the disgraceful situation he inherited when he became Secretary of the Smithsonian and found himself in the unenviable position of having to make an embarrassing decision. But it seemed as if he could not quite muster the courage to break away from the course the Institution had been following. Instead, he at first tried to justify the Institution's previous attitude, though he did concede that it was not true that the Langley plane had been flown at Hammondsport "without modification" as the Smithsonian had published. There were "many differences," he admitted. "*Some of the changes were favorable, some unfavorable, to success*," he declared. "*Just what effects, favorable or unfavorable, the sum total of these changes produced can never be precisely known.*" Orville Wright, on the other hand, insisted that the "effects, favorable or unfavorable" could easily be determined by experts if only the changes were made known to them. But Dr. Abbot still failed to publish the changes. Since then Orville Wright has more than once let the Smithsonian know what he thinks should be done to settle the controversy. In a letter he sent to Dr. Abbot on December 23, 1933, he wrote, "*The points involved in the straightening of the record are not on matters of mere opinion. They are on matters of fact, which at this time can be easily and definitely established. All that I have demanded in the past has been that there be an* impartial investigation of the matters in controversy and that the record then be made to agree with the facts. The suggestion made by me in 1925, three years before the plane left this country, that a committee be appointed to make an impartial investigation and settle the controversy, received from the Smithsonian no response. Nevertheless, I shall be most happy now to join with you in the selection of such a committee, with the understanding that the committee will fully investigate the matters in controversy and will make a full report of its findings." In a letter a few weeks later, Dr. Abbot suggested that, if it were agreeable to Orville Wright, he would ask three public officials each to name an expert to serve on "an impartial committee" of three to investigate and report on the experiments at Hammondsport in 1914, and their bearing on the capacity of the Langley machine for flight in 1903.

But all three of the Government officials that he mentioned were members of the Smithsonian. If the suggested plan had been followed, presumably Dr. Abbot himself would have had the naming of the investigating committee, for in organizations, such as the Smithsonian, appointing of committees by members is usually referred to the Secretary.

[Chief Justice Taft, Chancellor of the Smithsonian, had written that because he did not have the time, he let questions regarding the Institution be settled by the Secretary.]

It appeared to Orville Wright that Dr. Abbot did not have too much confidence in the findings of a committee, even if wholly appointed by the Smithsonian, for Abbot specified just what questions the committee was to investigate. And most of these were wholly irrelevant. A little later, Orville Wright, in reply to a letter from Dr. Abbot, made this suggestion, "That the Smithsonian publish a paper presenting a list of specifications in parallel columns of those features of the Langley machine of 1903 and of the Hammondsport machine of 1914 in which there were differences, along with an introduction stating that the Smithsonian now finds it was misled by the Zahm report of 1914, that through the Zahm report the Institution was led to believe that the aeroplane tested at Hammondsport was 'as nearly as possible in its original condition' that as a result of this misinformation the Smithsonian had published erroneous statements from time to time alleging that the original Langley machine, without modification, or with only such modifications as were necessary for the addition of floats, had been successfully flown at Hammondsport in 1914, that it ask its readers to disregard all of its former statements and expressions of opinion regarding the flights at Hammondsport in 1914, because these were based upon misinformation as the accompanying list of changes would show." [The accuracy of the list of changes was to be settled before publication by the Smithsonian, Orville Wright and a mediator.] But the suggestion was not followed. It will be noted that Orville Wright did not even ask that the Smithsonian should say it did not believe the original Langley machine could fly. All he asked was that the facts regarding the Hammondsport trials be made public by the Smithsonian. It has been his contention that if this information had not been withheld [and] anyone having a knowledge of the science of aviation could form for himself an opinion regarding the importance of the differences between the original Langley machine of 1903 and the Zahm-Curtiss-Langley machine of 1914. He [Orville Wright] has been willing to stake his and his brother's reputation on the conclusion that a committee of competent disinterested scientists would reach if they had all the facts.

  Dr. Abbot, in the years 1933 to 1942, proposed a number of times to issue a statement by the Smithsonian for the declared purpose of correcting the record. All these statements, however, except the final one, would have left the record as confusing as it was before. The first statement proposed was to contain, (1) A history of Langley's work up to December, 1903, which was entirely irrelevant to the controversy and would have filled hundreds, if not thousands, of pages of print, (2) a history of the Langley machine from 1903 to 1914, which, likewise, had no part in the controversy, (3) Alfred Francis Zahm's report of the tests of the Langley machine at Hammondsport in 1914, with no correction by the Institution of its many misrepresentations of fact about those tests, (4) Orville Wright's list of changes made in the Langley machine at Hammondsport in 1914, without any acknowledgement by the Smithsonian of its accuracy.

[The accuracy of the list was later acknowledged by the Institution.] (5) A long list of "amendments" by Alfred Francis Zahm to Orville Wright's list of changes. [These "amendments," or comments, had the appearance of being corrections of errors in Orville Wright's list, though a careful reading will disclose that they were not corrections.] Dr. Abbot's proposed statement thus would have dealt almost entirely with matters not involved in the controversy. About all that did touch on questions in the controversy would have been contradictory statements by Zahm and Wright. The reader, having no way of knowing which one was telling the truth, would have been more confused than ever. All the publications proposed later, except the final one, were similar to the first, though less voluminous. None of them would have clarified the situation any more than the first. Not until September, 1942, did Dr. Abbot submit a statement which, with some amendments, was satisfactory to Orville Wright. That statement, published by the Smithsonian on October 24, 1942, is given here as follows, THE 1914 TESTS OF THE LANGLEY "AERODROME" by Charles Greeley Abbot Secretary, Smithsonian Institution [*Note*—This paper has been submitted to Dr. Orville Wright, and under date of October 8, 1942, he states that the papers as now prepared will be acceptable to him if given adequate publication.] It is everywhere acknowledged that the Wright brothers were the first to make sustained flights in a heavier-than-air machine at Kitty Hawk, North Carolina, on December 17, 1903. Mainly because of acts and statements of former officers of the Smithsonian Institution, arising from tests made with the reconditioned Langley plane of 1903 at Hammondsport, New York, in 1914, Dr. Orville Wright feels that the Institution adopted an unfair and injurious attitude. He therefore sent the original Wright Kitty Hawk plane to England in 1928. The nature of the acts and statements referred to are as follows, "*In March 1914, Secretary Walcott contracted with Glenn H. Curtiss to attempt a flight with the Langley machine. This action* seems ill considered and open to criticism. For in January 1914, the United States Court of Appeals, Second Circuit, had handed down a decision recognizing the Wrights as "pioneers in the practical art of flying with heavier-than-air machines" and pronouncing Glenn H. Curtiss an infringer of their patent. Hence, in view of probable further litigation, the Wrights stood to lose in fame and revenue and Curtiss stood to gain pecuniarily, should the experiments at Hammondsport indicate that Langley's plane was capable of sustained flight in 1903, previous to the successful flights made December 17, 1903, by the Wrights at Kitty Hawk, North Carolina. The machine was shipped to Curtiss at Hammondsport, New York, in April. Dr. Zahm, the Recorder of the Langley Aerodynamical Laboratory and expert witness for Curtiss in the patent litigation, was at Hammondsport as official representative of the Smithsonian Institution during the time the machine was being reconstructed and tested. In the reconstruction the machine was changed from what it was in 1903 in a number of particulars as given in Dr. Wright's list of differences which appears later in this paper. On the 28th of May and the 2d of June, rg14, attempts to fly were made. After acquiring speed by running on hydroplane floats on the surface of Lake Keuka the machine lifted into the air several different times. The longest time off the water with the Langley motor was approximately five seconds. Dr. Zahm stated that 'it was apparent that owing to the great weight which had been given to the structure by adding the floats it was necessary to increase the propeller thrust.' So no further attempts were made to fly with the Langley 52 HP engine. It is to be regretted that the Institution published statements repeatedly to the effect that these experiments of 1914 demonstrated that Langley's plane of 1903 without essential modification was the first heavier-than-air machine capable of maintaining sustained human flight."

Publication of this statement in the Smithsonian Annual Report presumably should mark the end of the long controversy.

Afterword

Despite the passage of time the legacy of Sacajawea endures. There have been many attempts to tell her story and what happened to her but despite the best efforts, the truth remains lost to history. There have been multiple versions printed of the Lewis and Clark Expedition journals throughout the years since the 1904 edition was published by historian Reuben Gold Thwaites—but for whatever reasons most of the reprints remains largely unread by the general public. In 1978 novelist Anna Lee Waldo wrote a lengthy novel titled *Sacajawea* of which she explored the later years of Sacajawea's life. The novel was expanded in 1984 and is considered today a modern classic.

Throughout the United States, there are statues honoring Sacajawea. Many are of her alone, while others depict her with Lewis and Clark. Many paintings exist as well, but few bear little resemblance to what Sacajawea actually looked like. In 2000, a dollar coin with her image was put in circulation by the US mint. It was issued until 2008 and remains in circulation presently.

Despite the controversy surrounding the specific date of her death, the grave at Wind River Reservation is visited annually and remains the location where most history buffs believe the brave heroine of the Lewis and Clark Expedition lies buried.

Following endless decades of a smear campaign by the Smithsonian Institution against the Wright brothers and whether or not they were the first to fly, vindication was rewarding to Orville Wright in making sure he and his brother were given the credit due them in a report issued in October 1942. However, due to World War II the Wright Flyer wasn't returned to the United States until the middle of October 1948. Tragically, Orville Wright would never see his invention again. Orville Wright died in January 1948 at the age of 76 and his funeral was attended by many. Orville survived his brother Lorin by almost a decade. Lorin died in December 1939 at the age of 77. Orville outlived his sister Katharine by almost two decades. Katharine died in March 1929 at the age of 54. Prior to her death she married Henry Joseph Haskell in November 1926. Apparently Orville felt betrayed by his sister's marriage and refused to speak to her until she was dying of pneumonia. He was at her bedside when she died. Orville's older brother Reuchlin passed away in May 1920 at 59.

Milton Wright died in April 1917 at the age of 88. His death, like Wilbur before him, left a void in Orville's life that remained with him until he, himself joined his beloved family. The Wright brothers—so long an unbreakable team—was now together again, forever. Wilbur and Orville, together with their sister and parents are buried at the Woodland Cemetery in Dayton. Lorin is also buried at the same cemetery but at a different location. Reuchlin is buried with his wife at the Forest Hill Cemetery in Kansas City. On some occasions visitors will leave photographs of airplanes in honor of their invention.

Today, the Wright brothers are remembered for having created the first successful airplane and inspiring many in the coming decades. It can be assumed modern flight wouldn't exist if it hadn't been for the Wright brothers daring to go where no one else had gone before. Today, the original 1903 Wright flyer is housed at the National Air and Space Museum in Washington DC. The museum is a part of the Smithsonian Institution. The Library of Congress holds many of the original writings of the Wright brothers as well as vintage photos taken of their flights in Ohio and Kitty Hawk. In 1978 a movie called *The Winds of Kitty Hawk* starring Michael Moriarty as Wilbur Wright and David Huffman as Orville Wright aired on NBC. Both actors bore an uncanny resemblance to the Wright brothers as young men. If they had been alive to see the film about their exploits I'm sure they would have approved. The acclaimed biographical movie followed closely the events of what occurred during the first years of modern flight—but like all movies based on the lives of famous people—dramatic license was taken in some instances.

Over the years there have been many documentaries made about the events leading up to the first flight by the Wright brothers in 1903—as well as multiple biographies detailing select events in the lives of the Wright family. However, the 1943 biography, authorized by Orville Wright, remains the closest to how he would've liked events to be described pertaining to the lives of his brother and himself—and their first attempts to do what had never been done before. There are many monuments to the Wright brothers but the most prominent is at Kill Devil Hills in North Carolina. The Wright Brothers National Memorial was erected in the area where the brothers first flew in December 1903. Though Kitty Hawk is credited at where the first flights originated, it was actually at Kill Devil Hills just down the way from Kitty Hawk where history was made. The memorial is visited annually by tourists from as far away as South Africa paying homage to the brothers Wright and their extraordinary accomplishment. Nearly a century after the Wright brothers first arrived at Kitty Hawk to make history, scenes from Natalie Wood's last movie *Brainstorm* were filmed at the Wright Brothers National Memorial shortly before her tragic death in November 1981. The Kill Devil Hills location has also been used in other productions over the years capitalizing on its scenic beauty.

Additional Notes

An opinion on the controversy over Sacajawea's later years and death following the Lewis and Clark Expedition.

Statement issued by James Patten on whether or not the woman who stated she was Sacajawea was in fact the same woman mentioned in the Lewis and Clark Expedition journals and not an imposter as suggested by historians.

I believe most sincerely in the identity of this Shoshone woman and her being the guide to [Meriwether] Lewis and [William] Clark, and from the very first of my acquaintance with her (1874) I was sure of this fact. She must have been Sacajawea, for how could an old Shoshone squaw have known of Lewis and Clark, if she had not seen them and had not been associated with them at least for some time? Why should she claim as she did, that she introduced the first white men into this country, unless this was a fact, for in the eyes of her people, this would be considered not a meritorious action but treachery.

James Patten was a solder, gold miner, teacher, postmaster, legislator, Indian agent, fossil hunter, and documenter of early Wyoming history as well as a member of the Pioneer Association. Patten is reported to having met Sacajawea and verified she was the same Sacajawea who accompanied the Lewis and Clark Expedition in their westward journey during 1804-1806.

If the events mentioned above concerning the identity of Sacajawea were some obscure piece of fluff made for Netflix it would actually be considered too ludicrous to be believed. But since the publication of Grace Raymond Hebard's biography of Sacajawea in 1933, so-called "historians" determined to ignore decades of oral history from various Native American tribes have instead set out to discredit Hebard's writings in order to satisfy their own beliefs that William Clark, being a white man, though uneducated, was somehow an expert on history, and that the stories from Native Americans and other lesser-known white men were somehow not credible or outright lies. Some have even gone as far as to create a bizarre universe of alternative reality giving credence to conspiracy theories over actual facts.

This story has enthralled historians and history buffs for over a century. But despite facts being hard to come by from both sides, historians chose in most accounts to ignore oral histories from those who stated they knew a woman who may have been Sacajawea and believe that an uneducated man was somehow more credible. Whenever the name of William Clark is mentioned in association with Sacajawea's death, historians ignore the fact he made numerous incorrect statements previously about the supposed deaths of other members of the Lewis and Clark Expedition—and instead act like he was the absolute authority on her whereabouts regardless his previous misstatements. He wasn't. Clark's curious 1820s note on Sacajawea's "supposed" demise was based on questionable statements made concerning the death of an unidentified Indian woman in December 1812 or whether or not he assumed Sacajawea was dead since he had lost contact with her at the time he allegedly made his mysterious notation about her being dead by the late 1820s. Since he never made it clear in any of his writings from the years 1813 until his death in September 1838 that he knew for a fact Sacajawea was dead—there is no way to know for sure exactly what Clark was referring to—the 1812 alleged death of Otter Woman—or Sacajawea having left her abusive husband and assumed dead by the late 1820s. But how about another scenario—what if the note made, was forged over a century later by someone else—what then? Questions of this nature surround one of the so-called experts on the history of the Lewis and Clark Expedition, Blanche Schroer, who fancied herself a "historian" and "expert" on Wyoming history but in reality she was neither. If anything, she was self-anointed and delusional—no different than someone who calls themselves a film critic but in reality they are just someone who watches a lot of movies and has a YouTube channel—but without credentials of a qualified professional. Schroer, without a shred a proof, sought to debunk the story of Sacajawea's later years detailed by Grace Raymond Hebard in her biography gathered from the oral histories she diligently archived focusing on the 1884 death of the much-respected heroine.

    Schroer's own history is not impressive whatsoever. She spent most of her adult years working at a forgettable job with no prospects of a real future outside the mundane existence of meaningless employment. One can only imagine how dull and lonely her life was—but in order to make herself feel worthwhile she anoints herself a "historian"—and recreates her forgettable existence with outlandish tales about her supposed importance concerning one of the most curious events in American history. She was probably a fan of conspiracy theories and would have fit perfectly into the world of Qanon and the millions of crazies that follow every ridiculous piece of garbage that is put forth as factual information—but in reality is nothing more than foolish nonsense. Schroer, it should be noted, briefly attended college then dropped out because she assumed she was smarter than everyone else. She wasn't. Here is a quote that Schroer said about herself over dropping out of college, "*I entered that select college of self-education, limited to those who are so interested in so many things they become fanatical readers. I believe too much formal education may stifle creativity and, having no professors to ape, I was forced to do everything my way. I have been blessed or cursed with an intensely curious mind and curiosity is what set me off on the Sacagawea search.*" In order words, if one is to take what she said at face value, Schroer quit school because she didn't like what others said if it wasn't what she wanted to hear or what she believed. Obviously she applied that radical way of thinking when it came to the history of Sacajawea—and when she assumed she had found *evidence* about Sacajawea possibly being dead by the 1820s—she refused to admit that maybe she might have been wrong. So Schroer, for whatever reasons took a dislike to Hebard and her research about Sacajawea—which I might add took well over thirty years to accomplish and was quite detailed even by modern standards. With unparalleled duplicity, Schroer sought to discredit what Hebard presented and attempted to replace it with her own version of the mystery surrounding Sacajawea's demise. The question is simple—can I say without hesitation if all the material Hebard gathered was accurate? No. But Hebard never stated everything she found was credible as Schroer had wrongly repeated on various occasions. In Hebard's archived papers on Sacajawea, there was plenty of information she didn't include in her published book for whatever reasons.

Schroer, herself went through Hebard's files after her death in 1936 and cherry-picked interviews that Hebard didn't include in her book on Sacajawea to bolster her claim Hebard made up what she couldn't prove. Unfortunately for Schroer, her actions only made her look even more unhinged than she did previously. From my research, it seems to me Hebard's only purpose for writing a book about Sacajawea's later years was to compile what could have been the story of the legendary woman's life after the journey to the Pacific ended in a credible way. But does that mean everything Hebard was told wasn't truthful as Schroer has repeatedly said. One should wonder, what was Schroer's reasoning on her assumption that Hebard was wrong about Sacajawea's story? Well, it seemed that after Hebard's book on Sacajawea was published, Schroer became insanely jealous of the respect Hebard garnered and sought to damage her reputation by attempting to discredit the biography Hebard wrote about Sacajawea. Apparently, Schroer based her beliefs on a scrap of paper supposedly found with the writings of William Clark that stated Sacajawea was dead by the 1820s. It should be noted that no verification of the handwriting was done (or has been done) to prove it was actually Clark's. For all purposes, someone, working with Schroer could have found the "supposed" note by Clark with a list of the Expedition members who had died previous and simply added Sacajawea's name to the existing list in order to push Schroer's claims that Sacajawea had died before April 1884. Given her duplicitous behavior to prove her theory that Sacajawea died in December 1812 correct right up until her death in 1997 I wouldn't have put it past Schroer to have forged William Clark's handwriting herself. For the record as previously stated, William Clark never directly stated when Sacajawea "supposedly" died in the note that had garnered so much attention since it was discovered. Nevertheless, Schroer used this info as proof that Sacajawea died in 1812 and added that two previous explorers had also mentioned the death of Sacajawea in 1812. What she neglected to mention in her statements was that neither explorer ever directly stated it was Sacajawea who had died. They, like many other white men of the era never spent two seconds of their time paying any attention to the Indian wives of white men. They were always referred as "squaw" of "the squaw of" in reference to an Indian woman whose name they didn't know or never bothered to find out. In reality, it is very likely the woman referred to in both the journals of Henry Brackenridge and John Luttig was actually Otter Woman, the other wife of Toussaint Charbonneau, the French fur trapper husband of Sacajawea. As for the children of the "Indian Woman" referred to by both Brackenridge and Luttig, they were in reality the children of Otter Woman and not Sacajawea. Over and over again, lazy historians, unwilling to do their own research into Sacajawea's life have simply accepted what was incorrectly stated before, never checking to see if the information they were repeating was accurate. Yet, if they had looked closer, they would've seen many inaccuracies with Clark's "supposed" note about Sacajawea. First, Clark never specifically stated the year of Sacajawea's "death" as previously mentioned. It's very likely he assumed she was dead by the late 1820s when he allegedly made the notation after losing contact with Sacajawea once she left Toussaint Charbonneau after he assaulted her in front of one of his other wives. Nowhere else in his, or anyone's existing writings during the time period for the years 1812 and 1813 was it ever stated officially that Sacajawea had died in December 1812. This fact is always ignored for some reason by historians, one can only wonder as to why. Didn't they check records? Ask questions?

Clark had also stated previously that former Expedition member Patrick Gass and Sacajawea's husband Toussaint Charbonneau were dead by the 1820s as well. He was wrong on both counts. In actuality, both Gass and Charbonneau outlived Clark. Second, let's stop pretending that Clark was some sort of college professor. The man, though a skilled frontiersman, was illiterate. He had no formal education to speak of, his poor writing skills in the journals he kept during the expedition is proof of his not having writing abilities that an educated individual of his era would have had. Other notable frontiersmen such as Daniel Boone and Davy Crockett knew their way around the wilderness, but sadly they lacked formal education—which made most of what they wrote unusable without lots of editing. Third, was there ever any forensic efforts made to see if the handwriting was actually that of Clark? In a lot of Clark's writings from the Expedition, there were indications other people made numerous notations in his journals. Could this have been the case here too? Or, like I stated before, was Clark's handwriting forged at a later date? From what I have deduced about Schroer's dubious character, she was willing to do *anything* to prove her view about Sacajawea and wouldn't let a little thing like having Clark's handwriting forged detract her determined efforts of discrediting Hebard and her years of research on Sacajawea stop her. In doing my research for the republication of Hebard's biography on Sacajawea, what I have found out concerning Blanche Schroer's character have led me to believe she didn't care whose reputation she sullied as long as her view was the one people believed.

Later historians such as Ken Burns and Gary Moulton have never bothered to look at the facts surrounding Sacajawea's supposed 1812 death either. They simply ignored the oral histories focusing on her return to her people and her death in

April 1884. Ken Burns has a history of "revisionist" history-making with some of his documentaries. While some have been widely lauded, others like the documentary on the Lewis and Clark Expedition plays like one of those documentaries you see on YouTube that was made by people unaware of the actual research needed to make a competent documentary watchable and simply strung together a whole bunch of dull material that tells you nothing new and allows you to learn even less. Burns also repeatedly lauded disgraced "historian" Stephen Ambrose every chance he got in interviews about Lewis and Clark as if Ambrose was someone who should be respected for his views on history. It's a known fact that Stephen Ambrose was discredited prior to his 2002 death for repeated claims of plagiarism from works by other historians as well as fabricating a close friendship with Dwight David Eisenhower. Eisenhower's family stated numerous times Ambrose had no friendship with the former President and that they met only a few times over a book Ambrose was writing about Eisenhower and those meetings were always supervised. So, even if someone wants to claim Ambrose and Eisenhower were acquaintants, such a statement would be a massive stretch of reality. To simplify this idea, imagine a fan meeting their favorite film star at a movie premiere and then telling everyone they know that they were close friends with the film star they met only briefly. All of the works by Ambrose have fallen under harsh scrutiny since he was charged with plagiarism and the fact he refused to acknowledge his actions before his death does not change anything other than to show the kind of *character* he had right up to his death. It is certainly odd that Ken Burns continues to laud a known plagiarist despite knowing the truth. I guess it's easier for him to deny the truth than to admit reality about one of his peers. But yet, Burns, Moulton, Schroer, Ambrose, and others like them are nothing new when it comes to misrepresenting historical facts in order to bend specific events of history to their liking. Certain historians, much like crooked cops caught on video committing criminal acts, always side with their own and deny wrongdoing when exposed, even on camera, never challenging incorrect statements even when they know not all their brethren are credible. An anomaly of this type of ideology is a 2003 historical study by historian, Thomas P. Slaughter, which focused on history as it was—and not as we would've wanted it to have been. His book, titled, *Exploring Lewis and Clark, Reflections on Men and Wilderness*, dealt with the experiences of the Lewis and Clark Expedition and offered views not usually found in historical studies. Slaughter's account of the experiences of the members of the Expedition is not glossed over with embellished facts based only on what famous white men said and did.

History isn't always pretty or wonderful—sometimes it's a bit harsh and cruel too—very unpleasant. One can only wonder why Burns, Moulton, Ambrose, Schroer and others like them never attempted to research their writings about historical events before they published them as factual when in reality, their views are simply theirs, not actual history. To repeat, an opinion by a historian is not history, and should never be viewed as absolute fact no matter who stated them. History is only history when proven to actually have happened—not merely assumed to have happened because someone believes their own opinions.

Certainly Schroer and many others should have known better about saying something happened because they believed it did, while ignoring the fact they had no proof. In the case of the countless oral histories about the later years of Sacajawea's life gathered over a period of decades by Hebard, Schroer simply ignored everything that she didn't agree with. I'm the first to admit I don't know if the note by William Clark stating that Sacajawea was dead by the late 1820s was a forgery or not. But even if it was actually written by Clark, he NEVER indicated if he was referring to her supposed 1812 death, or the fact he assumed she was dead because he hadn't heard from her for years.

Schroer, as well as others, have repeatedly stated Clark knew because he "adopted" Sacajawea's children. Again, there is no evidence to support this theory because the children listed in the paperwork for "adoption" were listed as Toussaint and Lizette Charbonneau. Nowhere is Jean Baptiste Charbonneau listed in the archived records. Jean Baptiste was the son of Sacajawea, the same child that accompanied her on the Lewis and Clark Expedition. If Clark had truly filed a petition for "adoption" of the two children stated above, wouldn't he have listed Jean Baptiste Charbonneau's name correctly? How could he have made such a gigantic blunder? It doesn't make sense. Wouldn't he have known the name of Sacajawea's child if he was so close to her as has been widely reported? How could he not know the correct name of the little boy he watched grow up from baby to young boy?

Did historians ever ask these questions? No. Did it ever occur to them to wonder about Clark's blunder? No. It's clear that the "Toussaint" listed in the adoption paperwork by William Clark is Toussaint Charbonneau Jr., the son of Toussaint Charbonneau and Otter Woman. And what about Lizette Charbonneau—who was she? Lizette obviously was the daughter of Otter Woman and not Sacajawea is the assumed guess of most Native American oral historians. There is no note in any writings by Clark that exists stating Lizette was the daughter of Sacajawea. If he was so close to Sacajawea as historians have stated, wouldn't he have mentioned her daughter in his writings? What about the fact that there seems to be no record of Lizette Charbonneau as an adult? What happened to her after being "adopted" by Clark? If he was her adoptive father wouldn't he have acknowledged her marriage or death in a letter or some official record before his death?

In fact, after the Expedition ended, there is no notation in any writings by William Clark that he had a close association with Sacajawea. Of course, that odd fact has never stopped so-called "historians" from offering revisionist views on what they think is factual. They always ignore the fact that Sacajawea had a husband, and he wasn't Clark. Her husband was Charbonneau and he didn't particularly like civilian life or Clark for that matter. Charbonneau and Sacajawea were always on the move and while Jean Baptiste may have been left in William Clark's care in St. Louis whenever necessary, Clark obviously would've known Jean Baptiste's name and wouldn't call him by the name Toussaint as has been casually explained away by careless historians when it comes to the supposed "adoption" papers for Sacajawea's son. Over the years in an attempt to give credence to the story that Sacajawea had died 1812 and not 1884, some historians have sought to erase people from history by simply stating they never existed. When questions about the fact Otter Woman was the Indian woman who died in 1812 arose and not Sacajawea, suddenly Otter Woman was explained away as never having existed and that she was made up, despite written evidence stating to the contrary. When it was stated that it was Toussaint Jr. who was adopted by William Clark in 1813 and not Jean Baptiste, suddenly Toussaint Jr. somehow never existed either in order for revisionist history concocted by so-called "historians" to play out. Of course none of these fiction writers can explain how Clark could have incorrectly written down the name Toussaint and not Jean Baptiste—so they began saying Clark simply confused the names of father and son. But as stated before, it makes no sense since he knew Jean Baptiste well enough that he would never make such a careless mistake on official paperwork. No matter how many versions of reality played out over the years by so-called "historians" they can't seem to ever get their "story" straight about whether or not Jean Baptiste Charbonneau had an older half-brother and younger half-sister. Until actual evidence can be found to explain Clark's supposed error on the adoption paperwork for Toussaint Charbonneau Jr. and his sister Lizette Charbonneau, it can only be assumed they were the children of Otter Woman and Jean Baptiste Charbonneau was the son of Sacajawea. In preparing this book for publication I searched diligently on the Internet and libraries that might have some record of journals or letters that mentioned the confusion by Clark—but found nothing indicating that Toussaint Jr. and Jean Baptiste were the same person or if there ever was a situation where they were confused for being the same person by Clark.

    Notwithstanding, the attempt to rewrite the history of Sacajawea's life and times by eliminating people from her life in order to recreate reality justifying a statement made in 1812 by two explorers that had no clue who Sacajawea was or what she looked like seemed like a full time job for several historians. Schroer's view that Hebard's book was inaccurate proved to be harder than she assumed it would be. Most of the people Hebard interviewed for her book refused to say they were confused about their statements—or, that they were told what to say. But Schroer's behavior toward Reverend John Roberts was especially despicable. At the time Hebard originally interviewed him, Roberts was middle-aged. He remained in contact with her through the 1920s and was interviewed several times during that period—and from all accounts their relationship was warm and friendly. Nevertheless, after Hebard's death in 1936, in order to prove her theory that Sacajawea didn't live until 1884, Schroer like a spider waiting patiently in a web for its next meal to become ensnared, went after Roberts with extreme viciousness (despite his age) determined to force him to recant his story. But the old man, despite his age refused to give Schroer what she wanted to hear and maintained he had not said anything that wasn't true to Hebard. He made it clear his statements in Hebard's book was accurate and though he didn't know at the time that Sacajawea was the same woman who had been part of the Lewis and Clark Expedition when he had met her, he remained defiant that he had no reason not to think Sacajawea wasn't who everyone had said she was. His defiance must have irritated Schroer that Roberts remained true to his statements in Hebard's book. Following her failed attempts to discredit Hebard, Schroer went full throttle into denying reality. She already had convinced herself she was a "historian" and an authority on Wyoming history, making herself out to be more important than she actually was, but in attempt to make her views be accepted, she associated with several well-known historians whose studies of the Lewis and Clark Expedition were respected and proceeded to make it look like she had credibility. Again, for the preparation of this book I searched for articles by Schroer on the Internet and could find none. Her writings are supposedly archived, but seriously, if she was that good, wouldn't they be available for all to read, rather than packed away somewhere where no one can read them or care to? Her stubborn view had always been that no one could ever find evidence that Sacajawea lived after December 1812. However, the same could have been asked of Schroer. Was there any evidence Sacajawea didn't live to be an old woman? No. Not one piece of credible evidence exists presently to verify Sacajawea didn't live until early April 1884. Regardless, there is plenty of oral history stories indicating Sacajawea lived long after her supposed death in 1812.

The question actually for historians is simple—why are the oral histories of Native Americans ignored by white historians? It seems clear the reason Native American oral histories are ignored is actually about race and racism. There seems to be no other reason to ignore the oral histories presented to verify that Sacajawea didn't die in 1812 other than racism. It is one thing to ignore the oral histories of Native Americans by stating they were mistaken in their accounts of what may or may not have happened, but many historians have also carelessly ignored the research done by Dr. Charles Eastman in accordance with the later years of Sacajawea. In order to verify what Hebard had presented, Eastman was appointed to prove whether or not Sacajawea had indeed lived until April 1884 as had been stated. Eastman was college-educated and was a published author of numerous books. Yet historians have dismissed his qualifications and ignored his findings that the old woman who lived at the Wind River Reservation was Sacajawea. The question is why would historians dismiss the findings of a college educated author and believe an illiterate explorer named William Clark?

There seems to be no other reasoning other than to assume most historians chose to believe William Clark over Dr. Charles Eastman because Clark was white and Eastman was Native American. Unfortunately historians have a long history of believing a white man or woman over someone of black, Native American, Asian, or mixed raced heritage. Eastman, by all accounts should have been shown more respect for his views by historians than Clark since he was college-educated and Clark's education basically was equal to that of a third grader. Whether or not Blanche Schroer was basing her views on race is not known but certainly the idea she decided that Hebard book was not factual seems to be based on the theory she thought the word of Clark was worth more than the words of Native Americans.

Schroer was a self-anointed Wyoming "historian" and nothing more than that. She was not sought after for her opinions on Wyoming history during her lifetime and she's described as "controversial" in many Internet sites connected to her writings. Having a word such as controversial used to describe your character is hardly a compliment if truth be known. Just knowing she harassed an old man (Reverend John Roberts) during the final years of his life in her quest to prove that the woman who claimed to be Sacajawea was an imposter is appalling on so many levels. I don't know which is worse—the fact she was willing to harass an old man or the fact she wouldn't admit she had no way of ever verifying her opinions on whether or not an unknown Indian woman pretended to be Sacajawea.

Once Schroer realized she wouldn't be able to discredit the book Hebard wrote, she set out on a new quest of implying the woman who Hebard stated was Sacajawea was actually an imposter who played everyone for fools—both white and Native Americans alike. Schroer never had proof that some unknown woman pretended to be Sacajawea but nevertheless stated that Hebard's research was incorrect and the woman she claimed was Sacajawea was in fact an imposter. Of course for this ridiculous theory from Schroer to be true, imagine just how many people who encountered this woman at Wind River would have had to have been misled. Nevertheless, the idea her nephew (Bazil) who considered Sacajawea his mother wouldn't know the difference between an imposter and his actual aunt is something right out of an old soap opera plot. Seriously, are we supposed to also believe Sacajawea's biological son Jean Baptiste Charbonneau would let a stranger pretend to be his mother whom he knew was dead from 1812? I think not. And what about Chief Washakie who came to know this old woman really well during the years she lived at Wind River? Was he somehow so stupid he couldn't tell he was being lied to? But forget all the situations of someone being an imposter and think about this for a second. If someone did pretend to be Sacajawea during the years they lived at the Wind River Reservation, a few things should be explained. First, how did someone who never traveled with the Lewis and Clark Expedition have so much knowledge about what took place? The journals from the Expedition were first published in a heavily edited limited edition in 1814. The original journals edited by Reuben Gold Thwaites weren't published until 1904—and was unavailable until that point to the general public. So, how would this Native American woman have known about the things she mentioned over the years while she lived at Wind River if she wasn't who she said she was? It makes no sense that she would know what she knew in vast detail if she was an imposter. Much of the information the woman who claimed to be Sacajawea described during her last years at Wind River was only available in the 1904 published editions and not in the 1814 version. So, the question keeps coming back over and over, how would someone who was merely an imposter have known about such things?

Are we supposed to believe this person was a diabolical schemer who befriended surviving members of the Expedition and got them to tell her endless stories about Sacajawea and her exploits with the Lewis and Clark Expedition? Like seriously?

Second, are we supposed to believe this unknown imposter was such a good actress that she could fool everyone she came in contact with, including her own son and nephew?

Meryl Streep on a good day would have nothing on someone like this woman described. Imagine having to pretend to be someone else for decades? Just saying it sounds like an episode of an old soap opera like *Search for Tomorrow*. Third, if she didn't befriend Expedition members, how would she somehow get a copy of the unpublished journals? It is doubtful she would be able to read them regardless, so, are we supposed to also believe she had someone read them to her and she memorized what she heard? Why? What for? Simply repeating this out loud seems like something a delusional Qanon supporter would say. Can Schroer and others like her explain their motives—if any? I think not. The only possible way for historians to explain away Schroer's outlandish fantasy would be to raise the possibility that if it was Sacajawea who died in December 1812, then it was Otter Woman who pretended to be Sacajawea at Wind River. Such a far-fetched theory is certainly bizarre—but Otter Woman was the only other woman Sacajawea had a close friendship with and would have been the only one who would have known about what took place during the Expedition once it concluded. Fourth, even if that bizarre theory was examined, how would Otter Woman have been able to fool Sacajawea's nephew and son? It just doesn't make sense or seems plausible for someone to go to all that trouble other than for money. And yet, this "mysterious" woman didn't make one red cent pretending to be Sacajawea. There were no newspaper articles and no book. If such a thing occurred today, a book deal, a movie deal, or a TV series might make someone go to extreme means to get attention—but this was the nineteenth century—and there was no such things as movies, television or YouTube fame. So, the fact remains unchanged, Blanche Schroer was a pathetic individual who wanted to be someone important but ended up being someone described as controversial decades after her death because of her stubborn efforts to destroy the credibility of Grace Raymond Hebard's research. Why Schroer went about trying to rewrite long ago history remains unknown—it can only be assumed she knew she would never be remembered for anything she did or could do—and chose instead to tarnish the reputation of someone she was jealous of because they achieved something she couldn't ever accomplish. It should be noted that despite Schroer's diabolical attempts to ruin Hebard's reputation, she failed. Hebard's 1933 biography of Sacajawea is still respected today and hailed as the first credible attempt to examine the history of this remarkable woman. Were there issues with some of the events Hebard chose to include in her biography about Sacajawea's life and times that wasn't explained? Yes. Hebard stated that Sacajawea's son, Jean Baptiste Charbonneau, lived at

Wind River Reservation after he supposedly died in 1866 in Oregon. Was this "Baptiste" the same person? If the son of Sacajawea did indeed die in 1866 as has been reported, an explanation of who the "Baptiste" described in Hebard's book may have been Toussaint Charbonneau Jr. Available records of him after the 1840s are rare. It is possible Toussaint Jr. was assumed to be "Baptiste" by the residents of Wind River when in fact he was his half-brother. Obviously this theory has never been focused upon before—but it is a possibility—given the fact Bazil apparently never bothered to question the supposed identity of the "Baptiste" described in Hebard's book. But this idea would make sense since Toussaint Jr. was reported to have had a drinking problem during his adult years—and the man who lived at Wind River that was assumed to be "Baptiste" *had* a drinking problem as accounts in Hebard's book indicated—so there is a possibility the "Baptiste" described was actually Toussaint Jr.

For all the talk concerning the confusion about whether Sacajawea died in 1812 or 1884, it astounds me that not one credible historian has suggested exhuming the bones of both Sacajawea and her beloved son. If it is true that Jean Baptiste Charbonneau died in Oregon in May 1866 as had been stated and is buried there—why hasn't anyone made the effort to exhume his remains for DNA testing? Sacajawea's grave at the Wind River Reservation in Wyoming can be opened also to prove once and for all if the woman buried in the grave truly was Sacajawea.

Whether or not Hebard got everything right in her attempt to tell Sacajawea's story remains unknown, but until all journals, diaries, books of letters, notebooks, memoirs, and miscellaneous writings from the nineteenth century have been scanned and made available for research online, there will always be questions about what really happened to Sacajawea and whether or not she died in December 1812 or in April 1884.

About the Series Editor

Gary Brin was born in 1965 and has lived in the United States Virgin Islands, Hawaii and California. He has edited numerous original literary works over the years—both new and revised. In 2019 he established Standish Press to bring forth interesting fictional and historical material usually ignored by mainstream publishers because of specific views or content. In addition to publishing books, he also created the Nancy Hanks Lincoln Public Library (named after the mother of Abraham Lincoln) in 2014 to make available hard-to-find books to a worldwide audience.

Production Notes

Written by Grace Raymond Hebard and Fred C. Kelly
Manuscripts edited by Gary Brin
Front cover design and book layout by Gary Brin
Cover layout and additional design by Victoria Valentine
Additional help provided by Carlton J. Young
Series created by Gary Brin

For free public domain books please visit
www.nancyhankslincolnpubliclibrary.org

Marie Laplace
February 13, 1892
August 16, 1981

Robert J. Questel
June 22, 1911
August 4, 1990

Marie Anicia Berry Questel
January 13, 1912
April 9, 1997

Eugene Albery Brin
March 21, 1932
May 26, 1977

Lucille Questel Brin
February 21, 1940
December 10, 2000

They never got to have the dreams they wanted or expected but their lives were important nevertheless.

Sacajawea
and the
Wright Brothers

Published by
Standish Press

www.ingramcontent.com/pod-product-compliance
Lightning Source LLC
Chambersburg PA
CBHW062037120526
44592CB00035B/1077